AMERICAN INTERGOVERNMENTAL RELATIONS

AMERICAN INTERGOVERNMENTAL RELATIONS

A Fragmented Federal Polity

G. Ross Stephens
University of Missouri–Kansas City

Nelson Wikstrom
Virginia Commonwealth University

New York • Oxford
Oxford University Press
2007

Oxford University Press, Inc., publishes works that further Oxford University's
objective of excellence in research, scholarship, and education.

Oxford New York
Auckland Cape Town Dar es Salaam Hong Kong Karachi
Kuala Lumpur Madrid Melbourne Mexico City Nairobi
New Delhi Shanghai Taipei Toronto

With offices in
Argentina Austria Brazil Chile Czech Republic France Greece
Guatemala Hungary Italy Japan Poland Portugal Singapore
South Korea Switzerland Thailand Turkey Ukraine Vietnam

Copyright © 2007 by Oxford University Press, Inc.

Published by Oxford University Press, Inc.
198 Madison Avenue, New York, New York 10016
http://www.oup.com

Oxford is a registered trademark of Oxford University Press

Library of Congress Cataloging-in-Publication Data
Stephens, G. Ross.
     American intergovernmental relations: a fragmented federal polity / G. Ross Stephens,
Nelson Wikstrom.
     p. cm.
     Includes bibliographical references and index.
     ISBN-13: 978-0-19-517203-4
     ISBN-10: 0-19-517203-5
     ISBN-13: 978-0-19-517202-7 (pbk.: alk. paper)
     ISBN-10: 0-19-517202-7 (pbk.: alk. paper)
        1. Federal government—United States—Textbooks.   2. Intergovernmental fiscal
relations—United States—Textbooks.   3. United States—Politics and
government—Textbooks.   I. Wikstrom, Nelson.   II. Title.

JK325.S785 2006
320.473'049—dc22

                                                                            2005051805

Printed in the United States of America
on acid-free paper

To Delia and Anita

• C O N T E N T S •

Preface

Throughout much of the last seven or eight decades considerable concern and attention have been focused on the character and viability of the federal system and various aspects of intergovernmental relations in the United States. As government has become more pervasive, more important relative to the economy, and more intrusive in terms of our daily lives and as the nation has moved from rural to urban to suburban with over 90 percent of the population living in metropolitan and micropolitan urbanized areas,[1] many have become more and more concerned about intergovernmental relations and how the system actually works. Several presidents have made an effort to reshape the governmental system into something more akin to their vision of what it ought to be—President Roosevelt with his Committee on Administrative Management; President Truman with his Hoover Commissions; President Eisenhower with his Kestnbaum Commission and the U.S. Advisory Commission on Intergovernmental Relations; Presidents Nixon and Reagan with their visions of a "New Federalism"; President Clinton with his "Reinventing Government" by downsizing federal personnel; and President George W. Bush with his "Ownership Society," so-called compassionate conservatism, evisceration of the separation of church and state, and changes in tax policy that primarily benefit the corporate rich.

The one constant, in terms of intergovernmental relations and the operation of the American federal system, is change. Although some scholars view federalism as a midpoint in the trek from confederation to a unitary or centralized system of government, changes over the last century have not always followed this pattern. The first half of the twentieth century, with the crises of the Great Depression and two World Wars, was a period in which the federal system became more centralized and the tax structure more progressive. Down to about 1981, the country became more democratic, but starting in the 1960s and 1970s and accelerating later on, the tax structure became less and less progressive, culminating in a system that relieved corporations and the very rich of most of their tax burden during the first decade of the twenty-first century.

With the massive changes in population and residence that occurred over the course of the twentieth century and the layering of 934 metropolitan and smaller urbanized areas on what had once been a predominantly rural nation, the structure of government became far more complex, some would say more atomistic and amorphous. By the beginning of the twenty-first century, the governmental system in the United States has become the most complex that exists anywhere in the world today, and it is not only complex but is also multidimensionally fragmented—socially, politically, and jurisdictionally. One reason the system is so atomistic and amorphous is because of the attempts to provide needed public services to our urbanizing areas with the add-on ad hoc application of governmental mechanisms that evolved for the rural societies of the eighteenth and nineteenth centuries. Only a few states have been able to surmount this structural clutter. The system is so fragmented that it has enabled the largely unregulated and increasingly oligopolistic private sector to assume control of basic public policies and the delivery of many important public services for private profit at taxpayer expense.

With the passage of the Pendleton Act in 1883, the spoils system of the nineteenth century, in which the party faithful filled offices of government, gave way over the next century to the gradual development of rather competent civil service systems at all levels of government. While we have always had government at all levels contracting with private firms for the delivery of some public services, the actions and policies of President Reagan and his successors have had the effect of heavily privatizing the services of federal government, including such important services as defense and energy, with considerable privatization spillover to other agencies and to our subnational levels of government. Aided and abetted by the extremely high cost of media exposure on television and other mass media in campaigning for public office, this trend has accelerated under the aegis of George W. Bush to the point where the nation is now saddled with a new spoils system in which "to the private corporation belongs the spoils of office." If government is impotent, economic forces will dominate.

The subtitle to this book, *A Fragmented Federal Polity*, is aptly demonstrated by the chaotic response of government at all levels to Hurricane Katrina in New Orleans. The authors are persuaded that, as we move further into the twenty-first century, students of government need to know much more about how our federal system works —or doesn't work. They need a comprehensive understanding of intergovernmental relations, how the system has evolved over the course of the last century, the gains, the losses, and the prospects. Required is an understanding of not just theoretical constructs. Students of government must look beyond the patriotic fervor of those in power to the harsh reality of what is actually happening: Who benefits and who pays the price for the changes in public policy that have taken place in the past as well as those being proposed for the future?

Acknowledgments

As Professor Emeritus, Ross Stephens wishes to thank and acknowledge the support of the Political Science Department and its chair, Harris Mirkin; Ann Hubbard, departmental administrative assistant, for her help in back-and-forth digital communications with Nelson Wikstrom; Dean of Arts and Sciences Bryan LeBeau; and Dean of Graduate Studies Ronald A. MacQuarrie for the financial support of an Emeritus Faculty Research Grant at the University of Missouri–Kansas City. Just as important is the support received from my wife, Delia, in my continuing research and writing efforts. I also wish to acknowledge the complementary support and interaction with my coauthor in terms of comments and sources of information, which has been extremely helpful in this endeavor. His perseverance has helped keep this project on track. We go back a long way to our time at the University of Connecticut in the 1960s. Finally, considering the problems currently experienced because of declines in funding and personnel, I wish to thank William K. Koerber at the Census Bureau and others in the Governments Division for the provision of materials that were not otherwise available.

Nelson Wikstrom wishes to acknowledge the support of a number of individuals who have played a significant role in his professional development and stimulated his research and scholarship in the area of intergovernmental relations and federalism. First, I want to acknowledge my profound intellectual debt to my coauthor, who first introduced me to the subject of federalism and intergovernmental relations while I was a graduate student at the University of Connecticut and has continued to influence my research and scholarly efforts over the years. Second, I would be sorely remiss if I did not also acknowledge the profound impact of professors Karl A. Bosworth, Lowell Field, Fred Kort, Everett C. Ladd, and I. Ridgeway Davis in influencing and shaping my intellectual development during my period as a graduate student at the University of Connecticut. Third, I wish to warmly acknowledge the valued professional encouragement and support I have received over the course of my career from Joseph F. Zimmerman of the State University of New York at Albany. Next, I want to extend my sincere thanks to my faculty and staff colleagues of the L. Douglas Wilder School of Government and Public Affairs at Virginia Commonwealth University–Richmond. Each of my colleagues has profoundly influenced, much more than they realize, the manner in which I think and write about politics and government. And finally, I wish to acknowledge the support and love of my wife, Anita. She proved to be most understanding while I was writing my portion of the manuscript.

Collectively, we would like to thank Professor Joseph F. Zimmerman of the Rockefeller College at the State University of New York at Albany for providing his insightful research on intergovernmental relations.

We trust that this volume will constitute a valuable and useful addition to the literature on intergovernmental relations and federalism and prove helpful to our professional colleagues and students and to the general public. As is customary in any work of this nature, we assume responsibility for the information that we have conveyed as well as for any errors that we might have made.

G. Ross Stephens
Kansas City

Nelson Wikstrom
Richmond

American Intergovernmental Relations

THE UNITED STATES AS A FEDERAL SYSTEM: THEORETICAL INSIGHTS AND EXPERIENCE

The fifty American states, located between the powerful federal governments and the burgeoning local governments . . . , are the keystones to the American government arch. This was the case when the Constitution was adopted in 1789 and remains true despite the great changes that have taken place in the intervening years.

—Daniel J. Elazar, *American Federalism: A View from the States* (1966)

Intergovernmental relations are the activities and interaction that enable a federal system to function or not function. As Terry Sanford pointed out in 1967, the federal government cannot effectively reach its goals without the power of the states; states cannot serve all their people without the power of the national government; local governments cannot overcome problems without the power of the states and the nation; and states and the nation cannot serve residents without the authority of local governments.

Intergovernmental relations are the interactions and interrelationships between levels and units of government in a complex multilayered (federal) system of government. These interactions and relationships determine how well the federal system can work where power is divided between units and levels of government, as well as within units of government among different branches and agencies. Such interaction can be de jure or de facto (legal or extralegal), or both. In many cases, the extralegal informal relationships are just as important as those involving the more defined legal authority and structure in terms of the distribution of power. In the U.S. federal system, with its three or more levels of government, the separation of powers and checks and balances between branches of government involve both vertical and horizontal activities. Such interaction can encompass governments lobbying governments, cooperation, compromise, competition, conflict, and, at times, a higher level imposing mandates on a lower level; at other times interaction is at a stalemate. Contrary to popular view, intergovernmental contact, collaboration, competition, and conflict have existed among American governments since colonial times.

In 1964 W. Brooke Graves noted that intergovernmental relations in the United States may also involve the interaction of legislative-executive-judicial branches or relationships between different agencies at the same level and branch of government. Although more common in the nineteenth and early twentieth centuries, county governments, and some city governments in many cases, were more collections of separately elected officials, boards, and agencies operating on their own authority—who just happened to occupy the same county courthouse or city hall— than integrated units of a single unified government. For many local governments this is still the case. To a somewhat more limited degree, this has been a characteristic of state governments as well; many comprise separately elected administrative officials, boards, and commissions. Separate branches and some government agencies are established to operate independently. Some operate independently even though they were not established to operate that way. At the same time, we should not forget the more standard intergovernmental relationships of federal-state, federal-local, interstate, state-local, interlocal, and federal-state-local. At the local level, particularly in metropolitan areas, we commonly must consider relationships between a number of municipalities, sometimes townships, and perhaps dozens of school districts layered on top of other local governments, as well as numerous special districts also often layered on top of each other and other local governments —all of which may be layered on top of several county governments. With a few exceptions, local government is commonly a multilayered system rather than a single level.

DEFINING FEDERALISM

Carl J. Friedrich (1968) notes that the political order may and often does operate on many different levels of community—local, regional, national, and supranational. Nor is a government necessarily attached to each of these levels. The borders between them are diffuse and the levels are interactive—they may constantly associate, argue, fight, compromise, and cooperate. In a political sense, however, they have "a distinct and operational meaning, namely the range or territorial extension of power and authority." To this, Thomas R. Dye (1990) adds competition among governments.

Arthur W. Macmahon (1955) lists five "essential" attributes of a federal system, although these characteristics are always a matter of degree: (1) Power is divided between levels; (2) each level must have substantial independent authority; (3) each level must be able to draw authority from and operate directly upon individuals; (4) constituent governments (states) need procedural and organizational freedom; and (5) legal equality must exist among the states. The U.S. Constitution provides for federal and state governments, and a local level is almost always provided for in state constitutions, even though there is no mention of local governments in the federal Constitution, and, legally, local governments exist at the behest of the state government. To these items, we should add a written constitutional document or other basic documents that spell out relationships.

First, a federal system distributes power between at least two levels of government, a central government and constituent governments, which we call the federal government and states in this country. This distribution of authority cannot usually be changed by ordinary legislation, but requires a more stringent level of authorization, usually involving both the central government with extraordinary voting requirements and a significant, extraordinary majority of the constituent provincial or state governments.

Second, although it is always a matter of degree, the authority given to each level must be substantial, whether these powers are residual or delegated. The distribution of authority between the central or federal government and the states in the United States is in a constant state of flux, although the federal level is much stronger and more pervasive today than it was in the beginning of our nation. The same can be said concerning the distribution of power between state and local governments. In a number of American colonies, local governments were created prior to the establishment of the colonial government. Some would contend that federalism requires a written constitution in order to maintain an effective distribution of power between levels and among the constituent governments, one that is adhered to and reenforced by the political, judicial, and representational systems (Walker 1995).

Third, in a representative, two-level system, both levels must have the ability to draw their authority from and act directly upon individuals within their jurisdiction. Both the central and constituent governments must be able to act directly on residents in terms of such actions as collection of taxes and law enforcement, and in turn citizens elect representatives to the legislatures of both the central and constituent governments. The same would apply to a three-level federal system. In the United States we have a de facto three-level system with the states dividing their authority with duly constituted local governments, although there is no legal requirement that states must establish a local level of government.

The fourth characteristic of a federal system is that states or provinces should have considerable leeway in devising their forms of government and their procedures. Presumably, if a U.S. state chose to do so it could create a parliamentary system. States in the United States have fairly common arrangements in terms of the broad organizational structure of government. They all have what is called a "presidential system," with three branches of government—administrative, legislative, and judicial—plus a separation-of-powers arrangement, set terms of office, and checks and balances. States differ in many of the details and the manner in which they are structured. With reference to local governments, there are commonalities among some states, but also wide differences in how many states structure their systems of local government.

Fifth, there needs to be equality of legal status among the constituent governments, even though there are rather extreme differences in size of territory, population, wealth, and other characteristics. In the United States, legal as well as political equality among the states is reinforced by the fact that all states have equal representation in the U.S. Senate, no matter how small they are, and the Senate has legislative authority equal to that of the U.S. House of Representatives. In fact, the twenty-six smallest states, with less than 18 percent of the population, have 52 percent of the votes in the Senate; the nine largest states, with 52 percent of the population, have 18 percent of the votes. Small states seem to play a disproportionate role in Senate leadership and, in effect, have a veto over legislation favored by states with an overwhelming majority of the population (Stephens 1996 and later updates).[1]

VERTICAL AND HORIZONTAL BALANCE

In the U.S. federal system, power is divided both *horizontally* among branches and agencies of government and *vertically* between levels of government. Governments should not always be considered as unified or integrated entities. Executive, legislative, and judicial branches divide power; but even within each of these branches authority is divided and often unequal as it pertains to different branches, departments, and agencies. Some agencies operate independently of others and some are established to be independent or semi-independent. Different types of courts have different jurisdiction. A more obvious division of authority is the use of a two-house legislature, the Senate and the House of Representatives. The U.S. Senate and House of Representatives are unusual compared to national legislatures in other countries in that power is almost equally divided between these two legislative bodies. This type of division of authority carries over to most of state legislatures, although in the states both houses in bicameral legislatures must be based on population. Forty-nine states have bicameral legislatures; only Nebraska has a unicameral system, although the bicameral legislature in Alaska was originally designed to operate as a single body in five major areas of legislation.

The vertical division of power between the federal government and the states needs little comment. It is always changing and the central government has much more authority than when the current constitution was adopted. State power is divided between state and local governments, and there is usually some delegation of authority to local units in the state constitution, but local governments are not necessarily a single level of government. It is usually composed of discrete entities like municipalities and townships, and although discrete among themselves, county governments overlie municipalities and townships. Civil county government does not exist in Rhode Island and Connecticut. In Rhode Island, counties are merely judicial districts. Connecticut counties were abolished in 1960 because they did little other than provide a sheriff and jails. Where they exist, school districts usually overlie the previously mentioned units (municipalities, townships, and counties). Special district governments may be discrete or overlie one another and all of the other previously mentioned local governments. Residents may be served as well as regulated and taxed by several layers of local government. Many of these entities often operate quite independently from each other as well as from the state level of government. Daniel Elazar (1966) labels our system of government "noncentralized" rather than decentralized.

For large nations, the federal structure may be a necessity in terms of the administration, regulation, and the delivery of public services, even where all legal authority accrues to the national government. Territorially large, highly centralized nations must at least decentralize the delivery of services and the enforcement of law and other regulations to the regional and local levels.

PRINCIPLES AND MECHANISMS OF A FEDERAL SYSTEM

Daniel Elazar (1966) posits four principles of American federalism. The first is national supremacy in matters of national interest. Second, from the beginning Congress acquired broad authority to legislate and to appropriate money for public purposes under the Constitution, even though, until the 1930s, that authority was frequently diluted by the Supreme Court and by Congress itself. Because of its geographic scope, the central government is inherently a better regulator and collector of revenue as it is harder to evade or avoid federal taxes and regulations than those of state and local governments. This was particularly true after the Civil War and with the passage of the income tax amendment in 1913. Broad powers to legislate and appropriate money for a wide range of public purposes is reinforced by the principle of national supremacy in the Constitution and the ability of Congress to spend money for almost any public purpose.

Elazar goes on to emphasize noncentralized government with a maximum local control. The United States certainly has a system of noncentralized government, with fifty states and several nonstate, statelike governments: two commonwealths (Puerto Rico and the Northern Mariana Islands); the District of Columbia; four territories (American Samoa, Guam, Midway Islands, and the American Virgin Islands); nearly 88,000 local governments counting those in the nonstate, statelike entities; plus a number of federally recognized Native American Indian tribal councils. In the past, this system of organization has reinforced the existence of a noncentralized political party system, but there is a real question of whether or not this is currently being overridden by the influence of large amounts of centrally collected money for elections.

Elazar felt that the federal distribution of power was reinforced through the existence of a noncentralized political party system, routine legislative interference in administration, regular intergovernmental interaction, and a system of grants-in-aid from higher to lower levels of government. Political parties organize around the offices to be filled. Having 542 elective offices at the federal level, including five nonvoting members of Congress, almost 19,500 at the state level, and nearly 506,000 locally elected officials makes the organizational structure of the party system highly decentralized or, perhaps, noncentralized.

On the other hand, with the rise and consolidation of the mass media—radio, television, and newspapers, with a few newspapers distributed nationally—the cost of campaigning, even for state government and many locally elective offices, has risen exponentially. As a result, candidates and political party organizations in national elections, in particular, and state and local elections to a substantial but lesser degree, have become heavily dependent on assembling large amounts of money to run election campaigns. Because national party organizations and candidates are in a better position to secure contributions from wealthy individuals, groups, and organizations, the collection of campaign funds has become much more centralized; thus national party influence is considerably more centralized than in previous decades.

Not only has the mass media become extremely costly for candidates and critical to election of individuals to public office, it has become more profitable for the oligopolies that own and control the mass media. Lawrence Soley (2002) contends that oligopolistic ownership of the media amounts to a type of censorship where those with money and power to put their ideas and policies across are smothering ideas and policies that might threaten their position in the system. Corporate political action committees (PACs) have contributed massive amounts of "soft money" (money outside the limitations placed on campaign contributions) to federal and state election campaigns and political action committees—more recently to so-called 527 organizations, a newer type of PAC. Although both major political parties are involved in the collection of large soft money contributions, the Republicans have had much more access to these resources.

From the beginning, states and to some degree local governments have been involved in the administration of federal programs; local governments have played a similar role vis-a-vis states. Interlevel cooperation has been augmented with federal grants-in-aid to state and local governments and state aid to local governments. Federal grant programs date back to the Northwest Ordinance of 1785 under our first constitution, the Articles of Confederation, and were later reauthorized in 1787 and under the current constitution, which provided land grants for local public schools. Nineteenth-century federal aid was predominantly in the form of land grants, whereas twentieth-century grants came in the form of cash, or loan, credit, or insurance programs.[2]

Most federal aid is to pay for federal programs in which the service is delivered by state and local governments. Both federal and state governments pay for more services than they deliver. State and local governments administer more services than they pay for. State aid is sometimes pass-through federal aid, that is, money given to the state government where a federal program is being administered by local governments or where the federal government mandates the pass-through of these funds for local programs. States are free to accept or reject federal grants, but they seldom reject federal money. State grants are also for state programs, but state aid is more likely to contain some general financial support for local governments, that is, discretionary money. Land and money grants have been used by the federal government to become involved in activities that are primarily the prerogative of state and local governments as well as to fund state and local delivery of services that are primarily within the jurisdiction of the central government or the states. An important part of intergovernmental relations revolves around these financial arrangements.

PRECEDENTS FOR THE FEDERAL DISTRIBUTION OF POWER

We sometimes forget that in what is now the United States, organized governments have existed for well over four hundred years, and important portions of that time as colonies of Britain, France, Spain, Russia, and even the Dutch. Significant portions of the Southwest were at one time Spanish, French, or Mexican territory; Alaska was purchased from Russia; Hawaii was a monarchy before it became a U.S. territory and later a state; and Texas was briefly a republic after it seceded from Mexico before it became a state.

Colonial government provided something of a precedent for a two-level federal arrangement with a distant central government and colonies that were somewhat independent of the mother country. Colonial, and sometimes local autonomy, was fostered by three thousand miles of salt water, wilderness conditions, and slow communications. British colonial government in what is now the United States dates from the ill-fated settlement of Jamestown in Virginia in 1607.

The Mayflower Compact was drawn up by settlers while anchored off the New England coast on November 11, 1620. It appeared to accept both the divine right of kings and the contract theory of governance, that is, government as a compact between the governors and the governed. It could also be a precedent for locally conceived charter government. County government dates from 1634 in Virginia and 1643 in Massachusetts. In Connecticut, the towns of Windsor, Wethersfield, and Hartford were established successively in 1633, 1634, and 1635. The town of Deep River was also established in 1635, New Haven in 1638, and Milford in 1639. The first three towns drew up the Fundamental Orders of 1638–39 under the "Charter Oak" in Hartford, which became the first colonial charter of Connecticut. New York City was the first chartered municipality dating from 1686, although if a Dutch charter is counted, the city was established in 1652.

The New England Confederation, 1643–84, was something of a prototype for the later Articles of Confederation. After the war with the Pequot Indians, it brought together settlements in Massachusetts, Hartford, New Haven, and Plymouth in a loose union with equal representation from each for the protection against common enemies—the Indians, the Dutch on the West, the French on the North, and even against the mother country which was in the throes of the civil war. It was dissolved because of equal representation and the fact that Massachusetts was more populous than the other three settlements combined.[3] The Albany Plan of 1754, a confederation of the colonies, sought to remedy the equal representation problem by giving each member colony representation closer to the population of each of the eleven colonies to be included, but it was never consummated.[4]

British colonial governments provided a variety of precedents for later state and local governments, the Articles of Confederation, and the Constitution. Colonial charters certainly provided the precedent for written constitutions and the division of power between state and local governments, such as counties, municipalities, parishes in Louisiana, and New England–type towns. There were even precedents for special district governments as early as the 1600s. Colonial governments chartered private and public corporations to provide goods and services beyond the limited abilities of local governments for things such as roads, bridges, canals, and harbors (Foster 1997). Other features included election for the lower house of the legislature, limited executive power, common law, bills of rights, and, in a less restricted manner, the separation of powers.

Over the 169 years of colonial development in the British colonies, the structure of the thirteen colonial governments came to resemble one another in several respects. All had an elected lower house of the legislature, elected by white male property owners, although the stringency of property requirement varied among the colonies. In the eight "Royal Colonies" the governor and the governor's council were appointed by the king and Parliament. The governor's council functioned as the upper house of the legislature and the supreme court of the colony. The governor had an absolute veto. For the three "Proprietary Colonies" (Pennsylvania, Maryland, and Delaware), the charter was issued to a proprietor such as William Penn or Lord Baltimore, and the proprietor selected the governor and the council. Connecticut and Rhode Island operated under charters drawn up by the towns in these colonies and accepted by the Crown. Charter colonies were the most democratic in that the elected lower house of the legislature selected the upper house, and the two houses of the legislature selected the governor—a governor with only limited veto power.

The Continental Congresses

After the French and Indian War, 1754–63, the ministers of George III decided it was time to tighten the reins on the colonies, enforce commercial regulation, station British regulars in the colonies, and collect taxes to pay for it. But the colonies, living in wilderness conditions, separated by three thousand miles of salt water, with attendant slow communications, were not used to abiding by the wishes of the mother country and were doing pretty much as they pleased. These enforcement actions led to the Continental Congresses (1774 and 1775–81) and the start of the Revolutionary War, 1775–83.

A body of delegates from the colonies that met in Philadelphia in the fall of 1774 became known as the First Continental Congress. The Second Continental Congress met in Philadelphia the following year and served as the national government until March 1781. It was the national government until the adoption of the Articles of Confederation in 1781. On June 7, 1776, a resolution was introduced to declare the colonies free and independent states, and the Declaration of Independence was approved July 4 of that year. Shortly thereafter, our first constitution, the Articles of Confederation, was drawn up in just eight days, but it was not approved by the Congress until November 15, 1777. The Articles did not secure authorization from the requisite number of states for $3\frac{1}{2}$ years, until 1781.

Articles of Confederation

Government under the Articles consisted of a one-house legislature composed of delegates from each of the states. The Articles required the approval of nine of the thirteen states in order to effectuate any action. It lacked the power to tax and regulate commerce. The powers it did possess were limited and few. The powers it was given included asking the states for money and troops to conduct the war, borrowing money, issuing paper money, regulating trade with the Indians, and conducting foreign relations. It lacked authority to enforce its regulations. In effect, it was a league of sovereign states. States often violated provisions of the Articles by signing separate treaties with Indian tribes, entering into separate interstate compacts, and issuing paper money.

Government under the Articles was able to carry the Revolutionary War to a successful conclusion, and it did foster some cooperation among the thirteen states. Almost from the beginning, grants-in-aid from the national government to the states have been an important characteristic of intergovernmental relations. The one landmark enactment of the Congress under the Articles was the Northwest Ordinance of 1785, reaffirmed in 1787 and again under the current constitution in 1789. It was our first federal grants-in-aid program. It provided land for public schools, implied the eventual statehood for territories to the West, forbade slavery in the territories, and made fairly liberal provisions for local self-government, civil and political rights, and education.

Early State Constitutions

After war broke out in 1775, many of the Royal governors and other officials left the country. During the same year, the Continental Congress advised each colony to reconstruct its government, and in one colony after another affairs passed to rump legislatures, conventions, and other rather irregular bodies of officials. These actions varied, for example, from Connecticut, where references to the Crown and Parliament were simply struck out of the constitution, to far more complete revisions of colony charters.

A number of early state constitutions enumerated a clearer separation of power between legislative, executive, and judicial branches of government, as well as checks and balances, although in most the authority of the executive branch was reduced and the upper house of the legislature became elective. The judicial branch was separated from the other two branches, and new methods were used for selecting judges— appointment by the legislature or by the governor with legislative consent. Georgia was the first to elect judges. In general, the overall organization of the courts changed little with the transition to independence. The people were proclaimed to be the source of authority, but popular sovereignty was not construed to mean political democracy, even though prominence was given to civil rights and liberties. Legislatures were given rather extensive authority. The governor, at least for a time, was stripped of his veto power and in most cases was selected by the legislature and often limited to a one-year term of office; further, governors' appointments required legislative approval. The legislatures remained bicameral, although in three states (Maine, Massachussets, and New Hampshire), an elected Governor's Council carried over into the twentieth century as a sort of third house of the legislature to advise the governor on finance, political, policy, and patronage matters.

THE PHILADELPHIA CONVENTION AND THE RESULTING DOCUMENT

We have no intention of covering the details of the Philadelphia convention and the development and adoption of the Constitution, only to outline some of the results.

A failed attempt was made to bring the states together to deal with commercial problems between the states under the Articles of Confederation in Annapolis in 1786. Only four states attended. Some thought the project should be dropped, but James Madison and Alexander Hamilton called for a new convention to be held in Philadelphia in May 1787. In February 1787, the Congress proposed a new convention with representatives from all states for the sole purpose of revising the Articles of Confederation "to render the federal constitution adequate to the exigencies of government and the preservation of the Union" (Ogg and Ray 1948).[5] From the beginning there was no attempt on the part of the delegates to the Philadelphia convention to revise the Articles of Confederation. They started over from scratch.

The representatives that met in Philadelphia in May 1787 were the major political and economic leaders of the thirteen states and among the wealthiest. A number had helped frame the constitutions of their respective states. Many were lawyers, half had been members of Congress under the Articles, and nearly all had been active in the politics of their respective states. Most held the not so valuable securities that had been issued under the Articles; many were land speculators; others loaned money at interest; several had commercial, shipping, or manufacturing interests; and fifteen owned slaves (Beard 1935). There is no doubt that these delegates were among the best and most talented politicians of their time. In all probability they achieved as much of a national government and representative system as was possible at that time. Many were concerned with the economic situation and solvency of the country in terms of the need to pay off Revolutionary War debts and develop a sound currency. Nevertheless, no one at the Philadelphia convention could be said to represent the interests of the small farmer or wage earner.

The Constitution that resulted from the efforts of our "founding fathers" corrected these problems by creating a national government that could levy and collect taxes, pay off the debts that had accrued, regulate commerce among the states, enforce its laws and regulations, issue legal tender, and so on. In a sense, it was the world's first truly federal system with significant authority residing at both the central government and the level of the constituent (state) governments.

In effect, the Constitution originally created a mixed form of government, one in which the House of Representatives was designed to represent primarily the white male population with property for two-year terms of office and the Senate was designed to represent the states equally, with Senators appointed by the respective state legislatures for six-year terms. The courts were to be populated by judges appointed by the president and confirmed by the Senate, with tenure for life. The executive was to be selected in an indirect manner by supposedly elite electors meeting in the state capitols. The president was to be a kind of limited monarch selected for a term of four years. With power divided between the two-house legislature, the courts, and the president, provisions were inserted so that each entity could check the power of the others. The Constitution was not a small "d" democratic document—it was intended to limit the influence of the masses.

The Constitution included methods for changing the basic document, which involved the consent of extraordinary majorities of both houses of Congress, or a special national convention, and the constituent states. Giving each level of government an important role in changing the basic document is critical to the maintenance of a truly federal arrangement. In addition, because the Constitution is a relatively brief document that uses general terms outlining the authority of the central government, the power of the central government and the distribution of power between levels can also evolve through reinterpretation of the meaning of various provisions as conditions change.

The original document did not contain a Bill of Rights, and this deficiency was highlighted by opponents of the new constitution. In this regard, some 124 amendments were suggested by seven states in the process of accepting the Constitution. Pledges were made for a federal Bill of Rights by the proponents, and shortly after the first Congress met, seventeen amendments were passed by the House of Representatives; twelve passed the Senate, and ten were adopted by the states.

EVOLUTION OF THE FEDERAL SYSTEM

Currently continuing arguments over the proper distribution of authority date to colonial times. The history of the United States under the Constitution devised in 1787 can be viewed largely in terms of the changes in power and relationships among institutions and levels of government. It is the issue over which the Civil War was fought. The Constitution established a divided government, one that was bound to foment conflict: conflict over the distribution of power between the federal government and the states and conflict among the agencies and branches of government at all levels. It was full of compromises and was set up not to work very well.

The very early years, from 1789 to 1800, were spent exploring the meaning of the new constitution. It was a period of cooperation during which the federal government enacted land grants to the states and assumed the Revolutionary War debts of the states. State and national laws were brought into alignment, in some cases by federal adoption of state law and vice versa, and there was a substantial division of revenue sources between the national and state governments. A number of states adopted interstate compacts, and three new states were added by the separation of territory from existing states—Vermont from New York in 1791, Kentucky from Virginia in 1792, and Tennessee from North Carolina in 1796. There was cooperation between levels of government, particularly in the area of banking, and some national activities were performed by the states under contract. It appeared to be an initial period of "cooperative federalism" in which the federal government and the states operate and cooperate in the same activities, a sort of system of interlocking governments. But the cooperative approach could not last.

For a generation after the adoption of the Constitution, government employees were generally appointed on the basis of the skills necessary to do the job even though there was no civil service system. George Washington started out by announcing that he intended to appoint the best qualified persons to positions in the new government. There were few removals of personnel for partisan reasons. That changed with the rise of political parties and the adoption of the Tenure of Office Act of 1820, which set the stage for the "spoils system" of partisan appointment by limiting the terms of office to four years for district attorneys, collectors of customs, and other officials. The system of appointment changed direction with the election of Andrew Jackson of Tennessee and his conviction that any man of average intelligence could master the duties of public office. Jackson thought that more is lost by continuance in office than is gained by experience and that the older seaboard states had monopolized the federal positions available for far too long.

THE NINETEENTH CENTURY

The spoils system of partisan appointment to government positions became the primary method for selecting government employees at all levels during the nineteenth century. There were problems with the spoils system, not the least of which was corruption. Another was the fact that after a change in the political party in control took place in early November, the administration of government programs often came to a halt. Officeholders knew they were out of a job and left. The new president did not take office until the next March. There were a few weak attempts to remedy the situation in 1853, 1855, and 1871, but these efforts were largely unsuccessful. It was not until the assassination of President Garfield by a disappointed office seeker in 1881 that Congress passed a real civil service reform measure—the Pendleton Act of 1883. Originally, the civil service system covered only about 10 percent of federal employees, but it was extended over the next century to the point where 85 to 90 percent of federal government workers were included in some type of civil service program. To some degree state and local governments followed suit, in part at least because the requirements of federal grants that they employ qualified personnel to administer programs funded by the federal government.

The nineteenth century, on the other hand, was a period of major conflict culminating in the Civil War. Some states, particularly Southern states concerned with states' rights, pushed for a system of "dual federalism" in which the federal government and the states carve out completely separate spheres of influence and activity. The South was not the only region to be concerned about states' rights. Before they learned the outcome of the War of 1812, Federalist delegates from Massachusetts, Connecticut, Rhode Island, New Hampshire, and Vermont met in Hartford to consider secession. The Civil War and the Civil War amendments to the Constitution—those that abolished slavery, provided due process and equal protection of the law, and granted the right to vote—established the ultimate authority of the federal government in these matters and effectively wrote off the concept of dual federalism, even though full implementation of these amendments took nearly a century. The outcome of the Civil War certainly did not eliminate all of the appeals and adherents of dual federalism or appeals to states' rights when politicians believed the federal government had overruled state authority in some matter.

Nevertheless, throughout the nineteenth century there were forces pushing for more federal-state cooperation, and there continued to be federal-state cooperation in administrative matters. The admission of a large number of states over the course of the first six decades of the nineteenth century, as well as later, changed the influence of older states in Washington, DC. Starting with Ohio in 1802, as new states were admitted they were given land grants for public education. With the passage of the Morrill Act in 1862, land grants were given to states for colleges specializing in agricultural and mechanical arts, which had the effect of creating our system of land-grant public universities. After 1887, money grants were given to land-grant colleges for the establishment of agricultural experiment stations. Land grants were also given for the development of roads, canals, rivers and harbors, and railroads. During this period, some aid went from the states to the national government, particularly in terms of military and Indian affairs.

The thirteenth, fourteenth, and fifteenth amendments to the Constitution abolished slavery, imposed due process and equal protection of the laws, and granted the right to vote without regard to race or previous condition of servitude. The Civil War amendments to the Constitution, which went into effect in 1870, imposed these restrictions on states, although some states used extralegal and illegal measures to circumvent these requirements during the latter half of the nineteenth century and well into the twentieth.

THE TWENTIETH CENTURY

At the beginning of the twentieth century there were forty-six states with four more added over the next fifty-nine years—Oklahoma in 1907, New Mexico in 1912, and Alaska and Hawaii in 1959. No one knows how many local governments existed at the beginning of the twentieth century, but in 1932 there were 182,602 units—over 70 percent were school districts, most very small rural one-room schools. Over the course of the century, the number of local governments in the fifty states declined from the 1932 high to 78,218 in 1972, then increased to 87,525 by the year 2002.

Twentieth-Century Local Government

From 1932 to 2002, the number of county governments was very stable at a little over 3,000; municipalities increased from 16,442 to 19,429, while the number of townships declined from 19,978 to 16,504. Many of the disappearing townships were either absorbed by urban expansion or became municipalities. The really major changes in the numbers of local governments were those for school districts and special districts. Between 1932 and 2002, school district consolidation resulted in the elimination of nearly 90 percent of those that existed seventy years earlier, leaving only 13,506 at the start of the twenty-first century. The number of special district governments declined from 14,572 in 1932 to 8,299 by 1942, probably because of the exigencies of the Great Depression of the 1930s. Since 1942, however, special districts have been the most rapidly increasing type of local government both in number and activity. Over 90 percent are single-purpose units of local government. Between 1942 and 2002 their numbers increased 4.3 times to 35,052 (see Table 1.1). In addition, the 2002 *Census of Governments* lists 3,470 *types* of semi-independent special districts that do not meet the Census criteria for being fully independent local governments—two-thirds of them are local and one-third are under the aegis of state

TABLE 1.1. Number of Local Governments, by Decade, 1932–2002

Year	County	Municipal	Township	Special District	School District	Total
1932	3,062	16,442	19,978	14,572	128,548	182,602
1942	3,050	16,220	18,919	8,299	108,579	155,067
1952	3,049	16,778	17,202	12,317	56,346	105,692
1962	3,043	17,997	17,144	18,823	34,678	91,685
1972	3,044	18,517	16,991	23,885	15,781	78,218
1982	3,041	19,076	16,734	28,078	14,851	81,780
1992	3,043	19,279	16,656	31,555	14,422	84,955
2002	3,034	19,429	16,504	35,052	13,506	87,525

Sources: Governments Division of the Census Bureau; Graves 1964, p. 699. Note: there are some small inconsistencies in these numbers from different Census Bureau sources.

government, although most serve local areas. No one knows how many of these semi-independent entities exist, but there must be tens of thousands.[6]

Over the last half of the twentieth century, local government became even more fragmented with the development of residential community associations (RCAs), more commomly referred to as "homeowners associations" or "condominium associations." RCAs are organized as private, usually nonprofit corporations. Most provide services similar to those of local government along with maintenance of facilities and common areas to a development or condominium using compulsory fees and charges levied against homeowners. According to the U.S. Advisory Commission on Intergovernmental Relations, these private governments range in size from as few as 10 residents to nearly 70,000. Their numbers increased from a few thousand in 1960 to 160,000 in 1989 and an estimated 180,000 by 1995 (Dean 1989; Stephens and Wikstrom 2000). By 2005, there are 274,000 RCAs. These private associations further confuse the landscape of local government in the United States.

Local government in the United States is not only highly disparate and fragmented, but is also small. Over 90 percent of all local governments have fewer than 25,000 residents. In fact, over two-thirds of all local governments had a population of less than 2,500 in Census year 2000. Much of the work of all levels of government is contracted out to private firms. In 1997, 30 percent of all local governments, excluding RCAs, had no employee that constituted as much as a 0.5 full-time equivalent worker (Stephens and Wikstrom 2003). Yet much of the published information and scholarly attention concerning local government concentrates on large local governments.

TWENTIETH-CENTURY CHANGES

While it seems likely, except during times of war, that local governments had been the most active level in terms of the provision of public services from colonial times to the twentieth century, it was certainly true at the beginning of the twentieth century. In 1902, local governments were the most active level and states the least active. In fact, more than half, 56 percent, of all governmental activity was local; less than one-third, 31.9 percent, was federal; and only 12.1 percent was state, using Stephens's indices of state and federal centralization.[7] Discounting federal activity in

World War I, local governments were the most active level for the first three decades of the twentieth century.

In 1902, government accounted for only about 8 percent of gross national product (GNP). The twentieth century was a period in which major changes took place in the relative roles of government, not only in terms of the roles played by the three levels of government, but also in terms of the role of government in the economy. The intensity of activity at the federal level has risen rapidly in response to real and perceived crises, such as the two World Wars, the Great Depression, the Cold War, and other wars in various parts of the globe. Now there are the wars in Afghanistan and Iraq and the so-called war on terrorism. After each major crisis is past, the federal role tends to decline, never quite reaching its precrisis level. The federal role reached two-thirds of all governmental activity in World War I vis-à-vis subnational governments then declined rapidly in the 1920s. Both state and federal roles increased in relation to the economy during the Great Depression. In 1945, the last year of World War II, federal expenditures accounted for over 43 percent of GNP and nearly 85 percent of all governmental activity. When you add in state and local activity for 1945, government accounted for half of GNP for that year. At century's end, federal, state, and local governments combined comprised slightly over 35 percent of GNP (Stephens and Wikstrom 2003a).

Starting with the stock market crash in the late 1920s, states more than doubled their role vis-à-vis their local governments by 1942. It appears that state governments responded earlier to the exigencies of the Great Depression than did the federal government. In fact, the maintenance of state, federal, and local activity kept the nation's economy from sinking even deeper into the Depression of the 1930s. Between 1946 and the early 1980s, states increased their activity relative to their political subdivisions from 41 to 56 percent and remained in the 56 to 58 percent range throughout the rest of the century[8] (Stephens and Wikstrom 2003a).

Although there were ups and downs with hot and cold wars, by the end of the century, state and local government again accounted for half of all government activity, although that relative status was scheduled to decline early in the twenty-first century as a result of wars in Afghanistan and Iraq.

Government as a proportion of the economy increased more than 4.5 times over the course of the century. In these terms, local governments doubled, federal activity increased seven times, and state government, starting from a smaller base, achieved a rise of 11 times. The large post–World War II increase in state and local activity was largely because of increases in urban and rather massive increases in suburban residents needing the services provided by state and local governments.

THE CENTURY'S SECOND DECADE

[T]he tide of centralization will probably steadily sweep power from the localities to the states, and from the states into the hands of the national authorities.

—Leonard D. White, *Trends in Public Administration* (1933)

The second decade of the twentieth century witnessed major changes in the Constitution that also altered the division of authority between the central government and the states and a democratization of representation in Congress. The sixteenth amendment (1913) authorized the federal government to levy and collect taxes on income, which eventually led to a greatly enhanced ability to collect revenue and, therefore, *the ability to spend it for activities once considered the domain of the states and/or their political subdivisions.* Taxes on income became the dominant source of federal revenue by mid-century. Almost simultaneously, six days after the passage of the income tax amendment, the seventeenth amendment went into effect providing for the direct election U.S. Senators by the voters rather than appointment by the legislatures of their respective state governments. The nineteenth amendment, proclaimed in 1919, allowed women the right to vote. Actually, prior to the passage of the seventeenth and nineteenth amendments, a few states had held elections for the U.S. Senate, then the state legislature appointed the winner, and/or had given women the right to vote in state and local elections. This was also the decade of the proposal for the ill-fated eighteenth amendment (1920), which gave the federal government the authority, along with the Volstead Act, to prohibit the manufacture, sale, or transportation of alcoholic beverages. It was rescinded by the twenty-first amendment in 1933.

During the first three decades of the twentieth century federal grants-in-aid were largely for agriculture, roads, and the military. The manufacture and widespread use of the automobile led to a need for hard surfaced roads. The 1914 Smith-Lever Act for agricultural extension work set the pattern for rather highly specific conditional grants-in-aid to the states, grants we now refer to as project grants, program grants, or "categoricals." These grants usually require matching funds, the money can only be spent for the specified purpose, there must be a responsible administrative agency at the state or local level, and the federal government has the right to set standards of performance and inspect results.

The National Defense Act of 1916 was a further invasion of states' rights with reference to the state militia. The "camel's nose" was inserted further into the proverbial tent of states' rights by renaming and reorganizing state militias into the National Guard, thus creating a national auxiliary for the regular army. The Federal Aid Road Act of 1916 provided money for the construction of rural postroads subject to an even match of funds by the states, to be followed later by grants for a national road system and eventually, after World War II, the Interstate Highway System. All states have participated in these programs, even though participation has been "voluntary."

The major revenue source for state and local governments at the beginning of the twentieth century was the ad valorem property tax accounting for over two-thirds of own source revenue, although over the course of the next half-century, many states adopted sales and income taxes and there was a significant increase in the use of service charges. By the end of the century, property taxes accounted for less than 17 percent of state and local receipts; the revenue base for subnational governments became quite diversified with increases in all types of sales and gross receipts taxes, charges for services, and payroll and income taxes. Over the course of the century federal grants became an important source of state revenue, and state grants-in-aid became an important source of local revenue, particularly for education and highways. At times, significant portions of state aid was pass-through federal aid, that is, federal aid given to state governments that is passed on to local governments either as a federal mandate or because the services in question were performed by local governments.[9]

Federal aid to state and local governments was used to some extent during the Great Depression of the 1930s, but dropped off during World War II. Starting after the war, federal grants-in-aid escalated, doubling nearly every five years to about 1980. There were literally hundreds of federal aid programs for many different projects and purposes. Throughout most of the century, most federal aid, about 90 percent of the money, went to state rather than local governments. The major exceptions were urban renewal grants, planning and housing grants in the 1940s to 1970s, and General Revenue Sharing programs and anti-recession fiscal assistance grants in the 1970s, which were primarily directed toward local governments. From the end of World War II through the 1970s was a period of cooperative federalism, with the federal government funding and becoming involved in the problems of state and local governments. In the early 1980s, starting with the Reagan administration, federal aid was reduced, some programs like General Revenue Sharing and anti-recession fiscal assistance grants were eliminated, other programs were consolidated into block grants, and aid was redirected toward states rather than local governments.

FROM PROGRESSIVITY TO PLUTOCRACY: 1950 TO THE TWENTY-FIRST CENTURY

Much of what goes on in terms of intergovernmental relations in our federal system has to do with revenues, revenue sources, expenditures, and how and for what purposes money is expended. One way to understand the intergovernmental relations over time is to follow the money.

The first half of the twentieth century was a time during which state and local governments started reducing their reliance on the ad valorem property tax and diversifying their revenue structures by adding all kinds of sales and gross receipts taxes, income and payroll taxes, fees and franchise taxes, and service charges. This trend continued throughout the century, but almost universally, the trend toward ever more taxes on consumption and service charges continues into the twenty-first century. State corporate income taxes bring in a much smaller proportion of revenue today than they did at the mid-twentieth century. The property tax, although sometimes badly administered, was probably more a progressive revenue source than the more diversified system used by state and local governments today since what it taxed was a measure of wealth (Stephens 2003).

For the federal government, the first half of the twentieth century was one of greatly increased dependence on rather highly progressive corporate and individual income taxes. In 1952, the federal individual income tax brought in 42 percent of federal revenue while the corporate tax accounted for nearly one-third, 32 percent, of federal receipts. Payroll taxes, which like that for Social Security are all flat-rate, often tax only earned income (wages, salaries, and commissions), not other forms of personal income. The most important payroll levies, like Social Security, do not tax earned income above a certain level. They were a relatively minor source of revenue at mid-century, bringing in less than 10 percent of federal receipts. Taxes on some measure of income brought in 84 percent of federal receipts at that time (Office of Management and Budget 2002 through 2005).

The last half of the twentieth century witnessed a retreat from progressive income taxes. By the fiscal year (FY) 2001, the tax rate for the highest income, the top 1 percent of individual income taxpayers, had dropped by half, yet the tax still brought in half of all federal revenue for that year. The tax had become far less progressive. The same thing happened for corporate income taxes, except moreso. They declined to less than 8 percent of federal revenue as a result of exceptions, exemptions, loopholes, decline in tax rates, and taking profits offshore. Over the same period, payroll taxes increased from less than 10 percent of federal receipts to 37 percent. Alterations of the tax code over the last half of the century and beyond have not only changed who pays and who benefits, as well as the role of government, but have also altered the social and economic structure of the nation. Moreover, under the urging of President George W. Bush, taxes on corporations and the wealthiest individual taxpayers declined even more with tax cuts enacted during his first and second terms in office. There were large reductions in the top income tax brackets, capital gains taxes, and taxes on dividends—with more such reductions scheduled to go into effect over the next few years. Because of a decline in economic activity, the curtailing of federal aid, and federal tax cuts, state and local governments have had to cope with declining revenue. Many have enacted increases in service charges, sales and excise taxes, and fees and fines.

COMMENT

Over two hundred years ago, a group of privileged white property owners, plutocrats, met in Philadelphia charged with revising the Articles of Confederation, our first national constitution. They threw out the old constitution and wrote a new one. The government they created was a mixed form of government, often referred to as a federation and a republic, but one that curtailed the influence of the average citizen. The executive was to be a sort of limited term monarch and titular head of government selected by an indirect method called the electoral college. The judiciary was also an aristocratic arrangement, with judges appointed for life terms of office when nominated by the monarch and approved by the Senate. The Senate itself was a kind of aristocracy appointed by the legislatures of the several states, with each state having equal representation. The lower house of the legislature, called the House of Representatives, was to have representation according to the population of each state who were "free persons, including those bound for service for a term of years [indentured servants], excluding Indians not taxed, and three-fifths of all other persons [slaves]." States decided who could vote, and at that time only property-owning male free men could exercise the franchise. This was not a "democratic" or even a "republican" form of government in the strict meaning of those terms.

Over the next eight or nine decades it became more of a republic and over the following one hundred years it became more representative and more democratic.

These changes were brought about by the reinterpretation of the original Constitution that became operative in 1789 and with the Bill of Rights proclaimed in 1791, the post–Civil War amendments, elimination of property qualifications for voting, the direct election of Senators, women's suffrage, and giving the federal government the power to levy taxes on income.

Over the fifty years after its passage, the use of the progressive income tax, whereby those corporations and individuals with higher income pay a larger percent in taxes, not only leveled the playing field for the average citizen but also provided funds for various social programs and grants-in-aid to state and local governments. Who would guess that, after the sacrifices of World War II, our elected officials, the ones charged with protecting the system, would turn the clock back to a time when the United States was a plutocracy, ruled by the rich, pretending to be a republic or even a democracy? But that is precisely what happened over the last half of the twentieth century—and this trend continues unabated, even accelerated, into the twenty-first century.

If we "follow the money" over the last half-century, at tax time *the rich get richer and everyone* else gets poorer. As will be shown in Chapter 4, taxes and other government revenue in our multitiered federal system have been downloaded on middle- and lower-income residents. Where the overall federal-state-local tax structure was quite progressive in the mid-twentieth century, it is now flat-rate across classes of income and scheduled to become significantly regressive as a result of changes in the tax structure occurring during the tenure of President George W. Bush. Moreover, when you relieve high-income individual taxpayers and corporations of their obligation to pay taxes, you are redistributing income from low- and middle-income taxpayers to the corporate rich. This process has gone hand-in-hand with the destruction of a competent civil service system and the substitution of a new spoils system in which the beneficiaries are large influential private corporations rather than political parties. Deliberate government policies have altered the socioeconomic structure of the nation. Nearly all of the expansion of the economy over the last half-century has been financed by the expansion of credit—personal credit and mortgage debt, government deficits, and balance-of-payments deficits. In addition, the rise of the new plutocracy, the "corporate state," is creating a society of indentured servants, burdened by debt and beholden to the Fortune 500, rather than citizens with a voice and vote that counts. We now have a *de facto plutocracy masquerading as a democracy.*

THE FOLLOWING CHAPTERS

Chapter 2 discusses various concepts and models of federal systems, contrasting the U.S. system with more centralized systems of government. It details the complexity of the federal system in the United States and the monumental number of governments and elected officials. To some degree it analyzes the adaptations and changes that have taken place over time. It also lists how recent presidents have tried to impose their particular view of what the roles of the different levels of government ought to be.

Chapter 3 provides a broad overview of contemporary American federalism and intergovernmental relations, in both the vertical and horizontal dimensions.

Attention is devoted to the various socioeconomic and political factors that have shaped an intergovernmental system marked by both cooperation and conflict. Note is made of the increasing privatization of the federal system.

Chapter 4 uses a different approach to the study of our federal system. In order to understand what federal, state, and local governments are doing and what government is about, you need "to follow the money." The chapter discusses how revenues are divided among governments, how they are transferred between levels, and who pays the tab for government services. Also considered is how these things have changed over time and how the United States has become a debtor nation.

The narrative in Chapter 5 centers on the roles of the president, Congress, and the Supreme Court in the fragmented national policy process that shapes and sometimes distorts intergovernmental and intragovernmental policies and programs. Discussion is devoted to the roles of various federal, state, and local governmental and non-governmental groups that lobby in Washington to promote their fiscal and policy goals.

Chapter 6 stresses the decline of the "cooperative federalism" of the twentieth century and the rise of "coercive federalism" through the extensive use of various regulatory techniques by the federal government such as mandates, cross-cutting regulations, and partial preemptions. Also included is a discussion of mandates imposed by states on their respective local governments.

Chapter 7 focuses on the increasing role played by states in the federal system over much of the twentieth century. Attention is given to the provisions of the United States Constitution that structure the relationships between the states and the federal government, as well as between and among the states. Also discussed is the cooperative and competitive characteristics of interstate relations as well as interstate conflict. This chapter notes the various factors that promote policy diffusion among the fifty states.

State-local relations are the central theme of Chapter 8. Attention is given to the legal relationships between state and local governments, noting the declining significance of "Dillon's Rule," the home-rule movement, and the increased role of the state. Also included is a discussion of the various forms of state assistance to local governments as well as the various techniques states utilize to affect local governmental structures and policies. The chapter concludes by noting the phenomenon of state centralization over the course of the twentieth century and the common sources of tension between state and local governments.

Chapter 9 starts out with a discussion of the different systems of local government that exist in our fifty states. It delineates the very large number of very small governments in the United States as well as how we have layered the urban and suburban population of 922 metropolitan and micropolitan areas on a system of local government that evolved in a rural society. Included are small case studies of "republics in miniature," that is, municipalities and townships and special districts that operate without any full-time employees.

The last chapter summarizes some of the findings from the earlier parts of the book, traces what seem to be the important trends in the federal arrangement, and focuses on the problems that result from the multidimensional fragmentation of political and legal jurisdiction and the privatization of government at all levels. Periodically, governmental systems must break out of the ossified strictures that bind it.

In addition, at selected points throughout the book are five case studies. They take a look at topics relating to intergovernmental relations and the viability of the federal system. The first analyzes what has happened with the creation of the federal Department of Homeland Security after the terrorist attacks of September 11, 2001. Case Study 2 analyzes the intergovernmental implications and effects of the No Child Left Behind legislation passed by Congress in 2001. The third looks at the changes wrought by the so-called Welfare to Work legislation of the 1990s and the way it relates to the workings of the federal system. The shortest case study outlines what we know about the more than three thousand semi-independent *types* of special districts and authorities that have been created over the years. No one knows how many of these benighted entities exist, but they tend to make our governmental system even more diffuse and amorphous. The last case study pertains to Hurricane Katrina.

REFERENCES

Beard, Charles A. 1935, 1996. *An Economic Interpretation of the Constitution of the United States.* New York: Free Press, reissue edition. 74–149.

Council of Economic Advisors (CEA). 1991, 2002, 2003. *Economic Report of the President.* Washington, DC: Government Printing Office.

Dean, Debra L. 1989. Residential Community Associations: Partners in Local Governance or Headaches for Local Government. *Intergovernmental Perspective.* 15:1 (Winter 1989), 36–39.

Dye, Thomas R. 1990. *American Federalism: Competition Among Governments.* Lexington, MA: Lexington Books, D.C. Heath and Company. 19–33.

Elazar, Daniel J. 1962. *The American Partnership: Intergovernmental Co-operation in the Nineteenth-Century United States.* Chicago: University of Chicago Press.

———. 1966. *American Federalism: A View from the States.* New York: Thomas Y. Crowell Company. 1.

Foster, Kathryn A. 1997. *The Political Economy of Special-Purpose Government.* Washington, DC: Georgetown University Press. 15.

Friedrich, Carl J. 1968. *Trends of Federalism in Theory and Practice.* New York: Frederick A. Praeger. 3.

Graves, W. Brooke. 1964. *American Intergovernmental Relations: Their Origins, Historical Development, and Current Status.* New York: Charles Scribner's Sons. 4, 699.

Macmahon, Arthur W. 1955. The Problems of Federalism: A Survey. In Arthur W. Macmahon, ed., *Federalism: Mature and Emergent.* New York: Columbia University. 4–5.

Office of Management and Budget (OMB). 2002–2005. *Historical Tables.* Budget of the United States Government. Fiscal Years 2003–2006. Washington, DC: Government Printing Office.

Ogg, Frederick A. and P. Orman Ray. 1948. *Introduction to American Government.* New York: Appleton-Century-Crofts. 11–39.

Sanford, Terry. 1967. *Storm over the States.* New York: McGraw-Hill. 97.

Soley, Lawrence. 2002. *Censorship, Inc. The Corporate Threat to Free Speech in the United States.* New York: Monthly Review Press. 18–19, 257–58.

Stephens, G. Ross. 1974. State Centralization and the Erosion of Local Autonomy. *Journal of Politics.* 36:1, 44–76.

———. 1996. Urban Underrepresentation in the U.S. Senate. *Urban Affairs Review.* 31:3 (January), 404–18.

———. 2003. The Corporate State—to the Corporations Belong the Spoils. Paper prepared for publication.

Stephens, G. Ross and Nelson Wikstrom. 2003a. Institutional Centralization/Decentralization over the Course of the Twentieth Century. Working paper.

——. 2003b. "Republics in Miniature" and Other Toy Governments. Paper presented to the annual conference of the American Political Science Association. Philadelphia. August 29, 2003.

U.S. Bureau of the Census. 1961. *Historical Statistics of the United States*. Washington, DC: Government Printing Office. 139, 709–30.

——. 2001. State and Local Government. www.census.gov/govs/estimate/01s100us.html.

——. 2002. State and Local Government. www.census.gov/govs/estimate/02s100us.html.

——. 2002, 2003, 2004–5. *Statistical Abstract of the United States*. Washington, DC: Government Printing Office.

——. 1952–2002. *Census of Governments*. Vol. 1, No. 1. Government Organization (GC(1)-1). Washington, DC: Government Printing Office.

Walker, David B. 1995. *The Rebirth of Federalism: Slouching toward Washington*. Chatham, NJ: Chatham House Publishers. 20.

White, Leonard D. 1933. *Trends in Public Administration*. New York: McGraw-Hill. 140.

Wright, Deil S. 1982. *Understanding Intergovernmental Relations*. Monterey, CA: Brooks/Cole.

FEDERALISM AND INTERGOVERNMENTAL RELATIONS: CONCEPTS, MODELS, AND THE AMERICAN SYSTEM

The territorial principle of divided powers was and is the prime gift of the United States to the art and science of government. . . . Federalism . . . is a constitutional principle involving a distinctive territorial division of powers, usually a special approach to representation within the national government, and mechanisms—both legal and political—to settle interlevel disputes. Its embodiment as a system is not easily established and usually is even more difficult to maintain.

—David B. Walker, *The Rebirth of Federalism* (1995)

As Professor Walker implies, the concept of "federalism" per se too often involves a highly legalistic and structural approach since there is a tendency to forget about the political mechanisms, both formal and informal, that are necessary to make a complex system of government function. And the United States is the world's most extensive and complex federal system, with 57 state and statelike regional governments; nearly 88,000 discrete and overlying local governments; almost 88,000 legislative bodies; numerous court systems; uncountable—hundreds of thousands—federal, state, and local, often functionally discrete, administrative agencies; and over one-half million elected officials.

Further, many of the federal, state, and larger local government administrative structures have subordinate regional or subarea organizations. At the federal level alone there are over 150 departments, agencies, boards, and commissions concerned with specialized activities, along with a bicameral legislature and 115 courts (Office of the Federal Register National Archives and Records Administration 2003); there are probably well over 5,000 administrative agencies and fifty-odd court systems at the state level (CSG 2003b); and no one knows how many administrative agencies exist at the local level. In addition to the more than 35,000 independent special district governments tabulated by the Census Bureau as separate local governments in the 2002 *Census of Governments*, there are 3,470 *types* of semi-independent special districts and authorities at the state and local levels of government—probably more than the number listed as independent units of local government (U.S. Bureau of the Census 1997, 2002; Stephens 2003).

Our federal system requires a myriad of formal and informal public and private actions and activities in order to operate at almost any reasonable level of effectiveness. Sometimes government is ineffective and unable to accomplish its policy goals because of these multitudinous discrete and overlying jurisdictions. There are multiple points of access and a bewildering array of strictures. It is a wonder this system functions at all. In fact, a good portion of the time it *does not* work in the interest of a majority of the citizenry (see Figure 2.1). One example of how this can happen took place in Leawood, Kansas in 1979 during a dispute about a little taxing district for road improvements for 123rd Street and Mission Road, an improvement that was needed by three developers of new subdivisions who owned unimproved land. It placed most of the costs, based on assessed value of property, on the already developed subdivisions in the area. The vote was 187–3 against the project. The three won because the vote was by square footage of land owned by those who held the title to the land. The three developers had 51 percent of the land area. While this is but a minor example, it tells what can happen with our complex and diffuse system of local government.

A major example is the failure of government at all levels to perform adequately in a crisis is the 2005 disaster caused by Hurricane Katrina in New Orleans and communities along the Gulf Coast from Mobile, Alabama through Mississippi and Louisiana. Three states, hundreds of local governments, and numerous federal agencies were directly involved. There was ample warning of the severity of the storm, but it took several days for the federal government and some of the state agencies to gear up and face the situation. No one was in charge. Dereliction by all levels in not only planning for the possibility of a major hurricane, but also in terms of the maintenance and upgrading of the infrastructure goes back a number of years. It could be argued that many local and state governments simply lack the resources to cope with such a disaster, but the failure of the federal government to act immediately in light of the early warning of the pending crisis by its own weather bureau is inexcusable. Without making light of this event a former colleague, Thomas M. Magstadt, summed up the situation with a series of f-words, "Feuding feudal fiefdoms foster fragmented federal government and feckless federal policies."

In a series of lectures on public administration at the University of Alabama in 1945, published in 1947, John M. Gaus talked about the importance of the "ecology of government" and the interaction of government with its environment from the ground up—for example, how the elements of place, like soils, climate, the people who live there in terms of their numbers and composition, physical and social technology and organization, ideas and concepts, catastrophe, and even the personality affect government and its administration. In hindsight, he should have also included the ecology of governments vis-à-vis governments as an important ecological characteristic.

> **Federal**

Congress, the *Judiciary*, and the *President*, over 100 federal courts, plus at more than 150 different
departments, agencies, regulatory and advisory commissions, and government corporations.

> **Fifty states, plus four Territories, two Commonwealths, and the District of Columbia**

106 *Legislative* bodies, 56 *Governors*, about 300 separately elected administrative officials 52 *Judicial* systems,
about 5,450 administrative agencies, regulatory and advisory boards and commissions. In addition,
there are 1,149 state created *types* of semi-independent special districts and authorities some of
which serve local areas. There are over 19,500 elected officials at the state level.

> **Nearly 88,000 Local Governments**

3,034 **Counties**
19,429 **Municipalities**
16,504 **Town and township governments**
35,052 **Special districts and authorities**, plus 2,321 *types* of semi-independent special districts and
authorities and public corporations serving local areas. No one knows how many exist (see
paragraph under fifty states above and the following description).
13,506 **School districts**, plus 1,508 dependent school systems operated by counties, municipalities and
townships.
Nearly all local governments have a legislative body, although in the case of special district governments
about 84,700 or 48 percent of the 176,500 governing body membership is either appointed by
other local governments or by a state official like the governor, or serve *ex-officio* (see Table 2.1
on page 36). County, municipal, town and township, and school district governments are mostly
discrete entities with reference to each other, but they usually overlie one another. Special districts
and authorities are sometimes discrete with reference to each other, but virtually all overlie other
local units. Moreover, there are 2,321 *types* of semi-independent special districts and authorities,
probably as many as are listed as independent special district governments (see above), that are
subordinate agencies of counties, municipalities and town governments. No one knows how
many subordinate agencies of these local units exist. There are nearly 506,000 locally elected
administrative, legislative, and judicial officials. In addition there are about 274,000 private RCAs
that provide government type services. The number of administrative departments and agencies that
exist within the 88,000 local governments is unknown, but a crude estimate by the authors would
place it at almost 400,000.

FIGURE 2.1. The 2002 listing of federal, state, and local governments in the United States,
including nonstate, statelike entities. *Sources: U.S. Bureau of the Census 1997, 2002; Office of the
Federal Register National Archives and Records 2003–4; Council of State Governments 2003a, 2003b.*

The ecology of governments is particularly important in areas that have a congestion
of governments, like our 361 metropolitan regions—perhaps also for the 573 micropolitan urbanized areas recently defined by the Office of Management and Budget
(OMB). The manner in which a government operates affects not only those within its
own boundary, but also neighboring polities and those that underlie or overlie its
jurisdiction with primary and, perhaps, secondary and tertiary consequences.

There is another problem with federalism, particularly with the extreme complexity that is a major characteristic with the federal system in the United States. Such

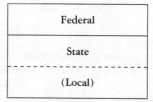

Federal
State
(Local)

FIGURE 2.2. The layer-cake model of federalism. This is the concept of a federal system in which the federal and state (or provincial) levels operate in almost exclusively different spheres, local governments are dependencies of the state level, and their independent activities are at the discretion of the state. Barring state constitutional limitations, local governments are creatures of the state subject to the discretion of the state in terms of their creation and/or abolition. It is the "Dillon's Rule" concept of local government (*City of Clinton v. the Cedar Rapids and Missouri River Railroad*, 24 *Iowa Law Review* 455, 1868).

complexity allows many *access points* where small determined and well-financed groups can, over long periods of time, do their will on major public policy issues by slow accretion without the average citizen even knowing such drastic changes have taken place. As will be seen in Chapter 4, "Fiscal Federalism," over the last fifty or sixty years the entire tax and revenue structure of the federal system has been drastically altered. These changes have altered not only the revenue structure and who pays or does not pay for government services, but also the manner in which government services are performed. It has even rearranged the social and economic structure of the nation, not to mention the way the political structure actually operates.

Legally the United States is a two-tier, layer-cake federal system with federal and state levels. Again, in a legal sense, local governments are considered dependencies of the states and operate at their discretion (see Figure 2.2). Barring state constitutional provision to the contrary, local governments exist at the discretion of state government. This is the federal model of "Dillon's Rule" (*City of Clinton v. the Cedar Rapids and Missouri River Railroad*, 24 *Iowa Law Review*, 455, 1868), which has been adhered to in court cases from time to time. This case says that local governments operate only on those powers that have been explicitly granted to it by the state legislature. There is no right of self-government in common law. It is also what Deil Wright (1978 and later editions) calls the separated authority model, in which the two major levels operate independently with clear distinction relative to the authority of the central and constituent (state) governments. This appears to have been the dominant pattern in very early years under the 1787 Constitution, although in the earliest times the national level did contract with states in some instances for the performance of federal services. James Bryce (1891) noted, "The distinct feature of the American Union is that it shows us two governments covering the same ground, yet distinct and separate in their action."

But it doesn't really work out that way today. This layer-cake model of the federal system is much too simplistic for most intergovermental relationships, although it does describe certain legal interactions in which the two levels are more or less autonomous with different spheres of authority and control. States do give local governments a degree of independence set out in the state constitution and statutes.

Just as Judge Dillon's Rule fails to capture the complexity of the American federalism, both Daniel Elazar (1962) and Morton Grodzins (1966) found that Lord Bryce was wrong in his analysis of the way the system works. Elazar found a great deal of intergovernmental cooperation among governments and levels of government even in the nineteenth century.

Nevertheless, the national government is still a government of delegated powers and the states governments of residual powers. The national government in the United States rests on delegated powers, those powers delegated to the federal level by the Constitution, plus other powers necessary to carry the authority so delegated by the states. The states have the residual authority, in theory at least. The reverse is true of the Canadian federation—the provinces have the delegated authority, the central government the residual powers. The extent of the powers delegated is open to interpretation and it has fallen to the federal courts and, to some degree, to Congress and the president, as to where to draw the line between the states and the federal government given the supremacy clause of the federal Constitution (Article VI, paragraph 2). Moreover, the central government has whatever "necessary and proper" authority required to carry out its delegated powers. The clause allowing federal regulation of interstate and foreign commerce and the provision to "provide for the common Defense and general Welfare," among other things, like the control of navigable rivers, have been utilized to expand the authority of our central government (Article I, section 8). The federal government used an income tax to finance the Civil War. Later when Congress tried to reauthorize the income tax, the U.S. Supreme Court declared it unconstitutional, so it took a constitutional amendment in order to levy taxes on income. Interpretation changes from time to time, usually, although not always, toward a broadening of the authority of the central government. We are dual citizens of a state and a nation. Each level has authority within its assigned functions relative to persons and property within its territorial jurisdiction and sphere of operation.

In spelling out the legislative authority, the Constitution gives Congress broad authority to appropriate and spend money—authority that has not been limited to the specific delegated powers listed in Article I, section 8. The inherent superiority of a national government to collect revenue is important when considering the divisions of authority between a national government and state or provincial levels. The national government has the revenue resources of the nation at its disposal, whereas state and local governments are mostly limited to the resources within their respective political jurisdictions. As a result, the national government has used its ability to spend money to influence the activities of state and local governments using grants-in-aid. Some would say the spending authority has been used to persuade, bribe, cajole, and affect what the state and local governments do.

In all states there are geographically discrete local governments. While it varies considerably among states and regions, in most states there are often many layers of local government that operate independent from one another. Moreover, social, economic, political, media, religious, and governmentally associated groups and actors are often involved in the policy-making process. At the same time, the United States is a federal system in which state and local governments and governmentally associated groups—types of elected and appointed officials, government employees, occupations associated with government, and even associations of types of governments—try to influence public policy, not only as it applies to their own level, but also at other levels of government. For these and other reasons, the emphasis in this book is on intergovernmental relations, rather than the federal structure per se. Nevertheless, we do spend considerable time discussing structure because it shapes the manner in which government and the carrying society interact, what government can and cannot do, and the territorial jurisdiction through which government policies and programs can be effective.

Let us briefly review the five attributes of a functioning federal system listed by Arthur Macmahon (1955) and referred to in Chapter 1, all of which are a matter of degree. (1) The distribution of power between a central and constituent governments (provinces or states) must be under an arrangement that cannot be changed by ordinary legislation. It requires extraordinary consent of both the central and constituent governments. (2) Matters entrusted to both the central and the constituent governments (whether those powers are residual or delegated) must be substantial. Trivial or ceremonial authority is not enough. The powers given to the central government under the Articles of Confederation were limited and few. (3) In a "republican" (small "r") form of federation, both levels must be able to draw their authority directly from the citizens in terms of elections and operate directly upon residents in terms of the enforcement of laws and regulations. (4) Member states need considerable leeway in devising their forms of government and procedures. (5) There must be legal equality among the constituent states even though they are likely to differ greatly in terms of other attributes such as population, territorial size, wealth, and tax capacity.

Macmahon goes on to say that the appearance of federal systems is related to attitudes that permit a union as close as a federation, but not complete integration that would eliminate the independence of the constituent governments in some important matters. A. V. Dicey (1915) wrote that federation requires two conditions: (1) a desire to unite, for at least some services, and (2) "a body of countries . . . so closely connected by locality, by history, by race, or the like, as to be capable of bearing, in the eyes of its inhabitants, the impress of a common nationality." In other words, a desire to unite, but not a desire for unity.

Some think of federation as a way-station on the path to a more centralized system of government. In 1933 Leonard D. White observed, "[T]he tide of centralization will probably steadily sweep power from the localities to the states, and from the states into the hands of national authorities." So far, while that has been the major long-term trend, it does not entirely explain the evolution of the federal system in the United States. There have been periods of regression. It is also possible for federations to disintegrate and fly apart, reverting to whatever existed prior to union or to something else. The Civil War was fought over the federal-state distribution of power within the union.

The one constant in the U.S. federal system has been change, change in the roles played by federal, state, and local governments. Over the more than two hundred years of our federation, much of this change has been toward a more centralized system, but

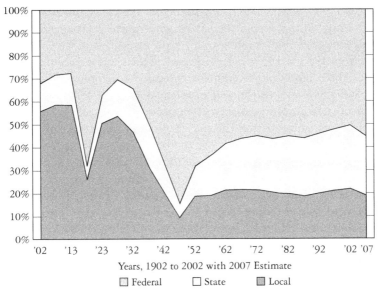

FIGURE 2.3. A century of change in the relative roles of federal, state, and local governments, 1902–2002, with 2007 estimate. The figure uses Stephens's indices of state and federal centralization based on three subindices—financial responsibility, service delivery, and personnel—adjusted for differences in relative inputs of labor versus cash and capital for interlevel differences in public services (Stephens 1974 and later updates). The most accurate data are available for the period from 1946 on. Some of the personnel data for 1902 through the early 1940s must be inferred from the types of public services provided. The effects of World War I and II can be seen on the graph.

that is not an entirely consistent or fully unidirectional pattern (see Figure 2.3). It should also be remembered that even large unitary or centralized governments must decentralize the administration and delivery of many regulatory activities and public services. In territorially large governments, the need for and the ability to pay for public services varies widely among different geographic and demographic areas. Financial resources and the need for public services are often not coterminous.

Many of the services regulated and paid for by the federal level of government in the United States are delivered by state and local governments; some of the services of state governments are delivered by local governments. The effectuation of public policy in the United States involves not only the actual legislation and the payment of money for the services delivered but also how these services are delivered and whether they are delivered by public agencies or private firms. How and how well service delivery is administered is just as important, maybe more important, than the actual legislative policy being implemented.

The changing roles of federal, state, and local government shown in Figure 2.3 clearly indicate that the role played by the federal level responded dramatically to the exigencies of two World Wars, eclipsing those of state and local governments. After the major expansion of the federal role during the two World Wars, the federal role declined rapidly, but never really returned to its prewar level. The war powers of the federal level have been used to greatly expand federal power and sometimes to suspend civil rights and control the activity of state and local governments. Although not shown very clearly on this graph, the federal government also expanded its role after the stock market crash 1929 in order to meet the exigencies of the Great Depression, particularly from 1933 to 1937. In fact, because of the relative stability of government revenues, all three levels of government expanded their roles in constant dollars (taking out inflation) vis-à-vis the total economy during the 1927–1932 time period, with the rise of state government activity the most pronounced.

It must be remembered that the role of government relative to the rest of the economy changed dramatically over the course of the twentieth century. In 1902, government constituted only 8.4 percent of the GNP, and it stayed at that level until World War I, when it reached 29.8 percent. Government expenditures declined to 11.2 percent of GNP by 1927 and increased steadily in the 1930s, then increased dramatically to 52 percent during World War II. From there it declined to 28.7 percent by 1962. With hot and cold wars, government was usually somewhere between 33 and 39 percent of GNP for the 1970s through the 1990s, topping out at around 40 percent of GNP for fiscal years 2004 and 2005 with hot wars in Afghanistan and Iraq.

Federation is not a new idea discovered by the United States. It goes back at least as far as the ancient Greeks. During much of the Roman Empire, Rome maintained a careful balance between matters that were imperially controlled and those that were left to its provinces and municipalities. The Swiss and the Dutch experimented with federal arrangements before the adoption of the U.S. Constitution. According to W. Brooke Graves (1964), "[I]t appears that central-local relations are age-old and universal in their application. They are not peculiar to the federal form of organization, although they may be more numerous and perhaps more difficult to cope with under such a system."

INTERGOVERNMENTAL RELATIONS

As Carl J. Friedrich (1968) pointed out, "[L]evels of community and government are never sharply divided." They interact, fight, cooperate, argue, and compromise. He goes on to say, " '[L]evels of government' has a distinct and operational meaning, namely the range or territorial extension of power and authority." This is important because for most purposes all governments—federal, state, and local—have a bounded geographic area or territory within which they can legally operate. These boundaries are not necessarily natural or appropriate boundaries in terms of the provision of specific governmental services. Therefore, there is considerable need for both vertical (interlevel) and horizontal (among states and/or among local units) cooperation among governments.

Historians and lawyers have studied the legal structure of the federal system from the time of its establishment in this country, but the concept of *intergovernmental relations* (IGR) is apparently of more recent and obscure origin. The more common use of this term may have had its origin in the 1930s with the concern about the effective delivery of public services during the Great Depression and the collaboration of state and local governments in the New Deal federal programs of that era (Snider 1937). The use of the term could have originated earlier involving concern over interstate relations and interstate compacts. A 1940 issue of the *Annals* edited by W. Brooke Graves, titled "Intergovernmental Relations in the United States," discussed federal-state, federal-local, regional, interstate, and interlocal relationships. Graves later produced his seminal work on the subject, *American Intergovernmental Relations*, in 1964.

As a result of President Dwight D. Eisenhower's concern about the status and viability of the federal system, Congress created a temporary agency, known as the Commission on Intergovernmental Relations (1953–55, Public Law 83–109), to study intergovernmental relations. The commission, more commonly known as the Kestnbaum Commission, conducted a broad, wide-ranging, eleven-volume study of federal-state-local relations. One result of this effort was the creation of a permanent intergovernmental relations agency in 1959, the U.S. Advisory Commission on Intergovernmental Relations, usually known as ACIR.

ACIR's twenty-eight member commission consisted of three members of the U.S. Senate, three from the House of Representatives, four from the administration, four governors, four mayors, four members of state legislatures, three elected county officials, and three private citizens. The staff usually had from twenty-five to forty professional and clerical employees conducting major research in intergovernmental relations, at least during the first twenty-odd years of its existence. The staff produced a large number of well-regarded studies of intergovernmental relations in the United States, plus some that compared the United States to other federal systems. Beginning with the appointees of the Reagan administration in the early 1980s, the commission started losing financial and congressional support and was phased out during the last years of the George H. W. Bush and first Clinton administration.

The use of the term intergovernmental relations (IGR), rather than federalism, as a concept became widespread in the 1960s and 1970s. IGR was recognized by congressional legislation in the Intergovernmental Cooperation Act (Public Law 90–577, 1968) and the Intergovernmental Personnel Act (Public Law 91–648). The former required regional and state review of grant applications by local governments, while the latter provided federal funds for the training of state and local personnel and the interchange of federal personnel with state and local career public officials. By the 1970s nearly all states, the White House, and most federal agencies had personnel whose primary concern was IGR. In fact, by the mid-1970s, most large city and county governments had personnel devoted to IGR (ICMA 1970; ACIR 1977).

MODELS OF FEDERALISM AND IGR

Even in political systems in which the ultimate authority is centralized—some call this arrangement "unitary"—it is usually practical to organize government into regional and local or municipal governments for purposes of administration. Many often delegate authority to these regional and local structures. This is particularly true of larger countries with more diverse regions and urban areas. At the central level, government is commonly organized functionally, as are the structures of whatever regional and local administrative areas that are established. More democratic systems usually delegate some discretionary authority to these regional and local governments

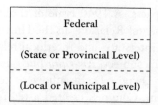

Federal
(State or Provincial Level)
(Local or Municipal Level)

FIGURE 2.4. The centralized or unitary system with ultimate authority at the central level. Larger nations will usually have a state or provincial level and local or municipal governments, if only for administrative purposes. In more democratic systems other authority will be delegated to the subnational governments and they will elect legislators and other public officials.

as well as establishing local and regional representative assemblies. In any event, the act of administering services and regulatory activities normally carries with it some discretionary authority (see Figure 2.4).

In what is now the United States, colonial governments started out with what can be considered a precedent for a federal system given their relationship with a country of origin. Separated by thousands of miles of salt water, living in a very different environment, with slow transportation and communications, the colonies got used to operating independently with only sporadic supervision by the mother country. This seems to be particularly true of federations that evolved from colonies, such as Canada, India, Australia, as well as the United States—although not limited to those under British rule.

All of the models of the U.S. federal system are inadequate to explain the overall complexity and interaction that takes place in the system, although Deil Wright (1978 and later editions) suggested a design that he called the "overlapping authority model," which captures some of the complexity of intergovernmental relations in the United States (Figure 2.5). It posits areas of exclusivity in terms of political authority and/or governmental activity for each of our three levels of government along with areas in which two or all three levels of government are involved—federal-state-local, federal-local, federal-state, and state-local. Wright describes this model as one in which the three levels have independent, interdependent, and overlapping authority with both cooperation and competition and a large degree of bargaining among the governments and levels involved. Areas of autonomy for each of the three levels are limited. In any case, autonomy is limited by both constitutional and statutory restraints and the resources available. Insofar as simple models are concerned, Figure 2.5 is probably the most descriptive of contemporary intergovernmental relations. It should be noted that we have rearranged Wright's model so the federal level is at the top of the diagram because, in practice, the national government is the ultimate arbiter of disputes on many issues.

While the areas shown for each of these relationships do not represent the actual amount of activity, there is a large area where all three levels of government are involved in the establishment of particular public policies, regulation, raising and spending money, and the delivery of public services. Moreover, within our *constitutional* system of government the amount of authority and influence available to any one level or jurisdiction is limited as are areas of autonomy. In addition, actions taken

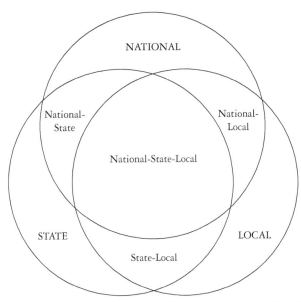

FIGURE 2.5. An adaptation of Deil S. Wright's overlapping authority model of intergovernmental relations. This model, in contrast to that of Wright, shows the national government at the top because, in practice, it is the national government that is the ultimate arbiter on many issues. *Source: Wright 1978.*

by one level or jurisdiction, whether or not that action is autonomous, often have primary and secondary consequences for other areas and jurisdictions. If a policy decision is to be carried out effectively, with few deleterious side effects, bargaining and compromise are almost always a necessary ingredient.

Although by no means limited to this area, much of the bargaining between governments, government agencies, and government officials involves federal and state grants-in-aid and federal loan, credit, and insurance programs. At least forty federal agencies are directly involved in the issuance of grants-in-aid and nearly all are involved in contractual relationships, either with other governments, government agencies, or private contractors.

Power in the overlapping authority model tends to be widely dispersed, making bargaining a necessary activity. Grants involve the transfer of resources, usually but not always the transfer of monetary resources, from one jurisdiction to another, which alters authority relationships among those officials and governments involved in the transaction. In the overlapping authority model power is dispersed. If the federal or state government involved sets the basic policy and provides the funds for carrying out a program or project, it wields a large stick in these negotiations—but how a program is administered by the recipient government can determine the manner in which the program or project reaches fruition and whether or not it succeeds. The granting government and the recipient government become more interdependent in what Wright calls "bargaining-exchange relationships." This process is characteristic of both cooperation and competition—cooperation among the governments involved, but also competition between recipient and grantor and between potential recipient governments for the money, the project, or the programs that are being funded (see Figure 2.5). Periodically over the last half-century, proposals for a "new federalism" (often positing a devolution of services and the responsibility for funding those services to state and local governments) has meant increasing competition among subnational governments for taxable resources given the highly unequal distribution of wealth and natural resources among the states (Stephens 1985).

A member of the Kestnbaum Commission once said that there are "too many governments, too little government." Competition for resources among state and local governments is often very intense. Many state and local governments try to export their taxes to residents and businesses in other states or other local areas by imposing taxes, fees, and service charges on tourists and travelers; severance taxes on extractive resources like oil, gas, coal, timber, and other minerals; or other taxes on items and goods that are likely to be exported to other jurisdictions. Florida emphasizes taxes on hotels, entertainment, and car rentals that are designed to tap the pocketbooks of tourists; Nevada, of course, does the same, plus its taxes on gambling. Many local governments also tap travelers through high selective sales taxes on hotels, ranging from 10 to 17 percent. Departure taxes at airports are another example (Stephens and Parsons 1989).

It is difficult to overstate the complexity of multiple jurisdictions. One of the authors once calculated (1959) that there were over 33,000 different taxing areas within the borders of Montgomery County (Dayton), Ohio. That was with only about fifty local governments. What would it be in Harris County (Houston), Texas, with 487 local governments or Cook County (Chicago), Illinois, with its 559 local governments? *Constitutional government* is defined as limited government, but given the extreme number of political jurisdictions in the United States, government is often incapable of attending to the needs of a majority of its citizens.

DECISION-MAKING AUTHORITY

In a technological, highly functionally specialized socioeconomic system, like that of the United States, lines of influence and authority don't always flow along the pathways envisioned by the authors of our many federal, state, and local constitutions. Because of this specialization, basic decisions are often made by what are called *functional triads*, sometimes referred to as *iron triangles*. Functional triads are made up of (1) specialized legislative committees and subcommittees, (2) specialized government agencies and their technical personnel, and (3) interest groups, both public (governmentally associated) and private, that have an interest in the specialized area of government activity. Congresspersons, state legislators, and even local council members of their respective governments often serve on committees for long periods of time and therefore become quite knowledgeable concerning the specialized legislation being considered. Other Congresspersons, other state legislators, and other local council members often defer to the expertise of these committee members when passing legislation. Some of the most important policy decisions made by government are frequently dominated by these functional triads. To a degree, this contravenes the concept of decision-making by a legislative body representative of the populace.

Another aspect of the way government sometimes works in practical terms that seems to violate the lines of authority established by those who wrote our constitutions is referred to as *vertical functional autocracy*. This also relates back to the very specialized socioeconomic system that has evolved. This is the concept that trained professionals, as a result of their training and professional interests, may be more amenable and responsive to the ideas, policies, projects, and programs of their counterparts at a higher level of government than to those of the representative legislators at their own level of government. This is particularly true when, for example, the local highway engineer is receiving grant-in-aid money for highway construction and maintenance from the state government or the state highway engineer, who is receiving money from the federal highway fund. This doesn't only apply to a function like highways; it is applicable to a whole host of specialized activities performed by government. It would appear that some of the activities involved in the operation of both functional triads and the relationships described as vertical functional autocracy contravene the attitudes and needs of the general public. It may also interfere with the manner in which we establish priorities. Some have described our system as a "picket fence federalism" arrangement because of the vertical functional flow of influence and responsibility from federal to state to local.

POLITICAL PARTIES AND THE ELECTORAL SYSTEM

The political organizations of a federal system need to be decentralized to the pattern of the federal system if one wants to maintain a federal arrangement over time. The Soviet Union was organized as a rather elaborate federation, but its one-party system was highly centralized, largely negating a federalized system of policy-making. In the later years of the U.S.S.R. there was some decentralized decision-making, but basic policy determination was centralized in Moscow.

Political parties in the United States have always been organized around the elective offices to be filled. In the past this has meant a rather highly decentralized or noncentralized political party system because the overwhelming majority of the offices to be filled are local. In 2002, there were only 542 federal elective offices, nearly 19,000 at the state level, and an estimated 505,800 locally elective positions—over 96 percent—for a total of nearly 526,000 elected officials in the United States and its territories.[1] According to Thomas P. O'Neill, Jr., Speaker of the U.S. House of Representatives from 1977 to 1987, "All politics is local." Historically, this has been the pattern. It has meant that even candidates for state and national office are often elected on the basis of local issues in their district or state.

During the twentieth century, two developments tended to weaken political party control over their members. The first was local nonpartisan elections that are common with the council-manager form of government; in a few states all local elections are nonpartisan. Even the unicameral state legislature in Nebraska uses nonpartisan elections. The other was the abandonment of the caucus and convention methods of selecting political party candidates in favor of the direct primary—the direct primary in which voters rather than party leaders select candidates weakens party control,

TABLE 2.1. Elected Public Officials by Level of Government, 2002 Estimates[1]

Level and Type of Government	Number of Governments	Total Number of Elected Officials	Legislatures and Other Governing Boards	Other Elected Officials, Boards, and Commissions
Federal	1	542	540	2
State	56	19,550	7,550	12,000
50 States	50	18,850	7,380	11,470
Other statelike entities[2]	6	700	170	530[3]
Local	87,525	505,800	356,000	149,800
Counties	3,034	58,700	17,200	41,500
Municipalities	19,429	136,600	108,400	28,200
Towns and townships	16,504	127,800	51,300	76,500
Special districts[4]	35,052	93,500	91,800	1,700
School districts	13,506	83,000	81,100	1,900
Dependent school systems[5]	(1,508)	6,200	6,200	n.a.
TOTAL	87,638	525,892	364,090	161,802

[1] The Governments Division of the Census Bureau no longer collects this type of data. These estimates are based on earlier Censuses of Government and projected on the basis of changes in the type and level of governments involved; CSG 2003a; and U.S. Bureau of the Census 2002 (*Census of Governments*).

[2] The District of Columbia, American Samoa, Guam, Northern Mariana Islands, Puerto Rico, and the U.S. Virgin Islands.

[3] This is really an estimate of the locally elected officials in Puerto Rico's municipios.

[4] Approximately 48 percent of the membership of special district governing boards are appointed by either the state or other local governments or serve ex-officio from other local governments. There are approximately 84,700 such members of special district governing boards.

[5] Dependent school systems are those run by counties, municipalities, towns or townships, and even one by state government (Hawaii). They normally elect a separate governing board subject to oversight by the government involved. In the past the Governments Division counted them when compiling the number of elected officials in the United States.

particularly when open primaries are utilized. One more recent development has tended to strengthen party control. That is the use of the mass media, specifically television, as the primary method of electioneering. Television requires massive amounts of money for election to national and state offices as well as to elective positions in our larger local governments. National and state parties are much better at collecting the funds required.

The only elected officials at the national level are the president, the vice president, and 535 members of Congress, plus five more from our nonstate statelike entities such as the Commonwealth of Puerto Rico and the District of Columbia. Those from the District, the commonwealths, and the territories do not have the right to vote on legislation (see Table 2.1).

Of the 19,550 elected state-level officials, nearly two-fifths, or 7,550, are members of legislatures, with another 1,300-plus elected to various boards and commissions. There are another 10,000 elected officials at the state level consisting of about 250 elected administrative officials, with most of the remainder elected judges from the various levels of the state court systems. Some of these judicial elections are nonpartisan, and some states have a mixture of partisan and nonpartisan elections for judicial positions depending on the level and type of the court. In eleven states most judgeships are appointive positions. Only six states, mostly southern, have strictly partisan elections for judgeships (CSG 2003a).

Of the 505,800 locally elected officials, 52 percent, or over 264,000, rather evenly divided, are elected to the governing boards of municipalities and towns and townships. They average seven to eight elected officials per unit of government partly because most municipalities and townships are quite small in terms of total population. County governments have the highest number of elected officials per unit of government, at over nineteen, mostly because of the large number of elected administrators and/or minor judgeships. Originally in many states, counties served as a decentralized arm of state government. This is still largely the role of more rural counties where county governments are more an aggregation of elected officials that just happens to occupy the same county courthouse rather than an integrated form of local government. Larger counties have increasingly become more integrated and evolved as urban and suburban service providers rather than simply performing as agents of the state (Benton 2002). Many local elections are nonpartisan, particularly where a council-manager form of government has been adopted.

School district governments average six elected members of their school board while dependent school systems average four. Dependent school systems are those that are part of another form of local government such as a municipality, New England town, or county government. Special district governments have governing boards that average five members, but only about half of the membership of these boards are elected. The other half are appointed by other local governments or the state or their membership serves ex-officio as members of the legislatures, councils, or executives of other local governments.

As campaigning for public office has become more expensive through the use of the electronic media as the primary tool of electioneering, especially television, the cost of running for office at the federal and state levels and for larger local governments has increased exponentially. This has led to some centralization of the funding of elections, particularly by national and state political party organizations. To some degree this has led to more federal and state party control over local party organizations by higher party organs and more influence by wealthy interest groups and the executives of corporate America.

In many instances, at all levels of government, the funding issue has led to the election of more individuals who are able to raise large amounts of campaign money, already have a considerable amount of media exposure, or are wealthy enough to finance their own campaigns—or some combination of these characteristics. The act of raising the necessary money to fund required media exposure in order to win an election means that the candidate is beholden to those who provide the campaign contributions. This indicates that money has become a critical variable in our electoral process and appears to restrict severely the kind of person who can successfully run for public office, especially for state and national office and for positions in many cities and larger suburban local governments. This situation would seem to run counter to, and have definite negative implications for, the prospect of maintaining a viable democratic federal system.

THE "NEW FEDERALISM," THE "NEW 'NEW' FEDERALISM" AND THE "NEW FEDERALISM, BY *DEFAULT*"

Federalism in the United States is continually trying to reinvent itself, a sort of constant reevaluation, reconstruction, and self-flagellation. Perhaps this is not just a tendency of the United States alone as similar activities seem to apply to the Canadian system (Saskatchewan Institute of Public Policy 2004). As the nation became more centralized over the course of the twentieth century, forces pushed against the tendency for the government in Washington, DC, to make more of the decisions, increase regulation, and provide more of the services, or at least to fund more of the services provided.

Over the course of the last century, many presidents have shown a concern for the role played by the federal government, including Presidents Taft, Wilson, and Harding. This concern sometimes started with proposals to evaluate and reorganize the administrative structure and activities of the federal government. In 1937, President Franklin D. Roosevelt appointed his Committee on Administrative Management, which resulted in the Reorganization Act of 1939 (Ogg and Ray 1945). President Harry S. Truman created the two Hoover commissions (headed by former President Herbert Hoover) to reevaluate and reorganize the activities of the federal government. President Eisenhower was concerned that the distribution of authority between the government in Washington and the states had gone too far and created three or four commissions to study the issue of the division of authority between levels of government, including the Kestnbaum Commission, which resulted in the more permanent ACIR from 1959 to the mid-1990s.

President Richard M. Nixon promoted his "New Federalism" as a method of returning more of the decision-making authority and freedom of action to state and local governments. Nixon's New Federalism primarily consisted of proposals to alter radically the system of grants-in-aid that had evolved over the course of the previous three decades. At that time, nearly all federal aid was in the form of highly specific federal grants for rather narrow projects and programs, commonly referred to as categorical grants. They usually required strict conformity to federal requirements, matching funds, and supervision by federal granting agencies. To some extent, Nixon's proposals were a response or reaction to the "Great Society" programs instituted by President Lyndon B. Johnson. These programs were intended to mitigate social welfare problems such as poverty, ameliorate inadequate medical care for the elderly and the needy, and provide education for disadvantaged children.

Nixon's New Federalism came in the form of General Revenue Sharing and six Special Revenue Sharing grants-in-aid that were to consolidate over one hundred categorical grants to state and local governments. The grants were to give more discretion to state and local governments in how they spent the funds received. Originally General Revenue Sharing (GRS) was to be general-purpose money given to the states with more per capita funding going to poorer states. There were no matching requirements or other strictures except that funds be spent for a public purpose and could not be spent for education, since the Nixon administration was also proposing a Special Revenue Sharing grant for education. Nor was there a provision that these funds be passed on to local governments.

Local governments and their lobbying organizations, known as "public interest groups," or PIGs, were up in arms about this since they wanted a share, too. (PIGs are organizations of state or local governments, officials, or occupations associated with local government, such as the National League of Cities, the U.S. Conference of Mayors, the International City Manager's Association, the National Association of Counties, and so on.) As a result, Congress decided these funds should be divided between states and so-called general-purpose local governments (municipalities, townships, and counties). Originally, this was to be a fifty-fifty division of funds between state and local government. In closed-door meetings with Wilbur Mills and other key members of Congress, New York Governor Nelson Rockefeller (later to serve a short time as vice president of the United States) persuaded them to change the division to two-thirds for local government and one-third for state.[2] This division was used for the State and Local Fiscal Assistance Act of 1971 (GRS) even though it was really only appropriate for New York and perhaps California in 1971. At that time a fifty-fifty division would have been much more appropriate. Other states were more centralized in terms of the funding and delivery of public services (Stephens and Olson 1979). At the time it was passed by Congress it was the largest federal grant-in-aid ever enacted.

Special Revenue Sharing (SRS) was designed to give broad functional-purpose grants to state and local governments that could be spent within six broad functional areas like education, welfare, and urban development. Only two of the SRS proposals were passed by Congress, although a number of block grants covering fairly broad fields were passed or renewed by Congress. Actually, however, the Nixon administration and the follow-on administration of President Gerald Ford, working with Congress, did more to fund domestic public services than any administration before or since. During this period grants to local governments were increased greatly compared to those for the state level. The overall thrust of Nixon's New Federalism was to return at least some decision-making authority to state and local governments.

President Ronald W. Reagan also proposed a new New Federalism, but with a different emphasis. In his 1982 State of the Union message, President Reagan proposed a New Federalism that would federalize Medicaid and turn responsibility for food stamps and aid to families with dependent children (AFDC) over to the states. It would also turn over to the states financial responsibility for some forty-three other federal grant-in-aid programs in the areas of transportation, revenue sharing (GRS), and so on. Over time, the federal government would withdraw support for these programs and vacate some tax sources used by the federal government so that state and local governments could levy taxes in these areas. According to the president, state and local governments would be able to exercise more discretion in both the levying of taxes and spending money for public services.

During the first year of Reagan's tenure, the Omnibus Reconciliation Act of 1981 (PL97-35) was passed by Congress. It consolidated seventy-nine grant programs into nine block grants, reduced funding by 25 percent, and channeled these funds through the states, thus eliminating some direct aid to local governments (Walker, Richter, and Colella 1982). This approach was a start toward what Reagan viewed as his New Federalism. Over the first few years of this approach, local government bore the brunt of the cutbacks in federal aid. Neither the Reagan or the George H. W. Bush administrations ever vacated any federal tax sources, but during the later years of both administrations federal aid to state and local governments increased somewhat.

The major problem with Reagan's New Federalism was, and still is, the maldistribution of tax capacity among the fifty states (see Chapter 4). Many states would have been incapable of funding some basic levels of public services if federal aid was abolished. During the period from the mid-1970s to the early 1980s fiscal disparities among the states were on the increase. No more than nine or ten states could have weathered the abolition of federal aid even if some federal tax sources were vacated (ACIR 1979–93; Stephens 1985). Unlike federal systems in Australia, Canada, and Germany, the United States has no grant system or shared tax that equalizes or levels up the finances of poorer state governments so that they are capable of providing a basic level of public services. Even the GRS of the 1970s and early 1980s did not accomplish this goal since the equalization provided was quite limited. And GRS no long exists.

President William Jefferson Clinton had his own New Federalism, but he labeled it "Reinventing Government." It was aimed at downsizing the federal government, particularly the federal bureaucracy, and making it more efficient under the direction of Vice President Albert Gore. Over the next eight years about 400,000 civil service positions were eliminated along with 456,000 active duty military personnel (U.S. Bureau of the Census 1995, 2003). In the aggregate, virtually all of the civilian positions eliminated were at the lower pay grades. General Service (GS) 13 to 15 positions increased 15 percent, while Senior/Executive positions increased over 49 percent. Moreover, most major agencies increased their contracting for outside personnel, which eliminated whatever savings were realized from the abolition of civil service and active duty military positions. Moreover, the lowering tide during the Clinton administration did not lower all boats. The judicial branch increased the number of civil service personnel by 30 percent and the Justice Department by 40 percent, while Federal Deposit Insurance Corporation (FDIC) personnel dropped by 53 percent despite increased workload given its consolidation with the Federal Savings and Loan Insurance Corporation (FSLIC).[3]

During the Clinton years, active duty military personnel declined by 27 percent from 1,705,000 to 1,249,000. This decline was also accompanied by an increase in contracting out for contract military personnel and services. In the early 1950s, only about one-fourth of federal direct expenditures for defense were in the form of procurement contracts. For most of the 1990s, contracting accounted for between 55 and 56 percent of direct outlays, but for FY2001 and 2002 it had reached 62.5 percent. In other words, most of the so-called savings from federal downsizing are illusory and have resulted in lower government services and increasing costs of government contracting. Many private corporations contract with the Department of Defense

(DOD) and other agencies involved in defense, but by 2003 there were at least sixty-two private corporations that provided military personnel (mercenaries) to DOD (Singer 2003; Wayne 2002).

Attempting to cut the federal government down to size and make it more *efficient* is not new. Nor is bureaucrat bashing. This was a major thrust of the Reagan administration and has been pushed by more conservative members of Congress for a very long period of time. Writing in *Scribner's Magazine* in 1933, Charles A. Beard and William Beard describe a similar situation: "Among the latest deliriums is that of waging war on the bureaucracy, full of noise and promise. Some of our best people are doing it, usually without discrimination, for discrimination takes the edge off propaganda" (Beard and Beard 1946). In the same vein, substantial misinformation has been conveyed as fact concerning both personnel downsizing and the state of the public bureaucracy in the United States—perhaps some of it originating from those who would benefit from government contracts. As Charles Goodsell noted in 1994, "Roughly 20 million Americans work for government. We recognize that this huge slice of the population does not consist solely of lazy bums, incompetents, or the psychologically malformed."

As was noted on the Reinventing Government website in 1999, "[T]he Administration's efforts [are] to reinvent government, making it work better, cost less, and get results Americans care about. Under his [Vice President Gore's] leadership, the size of the federal [civilian] workforce has been reduced . . . and common sense changes have been made that have saved the taxpayers $137 million."[4] These efforts are always made to sound like "the good, the true, and the beautiful." Given increases in procurement contracts for these agencies it is doubtful that any savings resulted from this process. In fact the cost of government appears to have increased with the downsizing of personnel and increases in procurement contracts.

The downsizing of personnel at the federal level has resulted in a diminution of federal services and abandonment of a considerable amount of information that was once published by the Census Bureau and other agencies. The authors notice this in the publications of the Governments Division of the Census Bureau, where much data is no longer collected about government at all levels, data that has been used for decades to evaluate the performance of the government in terms of public policy. It is also evident in the performance of other agencies. By turning government services such as this over to private contractors we are losing much of the institutional memory as well as the benefits of what was once a very good civil service system.

Perhaps Clinton's New Federalism should be labeled "New Federalism by default," since the intention was only to downsize the central government, not necessarily to turn services "back to state and local governments," with the exception of AFDC. Certainly when we appraise the administration of George W. Bush, it will also be New Federalism by default as the thrust is to handicap the federal government in such a way that it will be able to perform few services other than defense given the emasculation of the revenue capability of the federal government during the period between 2001 and 2006, the soaring debt and deficits resulting therefrom, along with the war in Afghanistan and the *preemptive war* in Iraq.

SUMMATION

> There has never been a time when it was possible to put neat labels
> on discrete "federal," "state," and "local" functions. Even before the
> Constitution, a statute of 1785, reinforced by the Northwest
> Ordinance of 1787, gave grants-in-land to states for [local] public
> schools. . . . More important, the nation, before it was fully organized,
> established by this action a first principle of American federalism:
> the national government would use its superior resources to initiate
> and support national programs, principally administered by the
> states and localities.
>
> —Morton Grodzins (1966)

Morton Grodzins called this arrangement "marble-cake" federalism. Nevertheless, most of the models of federalism do not seem to be sufficiently complex to delineate the situation in this country. While Deil Wright's overlapping authority model seems to best describe the governmental situation in the United States, the concepts of IGR seems more appropriate; perhaps IGR is not only more appropriate, but is even a necessary concomitant for any large nation with diverse regions and localities.

Since the beginnings, in the eighteenth and nineteenth centuries, and again in the twentieth century, there has been a pulling and hauling in terms of the roles played by the federal, state, and local governments; this continues in the twenty-first century. It is, however, still the case that the long-term trend has been, as Leonard White said, toward increased roles for the states vis-à-vis localities and central government vis-à-vis state and local governments, with the ultimate determination of the degree of centralization that is to be maintained, the purview of the national government. Wars and national crises have always had a centralizing effect.

Given the extreme complexity of the federal system in the United States, with its multitudinous and multifarious discrete and overlying jurisdictions, it is a wonder that this system works at all, much less accomplishes the tasks it sets out to do. And sometimes it doesn't. In a representative federal system, "Too many cooks may prevent the stew from ever being assembled in the pot." There are simultaneous counterveiling pressures for centralization and decentralization—the one constant in the federal system is change, change in the roles played by federal, state, and local governments—but always with a considerable amount of both cooperation and conflict. Moreover, the pattern of change can vary from one state to the next and/or in terms of the governmental functions at issue. Centralizing tendencies have prevailed over the long-term even though a number of presidents have worked hard to counter this trend and limit the role of the central government in Washington, DC.

On the other hand, the extreme dissection of the body politic into so many parts by the multitude of overlying and discrete local entities, legislative bodies, and functional administrative structures may well prevent the body politic from ever being assembled into a coherent mass to push for policies that benefit the public at large. In addition, this arrangement provides multiple access points where small, determined, well-funded groups can, over fairly long periods of time, work their will on the body politic—perhaps without the average citizen even knowing such a change in basic public policy has taken place.

Subnational governments need adequate financial resources in order to maintain their place in a federal system, and we have had only a few sporadic attempts to place a floor under the revenue base of poorer state and local governments, such as the GRS of the 1970s, Wisconsin's redistribution of revenue from the state income tax, or the redistribution of revenue from nonresidential land uses in the Minneapolis–St. Paul metropolitan area (see Chapter 4).

In terms of political parties, the phenomenal number of governments, legislatures, and elective offices to be filled at the state and local levels of government would seem to reinforce the maintenance of a federal system. But recent centralizing tendencies in terms of the financing of elections runs counter to this, as does the continuing consolidation of the electronic media and newspapers, thus giving those with the most money and power greater influence in the market of ideas. Access to the media has become much more limited (Soley 2002).

This, along with the consolidation of economic power, in terms of the influence of large corporations, such as those in the Fortune 500 and the multinationals, means that more of the decisions that shape what goes on at all levels of government is predicated on the decisions made in the private sector, which affects, even determines, what goes on in the public sector. A true federation may well require a more decentralized political, social, and economic system if a federal type governmental system is to be maintained. That does not seem to be the trend in the United States over extended periods of time, except, perhaps, for purposes of administration. Too many governments, too little access to government.

REFERENCES

Advisory Commission on Intergovernmental Relations (ACIR). 1977. *The Intergovernmental Grant System as Seen by Local, State, and Federal Officials*. Washington, DC: 1977, A-54. 45.

——. 1979–93. *Measuring State Fiscal Capacity*. Washington, DC. 1984–91.

Beard, Charles A. and William Beard. 1946. The Case for Bureaucracy. *Scribner's Magazine*, 1933. Republished in the *Public Administration Review*. 46:2 (March–April), 209.

Benton, J. Edwin. 2002. *Counties as Service Delivery Agents*. Westport, CT: Praeger.

Bryce, James. 1891. *The American Commonwealth*. 2nd ed. London: Macmillan. 318.

Council of State Governments (CSG). 2002, 2003a. *The Book of the States*. Lexington, KY: CSG.

——. 2002, 2003b. *Directory of Administrative Officials*. Lexington, KY: CSG.

Dicey, A. V. 1915. *Introduction to the Study of Law and the Constitution*. 8th ed. London: Macmillan. 137.

Elazar, Daniel J. 1962. *The American Partnership: Intergovernmental Cooperation in the Nineteenth Century United States*. Chicago: University of Chicago Press.

Friedrich, Carl J. 1968. *Trends of Federalism in Theory and Practice*. New York: Frederick A. Praeger. 3.

Gaus, John Merriman. 1947. *Reflections on Public Administration*. Montgomery: University of Alabama Press. 8–9.

Goodsell, Charles T. 1994. *The Case for Bureaucracy: A Public Administration Polemic*. Chatham, NJ: Chatham House Publishers. 167.

Graves, W. Brooke. 1964. *American Intergovernmental Relations: Their Origins, Historical Development, and Current Status*. New York: Charles Scribner's Sons. 11.

Grodzins, Morton. 1966. *The American System: A New View of Government in the United States.* Chicago: Rand McNally. 7, 17.

International City Managers Association (ICMA). 1970. Local Government Coordinators. *Urban Data Service.* 2 (August), 3.

Macmahon, Arthur W. 1955. The Problems of Federalism: A Survey. In Authur W. Macmahon, ed., *Federalism: Mature and Emergent.* Garden City, NY: Doubleday & Company. 4–6.

Office of the Federal Register National Archives and Records Administration. 2003. *The United States Government Manual 2003/2004.* Washington, DC: Government Printing Office.

Ogg, Frederick A. and P. Orman Ray. 1945. *Introduction to American Government.* 9th ed. New York: Appleton-Century-Crofts. 482–83.

Saskatchewan Institute of Public Policy/Centre for Research and Information on Canada. 2004. *Constructing Tomorrow's Federalism.* University of Regina, Regina, Saskatchewan.

Singer, Peter W. 2003. *Corporate Warriors: The Rise of the Privatized Military.* Ithaca, NY: Cornell University Press, 243–44.

Snider, Clyde F. 1937. County and Township Government in 1935–36. *American Political Science Review.* 32 (October), 909.

Soley, Lawrence. 2002. *Censorship, Inc.: The Corporate Threat to Free Speech.* New York: Monthly Review Press.

Stephens, G. Ross. 1974 and later updates. State Centralization and the Erosion of Local Autonomy. *Journal of Politics.* 36:1, 44–76.

——. 1985. New Federalism by Default, Little OPEC States, and Fiscal Darwinism. In Dennis R. Judd, ed., *Public Policy Across States and Communities.* Greenwich, CT: JAI Press. 49–68.

——. 2003. Special Districts Governments. *Encyclopedia of Public Administration and Public Policy.* New York: Marcel Dekker.

Stephens, G. Ross and Nelson Wikstrom. 1999, 2003. Institutional Change in the Roles of Federal, State, and Local Governments over the Course of the Twentieth Century. Working paper, earlier version presented to the 1999 annual conference of the American Political Science Association, Atlanta.

——. 2000. Reinventing Government and Federal Downsizing—or Whose Ox Is Being Gored. Pape-presented to the Southern Political Science Association Annual Conference. Atlanta. November 8–11, 2000.

Stephens, G. Ross and Gerald W. Olson. 1979. *Pass-through Federal Aid.* Report to the National Science Foundation. 2 Vols. University of Missouri–Kansas City.

Stephens, G. Ross and Karen T. Parsons. 1989. Rich States, Poor States: An Addendum. *State and Local Government Review.* 21:2 (Spring), 52–53.

U.S. Bureau of the Census. 1997, 2002. *Census of Governments, Government Organization.* Vol. 1, no. 1, GC97(1)-1 and GC02(1)-1. Washington, DC: Government Printing Office.

——. 2002, 2003. *Consolidated Federal Funds Report.* Washington, DC: Government Printing Office.

——. 1995, 2003. *Statistical Abstract of the United States.* Washington, DC: Government Printing Office.

Walker, David B. 1995. *The Rebirth of Federalism.* Chatham, NJ: Chatham House Publishers. 19.

Walker, David B., Albert J. Richter, and Cynthia Cates Colella. 1982. The First Fen Months: Grant-in-Aid, Regulatory, and Other Changes. *Intergovernmental Perspective.* 8:1 (Winter), 8–9.

White, Leonard D. 1933. *Trends in Public Administration.* New York: McGraw-Hill. 140.

Wayne, Leslie. 2002. America's for-profic secret army. *New York Times* October 13.

Wright, Deil S. 1978 and later editions. *Understanding Intergovernmental Relations: Public Policy and Participant's Perspectives in Local, State, and National Governments.* North Scituate, MA: Duxbury Press. 20–30.

CONTEMPORARY AMERICAN
FEDERALISM AND
INTERGOVERNMENTAL RELATIONS:
COOPERATION AND CONFLICT

Intergovernmental Relations, not always recognized as such and certainly not so denominated, have been a matter of concern to man living in organized society throughout the ages, regardless of race, creed, or color, or of time, place, or circumstance.

—W. Brooke Graves, *American Intergovernmental Relations* (1964)

Notwithstanding their general ambivalence toward government, Americans have created, as noted in Chapter 1, a large number of governments and quasi-governments. The former include the federal government, the fifty states, two commonwealths, four territories, literally thousands of local governments—cities, towns, counties, special districts, and school districts—and a number of federally recognized Native American tribal councils. Quasi-governments include a variety of federal government corporations and other entities, such as the Appalachian Regional Commission, the Tennessee Valley Authority, and the Columbia River Basin Authority, along with approximately 500 metropolitan and rural regional councils. More recently, due to the popularity of the concept of "privatization" in the public sector there are somewhat in excess of 270,000 condominium associations and RCAs, along with a multitude of for-profit and nonprofit entities, some of which provide services to the public.

This chapter is designed to provide the reader with a broad overview of the present nature of the American system of federalism and intergovernmental relations, which constitute what Daniel Elazar described some years ago as "non-centralized government" and "the American partnership" (1984, 2). Much of the subject matter covered in this chapter is elaborated upon in greater detail elsewhere in the volume. At the outset, attention is devoted to the various factors and developments that have shaped the contemporary nature of federalism and intergovernmental relations. This is followed by material centering upon cooperation among governments and the sources of competition and conflict between governments. The concluding section provides a summary of the major observations advanced in this chapter and of the future of the intergovernmental system.

Importantly, we would like to emphasize that we strongly prefer the terms "intergovernmental relations" and "intragovernmental relations," rather than federalism, in explaining the intricate web of the myriad relationships that exist between, among, and within governments and interest groups that lobby in the intergovernmental arena. This is simply the case because we believe that the term "federalism" is an excessively structural and legalistic concept that does not effectively "capture" the dynamic, especially human, essence of the interactions between and within governments. In contrast, the term "intergovernmental relations" underscores the process-oriented and human interactions of governments in the American polity. As William Anderson (1960) aptly phrased: "It is human beings clothed with office who are the real determiners of what the relations between units of government will be. Consequently the concept of intergovernmental relations necessarily has to be formulated largely in terms of human relations and human behavior" (4). And, as Deil S. Wright (1982) has succinctly written:

> Strictly speaking, then, there are no relationships among *governments*; there are only relations among *officials* who govern different units. The individual actions and attitudes of public officials are at the core of IGR. Their behavior is purposeful—for example, to obtain a grant or provide a program. And their actions are heavily influenced by how they perceive other participants' actions and attitudes. (11)

FACTORS SHAPING INTERGOVERNMENTAL RELATIONS

The present-day character of American intergovernmental relations has been shaped by a variety of developments and trends. The onslaught of the Great Depression in the early 1930s, accompanied by a host of economic and social domestic challenges, played a central role in permanently altering and shaping the character and dynamics of American intergovernmental relations. As a result of President Franklin D. Roosevelt's determination to end the nation's theoretical fixation with "dual federalism" and to usher in "cooperative federalism," the federal government and the states, and eventually local governments, agreed to a partnership of working together for coping with domestic, economic, and social challenges. Reflective of this new type of federalism, referred to as "marble-cake federalism" by Morton Grodzins (1960), the federal government, enlarging upon its earlier use of intergovernmental fiscal transfers, commenced to provide to the states financial assistance, through a wide variety of categorical grants, for providing social services for the less fortunate. Also in the 1930s, the federal government began to provide grants to local governments for emergency assistance and for the construction of public housing, and eventually for sharing with local governments the costs of the operation of public housing (Graves 1964, 858, 862). Since the administration of Roosevelt, the belief that the federal, state, and local governments should cooperate with each other has been "etched in the stone" in the

American system of intergovernmental relations (Walker 1981, 65–95). Indeed, this cooperation between the various levels of government has been a critical element in the success of our federal system of government.

In addition, the character of American intergovernmental relations has been altered by the overall changing nature of American society, evolving from rural to urban to metropolitan in nature. The vast majority of Americans presently reside in 361 metropolitan areas. It is of interest that many Americans reside in large metropolitan areas that are contiguous to each other. This type of geographically connected metropolitan area has been defined and labeled by social scientists as a "megalopolis." Although there are a number of these entities throughout the United States, the most prominent megalopolis, designated by the writings of Jean Gottmann, stretches along the East Coast from southern Maine and New Hampshire to the Tidewater region of Virginia (Gottmann 1961). It is of critical importance to note that the majority of our metropolitan citizens reside in the ever-burgeoning suburbs and more thinly settled fringe areas, often characterized as "edge cities," which surround our older central cities (Garreau 1991). We have become in essence a "suburban nation," with a national polity and, in most instances, state polities dominated by suburban interests scattered along the interstate highway system.

The rise and preeminent position of metropolitan America has served to play a defining role in shaping the present character of intergovernmental relations. Core cities, often described by social scientists as "fiscally stressed," have become increasingly dependent upon the federal and state governments for financial assistance for balancing their operating budgets and making necessary infrastructure improvements. This assistance has taken the form of intergovernmental transfers (grants) and a limited number of state and regional revenue-sharing programs. In addition, during the past fifty years, the federal and state governments have devised a bevy of policy initiatives, supported by a variety of grants-in-aid and block grant programs, designed to reverse the general deterioration of our core cities. The most of far-reaching and comprehensive of these urban policy initiatives were the "Model Cities" and "Demonstration Cities" programs of President Lyndon B. Johnson, which were part-and-parcel of his "Great Society" and larger "creative federalism" agenda (Walker 1981, 102–4). The increasing reliance of our core cities on higher levels of government for general fiscal assistance and for coping with their economic and social challenges underscores the fact that central cities have become rather permanent "dependent cities" in our intergovernmental system (Kantor 1995).

The rise of metropolitan America has had other consequences for our intergovernmental system, especially in terms of the provision of public services. The sheer inability or sometimes unwillingness of our cities and counties to provide a service has resulted in the establishment of ten of thousands of independent and semi-independent special districts and authorities. These developments have also been accelerated by economic feasibility and/or the need to provide a service on a semi-metropolitan or regional basis (Stephens and Wikstrom 1998). For example, mass transportation operations in our metropolitan areas are usually the province of a special district or authority, such as the Massachusetts Bay Transit Authority (MBTA), which is responsible for the provision of mass transportation in the Greater Boston region. The need to examine problems and fashion policies on a regional basis has led to the establishment of hundreds of regional councils. These bodies, alternatively referred to as council of governments, or COGs, are designed to promote a dialogue, and some measure of social capital, among local officials and to stimulate cooperation between governments. They are also centrally involved in physical and social regional planning efforts (Wikstrom 1977).

The explosive and continuing growth of private homeowners' associations, which typically provide a limited number of municipal-like services to their residents, has further fragmented the service delivery system of metropolitan areas. Homeowners' associations, which have experienced a 21 percent increase in number since 1998, deliver some services to about 20 million out of the approximately 106 million homes in the United States. Stated somewhat differently, about one in six citizens, or 50 million residents, resides in a community partially governed by a homeowners' association (Rich 2003, 1, 20).

The Role of the States

Elazar (1984) astutely noted that the resilient position of the states in the intergovernmental system is not only because of their protected constitutional status, but also because of the political ramifications flowing from their status as "civil society." He noted that each state has its own somewhat unique social patterns and traditions, political culture, and set of public policies. Elazar further advanced that the states constitute the "keystones" of the larger noncentralized, as he phrased it, American civil society (14–15). Notwithstanding their protected and important status, the states for much of our political history were roundly and continually criticized by many scholars for being ineffective and unresponsive, and in some instances hopelessly politically corrupt. For example, Robert S. Allen noted, as late as 1949, that: "State government is the tawdriest, most incompetent, and most stultifying unit of the nation's political structure" (vii). In an often cited published paper, Alan Campbell and Donna Shalala (1970) pointedly advanced that the states were the "fallen arches" in the federal system. This criticism against the states was advanced throughout the first half of the past century, notwithstanding the fact that the states on their own initiative during the early 1930s up to the start of World War II began to serve a much larger governmental role and exercise more functional responsibility. This was further stimulated by an infusion of federal grants brought into existence by President Franklin D. Roosevelt's New Deal and "cooperative federalism" policies.

Although the aforementioned charge was often levied in general against the states, it was advanced with particular force in regard to the continual deterioration of our core cities and the general unwillingness (or inability) of the states to deal with the pressing needs of disadvantaged urban citizens. Accordingly, the federal government, most particularly under the leadership of President Lyndon B. Johnson and his "Great Society" efforts, undertook to strengthen its fiscal and programmatic relationship with core city governments in order to (1) assist in their renewal and rehabilitation efforts, (2) provide a measure of political equity, (3) promote economic development, and (4) increase social services to the urban poor. Training programs for the unemployed were established at a variety of city training centers; social services, involving welfare, housing, health care, and education, were significantly enhanced. The "Model Cities" program, a more focused initiative of the Johnson administration, was designed to provide a targeted comprehensive approach to the needs of the poor in a limited number of cities. It should be noted that the administration of President Richard M. Nixon significantly expanded the urban initiatives of Johnson and cities were the recipients of an enhanced level of federal fiscal aid (Conlan 1998, 82–85). However, federal budgetary constraints, triggered largely by our military involvement and "moral crusade" in Vietnam, most crucially during the 1960s, ultimately turned Johnson's domestic war on poverty initiatives into, at best, a failed skirmish. Notwithstanding the fact that the federal government, especially during the administration of Ronald Reagan (1981–88), began to markedly reduce its programmatic and fiscal assistance to core cities, the demonstrated need for a strong federal-local relationship, circumventing the states, became a permanent feature of the American intergovernmental system.

However, as a result of the "modernization of state government," which commenced in the 1950s with the establishment of "little Hoover Commissions" in many states and was given further strong impetus by the historic United States Supreme Court reapportionment decision of *Baker v. Carr* 1962, the states, which by this date were largely dominated by suburban interests, over time assumed a much more prominent position in the intergovernmental system (Elazar 1984). Because of the reorganization and modernization of their executive, legislative, and judicial structures, states were soon hailed by scholars and practitioners as the "new keystones" in federal system because of their greater political and administrative capacity, along with their consequent ability to "govern well" (Bowman and Kearney 1986) and their willingness to confront problems and provide a much greater scope of services. In a more specific sense, the managerial capacity of the states was significantly enhanced by their emulation of the federal administrative structure, with the establishment of agencies resembling the federal departments of Housing and Urban Development and Transportation and the Environmental Protection Agency ("little HUDs, little DOTs, and little EPAs"). Taking recognition of this development, Presidents Richard M. Nixon, Jimmy Carter, Ronald Reagan, and, somewhat later, William J. Clinton championed what eventually became known as the "devolution revolution" (Nathan 1996) of responsibilities and—albeit, fiscal burden—and enhanced the role of the states in intergovernmental affairs. Reagan, for an assortment of reasons, including the adroit use of his political skills and his success in substantially reducing federal fiscal transfers to the states and localities, was considerably more successful than Nixon in implementing the devolution of responsibilities and shifting some federal decision-making to the states. However, Clinton's successful termination in 1996 of the Federal Aid to Dependent Children (FDIC) program, over the strenuous opposition of many of his fellow Democrats in the Congress, and replacing it with the Personal Responsibility and Work Opportunity Reconciliation Act and the Temporary Assistance for Needy Families (TANF) block grant represents the most recent spectacular and far-reaching example of the implementation of the devolution of powers in the intergovernmental system. As a result of the latter, the states were given new discretion and flexibility, although they also inherited onerous and prescriptive requirements (Kincaid 1990). States are now responsible for formulating and implementing "workfare" programs, designed to provide a mechanism for facilitating the movement of the disadvantaged and poor out of poverty and off the "welfare rolls." Although the aggressive posture of the states was somewhat curtailed in the beginning of the present century by their severe budget problems, they continue to be the dominant provider of domestic services, such as education, welfare, and public health. In essence, the more prominent position that the states gained in the intergovernmental system over the last seven decades of the twentieth century has not been substantially altered or reduced by developments reaching into the twenty-first century.

The Rise of the Conservative Ideology: Downsizing and Privatization

Commencing in the mid-1960s, the political dominance of liberalism, along with its belief in the virtue of strong and resourceful government, began to be challenged by an aggressive conservatism, which criticized, at base, the expansive role and utility of government. This new conservatism was championed and granted a considerable amount of political legitimacy by a number of scholars and prominent well-funded "think tanks," including the American Enterprise Institute, the Cato Institute, the Manhattan Institute, and the Heritage Foundation. These organizations sallied forth with an agenda calling for the "downsizing," or reduction, of government at all levels and for the public sector to make greater use of private firms for delivering services. President Ronald Reagan's election in 1980 and his re-election in 1986, the election of President George H. W. Bush in 1986, the election of President George W. Bush in 2000, along with the Republicans capturing control of both houses of Congress in 1994, provided further legitimacy and impetus for the eventual dominance of political conservatism. As a result, a distinctive feature of our present-day inter-governmental system has been the dramatic increase of "contract employees," provided by the private sector, working for the federal government. Also, all levels of government are making increasing use of private for-profit and nonprofit organizations for the delivery of services. Privatization and "private federalism" has emerged as an important component of our system of intergovernmental relations.

Technological and Economic Change

In addition, technological and economic change has had a tremendous impact in shaping the present character of American intergovernmental relations. Policy and programmatic governmental innovation and diffusion throughout the states (and localities), which was the focus of a seminal contribution by Jack Walker more than a quarter of a century ago (Walker 1969), has become more rapid and comprehensive with the enhanced level of communication between governments brought about by new systems of technology. The rise and the growth of the international global economy have resulted in increased competition between the states and among the localities for new and enhanced levels of domestic and foreign investment. Governors, in particular, are now assigned the daunting task of traveling throughout the world to seek and hopefully realize new foreign investment for their states.

The Rise of Presidential Dominance and
Intergovernmental Relations

All recent presidents have given some attention to and have been involved in matters relating to intergovernmental relations, although Deil S. Wright (1982) is certainly correct in his judgment that their involvement has been "at least cyclical, if not actually erratic" (137). For instance, President Franklin D. Roosevelt, in addition to generally advocating a new style "cooperative federalism," established in 1937 the Committee on Administrative Management, which although primarily was charged with making recommendations for improving the overall efficiency of the executive branch, devoted some attention to the subject of federal-state relations. In addition, Graves reported that Roosevelt encouraged Harold D. Smith, his director of the Bureau of the Budget, to participate in the formation and administration of the Council on Intergovernmental Relations (Graves 1964, 179). Similarly, Roosevelt's successor, President Harry S. Truman, established the Commission on the Organization of the U.S. Executive Branch, popularly known as the Hoover Commission, since it was chaired by former President Herbert Hoover. The Hoover Commission, which was in existence from 1947 to 1949 and whose primary focus centered on devising reforms for improving the efficiency and performance of the executive branch, devoted some attention to the issue of federal-state organizational relations. We should note that a second Hoover Commission, concerned with the need to reorganize the executive branch of government, functioned from 1953 to 1955.

Republican presidents, most notably Dwight D. Eisenhower, Richard M. Nixon, and Ronald Reagan, took a decided interest in intergovernmental relations through their innate belief that government should become more efficient and economical, their corollary belief in the "devolution of powers," and their consequent policy objective of enhancing the role of the states in the federal system. Although presidential interest and involvement in intergovernmental relations have been uneven, the long-term trend has been that of increasing the power of the president, especially in relation to Congress, in the shaping of intergovernmental relations policy. This was especially evident in regard to the leadership of President George W. Bush in the passage of the Homeland Security Act (P.L. 107–296) in 2002, which resulted in the creation of the Department of Homeland Security, along with the enactment of the USA Patriot Act, which limits civil rights and provides federal, state, and local law enforcement officials with additional powers for law enforcement and surveillance. Republican dominance of Congress has further "strengthened the hand" of President Bush in shaping intergovernmental relations policies.

THE WEB OF INTERGOVERNMENTAL
RELATIONS[1]

The growth of government, the increasing number of governments, and the utilization of profit and nonprofit entities for the delivery of services, along with the enhanced role or scope of the federal, state, and local levels of government, have resulted in an increasingly elaborate web of intergovernmental relations. Intergovernmental relations between governments in the American polity are of a vertical and horizontal nature. *Vertical intergovernmental relations* include federal-state, federal-local, federal-state-local, and state-local relations; in contrast, *horizontal intergovernmental relations* encompass state-state and local-local relations.

A variant of horizontal intergovernmental relations is that of horizontal *intragovernmental* relations, involving the interactions of the legislative, executive, and judicial components of the same federal, state, and local governmental entity. For example, Nelson W. Polsby in his work *Congress and the Presidency* (1986) provides us with a good understanding of the dynamics of the relationship between the Congress and the president, which is also the focus of Charles O. Jones's work *Separate but Equal Branches: Congress and the Presidency* (1999). Harold Seidman (1975) has noted that federal policy-making involving specific policy decisions is in actuality the product of "subgovernments," "iron triangles," or "functional triads" composed of Congressional committees, elements of the executive branch, lower levels of government, and interest groups, while Hugh Heclo (1977) describes these myriad policy relationships as more open and porous, constituting "issue networks."

Whether one is focusing on vertical or horizontal intergovernmental relations or on intragovernmental relations, we want to emphasize that, since governments per se are structures, in a practical and working sense these relations fundamentally involve human contact and interaction. In reality, intergovernmental and intragovernmental relations are largely the product of public and private officials acting on behalf and pursuing the interests and goals of their respective governmental entities or private constituencies.

COOPERATION IN THE INTERGOVERNMENTAL SYSTEM

In addition to its vertical and horizontal dimensions, intergovernmental relations may be described as *informal* or *formal* in character. In regard to the latter, elected and administrative governmental officials are often in regular contact and collaboration with each other via phone, cell phone, fax, and e-mail. As Elazar (1984) noted decades ago, "One of the ways in which problems are normally dealt with in any democratic system is through informal consultations designed to alleviate or eliminate them so that formal action will not be necessary" (57). Elected officials interact with their colleagues most often on broad policy matters or fiscal assistance. Local elected officials make repeated inquiries to federal or state officials to learn about the status of a grant request; similarly, state officials make inquiries to federal officials regarding grant requests or other matters. All states maintain and staff an office in Washington which has the responsibility, working in conjunction with their Congressional delegation, to monitor federal legislation and other developments, especially in terms of state economic and social interests as well as new grant and funding opportunities for their states. Many of the larger cities have also established an office in Washington with the same responsibilities. In a reverse sort of fashion, federal and state administrative officials, as part of their broad program-monitoring responsibility, maintain regular contact with subordinate governmental agencies regarding the implementation and expenditure of grant funds.

Local officials testify about pending legislation before state legislative committees and in the quest of advancing their political agenda retain a lobbyist during the legislative session. In addition, state associations of local governments annually adopt a legislative agenda for consideration, and hopefully adoption, by the state legislature. For instance, in Virginia local governments are represented in the state legislative process by the Virginia Municipal League (VML), which lobbies on behalf of its member cities, towns, and urban counties, and the Virginia Association of Counties (VACO), which represents the interests of counties. Succinctly stated, political actors representing governments lobby other political actors representing governments in the intergovernmental system.

Similarly, both local and state elected officials and representatives of their professional associations, such as the National Governor's Association (NGA), the Council of State Governments (CSG), the United States Conference of Mayors (USCM), the National League of Cities (NLC), the National Association of Counties (NACO), and many other PIGs, appear before Congressional committees. The testimony and advocacy of state and local officials on behalf of President Richard Nixon's GRS proposal played a crucial role in the passage of the State and Local Fiscal Assistance Act of 1972 (Conlan 1998, 65–70), which, however, was eventually terminated by the Reagan administration and Congress in the 1980s. Recently, state and local officials have traveled to Washington to testify before various Congressional committees, most prominently regarding legislation pertaining to elementary and secondary public education, mass transportation, and internal security and terrorism.

CASE STUDY 1

Homeland Security: Intergovernmental Response

Responding to the tragic events of September 11, 2001, and the opening of a new "policy window,"* Congress passed and President Bush signed into law the Homeland Security Act of 2002. This Act led to the establishment of the Department of Homeland Security (DHS) in January 2003, with Cabinet-level status (P.L. 107–296). The DHS has the awesome task of integrating twenty-two distinct agencies and bureaus, with a total workforce of about 180,000, each with its own employees, mission, and culture, into a single, unified department, whose overall mission is to secure the homeland. Because of its scale and complexity, Donald F. Kettl (2004a) described this reorganization as the most challenging ever attempted in America (1). Tom Ridge, a former governor of Pennsylvania and a close confidant of President Bush, was selected by President Bush to be the first secretary of the DHS, a position he served in for two years.

* The term "policy window" is drawn from the classic work of John F. Kingdon, *Agendas, Alternatives, and Public Policies*, 2nd ed. (New York: Longman, 1995).

Secretary Ridge informed President Bush that following the 2004 presidential election he intended to step down from the post. Consequently, President Bush nominated Bernard B. Kerik, a former police commissioner of New York City, for the position. However, the nomination of Mr. Kerik was met with a great deal of controversy, and eventually Mr. Kerik withdrew his nomination on December 10, 2004, amid legal and ethical questions. In turn, President Bush nominated on January 11, 2005, Michael Chertoff, a federal appeals judge and a former tough-minded prosecutor, to lead the department. Mr. Chertoff was unanimously approved by the Senate on February 15, 2005, to be the second secretary of the DHS (Stolberg 2005).

In addition, President Bush created the Homeland Security Advisory Council by Executive Order on March 19, 2002. The purpose of the council is to provide the president with advice on homeland security matters. The chair of the council, as of June 11, 2002, is Joseph J. Grano, Jr., of New Jersey, who is the chairman and CEO of UBS Paine Webber and a veteran of the U.S. Special Forces; the vice chair is William H. Webster, of the District of Columbia, a former director of the FBI. The remaining thirteen members of the council were drawn from the ranks of state and local government, the business community, public policy experts, and the nonprofit sector.

As stated in its strategic plan titled *Securing Our Homeland: Vision, Mission, Core Values & Guiding Principles* (2004), the mission of the DHS is stated as follows: "We will lead the unified national effort to secure America. We will prevent and deter terrorist attacks and protect against and respond to threats and hazards to the nation. We will ensure safe and secure borders, welcome lawful immigrants and visitors, and promote the free-flow of commerce" (4).

In seeking to accomplish this mission, the DHS is guided by the following goals, as set forth in its strategic plan:

Awareness—Identify and understand threats, assess vulnerabilities, determine potential impacts and disseminate timely information to our homeland security partners.

Prevention—Detect, deter, and mitigate threats to our homeland.

Protection—Safeguard our people and their freedoms, critical infrastructure, property and the economy of our nation from acts of terrorism, natural disasters, or other emergencies.

Response—Lead, manage and coordinate the national response to acts of terrorism, natural disasters, or other emergencies.

Recovery—Lead *national, state, local and private sector efforts* to restore services and rebuild communities after acts of terrorism, natural disasters, or other emergencies (emphasis ours).

Service—Serve the public effectively by facilitating lawful trade, travel and immigration.

Organizational Excellence—Value our most important resource, our people. Create a culture that promotes a common identity, innovation, mutual respect, accountability and teamwork to achieve efficiencies, effectiveness, and operational synergies. (9)

The strategic plan emphasizes an intergovernmental and wider partnership "approach to homeland security . . . based on the principles of shared responsibility and partnership with the Congress; state, local and tribal governments; the private sector; the American people; and our international partners" (3). After all, an intergovernmental approach to the challenge of homeland security is mandatory since, as Kettl has so well pointed out (2004b), all homeland security, at its core, is local (57). The need for an intergovernmental approach for combating terrorism is strongly supported by state and local officials, as conveyed in a report by Governor Mitt Romney, the leader of a national working group on homeland security, to Secretary Ridge (Belluck 2004). Among other endeavors, the strategic plan notes that the DHS will cooperate and work with the state, local, and tribal governments in the following areas: (1) collecting, aggregating, and analyzing all terrorism intelligence; (2) disseminating intelligence information to all relevant parties; (3) securing the safety of the transportation system; (4) reducing infrastructure vulnerability from acts of terrorism; (5) securing the physical safety of the president, vice president, and visiting world leaders; (6) protecting the marine environment and living marine resources; (7) strengthening nationwide preparedness and mitigation against acts of terrorism, natural disasters, or other emergencies; (8) providing search-and-rescue services to people and property in distress; (9) providing scalable and robust all-hazard response capability; and (10) leading and promoting e-government modernization and interoperability initiatives (10–43).

The twenty-two agencies that were consolidated into the DHS spent $13.1 billion in FY2000, which then increased to $15.6 billion for FY2002. Expenditures more than doubled to $32 billion for FY2003. Budgeted amounts appear to remain in the $32–$33 billion range for FY2005–FY2007, although it was a little less in FY2004 (see Figure CS1.1). Because of the carryover of unspent funds, budget authorization for FY2006 appears to be about $41 billion. Much of the doubling of expenditures appears to be in the form of procurement contracts to private companies (Office of Management and Budget, *Budget of the United States Government*, Fiscal Year 2006).

The budget revolves around five major themes: revolutionizing the borders, strengthening law enforcement, improving national preparedness and response, leveraging technology, and creating a twenty-first-century department.

In order to facilitate state and local involvement with the activities of the DHS, Secretary Ridge announced the establishment on July 1, 2003, of the State and Local Officials Senior Advisory Committee. This committee, consisting of thirteen members, was initially chaired by Governor Michael Leavitt of Utah, while Mayor Anthony Williams of the District of Columbia was

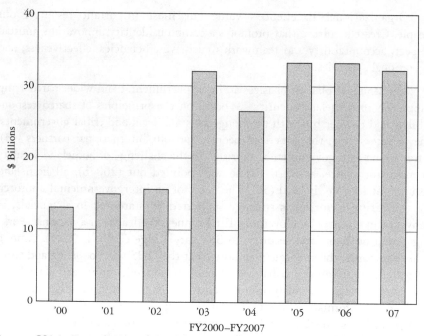

FIGURE CS1.1. Expenditures of the department of homeland security, FY2000–FY2004, and budgets, FY2005–2007. These are the expenditures and budgets of the twenty-two agencies that were consolidated into the department in 2003. *Source: Budget of the United States Government, Fiscal Year 2006,* Historical Statistics.

designated the vice chair. Other initial members of the committee included the governors of Arkansas, Connecticut, and Idaho; two state legislators; a state judge; a state administrative official; and four municipal officials. Eventually, representatives from the United States Conference of Mayors and the National Association of Counties were appointed to the commission.

Underscoring the intergovernmental nature of many of the functions and activities of the DHS has been the establishment within the department of the Office of State and Local Government Coordination and Preparedness (SLGCP), as identified in the organizational chart of the DHS in Figure CS1.2.

SLGCP was established to serve as a single point of contact for the facilitation and coordination of departmental programs that impact state, local, territorial, and tribal governments. In addition, SLGCP serves as a primary point-of-contact within the DHS for exchanging information with personnel associated with the various subnational governments. Further, the SLGCP identifies homeland security–related activities, best practices, and processes that are most efficiently accomplished at the federal, state, local, or regional levels. For FY2006, SLGCP will administer $3.6 billion in grants, training, and technical assistance for "first responder" state and local agencies, as they equip, train, exercise, and assess preparedness for emergencies regardless of scale or cause.

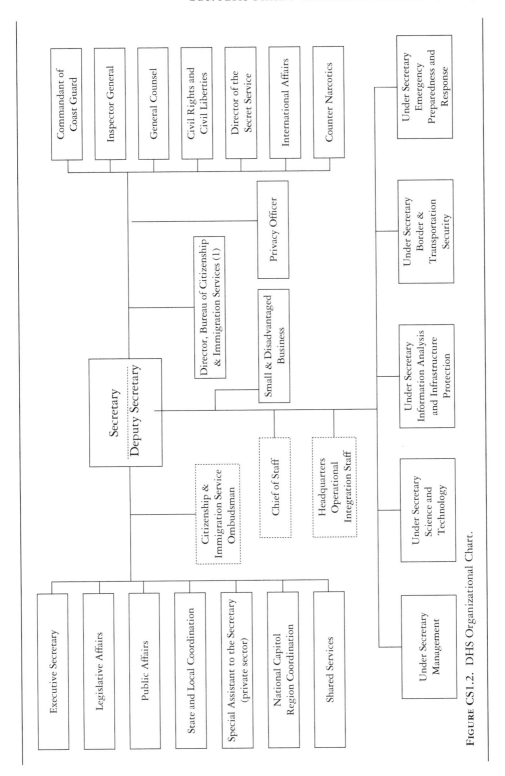

FIGURE CS1.2. DHS Organizational Chart.

ASSESSMENT

Former Secretary Ridge has been praised for his initial leadership in getting the DHS up and running and for making some meaningful progress in getting the twenty-two agencies and bureaus folded into the department to coordinate and work together in the effort to combat terrorism.[†] On the other hand, Kettl and his associates (2004a), while recognizing a variety of the accomplishments of the department, awarded the DHS an overall grade of C+ for its performance during its first year in operation (3). The reorganization of the various federal components has proved to be an awesome task, since each of the agencies and bureaus brought into the DHS has its own "work culture" and particularistic missions. In addition, the DHS had to resolve some "turf battles" with other federal entities, especially the Department of Justice and the FBI. Further, the "balkanized" nature of the DHS (described by one keen observer, because of its recent origin, as a "work still in the making") has made it somewhat difficult for the department to develop clear lines of authority and "operational policy space" with state and local governments. Nevertheless, as a result of the support of the DHS, individual states and localities have made significant progress in better equipping themselves and to responding to the challenge of terrorism. For instance, Governor Mark Warner of Virginia announced on June 5, 2003, that the Commonwealth had received a grant of $34 million to be used largely for implementing an enhanced public warning system, utilizing a new satellite system, to distribute much more rapidly the messages of its Emergency Alert System (EAS). The balance of the funds were dedicated for equipment purchases, training for first responders, and participation exercises to test first responders (Hardy 2003). In addition, as a result of a $275,000 DHS grant the Virginia National Guard has established a five-hundred-man rapid-reaction incident-response force to assist state and local law enforcement authorities in the event of of a terrorist attack in the state. Virginia's force is designed to give local authorities additional resources for guarding facilities and protecting the public. The National Guard has purchased equipment to alert the members of the force faster, protect them better, and enhance their operational capabilities. Special equipment purchased for the rapid-reaction force includes ballistic body armor, secure satellite communication systems, short-range walkie-talkies, checkpoint floodlights, and portable vehicle barriers (Bacque 2004). At the local level, Henrico County in Virginia, which received a $16,000 Certified Emergency Response Team (CERT) grant from DHS, provided the training for eight individuals to deal with various emergency challenges and situations. More than one thousand individuals residing in twenty-nine Virginia communities have received similar training (Martz 2003a).

[†] For an excellent analysis of the difficulties involved in coordinating the efforts of the various agencies and bureaus contained in DHS, see Donald F. Kettl, *System Under Stress: Homeland Security and American Politics* (Washington, DC: CQ Press, 2004), pp. 33–56.

A major and recurring criticism of DHS is that it has not fully met its responsibility of coordinating its activities with state and local governments. Reviewing its first year in operation, Kettl and his associates (2004a) awarded the department a grade of "C" on this measure and noted that "federal promises to improve coordination with state and local governments have gone unmet" (17). The department has been faulted particularly for being dilatory in sharing clear and concise information about potential terrorist threats with the states ("States Fault Sharing of Threats" 2005).

A second major criticism of the DHS initiative is that an inordinate amount of the homeland security grants have been distributed to rural states, where the threat of terrorism appears to be less acute. A study conducted by the Congressional Research Bureau found that Alaska received nearly $92 per resident in homeland security funds in FY2002–FY2003, while the respective figure for the following much larger populated states was as follows: New York ($32), California ($22), Texas ($21), and Florida ($21). The remaining states with the highest per-resident spending of homeland security funds are the predominately rural states of Wyoming, North Dakota, South Dakota, and Vermont. The inordinate amount of homeland security funds bestowed upon the less populous states is the result of a provision in the USA Patriot Act passed in Congress in 2001 which guarantees that each state will receive at least 0.75 percent of the total in terrorism preparedness grants for states and a minimum allocation for territories as well, in addition to the disproportionate political influence of the smaller states in the workings of the U.S. Senate. As Kettl (2004a) has advanced, DHS "money has been distributed more on the basis of pork than on the basis of need" (18). The *New York Times* reported: "Despite repeated efforts in Congress to address the situation . . . federal money continues to be distributed by a formula that places a higher value on spreading the wealth among the states than on assessing where the risk of terrorist attack is greatest" (Murphy 2004). In an editorial published the following year entitled "Security Loses; Pork Wins," the *New York Times* noted that, despite a strong plea registered by Secretary Chertoff to shift homeland security money from low-risk areas to high-risk areas, the "Senate voted, disgracefully, to shift homeland security funds from high-risk areas to low-risk areas" and that ". . . small-state representatives, put political pork ahead of national security" (*New York Times* 2005a).

Responding to the repeated concerns of big city mayors, the DHS in December 2004 began shifting a larger share of its annual $3.5 in antiterrorism grants to the nation's largest cities, allowing them to accelerate the purchases of equipment and implement the training needed to better defend against—or at least more rapidly respond to—a possible attack. The major beneficiary of this shift in funding was New York City, which was awarded a $208 million grant for FY2005, far surpassing the $47 million which it received for FY2004. As a result, New York City was able to purchase additional devices that can detect chemical, biological, or other hazards; increase training for its police and firefighters; and allocate additional funds for its intelligence center, where it analyzes possible terrorist threats. Other major cities that gained more fiscal aid from the funding shift included Washington, DC; Los Angeles; Chicago; and Boston. Conversely, cities that lost funds from this funding source included Memphis, New Haven, Orlando, St. Paul, Fresno, Albany, and Richmond (Lipton 2004). Under his leadership, Secretary Chertoff has underscored that the DHS will allocate more grants to states and cities that are considered the most likely terrorist targets (Lipton 2005a).

A third major criticism of DHS initiatives is that various localities around the nation have not consistently been the timely recipients of homeland security funds, nor have they been adequately involved in the homeland security planning process of their state. A study completed by the U.S. Conference of Mayors and released in March 2004 found that 76 percent of the cities had not received from their respective states any funds from the largest homeland security program designed to assist "first responders," such as police, fire, and other local officials. Further survey findings included in the study found that: (1) 64 percent of the cities had not received domestic preparedness funding; (2) local officials in 46 percent of the cities had not been involved in the state planning process for the use of urban area security initiative funds; (3) officials in 41 percent of the cities were of the belief that their city government or health department did not have an adequate opportunity to participate in their state's planning process for the distribution of funds regarding public health and hospital preparedness activities; and (4) officials in 22 percent of the cities stated that they had not been requested to submit a needs assessment to their state. The overall thrust of the report emphasized that local officials believed that they were not adequately involved in the homeland security planning process in their state and that their communities were being short-changed by DHS funding initiatives (U.S. Conference of Mayors 2004).

Seeking to improve the performance of the DHS, Secretary Chertoff announced in July 2005 his plans for a number of organizational changes in the Department. These changes include the appointment of a new intelligence chief, responsible for collecting information from the twenty-two agencies in the Department, and the appointment of an Assistant Secretary for cyber and telecommunications security. Additional changes included the hiring of a Chief Medical Officer responsible for devising a response plan for the thousands of casualties that might result from a biological, chemical, or nuclear attack. Chertoff also indicated that he planned to appoint a Secretary of Policy and a Director of Operations Coordination.

In addition, Chertoff noted that under his reorganization proposal the Federal Emergency Management Agency would focus exclusively on responding to catastrophes, instead of assisting state and local governments in their prevention. All prevention duties are to be assigned to a new Directorate for Preparedness, responsible for the distribution of billions in grants to state and local governments, and also for devising plans for protecting crucial national buildings and infrastructure from attack.

These organizational changes, Chertoff advanced, will improve the ability of DHS to better identify possible terrorists, screen airline passengers at a faster pace, retard the flow of illegal immigrants, render more quickly the student and tourist application process, and better sift cargo for unconventional weapons (Lipton 2005b).

SUMMARY AND CONCLUSION

Following the tragic events of September 11, 2001, the Congress passed and President Bush signed into law legislation establishing the Cabinet-level DHS, which is charged with protecting the nation against further terrorist attacks. The very nature of this mission required the DHS to adopt an intergovernmental response, coordinating and working in concert with the various states, local governments, tribal governments, and the private sector. Although the DHS has enjoyed a measure of success in its mission, its success has been moderated by a number of challenges, including (1) providing on a timely basis intelligence information to state and local governments; (2) the difficulties involved in fully coordinating the activities and efforts of the twenty-two agencies and bureaus housed in the department; (3) the difficulties involved in structuring and coordinating the homeland security efforts of the various governmental entities and private sector with those of our larger federal system of government; (4) the "mismatch" of a good deal of the homeland security funding, that is, the inordinate distribution of these funds to rural areas at the expense of the more terror-prone metropolitan areas; and (5) the often failure of the states to integrate localities into their homeland security planning process and to rapidly distribute homeland security funds to their localities. Nevertheless, the various initiatives of the DHS have stimulated further vertical and horizontal cooperation between our various units of government and have promoted the concept of regional cooperation, primarily through the use of mutual aid agreements, between local governments in our metropolitan areas (Martz 2003b; Poulin 2005).

The *New York Times* in a lengthy editorial titled "Our Unnecessary Insecurity," published on February 20, 2005, panned the Bush administration and Congress for not adopting more proactive measures to protect the national security. The editorial stated in part:

> "Sept. 11 changed everything," the saying goes. It is striking however, how much has not changed in the three and a half years since nearly 3,000 people were killed on American soil. The nation's chemical plants are still a horrific accident waiting to happen. Nuclear material that could be made into a "dirty bomb," or even a nuclear device, and set off in an American city remains too accessible to terrorists. Critical tasks, from inspecting shipping containers to upgrading defenses against biological weapons, are being done poorly.

And, further:

The biggest obstacles to making the nation safer have been lack of political will and failure to carry out the most effective policies. The Bush administration and Congress have been reluctant to provide the necessary money—even while they are furiously reducing revenue with tax cuts. The funds that are available are often misdirected. And Washington has caved to pressure from interest groups, like the chemical industry, that have fought increased security measures.

Most of all, the government has failed to lay out a broad strategy for making the nation more secure. Among the most troubling vulnerabilities that have yet to be seriously addressed: chemical plants . . . nuclear materials . . . nuclear power plants . . . [p]ort security . . . hazardous waste transport . . . bioterrorism. . . .

Given these serious gaps, it is disturbing to see limited resources used as inefficiently as they have been. Fighting the last war, the Bush administration is devoting far too great a proportion of domestic security spending to preventing the hijacking of commercial aircraft. For a long time, it engaged in a draconian crackdown on academic visas, while the nation's borders—the likeliest entry points for future terrorists—remained as porous as ever. And with the stakes literally life or death, the pork-barrel politics that have controlled domestic security funds—giving Wyoming more per capita than New Jersey—are simply unconscionable.

Given this assessment, it is clear that the DHS and its intergovernmental allies—state, territorial, local, and tribal—and private partners have to make a more focused and strenuous effort to protect the nation's security.

REFERENCES

Bacque, Peter. 2004, November 6. Force Set Up to Counter Terrorism. *Richmond Times-Dispatch.* B1, B4.

Belluck, Pam. 2004, December 15. States and Cities Must Hunt Terror Plots, Governor Says. *New York Times.* A15.

Hardy, Michael. 2003, June 6. $34 Million to Help Virginia Fight Terror. *Richmond Times-Dispatch.* A1, A11.

Kettl, Donald F. (ed.). 2004a. *The Department of Homeland Security's First Year: A Report Card.* New York: The Century Foundation Press.

——. 2004b. *System Under Stress: Homeland Security and American Politics.* Washington, DC: CQ Press.

Kingdon, John F. 1995. *Agendas, Alternatives, and Public Policies.* 2d ed. New York: Longman.

Lipton, Eric. 2004, December 22. Big Cities Will Get More in Antiterrorism Grants. *New York Times.* A14.

——. 2005a, March 17. New Homeland Security Chief Plans Retreat From "Sky Is Falling" Approach to Terror. *New York Times.* A26.

——. 2005b, July 14. Homeland Security Chief Announces Overhaul. *New York Times.* A17.

Martz, Michael. 2003a, September 11. Homeland Defense Comes to Henrico. *Richmond Times-Dispatch.* A10.

——. 2003b, November 1. Terror May Require Regional Approach. *Richmond Times-Dispatch*. B8.

Murphy, Dean E. 2004, October 12. Security Grants Still Streaming to Rural States. *New York Times*. A1, A23.

Our Unnecessary Insecurity [Editorial]. 2005, February 20. *New York Times*. WK8.

Poulin, Thomas E. 2005. National Threat—Local Response: Building Local Disaster Capacity with Mutual Aid Agreements. *PA Times*. 28 (March), 3.

States Fault Sharing of Threats. 2005, March 12. *Richmond Times-Dispatch*. A2.

Stolberg, Sheryl Gay. 2005, February 16. Senate Unanimously Confirms Chertoff as Security Chief. *New York Times*. A16.

United States Department of Homeland Security. 2004. *Securing Our Homeland: Vision, Mission, Core Values & Guiding Principles*. Washington, DC: DHS.

United States Office of Management and Budget. 2005. *Budget of the United States Government: Fiscal Year 2006*. Washington, DC: OMB.

U.S. Conference of Mayors. 2004. *Second Mayors' Report to the Nation: Tracking Homeland Security Funds*. Washington, DC: U.S. Conference of Mayors.

A host of studies have found that elected and administrative officials in metropolitan areas have long valued the benefit of and practice informal interaction and collaboration. For instance, in his well-documented and intensive study conducted in the 1960s, H. Paul Friesema (1971) noted that local officials in the Quad Cities metropolitan area of Illinois and Iowa maintained regular telephone or personal contact with each other. More recently, George Frederickson and his colleagues (1999) at the University of Kansas have found that local administrative employees in the Kansas City bistate metropolitan area of Kansas and Missouri routinely seek technical information, advice, or a point of view from counterparts practicing the same profession in other governmental jurisdictions. Frederickson and his colleagues have labeled this widespread interaction the practice of "administrative conjunction." Informal interaction between governmental functional specialists, such as police, fire, public works, budget, and economic development personnel, in American metropolitan areas has become more prevalent with the advent and routine use of the newer forms of electronic communication. In addition, personal, or face-to-face, contact and collaboration among elected and administrative officials are stimulated by "luncheon affairs," general conferences, professional associations and meetings, and quasi-governmental structures. An example of the latter includes the multitude of regional councils that have been established in virtually every metropolitan area, and some nonmetropolitan areas, of the United States. These organizations engender an informal dialogue among local officials, serving to build a measure of social capital and trust among officials throughout the region[2] (Wikstrom 1977).

Formal Intergovernmental Relations

The most salient, and most important, example of formal cooperation between governments in the American polity involves the cost sharing between governments of various programs and projects. Federal grants-in-aid, technically labeled "federal intergovernmental transfers," have been present virtually throughout the history of the American polity, as underscored by W. Brooke Groves in his seminal work *American Intergovernmental Relations* (1964, 477–573). However, commencing in the 1930s and even more substantially in the 1960s and 1970s the federal government increased its fiscal aid, through categorical and project grants, block grants, loans, and loan guarantees, to state and local governments; this federal fiscal assistance was augmented in the early 1970s by a revenue-sharing program with the states and localities, which was terminated in the 1980s. The number of federal categorical grant programs increased from 51 in 1964 to 530 in 1971 and ultimately to 618 by 1995; in contrast there were 17 federal block grant programs in 1995 (Dilger 2000; Vines 1976). The federal government provides a wide variety of categorical and block grants to state governments; it also provides a limited amount of fiscal assistance to local governments, primarily for community development, law enforcement, and public education. In a parallel fashion, states usually play a major financial role in the provision of local elementary and secondary public education, with New Hampshire constituting a somewhat notable exception. Since New Hampshire has enacted neither a general sales tax nor an income tax, school financing is heavily derived from local property taxes. Through the block grant approach, the federal government provides to the states financial support for designing and implementing "workforce" initiatives and policies and for the provision of mental and physical health and social programs. The federal and state governments provide on a project grant basis financial assistance to local governments for the construction of public works facilities, such as water treatment plants, sewer and water lines, and mass transportation stations and facilities. Some states provide additional funding to their local governments through various general and special revenue-sharing programs. In some metropolitan areas, most notably Minneapolis–St. Paul, the local governments are the beneficiaries of a regional revenue-sharing program (Harrigan and Johnson 1978). A much more detailed discussion of fiscal federalism is found in the following chapter.

Local governments in metropolitan and nonmetropolitan areas are increasingly entering into agreements and contracts with neighboring governments for the provision of police, fire protection, water, sewer, and mass transportation services, or for the construction and operation of a joint county-municipal building. Graves took note of this development more than forty years ago when he wrote: "Whatever the precise terms in which the concept of interlocal relations is defined, the fact remains that an increasing number of interlocal contracts and agreements have been coming into existence, both within a single State and between units in different States" (Graves 1964, 739). Among the metropolitan areas where the use of the contract approach for the delivery of services is most heavily utilized is Los Angeles. Los Angeles County, through what has become popularly known as the "Lakewood Plan," provides a wide range and varying number of municipal type services to the more than seventy-five municipalities in the county. It is becoming more common for counties in metropolitan statistical areas (MSAs) to provide this kind of service to municipalities. Local governments in the Richmond, Virginia, metropolitan area have entered into a score of intergovernmental agreements involving planning, transportation, public safety, criminal justice, health, human services, libraries, utilities, solid waste, economic development, leisure services, and tourism (County of Henrico 1998).

Another example of formal intergovernmental cooperation between the various levels of government in the American polity involves technical assistance. The United States Department of Agriculture has long provided funding and technical assistance to the states and localities for research projects and various extension services. The Federal Bureau of Investigation (FBI) provides its expertise and resources to state and local officials for criminal investigations, which are interstate in character, and provides specialized training for state and local police personnel and laboratory analysis for state and local police departments. The Bureau of Alcohol, Tobacco, and Firearms (ATF) also provides federal assistance to state and local law enforcement officials. Law enforcement officials from all three levels of government worked closely together and were collectively credited for bringing to an end to the notorious "serial sniper terror," which plagued the District of Columbia, Maryland, and Virginia during the fall of 2002 and claimed a total of thirteen lives.

As a result of a rising homicide rate, Richmond, Virginia—which recorded 160 slayings in 1994—was the beneficiary in 1994 of police manpower assistance from the Commonwealth (State) and Henrico County, a neighboring suburb. This assistance, provided under the rubric of Operation Full Alert, involved thirteen state troopers and an equal number of police officers from the county. Again, almost ten years later, specifically in 2003, the Virginia State Police, drawing an undisclosed number of personnel from its Counter-terrorism and Criminal Interdiction Unit, provided assistance to the Richmond city police in its search for guns and drugs (Akin 2003).

Emergency situations and the need to maintain public order often result in formal intergovernmental cooperation. The Federal Emergency Management Agency (FEMA) provides assistance to states and localities upon their designation as disaster areas by the president to assist them in dealing with the havoc and damage caused by hurricanes, tornadoes, and other natural disasters and to rebuild publicly owned infrastructure. Such infrastructure includes public buildings, equipment, roads, water facilities, and utilities. Upon the formal request of the governor, the president will mobilize and provide military personnel to secure public order in an area of civic disorder and unrest.

Over the years, the federal and state governments have jointly provided a number of programs most prominently in regard to interstate highways, environmental protection, conservation, recreation and parks, consumer protection, and crime. For instance, the City of Richmond, the Commonwealth of Virginia, and the federal government have operated in the Richmond area an initiative known as "Project Exile" designed to get handguns off the streets. More recently, the federal National Rail Transportation Corporation, more popularly known as AMTRAK, has entered into numerous agreements with state and local agencies to provide long-distance rail service and mass transportation. AMTRAK, supported by state funding (what might be described as a form of reverse grants to the federal government) from Illinois and Wisconsin, provides passenger rail service between Chicago and Milwaukee. In a more recent venture, AMTRAK commenced passenger rail service between Boston and Portland, Maine, partially funded by subsidies provided by Maine, Massachusetts, and New Hampshire. In addition, the federal government has made substantial use of state universities for various research programs, including education, agriculture, defense, and so on. On this score, however, it should be noted that the vast majority of federal spending for research on defense-related matters is contracted with private agencies; more specifically, the percentage of federal contracting for defense-related research with the private sector increased from 60 percent in 2000 to about 63 percent in 2002. It is estimated that toward the end of President Bush's second term in office this figure will increase to between 70 and 75 percent.

Profit and Nonprofit Entities as Service Providers

The currently prevailing politically popular interrelated virtues of "downsizing government" and "privatization" have stimulated the use by government of profit and nonprofit organizations for the provision of services and have introduced with more force the concept of "private federalism" into the swirl of intergovernmental relations. This development, of course, has served to increase the complexity of intergovernmental relations and has somewhat blurred the distinction between the public and private sectors. The federal government, in its goal to downsize its permanent civilian workforce, has retained a large number of "contract employees." State social service agencies utilize, often on a competitive contract basis, private organizations, such as various religious, or faith-based, groups and other nonprofit agencies, for providing various forms of rehabilitative services to juvenile delinquents and older troubled youths. In addition, states, through the contract approach, utilize for-profit business concerns to construct and operate penal facilities and provide road construction and maintenance. Increasingly, local governments are contracting with private profit and nonprofit agencies for public works/transportation services, public utilities, public safety, parks and recreation, health and human services, and cultural and arts programs (Miranda and Anderson 1994).

Supporting Legislation

Higher levels of government have passed and implemented legislation that serves to reinforce policies adopted by lower levels of government. For example, Congress has enacted legislation prohibiting the movement of individuals and items through the mail or across state lines in order to support state laws and decisions regarding stolen cars, prostitution, gambling, and child support. In a similar fashion, states have passed laws that serve to reinforce local ordinances (laws) and policies regarding community development and planning, elementary and secondary education, and criminal activity.

Mandates

Adding to the complexity of intergovernmental relations is the practice of higher levels of government imposing a variety of policy *mandates*, a form of forced cooperation, on lower level(s) of government, requiring the recipient government to adhere to a certain practice or provide a certain service. The federal government has imposed upon the states a maze of "cross-cutting" requirements obligating the states to adhere to equal opportunity practices, especially with regard to employment and the issuance of contracts. The states, in turn, have imposed upon their local governments a wide variety of mandates relating to such matters as land use and comprehensive planning, clean air and water, budgeting and accounting practices, personnel policies, record-keeping, and elementary and secondary education. Mandates have often proved to be an irritant to lower levels of government and have provoked a measure of political controversy because of the often unwillingness of the government imposing the mandate to provide sufficient funds for its implementation (Rivlin 1992, 107).

As a result of the political controversy generated by unfunded mandates, the federal government and many of the states have enacted legislation designed to provide various forms of mandate relief. For instance, the Republican-dominated Congress, with the strong support of President Clinton, passed in 1995 the Unfunded Mandates Reform Act. The bill provides that Congress is required to define the costs and consequences of mandates, but it does not prohibit Congress from imposing new mandates. The effect of this legislation has been to render new federal mandates less extensive and more narrowly written (Posner 1997). As Robert Jay Dilger (2000) has reported on this matter, "[D]espite the passage of the Unfunded Mandates Reform Act of 1995, the national government's use of full and partial preemptions, direct orders, crossover sanctions, and other forms of governmental mandates to influence state and local government behavior," the behavior of our lower levels of government has remained relatively unchanged (99).

COMPETITION AND CONFLICT IN THE INTERGOVERNMENTAL SYSTEM

Although the American polity is marked by a substantial amount of intergovernmental cooperation, there is also a significant amount of competition and conflict between the array of governments. Some scholars, most prominently Thomas R. Dye in his work *American Federalism: Competition Among Governments* (1990), have praised the inherent competitive nature of our federal or intergovernmental system by arguing that such competition and conflict result in a more efficient and responsive government overall.

Some intergovernmental competition and conflict is vertical, between the national government and the states, the national and local governments, or the states and their local governments. On the other hand, considerable competition and conflict is horizontal, involving conflict between the states, among local governments, and among agencies within the same governmental entity. For instance, American metropolitan areas have long been the locale of intergovernmental conflict, most commonly between the core cities and neighboring suburban jurisdictions, but sometimes between suburban jurisdictions. The following are some examples, hardly exhaustive in nature, of vertical and horizontal intergovernmental conflict.

Public Policy and the Grants-in-Aid System

At times, Congress has passed and the president has signed legislation that some states have viewed in a hostile fashion. During the administration of President Ronald

Reagan the federal government enacted legislation requiring the states to adhere to various policies relating to the transit of trucks on their highways or risk losing a portion of their federal highway funds. Many states reacted to this legislation with great hostility, and eventually compromises on these policies were agreed to by the federal government and the states (Conlan 1998, 207–8).

More recently, Republican lawmakers from the National Conference of State Legislatures have voiced their strong opposition to the "No Child Left Behind" legislation, passed by Congress and signed by the president in January 2002, which they consider a violation of states' rights (Dillon 2004). Further, a number of localities, situated in Connecticut and Vermont, have rejected Title I federal fiscal assistance to elementary and secondary schools, designed to improve the reading and math abilities of their poorest students, since this funding was subject to the accountability rules of the "No Child Left Behind" legislation. The Superintendent of the Public Schools of Suffolk, Virginia, strongly recommended to the members of his school board that they follow the same course of action since the acceptance of the federal funds, approximately $3.5 million, was not worth the effort and time of bureaucratic compliance and that acceptance of the funds presented the possibility of financial sanctions by the federal government ("Educator" 2003).

Some practitioners and observers of the federal grants-in-aid system have been critical of grant programs that require, according to their perspective, frivolous spending requirements. For instance, in 1991 Congress amended the Surface Transportation Program to include a transportation enhancement initiative, requiring that 10 percent of the federal funding provided to a state under this program must be utilized for twelve categories of transportation enhancements relating to surface transportation. In Virginia in 2003, at a time when the state was being severely pressed to provide adequate funds for highway repair and improvements, the requirement of this law resulted in expenditures for a wide variety of items, including the construction of a wooden sailing schooner and the restoration of twelve old rail depots and numerous homes, churches, taverns, and courthouses. In response, the State Transportation Secretary stated: "Given the type of revenue constraints under which we are operating, if this program were discretionary, I doubt that the Commonwealth Transportation Board would choose to use these federal dollars in the way we are required to use them" (Bacque 2003).

On the other hand, the federal government has often viewed with frustration its inability to ensure that state and local governments, which are the recipients of federal assistance, allocate their fiscal assistance in accordance with federal goals. For example, Congress passed the Elementary and Secondary Education Act of 1965, which provided, in particular in Title I, that the local governments were to spend the money on behalf of disadvantaged children in poor areas. However, contrary to this requirement many recipient governments simply allocated their share of funding into their general operating school budget (Murphy 1973). In their classic study *Implementation*, Jeffrey L. Pressman and Aaron Wildavsky (1984) found that the multitude of federal grants awarded to the City of Oakland, California, in the 1960s designed to rebuild the community, and especially to engender economic investment and create jobs, were largely never realized.

In a rather ironic sense, the federal grants-in-aid system designed to promote cooperation between the federal government, the states, and localities has been the cause, or instigator, of political and intergovernmental controversy and conflict. The federal grant system, in general, has been repeatedly criticized for providing the states of the South and Southwest with an inordinate share of federal funds, as well as awarding to the small states a disproportionate per capita amount of grant funds (Stephens 1996). In a similar fashion, some observers have charged that the least populated states benefit to a much greater extent from the federal grants-in-aid system than their more populated counterparts, which greatly increases their per capita funds because of the usual requirement that all states receive a minimum percentage of program grant funding. In Virginia, as well as in several other states, state aid formulas that are utilized to determine the amount of state funding provided to local school systems have been criticized for favoring suburban school systems over those operated by core cities. Because of the limited amount of funding available, federal and state project grants, in particular, have created a good deal of competition and conflict between and among the states and localities. In addition, it has been noted that smaller communities have never received their fair share of federal and state fiscal assistance because they lack the adequate staff for practicing "grantsmanship" and securing federal and state grants.

Supreme Court Decisions

Decisions made by the United States Supreme Court have engendered conflict, at times very bitter and rancorous conflict, between the federal and state governments. For instance, in its famous decision of *Brown v. Board of Education* (1954) the Court required that the Southern states dismantle their racially segregated public school systems in favor of integrated public school facilities. In response to the ruling of the Court, North Carolina devolved its state system of public schools to counties and large cities, an action designed to thwart racial integration. In a parallel action of defiance, Virginia adopted a policy of "massive resistance" designed to impede racial integration in its public schools, a policy that delayed school integration but ultimately failed. Almost a decade later, the Court handed down its historic decision of *Baker v. Carr* (1962), which, augmented by a massive number of succeeding cases, forced the states to reapportion the district boundaries of their state legislatures according to the dictum of "one man, one vote." The consequence of *Baker* was to shift dramatically political power in the states from rural areas and core cities to rapidly expanding suburban regions.

In a somewhat reverse sort of fashion, however, commencing in the last quarter of the past century the Court has issued a series of rulings favoring the position of the states in the intergovernmental system at the expense of the federal government. The most salient of these rulings involved the case of the *National League of Cities v. Usery* (1976), in which a slim majority of the Court decided that the Congress did not have the power to apply the minimum wage and overtime provisions of the Fair Standards Labor Act to the states and localities in "areas of traditional governmental functions." Although the Court in *Garcia v. San Antonio* (1985) eventually overruled this decision, the Court beginning in the late 1990s issued a series of rulings in favor of the states.

As a result of these decisions, state employees may not bring a suit against the state for failure to abide by federal laws protecting employees, unless the state permits such suits. In addition, state employees cannot claim the right to minimum wages from the state, protection against age discrimination, or guarantees provided by the Americans with Disabilities Act.

HORIZONTAL INTERGOVERNMENTAL COMPETITION AND CONFLICT

Although there is a significant amount of important horizontal cooperation between governments in the United States, that is, between the states and among local governments, there is also a continuing degree of competition and conflict. Some of this competition and conflict is episodic and of a temporary nature and time-bound; other types of competition and conflict are ongoing or permanent in character. The following are a few prominent examples of horizontal intergovernmental conflict between the states and among local governments.

Interstate Competition and Conflict

In what has been often referred to as a "zero sum" game, the states continually and vigorously compete with each other for new economic investment, seeking to attract additional firms to the state or encouraging businesses already situated in the state to remain and increase their investment by enlarging their facilities and thereby generating additional employment opportunities and tax revenues. The basic public policy concern that states have for their economic well-being is of long duration, as noted by Elazar some two decades ago (Elazar 1984, 22). Especially in terms of attracting new commercial investment, the states (and local governments) offer to potential businesses infrastructure improvements, various tax abatements, lower income taxes, outright payments, training grants, and wage subsidies. In addition to economic competition between the states, other sources of interstate conflict include matters relating to boundary disputes, water disputes, air and water pollution, and social policies. A more complete presentation of the sources of interstate competition and conflict, along with the various ways in which these disputes are resolved, is found in Chapter 7.

Conflict Between Local Jurisdictions

Similar to the states, localities are engaged in ongoing competition and conflict with each other in the quest for new commercial investment. As one report noted: "Across the country, communities are competing with one another to offer the most lucrative incentives to lure good payrolls, from the giant assembly jobs at Boeing to small centers for processing credit cards, despite some studies that question the effectiveness of such tactics" (Egan 2004, A1). Larger localities, such as Boston, New York, Chicago, and San Francisco, regularly compete in the larger international business arena for new economic investment. Local governments seek new commercial investment because of the added tax revenues and employment opportunities it provides for the community. In order to be competitive and successful, cities and counties provide a range of incentives, including the donation of land or a facility; infrastructure improvements, such as new water lines, roadways, and entrance facilities; a reduction in property and other taxes for a certain stated period of time; and tax increment financing (TIF). The latter sometimes involves the creation of a semi-autonomous economic development district by and within a locality designed to attract commercial development through various TIF policies. It should be noted however, in an ironic twist of fate, that some communities which have provided a sizeable amount of tax breaks and other forms of financial assistance to a corporation for upgrading its manufacturing facility and remaining in the locality have ultimately witnessed the corporation closing its facility and abandoning the community. Such was the instance in Galesburg, Illinois when the Maytag Corporation, despite receiving large property tax breaks and other forms of financial aid from the community in the 1990s for upgrading its refrigerator manufacturing facility, ultimately closed its facility and left the community in 2004 (Egan 2004, A24). In the rivalry for commercial investment, affluent suburbs usually have a decided advantage over inner suburbs and core cities because of their higher quality of life, lower property tax rates, easy and quick access to interstate highways and rail facilities, and large available tracts of underdeveloped land suitable for commercial development. All of this has resulted in the lateral spread of metropolitan areas characterized by economic decentralization and expansive land use, the relative decline of the economic importance of core cities, and some measure of political tension between core cities and their surrounding suburbs.

The demand by core city officials that suburbs provide a higher amount of subsidized and/or public housing for the disadvantaged, especially for racial minorities, has provoked a significant amount of recurring political conflict between jurisdictions in the metropolis. In regard to this matter, the repeated pleas of core city officials have often been met by suburban resistance and, in some instances, by overt political hostility. However, in a number of metropolitan areas suburbs have voluntarily agreed to provide additional housing for the disadvantaged; this is the case in the Washington, DC, metropolitan area, where the Washington Metropolitan Council of Governments (MWCOG) was instrumental some years ago in successfully implementing a "fair-share" housing plan for the disadvantaged throughout the region.

In many metropolitan areas, the operation of large parks, sport stadiums, and other public facilities are administered and operated by a variety of special purpose districts or authorities or by the county government. For instance, in the Boston metropolitan area the Metropolitan District Commission (MDC) is responsible for the operation of large parks and zoos, as well as water supply and the operation of wastewater facilities. In contrast, Milwaukee County is largely responsible for these facilities and services in that metropolitan area, as well as airports. However, in some metropolitan areas, such as Richmond, Virginia, the operation and costs of many large parks and other public facilities in the core city remain the responsibility of the city. Richmond political leaders, acting on the premise that since suburban residents utilize their facilities, it is only reasonable that suburbanites bear their fair share of the costs, have been largely unsuccessful in making the operation and cost of these facilities a regionwide matter.

Matters relating to water supply and use have not only engendered serious conflict between the states, as noted previously in this chapter, but have also been the source of serious conflict between local jurisdictions. For instance, the City of Milwaukee, which historically has provided water on a contract basis to many of its suburbs, was charged in the 1940s and 1950s with using its provision of water as a "political weapon" or "carrot and a stick" on behalf of its annexation goals (Gladfelter 1971). Much more recently, a water dispute, dubbed a "water war," took place between the City of Richmond, Virginia, and Henrico County, which borders, in a semi-circular fashion, a large portion of the city. Throughout much of its history, Henrico has met all of its water needs, on a contract basis, from the city. However, Henrico's political leadership in the late 1980s decided to construct its own water treatment plant in order to meet at least some significant portion of its water needs. Richmond strongly objected to this decision by Henrico, arguing that it had the continuing capacity to supply all of the water requirements of the county and that, further, Henrico's construction of its own water treatment facility, drawing water from the same source as Richmond, would place in serious jeopardy a portion of the city's downtown redevelopment efforts. After lengthy and difficult negotiations, the city and the county reached an agreement in 1995 that allowed Henrico to construct a water treatment plant, provided it would continue to purchase some of its water needs from the city for a stated period of time. Henrico's water treatment plant was largely completed by 2003 and began operation the following year (Wikstrom 2003, 167–76).

SUMMARY AND CONCLUSION

In discussing the relationship between governmental and quasi-governmental entities, we have stressed that we maintain a strong preference for the term "intergovernmental relations," rather than federalism. This is simply the case because we believe that the term "federalism" is an excessively structural and legal concept that does not effectively capture the essence of the human interactions between, among, and within governments. In contrast, the term "intergovernmental relations" emphasizes the process-oriented and human interactions of governments and nongovernments in the American polity.

Importantly, as we have stressed, the nature of American federalism and intergovernmental relations changes as a result of a variety of demographic, economic, technological, and social forces. These have included the onslaught of the "Great Depression" of the 1930s, war and threat of war, and the continuing urbanization and suburbanization of the population. In addition to these characteristics, the changing roles of government at all levels, including the enhanced policy and managerial capacity of the "resurgent" states have put in place a paradigm of intergovernmental relations marked by a system of mutual dependency among and between federal, state, and local levels of government. Other factors shaping the current nature of American intergovernmental relations include the ascendancy of political conservatism, the more widespread use of "private federalism," the rise of presidential dominance, and worldwide technological and economic change.

The "web of intergovernmental relations" is of both a vertical and horizontal dimension. Vertical intergovernmental relations include federal-state, federal-local, state-local, and federal-state-local relations. In contrast, horizontal intergovernmental relations encompass state-state and local-local relations, not to mention the relations among agencies within our not so monolithic units of government. We have advanced that a variant of horizontal intergovernmental relations is that of intragovernmental relations, involving legislative, executive, and judicial relations in the same governmental entity.

Cooperative relations between governmental entities are of an informal or formal character. Informal relationships between governments most prominently involve the personal and electronic contact between elected and administrative officials, seeking information, technical assistance, and policy advice. The major features of formal cooperation include fiscal federalism, contracts and agreements, technical assistance, emergency assistance, supporting legislation, and mandates.

A substantial degree of vertical and horizontal competition and conflict exists between governments in the American polity. Prominent examples of vertical conflict involving the federal government and the states center on the grants-in-aid system, policy implementation, and decisions made by the United States Supreme Court. Conflict between the states, an example of horizontal conflict, largely involves economic conflict and competition, boundary disputes, and the control of natural, or "common ground," resources, primarily minerals, air, and water. Horizontal conflict between localities is the result of economic competition, matters relating to the location of low income housing, the financing and operation of public facilities and parks, and infrastructure disputes.

As in the past, broad economic, political, social, and technological forces will shape the future of American intergovernmental relations. Like the present, this will result in what we might describe as the "two faces" of intergovernmental relations. One face, of a centralizing dimension, emphasizes the central and critical importance of the federal government in the governmental matrix and the virtue of cooperation between all levels of government. This centralizing tendency is stimulated by the recognition that increasingly problems like terrorism, international economic competition, and air and water pollution are of a national scope and must be responded to in a cooperative fashion by the national government and its state and local governmental partners. The continued fiscal dependency of our lower levels of government on the federal government also serves to augment this centralizing dimension. On the other hand, the other face of our system of intergovernmental relations is of a decentralizing character, bent on achieving the "devolution revolution," with the movement of power and decision-making out of Washington to the states and their localities. This dimension is aided by the inherent forces of competition and conflict, largely motivated by self-interest, which are a part-and-parcel of our federal system of government and serve to undermine intergovernmental cooperation. We are continuing to witness the evolving nature of our bifurcated system of intergovernmental relations.

REFERENCES

Akin, Paige. 2003, November 5. City to Get Help Fighting Crime. *Richmond Times-Dispatch.* A1, A6.

Allen, Robert S. 1949. *Our Sovereign State.* New York: Vanguard Press.

Anderson, William. 1960. *Intergovernmental Relations in Review.* Minneapolis: University of Minnesota Press.

Bacque, Peter. 2003, October 11. Worthwhile or Waste? *Richmond Times-Dispatch.* A1, A10.

Bowman, Ann O'M. and Richard C. Kearney. 1986. *The Resurgence of the States.* Englewood Cliffs, NJ: Prentice-Hall.

Campbell, Alan and Donna Shalala. 1970. Problems Unsolved, Solutions Untried: The Urban Crisis. In Alan Campbell, ed., *The States and the Urban Crisis.* Englewood Cliffs, NJ: Prentice Hall. 4–26.

Conlan, Timothy. 1998. *From New Federalism to Devolution: Twenty-Five Years of Intergovernmental Reform.* Washington, DC: The Brookings Institution.

County of Henrico, Virginia. 1998. *Regional Cooperation in the Metropolitan Jurisdictions.* Henrico County Public Information Office.

Dilger, Robert Jay. 2000. The Study of American Federalism at the Turn of the Century. *State and Local Government Review.* 32 (Spring), 98–107.

Dillon, Sam. 2004, January 2. Some School Districts Challenging Bush's Signature Education Law. *New York Times.* A1, A13.

Dye, Thomas R. 1990. *American Federalism: Competition Among Governments.* Lexington, Massachusetts: D.C. Heath and Company.

Educator: Reject U.S. Money. 2003, October 15. *Richmond Times-Dispatch.* B2.

Egan, Timothy. 2004, October 10. Towns Hand Out Tax Breaks, Then Cry Foul as Jobs Leave. *New York Times.* A1, A10.

Elazar, Daniel J. 1984. *American Federalism: A View from the States.* 3d ed. New York: Harper & Row.

Feiock, Richard C. and Hyung-Jun Park. 2003. Social Capital and the Formation of Regional Partnerships. Paper presented at the Annual Meeting of the American Political Science Association. Philadelphia. August 27–30, 2003.

Frederickson, H. George. 1999. The Repositioning of American Public Administration. *PS: Political Science and Politics.* 32 (December), 701–11.

Friesema, H. Paul. 1971. *Metropolitan Political Structure: Intergovernmental Relations and Political Integration in the Quad-Cities.* Iowa City: University of Iowa Press.

Garreau, Jean. 1991. *Edge City: Life on the New Frontier.* New York: Doubleday.

Gladfelter, David D. 1971. "The Political Separation of City and Suburb: Water for Wauwatosa." In *Metropolitan Politics: A Reader,* edited by Michael N. Danielson. Second edition. Boston: Little, Brown: 75–85.

Gottmann, Jean. 1961. *Megalopolis: The Urbanized Northeastern Seaboard of the United States.* New York: Twentieth Century Fund.

Graves, W. Brooke. 1964. *American Intergovernmental Relations: Their Origins, Historical Development, and Current Status.* New York: Charles Scribner's Sons.

Grodzins, Morton. 1960. The Federal System. In *Report of the President's Commission on National Goals; The American Assembly, Goals for America.* Englewood Cliffs, NJ: Prentice-Hall.

Hardin, Peter. 2003a, October 8. Va v. Md as River Dispute Goes to Court. *Richmond Times-Dispatch.* B2.

———. 2003b, December 10. Ruling a Victory for Va. *Richmond Times-Dispatch.* B1, B4.

Harrigan, John H. and William C. Johnson. 1978. *The Metropolitan Council in Comparative Perspective.* Minneapolis: University of Minnesota Press.

Heclo, Hugh. 1977. *A Government of Strangers.* Washington, DC: The Brookings Institution.

Jones, Charles O. 1999. *Separate but Equal Branches: Congress and the Presidency.* 2d ed. New York: Chatham House Publishers.

Kantor, Paul. 1995. *The Dependent City Revisited: The Political Economy of Urban Development and Social Policy.* Boulder, CO: Westview Press.

Kincaid, John. 1990. From Cooperative to Coercive Federalism. In *American Federalism: The Third Century*, 139–52. Special issue of the *Annals of the American Academy of Political and Social Science.* John Kincaid, ed. Newbury Park, CA: Sage.

MacIver, Robert M. 1947. *The Web of Government.* New York: Macmillan.

Miranda, Rowan and Karlyn Andersen. 1994. "Alternative Service Delivery in Local Government." In *The Municipal Year Book 1994*, Vol. 61. Washington, DC: International City/County Management Association. 26–35.

Murphy, Jerome. 1973. The Education Bureaucracies Implement Novel Policy: the Politics of Title I of ESEA, 1965–72. In Allan Sindler, ed., *Policy and Politics in America.* Boston: Little, Brown. 160–99.

Nathan, Richard P. 1996. The Devolution Revolution: An Overview. *Rockefeller Institute Bulletin 1996.* Albany, NY: Nelson A. Rockefeller Institute of Government.

Polsby, Nelson W. 1986. Congress and the Presidency. 4th ed. Englewood Cliffs, NJ: Prentice-Hall.

Posner, Paul L. 1997. Unfunded Mandates Reform Act: 1996 and Beyond. *Publius.* 27 (Spring), 53–71.

Pressman, Jeffrey L. and Aaron Wildavsky. 1984. *Implementation.* 3d ed., expanded. Berkeley: University of California Press.

Putnam, Robert D. 2000. *Bowling Alone: The Collapse and Revival of the American Community.* New York: Simon & Schuster.

Rich, Motoko. 2003, July 27. Homeowner Boards Blur Line of Just Who Rules the Roost. *New York Times.* 1, 20.

Rivlin, Alice. 1992. *Reviving the American Dream.* Washington, DC: The Brookings Institution.

Seidman, Harold. 1975. *Politics, Position, and Power.* London: Oxford University Press.

Stephens, G. Ross. 1996. Urban Underrepresentation in the U.S. Senate. *Urban Affairs Review.* 31 (January), 404–18.

Stephens, G. Ross and Nelson Wikstrom. 1998. Trends in Special Districts. *State and Local Government Review.* 30 (Spring), 129–38.

Vines, Kenneth. 1976. The Federal Setting of State Politics. In Herbert Jacob and Kenneth Vines, eds., *Politics in the American States.* 3d ed. Boston: Little, Brown. 3–48.

Walker, David B. 1981. *Toward a Functioning Federalism.* Boston: Little, Brown.

Walker, Jack. 1969. The Role of Innovation Among the American States. *American Political Science Review.* 63 (September), 880–99.

Wikstrom, Nelson. 1977. *Councils of Governments: A Study of Political Incrementalism.* Chicago: Nelson-Hall.

———. 2003. *County Manager Government in Henrico County: Implementation, Evolution, and Evaluation.* Richmond, VA: County of Henrico.

Wright, Deil S. 1982. *Understanding Intergovernmental Relations.* 2d ed. Belmont, CA: Brooks/Cole.

Zimmerman, Joseph F. 1996. *The Neglected Dimension of Federalism: Interstate Relations.* Westport, CT: Praeger.

———. 2004. *Interstate Economic Relations.* Albany: State University of New York Press.

• 4 •

FISCAL FEDERALISM

[Federalism is] the method of dividing powers so that the general
and regional governments are each, within a sphere, coordinate and
independent.

—Kenneth C. Wheare, *Federal Government* (1964)

As Wallace Oates notes in his book on *Fiscal Federalism* (1972), one of the major problems with a federal system is determining where along the centralization continuum a particular public sector (public service or revenue source) should be located. Public services and revenue sources may be on different levels. Finances are one of the critical variables in the operation and maintenance of a federal system. Without adequate and independent financial resources, or some guarantee of adequate resources at each level of government, the federal structure will not operate as a truly federal system. Large and geographically diverse federal systems, such as that in the United States, are bound to have a highly uneven distribution of resources, tax and revenue capacity, and need for public services.

In order to operate independently, each level of government must be assured of adequate financial resources, that is, resources adequate to the maintenance of some minimum level of public services independent of the consent of the other level(s) of government. This can be accomplished through the constitutional division of revenue or separate revenue sources for each level of government. At the beginning of the twentieth century, the federal and state/local levels of government relied on a largely separate tax base, although this could not be said to be the case at the end of that century.

At the beginning of the twentieth century, state and local governments in the United States obtained over two-thirds of their revenue from the property tax, with small amounts from special assessments on property and excise taxes. The federal level obtained 92 percent of its revenue from customs duties, excise taxes, and the postal service, so there was a reasonably clear separation of revenue sources. (See Appendix Table 4.1, p. 104). Such a clear separation of tax base does not exist today. Nor does the United States have a system for placing a floor under the revenue of poorer state/local revenue systems as exists in other federal systems like Australia, Canada, and Germany (U.S. Advisory Commission on Intergovernmental Relations [ACIR] 1981).

The latest study of revenue capacity of the fifty states by ACIR (1993) indicates that the richest state, Alaska, had 3.5 times the per capita revenue capacity and 3.3 times the revenue collection of the poorest state, Mississippi. While ACIR no longer exists, very wide disparities in revenue base and revenue collection still exist among the fifty states, judging by the Census data for FY2001–FY2003, with Alaska still collecting three times the per capita revenue of Mississippi;[1] also, the richer states usually exhibit less tax effort than poorer states like Mississippi.

The U.S. system of federal aid to states and their local governments does not provide grants-in-aid that tend to equalize resources for poorer states. In fact, it does just the opposite by giving larger per capita amounts to small states and to rich states.[2] Moreover, because of the selective distribution of oil and gas production, other mineral resources, and tourism, some states are able to export the burden of significant tax revenues to consumers and businesses in other states. Nearly every state and many local governments try to export their taxes to consumers in or from other states or localities (Stephens 1985, 1989, 1996).

FEDERAL, STATE, AND LOCAL REVENUE SOURCES OVER TIME

The twentieth century was a period of major change in fiscal federalism in the United States. As mentioned earlier, state and local governments were heavily dependent on property as their tax base at the beginning of the century, and the federal government derived over 92 percent of its resources from customs, excises, and postal receipts, but this situation was about to change. In the 1960s, Nebraska was the last state to eliminate the property tax as an important state-level revenue source. Major changes in revenue sources portend changing roles for the different levels of government in a federal system.

Such change occurred in the first and second halves of the twentieth century. During the first half, the major change was the adoption of progressive income taxes, inheritance taxes, and payroll taxes, along with state adoption of general sales taxes and the diversification of state and local revenue sources. Change during the second half involved the erosion of income taxes on corporations and high-income individual taxpayers, along with the escalation of flat-rate payroll taxes and the continuing diversification of state and local revenue sources. A third major alteration, exacerbating the trends of the last few decades of the past century, occurred with the election of George W. Bush and a Republican Congress in the early twenty-first century. This change was aided by a spurious projection of federal revenue surpluses for the first decade of this century. This year 2000 projection was the most optimistic scenario by the Congressional Budget Office (CBO). It assumed that (1) the boom times of the 1990s would continue unabated for at least another decade, and (2) federal tax rates would remain at their current levels. Neither assumption proved valid.

At the turn of the twentieth century and for the first three decades on the 1900s, leaving out the perturbations caused by World War I, local government was the most active level in terms of both the collection of revenue and the provision of public services, with states the least active. In 1902, local governments brought in 51 percent of total government own source revenue and accounted for 58 percent of direct expenditures. States accounted for 11 percent of own source revenue and only 8 percent of direct expenditures, while the federal level constituted 38 percent of revenue and 34 percent of direct expenditures. Government at all levels was much smaller at that time, comprising only about 8 percent of GNP (U.S. Bureau of the Census, 1961).

At the dawn of the last century, local governments received 73 percent of their own source revenue from property taxes and an undetermined amount from special assessments against property, probably in the range of about 5 percent, with service charges another 7 percent, and an undetermined amount from excises. Property, at that time, was the preeminent form of wealth. As an ad valorem tax, even though sometimes badly administered, property taxes were probably a more progressive form of taxation than the system that evolved by the end of the twentieth century. By FY2001, the property tax had declined to less than 36 percent of local own source revenue nationally, with payroll taxes, local income taxes (which apply only to earned income and are almost always flat-rate), sales and excise taxes, and service charges accounting for half of all local own source revenue (see Table 4.1). While the proportions vary from one state to the next, these revenue sources carry a larger burden for low- and middle-income taxpayers. The net effect of twentieth-century diversification of revenue sources by both state and local governments has been to download the tax burden onto low- and middle-income residents.

The major development of the first half of the twentieth century was the passage of the income tax amendment to the Constitution in 1913, the sixteenth amendment, which enabled the imposition of income taxes on both corporations and individuals and payroll taxes on wages and salaries. The progressive income tax was used to wage two World Wars and became the mainstay of federal revenue by mid-century,

TABLE 4.1. Own Source Revenue as a Percentage of Total by Level of Government, 1902, 1952, and FY2001

	Local			State			Federal		
	1902	1952	FY2001	1902	1952	FY2001	1902	1952	FY2001
Customs duties	0	0	0	0	0	0	37.2	0.7	1.0
Property taxes	72.7	58.7	35.9	44.8	2.6	1.1	0	0	0
Individual income tax	0	0.6	1.7	0	6.4	19.7	0	42.2	49.9
Corporate income tax	0	0.1	0.4	0	5.9	3.3	0	32.1	7.6
Payroll taxes	0	1.9	6.6	0	17.2	27.1	0	7.2	34.9
General sales tax	0	4.4	6.1	0	15.6	17.7	0	0	0
Selective sales taxes	0	3.1	2.5	15.3	24.4	7.9	36.1	12.3	3.0
Other taxes	9.3	4.8	3.1	25.1	6.3	5.0	6.7	1.8	1.5
Service charges	7.0	22.5	32.9	13.7	13.4	9.6	18.9	2.7	2.0
Other revenue	11.0	3.9	10.8	1.1	8.2	8.6	1.1	1.0	0.1
TOTAL	100.0	100.0	100.0	100.0	100.0	100.0	100.0	100.0	100.0
As percent of GNP	4.54	4.07	6.83	0.97	4.13	9.66	3.46	20.69	19.50

U.S. Bureau of the Census 1941; www.census.gov/govs/estimate01.html; OMB 2003.

bringing in as much as three-fourths of all federal receipts with far smaller proportions at the state and local levels of government. When applied to tax sources, "progressive" means that individuals and corporations with higher levels of income pay a higher percentage of that income in taxes. The use of the progressive income tax reached its apex in the 1940s and early 1950s.

The passage of the Social Security Act of 1937, which included a provision for unemployment compensation, initiated the use of payroll taxes on earned income —applying only to wages, salaries, and commissions, but not to interest, dividends, capital gains, or inheritance. States followed suit with payroll taxes for unemployment compensation, workmen's compensation, and employee retirement. The first local payroll tax on earned income, usually called an earnings tax, was passed by Philadelphia in 1939. New York City was one of the earliest cities to use this as a revenue source and is one of the few where the tax is progressive. Earnings taxes were used by less than 4,000 out of the 87,525 local governments in 2002. The use of the local earnings tax is concentrated in Pennsylvania and Ohio and is used by a scattering of larger cities and by a few counties and school districts elsewhere. By mid-century, states were receiving nearly 30 percent of their revenue from income and payroll taxes, while sales and excise taxes increased from 15 to 40 percent of own source revenue (see Table 4.1).

LATER TWENTIETH-CENTURY DEVELOPMENTS—STATE AND LOCAL

The last half of the century witnessed both an increased role and the diversification of revenue sources at the state and local levels of government. It took a long time after World War II for the role of the federal government to decline relative to state and local government, partly because of the so-called cold war. Because of the increase in population, urbanization, and suburbanization, state and local governments almost achieved parity with the federal government by the turn of the twenty-first century (see Figure 4.1). Most domestic services are the responsibility of state and local governments, so there were large increases in the activity of our subnational governments providing services to millions of new residents (Stephens and Wikstrom 2000).

One way of looking at the changes in state and local finances is to analyze per capita revenue increases in constant dollars, taking out inflation. Between 1952 and FY2001, the (FY2001) constant dollar increase in gross domestic product (GDP) was 146 percent, but state and local own source revenue almost quadrupled, up 279 percent. (Fiscal year 2001 is from July 1, 2000 to June 30, 2001.) While property taxes and utility charges rose 110 and 112 percent, respectively, selective sales taxes went up 139 percent, with general sales taxes increasing 332 percent. The corporate income tax increased by 187 percent. Service charges reached five times their 1952 level by FY2001, the income tax eight times, and payroll over 6.5 times the earlier level (see Figure 4.2). Although not documented here, there has been a massive increase in the use of sales taxes and service charges by local governments from the 1980s into the first few years of the twenty-first century.

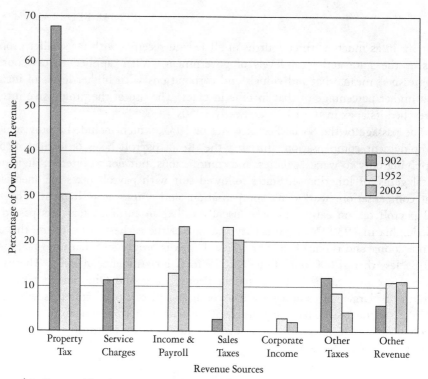

FIGURE 4.1. State and local revenue as percentage of own source revenue, 1902, 1952, and 2002. *Sources: U.S. Bureau of the Census 1961 and www.census.gov/govs/02us.html.*

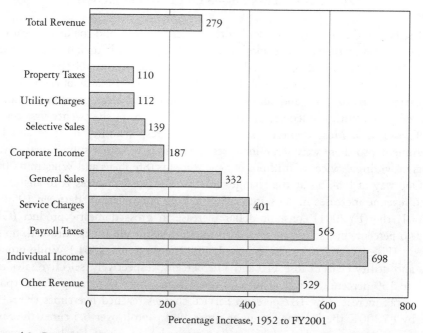

FIGURE 4.2. Per capita increase in state and local revenue by source, 1952 to FY2001 in FY2001 constant dollars. *Sources: U.S. Bureau of the Census, 1961; Council of Economic Advisors (CEA),* Economic Report of the President, *1991 and 2003; www.census.gov/govs/estimate/01s100us.html.*

Service charges, general and selective sales taxes, and payroll taxes take a larger percentage of income from low- and middle-income residents than from those with higher levels of income. Local earnings (income) and state and local payroll taxes are almost universally flat-rate. Seven states have no state individual income tax, and two tax only interest and dividends. In another seven states, the state income tax is flat-rate. The remaining state income taxes are progressive, but most are not very progressive (CSG, 2002, 2003). Of the constant dollar increases in state revenue over this time period, about 30 percent was proportionate or neutral across the range of income, 16 percent progressive, and 54 percent regressive, meaning the overall revenue structure of state and local governments became more regressive over the last half-century.

Nevada, Washington, and Wyoming have no state corporate income tax or anything comparable, such as the Texas corporate franchise tax of 4.5 percent on earned surplus or Michigan's 2 percent value-added tax. In thirty-one states and the District of Columbia the corporate tax is flat-rate. The remaining states have progressive rates, but they are not very progressive (CSG 2002, 2003). As with the federal corporate tax, the state corporate income tax has been declining as a proportion of state own source revenue over the last half-century as the net worth of corporations has multiplied.

TWENTIETH-CENTURY DEVELOPMENTS—FEDERAL

The last half of the twentieth century witnessed a precipitous decline in the use of the corporate income tax as a major source of federal revenue, as well as a similar decline in the progressivity of the individual income tax on high-income taxpayers (see Figure 4.3). Over the last half of the century corporate lawyers have found loopholes in the tax law and Congress has given so many concessions and included so many exemptions in the corporate income tax that few large corporations and multinationals pay anything at all. Not only foreign corporations but many U.S. corporations take their profits to offshore tax havens. One of more recent is the $136 billion reduction in the corporate income tax occurred in October 2004.

A report by the General Accounting Office (GAO) indicated that for the period 1996–2000, five years of increasing prosperity, over 60 percent of U.S. corporations paid no federal corporate income tax at all. In addition, over 70 percent of foreign corporations paid no federal income tax on the profits they made in the United States. Moreover, the percentage of these corporations completely avoiding the corporate tax increased over this five-year period and continues to increase under the George W. Bush administration (McKinnon 2004). This, however, is only the tip of the iceberg. Because of the loopholes and exemptions passed by Congress, those corporations that pay the income tax pay very little on the actual profits they make.[3] This situation appears to be particularly true for large national and multinational corporations. Moreover, in the 1940s and early 1950s an excess profits tax for corporations that did business with the government on procurement contracts limited profits to 10 percent above cost. This provision no longer exists. In 1952, the corporate income tax provided 32.1 percent of all federal revenue; by FY2001 (based on Calendar Year 2000

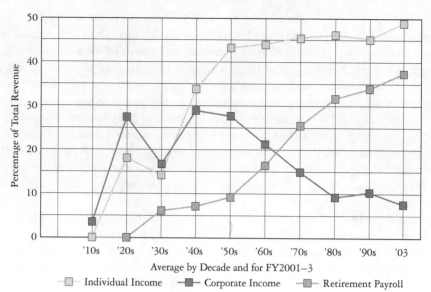

FIGURE 4.3. Average percentage of federal revenue by source by decade and for FY2001. For individual income, corporate income, and payroll retirement taxes. *Sources: U.S. Bureau of the Census 1961; OMB,* Historical Tables, *Budget of the United States Government 2004 and 2005.*

income), this source had declined to 7.6 percent (OMB 2003, 2004). For FY2006, the revenue from corporations is likely to be 4 percent or less. In constant dollars, taking out inflation, corporate net worth increased nearly fourteen times over the last half of the twentieth century, up 1,271 percent (U.S. Bureau of the Census 1953a–2003a).[4]

The effective tax rate for highest 1 percent of individual income taxpayers, as a percent of adjusted gross income (AGI), dropped from 60.1 percent in 1950 to 27.4 percent for tax year 2000. In the years 1950 and 2000, in 2000 constant dollars, the top 1 percent of taxpayers had AGI incomes that averaged an adjusted gross income in excess of 1 million (U.S. Bureau of the Census 1953a–2003a; OMB 2003, 2004, 2005; www.taxfoundation.org 2004; CEA 1991, 2003).

The tax year 2000 rate, 27.4 percent, has declined even more under the tax cuts passed by Congress during the period from 2001 to 2005. Particularly for high-income individual taxpayers, those in the top three tax brackets, these reductions cut the tax rates and reduced top tax rates for taxes on income, capital gains, dividends, and inheritance for tax years 2003 and beyond. Capital gains, dividends, and inheritance income, sometimes called "unearned income", accrues largely to the top 10–20 percent of taxpayers. According to David Cay Johnston (2003), taxpayers with the highest levels of income have significant proportions in "unearned income" and many ways to avoid paying income taxes. The top 1 percent of individual taxpayers average taking only half their income in the "earned income" category (wages, salaries, and commissions).

Further, tax avoidance and evasion have increased among individual high-income taxpayers over the last half-century (Johnston 2003). Over these five decades, the revenue from the personal income tax has continued to increase, from 42 to 50 percent of federal receipts between 1952 and FY2001 (OMB 2003, 2004). For this same time span, constant dollar median family income rose only 55 percent while GDP increased 146 percent. All of this means that the income tax burden has been downloaded on low- and middle-income residents.

Not only has the individual income tax been downloaded on low- and middle-income residents, over the same time span federal payroll taxes for retirement and Medicare displaced the corporate income tax as the second major source of federal revenue, increasing from 7.2 percent of federal revenue in the early 1950s to an average of 37.4 for the first three years of the new century (see Figure 4.3). Payroll taxes are almost universally flat-rate in their application, that is, the same tax rate applies to all levels of earned income without exemptions or deductions. However, payroll taxes like Social Security, the largest payroll tax, have a cutoff point where income above a certain level is not taxed. For tax year 2003, the Social Security tax dropped to zero above $87,000 of earned income for individuals. Across the spectrum of total income, this makes the incidence of payroll taxes highly regressive.

Looking at changes in the financing of the central government in terms of the per capita revenue collected from different revenue sources using FY2001 constant value dollars, taking out inflation, there have been rather massive changes in who pays the taxes. To do this over the last half of the twentieth century, we correlate the appropriate implicit price deflators and chain-type indices reported by the President's Council of Economic Advisors (CEA 1991, 2003, 2004).

In per capita constant dollar terms, total federal revenue increased 91 percent between 1952 and FY2001. Yet, remembering the changes mentioned earlier, the federal per capita personal income tax increased 125 percent, while excise taxes reached five times their 1952 level and retirement taxes reached almost nine times the earlier amount. Corporate per capita income taxes dropped by 55 percent (see Figure 4.4).

INTERGOVERNMENTAL TRANSFERS

As mentioned earlier, other democratic federal systems, notably Australia, Canada, and Germany, equalize or place a floor under their poorer state-level governments through the use of intergovernmental transfers, more commonly known as grants, grants-in-aid, or state aid and federal aid. In some instances these monetary transfers are in the form of shared taxes in which each participating level gets a portion of the total. The data given in Table 4.1 does not show federal aid to state and local governments and state aid to local, only own source revenue by level of government.

During the first half of the twentieth century there was little federal aid to states and what there was was largely for agriculture and roads, with the exception of the mid-1930s when aid was used as one of the methods of attempting to deal with the problems of the Great Depression. Again, with the slight exception of the 1930s, local governments received very insignificant amounts of federal aid prior to World War II. After the war, federal aid to state and local governments in current dollars nearly doubled every five years to the late 1970s. With the exception of the so-called

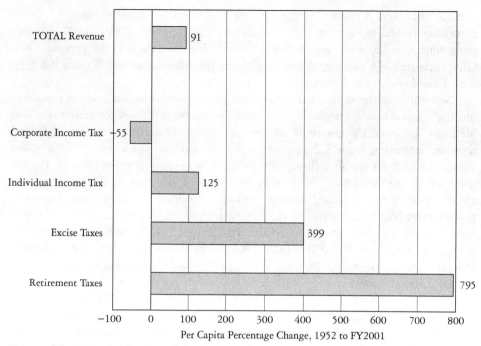

FIGURE 4.4. Per capita change in federal revenue by source, 1952 to FY2001 in constant dollars. Uses FY2001 constant dollars. *Sources: U.S. Bureau of the Census 1961; OMB 2003, 2004; CEA 1991, 2003.*

revenue-sharing and antirecession federal grants of the 1970s, states received about 90 percent of this largesse, although some of these monies were passed-through to local governments. Federal aid to state and local governments reached their peak in 1978 at 26 percent of state and local budgets and over 16 percent of the federal budget, then, in these terms, fell off to 14 percent of state and local revenue and about 12 percent of federal expenditures by 1987. By the turn of the twenty-first century, federal grants represented 17 percent of state and local outlays and 19 percent of federal expenditures (Shannon 1984; U.S. Bureau of the Census 1980b–2004b, 2004c, 2004d).

Grants-in-aid have existed since before the adoption of the present Constitution in 1789. The first, the Northwest Ordinance, was passed by the Congress under the Articles of Confederation in 1785 and was later readopted by the by first Congress under the present Constitution. The Ordinance provided for statehood in the territories (outside the then-existing states) once they acquired sixty thousand residents, local self-government, civil and political rights, and education. For most eighteenth- and nineteenth-century federal grants, the aid was in the form of land grants. The Northwest Ordinance established the important policy that the territories were not to be kept in subjection to the federal government, but were to be developed as states on an equal footing with the original thirteen (Young 1962). Originally, the territories covered the area north of the Ohio River west of New York to the Mississippi River— later to be extended to cover the Louisiana Purchase and other acquisitions. Most land grants were given out for the development of public education, higher education (Morrill Act of 1862, for state Agriculture & Mechanical Arts colleges), and transportation—roads, canals, and railroads.

While the federal government started giving cash grants in the nineteenth century, this became the principle form of federal grant in the twentieth century, although there are also credit, loan, and insurance programs that benefit state and local governments (Census, CFFR 1980–2004). There are several different types of federal grants. Some require the recipient government (state or local) to come up with some sort of matching fund, either cash or in kind; others do not. Where matching is required, it usually ranges from 10 to 50 percent of the cost of a project or program. Most federal grants are for a *specific-purpose* or project. These are usually called *categoricals*. While most categoricals go to states, some go to local governments. With the exception of the 1970s and early 1980s, 86–90 percent of all federal grant money has usually gone directly to states, although some of these monies are passed-through to local governments. These grants may or may not be distributed on the basis of formulae. Categoricals account for about 90 percent of the money given out by all federal grants. For several years, the largest federal grant has been Medicaid, at about $160 billion in FY2004 (OMB 2004).

A second type, usually called *block grants*, are for a broader *functional purpose* such as housing and community development, health, criminal justice, and social services. Today, out of nearly six hundred federal grants only fourteen or fifteen can be classified as block grants. A few grants to states have required a mandatory pass-through to local governments. During the 1960s and 1970s, between 30 and 40 percent of federal aid to states was passed-through to local governments, but this was a period of relative federal generosity. Federal aid for education has been the largest segment of pass-through money (Stephens and Olson 1979). About 30 percent of categoricals and nearly all block grants are distributed on the basis of a formulae.

Currently, less than 2 percent of all federal grant funds are *general purpose*. In other words, the money can be spent for any public purpose by the recipient government. From 1971 to the mid-1980s, there was a general-purpose grant, called General Revenue Sharing (GRS), that gave money to state and local governments with about two-thirds of the funds allocated to local governments (State and Local Fiscal Assistance Act of 1971)—this despite the fact at that time states had 51 percent of the service delivery responsibility and 57.5 percent of the financial responsibility for state and local public services (Stephens and Olson 1975). GRS funds went to states and so-called general-purpose local governments, that is, some 3,000 counties, 18,500 municipalities, and about 17,000 townships. The money was passed out on the basis of two different formulae, and each state could select the formula that gave it the most money. Only a few of these local units did not receive money, those whose allocation would have been less than $200. In fact, one of the authors calculated that nearly eleven thousand of these recipient local governments operated without employees, that is, they did not have as much as a 0.5 full-time equivalent employee (Stephens and Olson 1979).

At the time it was enacted, GRS was the largest federal grant ever passed by Congress, giving out as much as $6.9 billion in the late 1970s. Medicaid easily occupies that position today. There were, however, constraints in the GRS formulae that limited the per capita amounts that the poorest state and local governments could receive and assured the richest state and local units that they would get a share of this largesse. In other words, the redistribution was limited so that nearly all local governments, no matter how rich, would receive some money. One purpose seems to have been to pass the money around. Nevertheless, it was the first federal grant that seriously tried to give a bit more money to poorer states and localities. This grant was phased out in the 1980s. The remaining general-purpose grants are very small and usually involve the sharing of certain revenues from public lands or government corporations like the Tennessee Valley Authority (ACIR 1992, and 1993).

The late 1960s through much of the 1970s was a period in which Congress passed a number of block grants, with a total of about twenty-five, allocating more of the distribution to local governments. These were sometimes called Special Revenue Sharing. Three of these were called "antirecession" grants and included money for state and local projects and extra "revenue-sharing" money passed out on the basis of measures of unemployment. This was also a period in which public interest groups, often referred to as PIGs, had a great deal of influence in Congress, groups like the National Association of Counties (NACo), the U.S. Conference of Mayors (USCM), the National League of Cities (NLC), the Council of State Governments (CSG), and the National Association of Towns and Townships.

Table 4.2 illustrates the many complex forms of intergovernmental transfers. Both grants-in-aid and shared taxes can be for general purposes, for a functional purpose like health or education, or for a specific project or program. General-purpose grants are largely unconditional. In other words, the money can be spent for any public purpose at the discretion of the recipient government, although in most cases the recipient must account for the way it is spent and it must be for a public purpose. Most grants, however, are given out with a number of conditions, some of which have little relationship with the purpose of the grant. There may be matching requirements where the recipient government must come up with a certain share of the cost, either a dollar amount or a percentage of the total cost. Matching requirements can be in dollars or in-kind. In-kind matching may be where a local or state government provides land or some other facility in payment for their share of the project or program.

Contracts are another method whereby monies are transferred among governments. Contracts can be vertically among levels of government or horizontally between states or among localities. These arrangements are by negotiated agreements. Municipalities often contract with each other for the provision of services such as water or sewage treatment. It is not unusual for municipalities to contract with county governments for the delivery of selected services. Sometimes, there are agreements for the interchange of personnel or the use of one government's employees by another.

Services-in-aid are another aspect of intergovernmental relations in which one government uses the services of another. Local law enforcement often uses the facilities of state law enforcement agencies and the FBI. This is also the case with state and local agencies involved in agriculture who use the expertise of the U.S. Department of Agriculture (USDA). States often lend their expertise to smaller local governments in terms of land-use planning. Sometimes services-in-aid goes the other way and a

TABLE 4.2. Types of Intergovernmental Monetary Transfers Among Governments Within the U.S. Federal System

Type of Transfer	Common Names	Conditions	Allocation	Limitations
1. *Grants-in-Aid*		1. *Unconditional*	*Allocation can be by:*	*Transfers can be:*
(a) General-purpose	General revenue sharing	2. *Conditional*	(a) Project approval	(a) Open-ended in terms of the money involved
(b) Functional-purpose	Block grants or special revenue sharing	(a) Matching requirements set in dollars or percentages	(b) Program approval	(b) Closed-ended with strict limits on the amount of money available
(c) Specific-purpose	Categorical grants, project grants, or program grants	(b) Share of cost, percent cost, or set dollar amount	(c) Formula	
		(c) Share or percent of the revenue collected	(d) Project and formula	
			(e) Program and formula	
		[*Note:* Virtually all intergovernmental transfers have requirements in terms of accounting for the monies received and spent.]	(f) By some political or other extraneous criteria[2]	
2. *Shared Taxes*[1]				
(a) General-purpose	Revenue sharing or named shared tax			
(b) Functional-purpose	A named function			
(c) Specific-purpose	A named project or program			
3. *Contracts*		Negotiations concerning contractual arrangements between state and local, among local units, or between states		
4. *Services-in-Aid*[3]		Usually no money is involved, although on occasion there is a small fee that does not cover the costs. Often a higher level of government performs a service for a subordinate level, but sometimes it is the other way around.		
5. *Loan, Credit, and Insurance Programs*				

[1] States often share motor fuel taxes with their local governments on some kind of pro-rated basis for road maintenance. A number of states share state-collected fees on fire insurance with local fire departments. Maryland allows county governments to piggyback a county-determined percentage of the state income tax on top of the state income tax. It is then collected by the state and given to the county government. For decades Wisconsin has shared 50 percent of its state income tax with its local governments. In recent years it has been on a redistributed basis where property tax–poor localities receive a larger allocation.

[2] Throughout much of the last half-century no state receives less than one-half of 1 percent of most federal grants. Starting in 2003, this percentage was changed to three-fourths of 1 percent. This gives small states a much high per capita allocation. In 2000, twenty-six small states had 18 percent of the population and 52 percent of the votes in the U.S. Senate; the nine largest states had 52 percent of the population and 18 percent of the Senate votes (Stephens 1996, updated).

[3] The FBI performs technical services for state and local police agencies. Likewise, state bureaus of investigation also perform services for local police agencies. State departments of urban or local government often provide some land-use planning services for smaller local governments.

state or federal agency will use the personnel of a local government, such as a city or county.

Monies involved in intergovernmental transfers can be allocated in a variety of ways. State and federal grants can be allocated strictly on the basis of a formula, as was done under the federal GRS grants or in Wisconsin's sharing of half of state income tax revenues with local governments. Strict formula allocation is usually used only for general-purpose grants, although it is occasionally used for some shared taxes such as the motor fuel excise tax. Some grants are allocated on the basis of the granting government's approval of a project or program. Other grants allocate funds among states and/or local governments and also require approval of the projects or programs of the recipient governments. At times political or even extraneous criteria are involved in the allocation of funds. The granting government may require the recipient government to conform to certain professional and accounting standards, but they may also be required to do things totally unrelated to the project or program involved, such as making various facilities available to the handicapped. Grants can be open-ended in terms of the amount of money involved or strictly limited in the amount allocated.

Allocation of funds can also be political. Insofar as federal grants are concerned, most have a requirement that no state will receive less than one-half of 1 percent of the total funds dispensed. Starting in 2003, in some cases, the rule was changed to three-fourths of 1 percent. The result is that small states receive far higher per capita allocations of federal money than large states. Small states and rich states receive disproportionate shares of federal grants. This is because of the dominant position of small states in the U.S. Senate as well as the ability of rich states to pressure Congress for more money. The twenty-six smallest states with 18 percent of the population have 52 percent of the Senators, while the nine states with 52 percent of the population have 18 percent of the votes in the Senate. Senators from small states also dominate the political leadership in the Senate. High state/local tax capacity and small numbers of residents explain as much as 70 percent of the variation in per capita federal aid to state and local government (Stephens 1996, data updated to 2000).

State aid to local government has almost always exceeded federal aid to state and local government in total amount. Moreover, state aid has been much more constant in terms of functional purpose, heavily emphasizing education and roads, although in most cases road funds are a share of the state excise tax on motor fuels. Elementary and secondary education are almost always a local service, with the exception of Hawaii, where it is state administered.[5] State support for K–12 education increased considerably over the course of the twentieth century, although it seems to have leveled off or even declined somewhat in the late twentieth and early twenty-first centuries. Higher education has largely been a state-provided activity, but state support for higher education has declined considerably over the last three decades. The rationale for declining state support of higher education is that the individual benefits so much from the education that students ought to pay the costs—sort of a service charge for higher education. As a result, many students are heavily in debt when they graduate. As some wag once said, "We used to have a *state university*, then we had a *state supported* university, next it was a *state assisted* university, now it is a *state named* university."

Prior to the New Deal of the 1930s, public welfare services, insofar as there were any, were predominantly local. From the 1930s through the mid-1950s there was a considerable amount of federal pass-through money for welfare as it was largely a locally administered service. Since that time, public welfare has become almost universally a state-administered service, with the exceptions of New York City and about three-eighths of the expenditure for this service in California. The functional purposes of federal grants-in-aid seems to alter with changes in emphasis of whoever is in control of Congress and the presidency in Washington, DC. About 8–10 percent of state aid to local units is for general purposes without specificity as to how it will be spent.

Wisconsin is one of the few states that has ever had major redistributive state aid to its local units, giving higher per capita general-purpose aid to poorer municipalities, townships, counties, and school districts. Historically, Wisconsin has given half of the revenue from the state income tax to its local governments. Originally it was given back to the local unit of residence of the income taxpayer and as a result rich local governments got richer and the poor, poorer. In the 1970s the distribution was changed to give more money to local units with a lower than average per capita property tax base.

In FY2002, local governments received $355 billion in state aid and $43 billion from the federal government; states received $318 billion from federal and another $18 billion in local to state payments. The latter is usually state revenues collected by local governments, mostly by county governments in their capacity as agents of the state. In FY2002, per capita state intergovernmental revenue was $1,128 from federal and $63 from local governments. Local governments received $153 per capita from federal and $1,263 from the state (see Table 4.3). It should be pointed out, however, that the amounts of federal aid received by state and local governments and the amounts of state aid local governments receive vary widely from one state to the next. In FY2002, state aid to local averaged $1,263 per resident with a range from a low of $127 in Hawaii to a high of $1,992 in New York, but both states are somewhat exceptional. In New York we find pass-through federal welfare aid to New York City, while Hawaii is, by far, our most centralized state, with most state and local revenues and service delivery at the state level of government.[6]

Federal and state aid often comes with mandates as to just how such monies will be spent. In fact, grants-in-aid are the principle mechanism for enforcing mandates on the recipient state or local governments. Moreover, state and sometimes federal legislation mandates certain activities and procedures for recipient governments, on occasion without providing the necessary funds for compliance by the receiving units of government. Starting in the 1960s, these edicts led to considerable pressure by recipient governments to outlaw unfunded mandates. Major federal regulation of state and local governments using mandates date principally to the Civil Rights Act of 1964 and involve everything from highways to the environment, air and water pollution, flood disasters, education, occupational safety, health, energy, surface mining, the transportation of hazardous materials, and facilities for the handicapped, as well as voting rights, civil rights, and a host of other activities. Some of these are *cross-cutting requirements* that apply to anyone, any institution, or any government receiving federal

TABLE 4.3. Intergovernmental Transfer Payments in Current Dollars (Millions), 1902–2002

Year	Total Federal	State from Federal	State from Local	Local from Federal	Local from State
'02	7	3	6	4	52
'13	12	6	10	6	91
'22	108	99	27	6	312
'27	116	107	51	9	596
'32	232	222	45	10	801
'37	874	676	44	198	1,467
'42	858	802	56	56	1,780
'47	1,359	1,223	80	136	2,687
'52	2,566	2,329	156	237	5,044
'57	3,843	3,500	427	343	7,196
'62	7,871	7,108	373	763	10,879
'67	15,370	13,616	673	1,753	18,434
'72	31,342	25,791	1,191	4,551	34,143
'77	62,444	45,870	2,737	16,554	60,277
'82	87,282	66,026	3,139	21,256	95,363
'87	114,857	102,381	6,918	19,395	136,869
'92	179,209	159,068	10,861	20,141	195,845
'97	244,607	215,859	15,020	28,768	258,235
'02	360,534	317,581	17,841	42,953	355,544

Sources: U.S. Bureau of the Census 1961; 1957e–2002e Census of Governments, Washington, DC; Government Printing Office.

funds. There are also what are called *crossover sanctions*, where failure to comply with the regulations for one mandate may result in termination of funds for another completely separate program or grant (Beam 1983). A report by ACIR in 1992 found there were some seventy-three federal statutory mandates for recipient state and local governments enacted through 1990 (Conlan and Beam 1992). A much more recent mandate that has received a lot of attention is the "No Child Left Behind Act" of 2001.

Given the legal status of local government in the United States, state mandates for local government have existed since colonial times, as have counties, municipalities, special districts, and townships, even though some local governments preexisted the establishment of colonial government. State mandates applying to local government are no less contentious and have received quite a bit of attention over the last few decades. By 1994, twenty-nine states had either constitutional or statutory limitations on the imposition of mandates, fifteen constitutional and fourteen statutory. Four states have both constitutional and statutory limits (Zimmerman 1994). Even so, some of these states, like Missouri, at times seem to ignore the limits placed on state mandates for local government.

PROGRESSIVITY/REGRESSIVITY OF THE *FEDERAL* REVENUE STRUCTURE

Scholars often analyze the impact of a particular tax, tax change, or tax system on individuals with different levels of personal income. Seldom does anyone look at the changes taking place in the overall federal, state, and local revenue structure. This chapter attempts to do just that; the results are not too salutary in terms of changes in the *federal* (federal meaning federal *plus* state *plus* local) revenue structure over the last five or six decades.

The method used to measure how *progressive* or *regressive* a tax, tax system, or revenue structure is by developing a *simplified regression-line index*. A *progressive tax* or revenue source is one in which those with higher levels of income pay a higher percentage of their income in taxes than those with a lower level of income. The terms *tax* and *revenue source* are used interchangeably in this discussion. A *flat-tax* is one in which the same percentage of income is paid by individuals with different levels of income. A *proportionate tax* or tax structure is one that essentially takes the same percentage across different levels of income, sometimes called *flat-rate*. A *regressive tax* or tax system is one in which those with lower levels of income pay a larger percentage of their income in taxes and other revenues than those with higher income.

Using this index, a rating of 1.00 is a flat-tax that takes the same percentage of income across different levels of income. A rating of 2.00 indicates that the top category of income pays twice the percentage of those at the bottom, whereas a rating of 5.00 means that the top group pays five times the percentage of income as those in the lowest category. On the other hand, a score of 0.50 indicates the lowest category pays twice the percentage of those at the top, while 0.33 means they pay three times the percentage of those with the highest level of income.[7] These measures apply to the personal income of individual taxpayers.

In 1950, the federal individual income tax had a rating of 11.49, meaning that the top 1 percent of tax returns, on average, paid 11.5 times the percentage than the average for the bottom 50 percent of taxpayers across the range of income. The income tax dropped to a calculated (straight-line) rating of 6.22 for tax year 2000. Federal payroll taxes supplied only a minor proportion (7 percent) of federal revenue in 1950, but increased to over one-third by 2000. These payroll taxes were regressive in 1950 and have become even more so over the intervening half-century. In 1950, on average, using the revenue sources of the federal level, the top income group paid in over five times the percentage of AGI compared to the bottom 50 percent. By 2000, it was only 28 percent more on income that averages 71 times that of the bottom category. In tax year 2000, the top 1 percent had an average AGI income of $1,042,000 while the bottom 50 percent of tax returns averaged $14,600 AGI. The top 1 percent of tax payers often have a much higher proportion of their income in forms of income that are taxed at lower rates or not at all, so-called unearned income (from interest, dividends, tax exempt investments, capital gains, or inheritance). Unearned income constitutes about one-half of the earnings of the top 1 percent of tax returns. Constant dollar incomes for these groups in 1950 are comparable to those shown for CY2000 (see Table 4.4).

On this scale, the average state/local government system had a rating of 0.70 in 1950, meaning the bottom 50 percent of taxpayers paid 1.43 times the percentage of income into state and local coffers as did the top 1 percent. By tax year 2000, this had increased to 2.5 times the percentage paid by those with the highest level of income, with a rating of 0.40. It should be pointed out that there is wide variation among the

TABLE 4.4. Simplified Regression-line Index as It Applies to Personal Income

Tax or Revenue System	1950[1]	2000
Federal Revenue		
Individual income tax	11.49	6.22
Retirement payroll taxes	0.40	0.29
Total federal[2]	5.19	1.28
State and Local Revenue	0.70	0.40
TOTAL *Federal + State + Local*	4.20	0.90

[1] 1950 data taken from Stephens and Wikstrom 2000, p. 154.
[2] Includes selective sales taxes and estimates for service charges for each income group re AGI.

fifty states and their local governments in this respect, with the Oregon revenue structure as one of the least regressive and Texas the most regressive.

When we analyze the total own source revenue structure for federal plus state plus local in 1950, those with the highest income paid on average 4.2 times the percentage of their AGI in taxes and other charges to government compared to the average for the bottom 50 percent of taxpayers. By the turn of the twenty-first century, this had changed radically to where the bottom 50 percent, on average, paid in 11 percent more than the top 1 percent. State and local governments are a much larger share of the mix by the year 2000.

With tax changes passed by the Bush administration and Congress in 2001–2005, the percentage paid by the average low- to middle-income taxpayer will have increased markedly compared to top 1 percent of taxpayers, those with incomes averaging over 1 million annually.[8] Increases in regressive state and local taxes will have offset the small tax reductions given to low- and middle-income taxpayers. As we pass through the first years of the twenty-first century, individuals and families who depend on earned income (wages, salaries, and commissions) are doubly taxed compared to those whose income is heavily based on unearned income (interest, dividends, capital gains, tax free municipal bonds, and inheritance). Moreover, because of the interaction of federal and state income tax structures, as the federal government reduces its income and other taxes, this has the net effect of reducing state tax revenue unless each state takes action to change the manner in which its income tax is collected—and most have not done so. Moreover, federal tax cuts and the recent recession of 2001–3 have caused a revenue shortfall for most state and local governments. Many have increased service charges, sales, excise and gross receipts taxes, fines, and franchise fees—all of which tend to adversely impact low- and middle-income residents.

PRIVATIZING GOVERNMENT

Since the 1950s, but principally since the early 1980s, there have been moves to privatize government services at all levels, but more aggressively at the federal level.

Some public services have always been provided by contracting with private firms or individuals for service delivery, but recent moves to privatize more and more public services are unprecedented. While many state and local governments have privatized some services, like prisons by state governments, both state and local governments sometimes find it cheaper to privatize some services, as private contractors often do not provide benefits like health insurance and retirement programs for their employees. The arguments for privatization don't always hold water. Using health care as an example, the cost of administration and profits for private health insurance is almost always from one-fourth to one-third of the premiums paid in by the insured, whereas the overhead costs for Medicare are just 2 percent of the payout. The cost of administering health care by private insurers in the State of Massachusetts is higher than that for the entire Canadian health care system.

Many of these moves to privatize services, particularly at the federal level, start by denigrating the civil service, calling for deregulation of private business, criticizing government as a sea of waste, claiming private business can do the job more efficiently than civil servants, and extolling the virtues of unregulated capitalism. This activity was particularly prevalent under the administrations of Reagan and Bush in the 1980s. Criticizing the civil service is not new. Charles A. and William Beard noted this phenomenon in 1933 in an article for *Scribner's Magazine* ([1933]1986).

The Clinton administration had a program under Vice President Gore to downsize government employment, which eliminated some 400,000 civil service and 600,000 military positions, mostly at lower-level pay grades. Actually, over a seven-year period from 1990 to 1997, for high-level federal General Service (GS) grades 13–15, the number of civil servants employed increased 15 percent, while senior/executive positions increased nearly 50 percent. Some 300,000 of the positions eliminated were lower-level "wage pay" and GS 1–8 positions. Downsizing was not a zero-sum game; some federal agencies experienced significant increases in personnel during the 1990 to 1997 period—notably FEMA (+ 56 percent), the Justice Department (+ 40 percent), and the judicial branch (+ 30 percent). Most of the federal agencies that experienced significant declines in the number of civil servants had many, if not all, of their downsized employees replaced by contract workers (Stephens and Wikstrom 2002). Actually, between 1990 and 2001, 1,077,000 civilian and active duty military positions were eliminated (U.S. Bureau of the Census 1996a, 2002a).

State and Local Privatization

Thirty percent of our local governments in the United States operated without civil servants in 1997; some 26,313 function without so much as a 0.5 full-time equivalent (FTE) employee. These entities included 14,951 special district governments, 3,860 municipalities, 7,296 townships, 205 school districts, and one county government. Most, but by no means all, of these zero FTE local governments are quite small. Many operate by contracting for the services they provide, if they provide services, although some use volunteer workers, like volunteer firemen, or have a few people that work less than a twenty-hour workweek. Over two-thirds of all municipalities (68.1 percent) and over three-fourths of all townships (75.4 percent) have fewer than 2,500 residents. Population data are not available for special districts, although it is estimated that well over 80 percent have fewer than 2,500 residents (Stephens and Wikstrom 2003).

It has long been recognized that a perennial problem in federal systems is the maldistribution of taxable resources, which denies some states and many local governments the ability to finance a basic level of public services. Also well known is that the ability to tax business income and property, as well as their employees, can make it easier to finance necessary state and local public services. As a result, there is considerable competition among local governments and states for new economic development. In a federal system with close to 88,000 local governments in fifty states and several statelike entities, the competition for new business can be fierce. Moreover, where our federal government spends its money for defense (with its ever expanding expenditures for procurement) and grants-in-aid explains 80 percent of the variation in tax capacity of our fifty state/local systems—so the competition for federal dollars is also intense. The federal government spends more money in small states and tax-rich states, and, as a result, these expenditures are directly related to the ability of state and local governments to raise revenue (Stephens 1996; Stephens and Parsons 1989).

State and local governments often give incentives to private firms for economic development. These include direct government contributions for projects and tax incentives in the form of TIFs. The latter reduces or eliminates the taxes paid by the developer over a period of years. Because the net effect of TIFs and other incentives is to reduce the basic business tax capacity of the state or local governments involved, these incentives are often counterproductive. Another method is the use of a special district governments for a similar purpose, for example, to provide public facilities needed for a private business activity. In some cases these districts, in effect, give private developers the ability levy taxes and/or service charges and borrow money at tax-exempt rates for adjunct "public" facilities using revenue bonds, public facilities that largely benefit the private developer.[9] Both of these methods shift the tax burden from the developer and new businesses to older businesses, consumers, and residential taxpayers. Sometimes they are used to provide a public facility, like sports stadiums and convention centers, for use by privately owned businesses.

Kurt Thurmaier and Curtis Woods (2002) surveyed 28 services of 46 municipalities in the Kansas City metropolitan area and found 253 instances of contracting out for the provision of these activities. All contracted out for solid waste collection and disposal, with about half contracting for child care, economic development, and tourism activities. That is an average of 5.5 services per municipality. With their own personnel, they directly provided 475 services or 10.3 per government. The most common in-house services provided with their own personnel were contractor licensing, 22; water supply, 23; sewers and fire protection, 25 each; storm drainage, 28; parks, 34; recreation, 36; police and purchasing, 38 each; and land-use, 44.

Another way local government has become more privatized is the development of RCAs, more commonly known as homeowners' or condominium associations. These entities have private governing boards that often provide services normally associated with local government. Services are provided by assessing condominium owners or homeowners for the cost using a monthly or annual assessment. In many RCAs, the homeowners pay the same dollar assessment without reference to the differences in value of the property or use of the services provided, although some base it on square footage or number of rooms. The number of RCAs increased from somewhere between 1,000 and 4,000 in 1960 to an estimated 180,000 by the mid-1990s to 274,000 by 2005. RCAs usually use private contractors for the provision of services, although occasionally they may contract with a local government. According to ACIR, in 1989 RCAs ranged in size from as few as 10 residents to 68,000 (ACIR 1989; Stephens and Wikstrom 2000). RCAs are sometimes used to maintain property values and/or the exclusivity of certain types of residential development. At other times, RCAs are used to thwart annexation to a municipality where they would be taxed at a higher rate than the annual or monthly assessment against homeowners.

The Privatization of Federal Services

As near as can be determined, the contemporary effort to privatize federal services really started in the 1960s, but we have experienced three periods of acceleration of this trend: the 1980s under Presidents Reagan and George H. W. Bush, the 1990s under President Clinton, and 2001 and beyond under President G. W. Bush. The escalating use of private corporations to provide public services is most noticeable for the Defense, Energy, and Homeland Security departments, but has also occurred in most of the larger federal agencies.

In the early 1950s, only about one-fourth of the direct expenditures by the "War Department," which we euphemistically call the Department of Defense (DOD), were in the form of procurement contracts (U.S. Bureau of the Census 1953a, 1954a). By the mid to late 1990s, DOD procurement averaged between 55 and 56 percent of direct expenditures, and by FY2000 it had reached 60 percent. For FY2002 it was 62.5 percent, and with the wars in Afghanistan and Iraq it is expected to be 70 percent or more of a very much larger defense budget for FY2005–FY2006 (U.S. Bureau of the Census 1980b–2004b). The budget for DOD, counting supplemental appropriations, doubled between FY2001 and FY2005, not including massive increases for agencies included in DHS. Much of the extra portion of the $38 billion that went to agencies included in DHS when it was created was for procurement contracts to private corporations.

Military expenditures averaged about 70 percent of the activity of the Department of Energy (DOE), and 90 percent or more of DOE direct expenditures over the last decade were for procurement contracts. The Office of Management and Budget (OMB 2004) reported that for FY2002, DOE total expenditures were $17.7 billion, while, for the same year, the *Consolidated Federal Funds Report* indicated DOE spent over $19 billion on procurement contracts. As we throw more and more money at the military and military contractors, there is a very real question as to whether these agencies know how much they actually spend or where the money is going.

Moreover, as we have escalated DOD expenditures, downsized civil and military personnel, and increased spending on contracts, the personnel available to manage those contracts have declined precipitously. According to Michael Scherer (2004),

TABLE 4.5. Increasing Federal Procurement Contracts, FY1997–FY2002

	Contracts, $ Millions 1997	Contracts, $ Millions 2002	Percentage Increase, 1997–2002	Change in $ Millions
DOD	119,859	165,879	38.1	45,720
Total, Other Agencies	73,216	105,387	43.9	32,171
Total Federal	193,074	270,965	40.3	77,891
Other Agencies				
HUD	226	928	310.6	702
State	451	1,702	277.4	1,251
H&HS	2,686	5,866	118.4	3,180
GSA	6,086	13,193	116.8	7,107
Commerce	755	1,584	109.8	829
Transportation	3,485	7,217	107.1	3,732
Veterans	2,922	5,963	104.1	3,041
Labor	812	1,618	99.3	806
Education	485	941	94.1	456
Treasury	1,797	3,447	93.5	1,680
Justice	2,472	4,586	85.5	2,114
Agriculture	2,236	3,645	63.1	1,409
EPA	909	1,164	28.1	255
Energy	15,128	19,009	25.7	3,881
Postal Service	11,037	13,866	25.6	2,829
FEMA	264	311	17.8	47
NASA	11,000	11,611	5.6	611
Interior	876	812	−7.3	−64
Others, not listed	9,589	7,924	−17.4	−1,665

Source: U.S. Bureau of the Census 1980b–2004b.

"federal oversight of contracts has been eviscerated." Over the five-year period from 1997 through 2002, contracts let by DOD increased from $117 billion to $168 billion while the number of contract managers declined from 14,353 to 11,709 and the dollar value of DOD contracts let without competitive bidding increased from $47 to $72 billion. This is only the tip of the iceberg when we consider fiscal years 2003 and beyond. Since FY2002, with wars in Afghanistan and Iraq, the creation of DHS, the dollar value of DOD procurement contracts, and the increase in contracts let without competition, the government is losing control of its expenditures. Table 4.5 lists the increases in procurement contracts for FY1997–FY2002 before the escalation of expenditures for the wars in Afghanistan and Iraq. In FY2002 over $190 billion was spent for defense contracts by the different departments involved, not counting the appropriations for the new Department of Homeland Security (U.S. Bureau of the Census 1980b–2004b).

We say we have a voluntary military, but is it really a mercenary military? Leslie Wayne, writing in the *New York Times* (2002), said that DOD and the CIA employ some thirty-five private armies, many run as subsidiaries to Fortune 500 corporations. These firms were used in Bosnia and are being used in Afghanistan and Iraq. Peter W.

Singer in his book *Corporate Warriors* (2003) has a "partial listing" of the e-mail addresses of sixty such corporations.

According to Paul C. Light, the federal government employed nearly six million workers on contract in 2002.[10] This compares to 2.7 million regular civilian employees and 1.4 million active duty military (U.S. Bureau of the Census 2003a). When you add in the two million workers employed on federal grants, our central government was employing twice as many workers on grants and contracts as the total of the civil and military services for a grand total of twelve million employees.

The mantra from the private sector has been that federal civil service employees are inefficient and ineffective in the provision of public services, yet the contractors "supplementing" the military in Iraq and Afghanistan pay their employees in both civil and military positions several times that which a civil servant or member of the military would receive. In fact, in FY2003 the DOD spent 2.5 times as much on procurement contracts as it spent for all military and civilian employees combined in salaries and wages. We have privatized not only the defense of the country, but virtually all federal public services. Practically all of the activity of the National Aeronautics and Space Agency (NASA) and DOE, both of which are involved in defense, is done on contract. NASA spends 7.5 times as much on contracts as it pays out in wages and salaries for its own personnel; DOE spends 16.3 times as much for contracts as wages and salaries. Without going through all federal agencies, other agencies spending more on contracts than on personnel include the Department of Education, at 2.8 times, and the General Services Administration, at 16.5 times. One of the few federal agencies still relying primarily on its own personnel is the Postal Service, which spends 3.7 times in salaries and wages as for its own personnel as on contracts, although it still managed to let nearly $14 billion in procurement contracts in FY2003. In American government it is very clear "that to the corporations belong the spoils," whichever political party is in power (U.S. Bureau of the Census 1980b–2004b).

The virtual elimination of the corporate income tax comes at a time when federal services have been turned over to for-profit corporations—many of which take their profits to offshore tax havens like the Cayman Islands. This means they have no obligation to pay taxes on the profits given them by the American government and the American taxpayers. Do we need to ask, "Who is running the country?"

THE REDISTRIBUTION OF INCOME TO THE CORPORATE RICH

As was pointed out earlier in this chapter, the major trend of the first half of the twentieth century was the adoption and use of the progressive income tax, along with inheritance taxes. The major trend of the last half of the century, particularly the period from 1952 through the first years of the twenty-first century, has been the abandonment of the progressive features of the individual income tax and the virtual elimination of the corporate income tax for large corporations. Moreover, for the first few years of the twenty-first century, taxes on unearned income (interest, dividends, capital gains, and inheritance) are being drastically reduced or eliminated. At the same time, federal and state flat-rate payroll taxes; sales, excise, and gross receipts taxes; franchise fees and service charges; and all levies that more heavily impact earned income (wages, salaries, and commissions) are being increased, particularly at the state and local levels of government.[11] This, of course, means that income and wealth are being redistributed from low- and middle-income taxpayers to those at the top of the income scale through the use of the tax code and the federal-state-local revenue structure.

Professor John W. Sloan (1997) documented the rather even percentage increases in income across the range of family income, by quintile, for the period from 1947 to 1973, as well as the reversal of this trend between 1973 and 1992 when only the top 40 percent gained and the bottom 60 percent lost ground, with the greatest losses for the bottom 20 percent of families. He attributed this reversal to the tax policies of the Reagan administration and the reduction of taxes on businesses and high-income individual taxpayers.

Another way of looking at this issue is to document the changes that have taken place in the shares of family income from the bottom 20 percent (quintile) of families and the top 20 percent over time. As Figure 4.5 indicates, between the years 1980 and 2001, only the top 20 percent gained in its share of family income, while proportionate losses in shares increase as we go down the income scale. The top quintile now receives nearly half of all family income, while the bottom 20 percent of families receive only slightly over 4 percent of the total. In fact, the most gains were made by

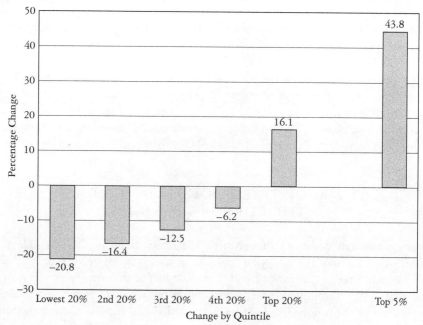

FIGURE 4.5. Percentage change in shares of family income by quintile and for the top five percent of families, 1980–2001. *Source: U.S. Bureau of the Census, 2003a, c. 459.*

the top 5 percent of families, a 44 percent increase in their share, 14.6 to 21 percent, over the two decades from 1980 to 2001 (U.S. Bureau of the Census 2003a). With the tax reductions of the George W. Bush administration and the Republican Congress, it appears that this trend is set in concrete for at least the next several years.

THE UNITED STATES AS A THIRD-WORLD DEBTOR NATION

Debt and deficits are giving the United States the credit status of a badly indebted Third-World country. It's not only the deficit in the federal budget and the national debt, but also the balance-of-payments deficits, the debts of state and local governments, and the mortgage and consumer debt, all of which have reached record levels in 2004. One wonders if the United States could get a loan from the World Bank if they really looked at the total debt obligation of the government and citizens of the United States.

At the end of World War II, the national debt stood at 127.9 percent of the gross domestic product (GDP). From there it declined erratically to 32.5 percent of GDP at the end of FY1981, President Carter's last budget year. We were outgrowing our national debt. From there, however, the national debt doubled during the Ronald Reagan and George H. W. Bush administrations, reaching 66.3 percent of GDP during G. H. W. Bush's last budget year, FY1993. (See Appendix Figure 4.1.) Most of the economic growth we have achieved since 1981 has come from the expansion of debt.

Under President Clinton the national debt leveled off and declined to 56.8 percent of GDP for Clinton's last budget because of continuing prosperity through FY2001. Despite all the ballyhooing, there was really only one year of actual budget surplus during the Clinton administration if one sets aside the surpluses in the Social Security and Medicare trust funds—that surplus was only $17.9 billion in FY2000. This was a surplus of exactly 1.0 percent of federal expenditures if one follows the U.S. Treasury Department's reports on changes in the national debt.[12]

Enter George W. Bush, and the deficits and debt have escalated at a rate not seen since the total war effort of World War II. The Bush administration has pursued massive tax cuts, spurred on by a spurious projection of massive federal budget surpluses. This at the same time as we became involved in wars in Afghanistan and Iraq and the "war on terrorism." The OMB originally said that the deficit would be $307 billion for FY2004, but by the end of FY2004 it had reached $596 billion. For FY2005, the national deficit as projected by the 2006 federal budget will be significantly higher as a result of the continuing war in Iraq, at $676 billion, with $677 billion for FY2006. It could be significantly higher than that because of hurricane Katrina, an additional $136 billion cut in the corporate income tax passed by Congress in the fall of 2004, and because the administration has not really accounted for all of the cost of these foreign excursions. The national debt was almost $8.0 trillion in FY2005.[13] That is about 70 percent of GDP (CEA 2005). Perhaps because they are expecting an unprecedentedly large deficit for FY2005, Congress increased the national debt limit by $800 billion in November 2004. The actual deficit would be significantly higher if the surplus from the Social Security and Medicare trust funds were excluded from the budget (OMB 2003, 2005). The deficit and national debt along with the debts of state and local governments could be much higher for FY2005 and FY2006 as the result of expenditures caused by hurricane Katrina. Many great nations have gone into decline as a result of war debt.

Because of the recent recession and the deleterious effect of federal tax cuts on state and local government revenue, state and local debt is another $2 trillion.[14] When we add in state and local government debt, the United States is over 85 percent, approaching 90 percent of GDP during FY2005. Along with this, we had a record-breaking balance-of-payments deficit in calendar year CY2003 of nearly $500 billion, $610 billion in CY2004, and an estimate of nearly $700 billion for CY2005 for a total of well over $5 trillion by that time. It is still going up as the result of the continuing high levels of imported goods and the price of oil (CY2004 and CY2005)—not to mention the precipitous decline in the value of the dollar. In effect, we are mortgaging this country to the countries providing these goods, like China, Japan, the European Union, and Saudi Arabia.

Over the last half-century, and particularly over the last twenty or thirty years, growth of the U.S. economy has been fueled by the expansion of consumer and mortgage credit—credit owned by the nation's banks, the *Fortune five hundred*, and the multinationals amounting to over $7.1 trillion in CY2001. Over the period from CY1950 to CY2000, in constant dollars, taking out inflation, consumer credit rose nearly eight times, up 677 percent; mortgage credit increased to over ten times the earlier figure, up 933 percent.

More recent data indicate that personal debt is soaring—increasing at an even faster rate than that indicated earlier. Between 1990 and 2003, the number of credit card holders in the United States increased from 82 to 144 million, up 76 percent in 13 years.[15] The average balance on these cards increased from $2,549 to $7,549. In constant dollars this was an increase of 123 percent using chain-type price indices for personal consumption (CEA 2004). This meant the constant dollar total for credit card debt increased nearly 300 percent to $1.1 trillion. For this same period, median family income increased only 13 percent in current dollars, but declined nearly 15 percent in constant dollars taking out inflation (2003a and 2004–5a).

As of the year 2004, the personal and public debt stands at about $18 trillion, about $60,000 for each person residing in the United States, or $189,000 per family unit. This aggregate debt is about 148 percent of GDP. As the song says, "We owe our soul to the company store," but the company store is the *Fortune five hundred*, the banks, and the multinationals, as well as foreign countries and nationals who own significant portions of our debt.

THE RICH GET RICHER, AND . . . THE POOR PAY THE TAXES

To recapitulate, changes of the last half-century or so have greatly reduced taxes on the profits of corporations, high-income individuals, and, particularly, unearned income.

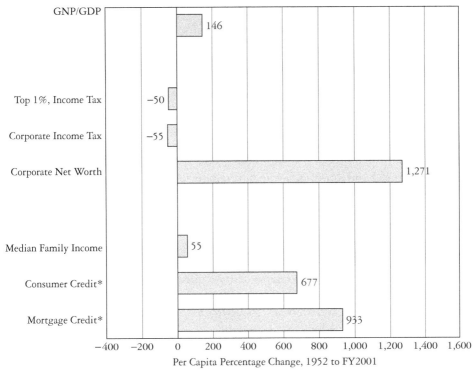

FIGURE 4.6. Per capita change in income and other characteristics, 1952–FY2001, in constant dollars. Uses FY2001 constant dollars. *Sources: U.S. Bureau of the Census, 1953a–2003a; 1941; CEA 1991, 2003; OMB 2003, 2004. Consumer and mortgage credit data is for 1950 to 2000.*

At the same time, taxes on earned income and on consumption have escalated. As a result, corporate net worth has soared, as have the balance sheets of the top income-earners who take their money mostly in forms of remuneration that are untaxed or enjoy much lower tax rates than that for earned income. The individual income tax reductions that went into effect in 2004 apply only to the top three income tax brackets. In the process, we are destroying the middle class and impoverishing the working class. If a large and prosperous middle class is a requirement for a democratic system of government, we have critically altered the social, economic, and political structure of the nation (see Figure 4.6). The virtual elimination of the corporate income tax at the same time public services have been turned over to private for-profit corporations is unconscionable.

Partly fostered by the complexity of our federal system, taxes have been downloaded onto low- and middle-income citizens. The system is so complex, with one very complex federal government, fifty states, several statelike entities, nearly 88,000 discrete and overlying local governments, and 274,000 private homeowners' associations delivering some public services, that almost no one knows who is responsible for what. The *federal structure* is further complicated by the fact that the federal and state levels, as well as larger local governments, are administered by dozens of agencies operating on the same territory. It is no wonder that so few citizens are well-informed about how they are being taxed, who is benefiting from the tax and revenue structure, how the services are delivered, and who is being left out in the process. In terms of fiscal federalism, the structure in the United States has become almost impenetrable for the average citizen.

At the same time, while for-profit corporations are delivering a huge share of our public services, corporations and wealthy individuals have been largely relieved of their obligation to pay taxes. This is redistribution of wealth from the poor and middle classes to the corporations and the corporate rich using the federal tax structure.

Between 1952 and 2001, in per capita constant dollar terms, GDP increased 146 percent while median family income rose a meager 55 percent, even though by 2001 there were one-third more workers per household bringing in money. Much of the so-called prosperity of the last half-century is based on the expansion of consumer and mortgage credit and government debt. The average worker is rapidly becoming an indentured servant to the *Fortune 500 and the multinationals.* As the rich get richer and the poor pay the taxes, economic equality and equality of opportunity are being eliminated. Intentionally, and unintentionally, income and wealth are being redistributed from the poor and middle classes to the corporate rich using the federal (meaning federal + state + local) tax structure.

To some extent, this situation can be blamed on a privatized oligopolistic media. It takes so much money to run for public office that candidates must rely on the corporations and the wealthy for contributions to their campaigns in order to stand any chance of being elected. Candidates must either be rich in their own right or become beholden to their contributors. As the saying goes, "The man who pays the piper calls the tune." This is true almost without reference to what level or what office a candidate seeks to obtain (Soley 2002).

Nearly 220 years ago, a group of privileged white property owners, plutocrats, decided that the government under the Articles of Confederation was not working, so they called a meeting in Philadelphia to draft a new constitution and created a mixed form of government—often referred to as a *republic*, but one that restricted the influence of the average citizen. Over the next eight decades or so, it became more of a republic and over the hundred years following the Civil War it became more representative and more democratic—as a result of reinterpreting the Bill of Rights passed in 1791, passing the Civil War amendments, eliminating property qualifications for voting, electing Senators directly, allowing the federal government to progressively tax income and inheritance, giving women the right to vote, legislating the "one man, one vote" series of court cases, establishing a substantial middle-class, and so on. But who would guess that, after the sacrifices of World War II, our elected officials, the ones charged with protecting the system, would turn the clock back to a time when the United Stated was a plutocracy, ruled by the rich, pretending to be a republic. But given the policies of the Congress and the George W. Bush administration, this trend toward rule by the corporate rich continues unabated and even accelerated into the twenty-first century.

POSTSCRIPT

As of the November–December 2005 period, the George W. Bush administration and Congress have made additional changes to the tax code that further exacerbate the trends of recent years. They want to make all the tax cuts of Bush's first and terms second permanent.

Their proposal for reforming Social Security by privatizing at least a part of it for younger workers has not made much headway in Congress. This would be a windfall of hundreds of billions of dollars for Wall Street and would subject Social Security to the whims of the stock market. It raises many questions, one of which is, would the government still guarantee some level of payout for the recipients even when the market is in a slump? What if Social Security is invested in companies like Enron? Would these funds be invested abroad? What happens if the stock market crashes? As Daniel Altman pointed out in the *New York Times* (2004), "In Chile, whose pension system has been cited by President Bush as a model . . . retirees saw their benefits drop by 7 percent in 2003." Similar problems have erupted in Britain when it privatized the retirement system under the Thatcher government. Whether guaranteed or not, this could lead to very large deficits in the Social Security accounts of individual recipients. As a percent of payout, Social Security and Medicare costs almost nothing to administer, but with privatization of accounts, administrative costs will soar if one includes the profits made by Wall Street brokers.

"Tax reform" and "tax simplification" are additional trial balloons being floated by the administration, post reelection of George W. Bush. A lot of nefarious activity has taken place under the rubrics of "tax reform" and "tax simplification" in the past. Because of the huge deficits being accumulated, the administration is considering a national sales tax or a national value-added tax. A value-added tax is one that applies to each step of the production of goods or services from the raw materials supplier to the manufacturer to the wholesaler to the retailer to the consumer and any stages in between. It is a huge sales tax. Either tax would be justified as a means of bringing down the huge deficits being run up as a result of the earlied tax cuts and the wars in Afghanistan and Iraq. Furthermore, either tax would be levied on the top of state and local sales and excise taxes, service charges, and franchise taxes. Given the fact that over 70 percent (70.6% according to CEA 2004) of the U.S. economy was based on consumption expenditures in 2003, such a levy of federal sales or value-added taxes could greatly reduce consumption by those at the bottom and the middle of the income scale. With the exception of the corporations supplying men and materials to the wars being conducted by this administration and for rebuilding along the Gulf Coast, it could throw the country into a recession. State and local governments might oppose new levies on consumption as they are an important source of revenue for our subnational governments.

Other suggestions that have been made have included allowing the taxpayer to funnel as much as $15,000 per year into Roth IRAs in a special portfolio that allows tax-free return of the money as well as making corporate dividends completely tax free. These measures would benefit few other than the top 20 percent of taxpayers.

Another suggestion being floated in 2005 is the "flat-tax," meaning a flat-rate income tax where all taxpayers pay the same percent of taxable income. Further, taxable income could be redefined as "earned income" leaving those with the highest incomes contributing very little to federal coffers. This is often called "tax simplification". It alone would make the entire federal tax structure highly regressive. When you add in how Social Security and Medicare are funded, the poor and the middle class would be paying a far higher percentage of their income than the top 20 percent of Taxpayers.

All of this, or several parts, could be packaged as a 1,000-page "Omnibus Tax Reform and Tax Simplification" bill to confuse everyone, including members of Congress, about what is really being done. Moreover, all of the tax cuts that have been made to date, as well as the additional ones being proposed, may well be for the ultimate purpose of eviscerating most federal domestic services at the same time taxes that affect the very wealthy are further reduced while everyone else gets a disproportionate share of the remaining tax burden.

> Deftly, year by year, step by step, the Bush administration has been re-inventing the American system of taxation. And the true story of this revolution is not over.
>
> —Nicholas Confessore (2005)

Appendix 4.1

OWN SOURCE REVENUE: STATE AND LOCAL, FEDERAL, AND TOTAL UNITED STATES

	State and Local			Federal			Total		
	1902	1952	FY2001	1902	1952	FY2001	1902	1952	FY2001
Customs duties	0	0	0	37.2	0.7	1.0	14.7	0.5	0.5
Property taxes	67.8	30.4	16.8	0	0	0	41.7	8.7	7.4
Individual income tax	0	3.5	14.4	0	42.2	49.9	0	31.2	34.3
Corporate income tax	0	3.0	2.2	0	32.1	7.6	0	24.0	5.2
Payroll taxes	0	9.5	8.9	0	7.2	34.9	0	7.9	23.4
General sales tax	0	12.5	14.3	0	0	0	0	2.9	6.3
Selective sales taxes	2.7	9.8	6.2	36.1	12.3	3.3	15.6	12.7	4.6
Other taxes	12.1	8.7	4.4	6.7	1.8	1.4	10.0	3.0	2.7
Service charges	11.4	11.5	21.4	18.9	2.7	1.3	11.0	7.0	10.2
Other revenue	6.0	11.1	11.4	1.1	1.0	0.6	7.0	2.1	5.4
TOTAL	100.0	100.0	100.0	100.0	100.0	100.0	100.0	100.0	100.0
As percent of GNP/GDP	5.51	8.20	15.55	3.46	20.69	19.62	8.97	28.89	35.17

Sources: U.S. Bureau of the Census 1961; www.census.gov/govs/estimate/01us.html; OMB 2003.

Appendix 4.2

THE NATIONAL DEBT AS A PERCENTAGE OF GROSS DOMESTIC PRODUCT, 1955–2005

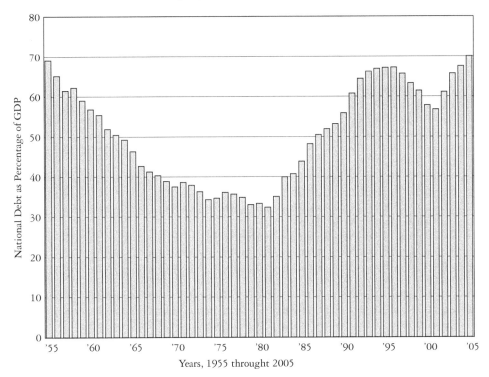

Sources: U.S. Bureau of the Census 1961; 1953a–2004–5a; U.S. Treasury Department, 2005. www.publicdebt.treas.gov.

REFERENCES

Altman, Daniel. 2004. Taxes and Consequences: The Second Term Begins. *New York Times*. www.nytimes.com/2004/11/7/business/yourmoney.

Beam, David R. 1983. From the Law to Rule: Exploring the Maze of Intergovernmental Regulation. *Intergovernmental Perspective*. 9:2, 7–22.

Beard, Charles A. and William Beard. 1986. 1933 article reprinted from *Scribner's Magazine* in the *Public Administration Review*. 46:2 (March–April), 209.

Brookings Institution. 2004. www.brookings.nap.edu/books/0815752652/html22.html.

Confessore, Nicholas. 2005, January 16. King Code. *New York Times Magazine*. 35–39.

Conlan, Timothy J. and David R. Beam. 1992. Federal Mandates: The Record of Reform and Future Prospects. 18:4, 1–11.

Council of Economic Advisors (CEA). 1991, 2003–2005. *Economic Report of the President*. Washington, DC: Government Printing Office. Appendix B.

Council of State Governments (CSG). 2002, 2003. *Book of the States*. Lexington, KY: CSG.

General Accounting Office (GAO). 1992, 2003. *1991 and 2002 Economic Report of the President*. Washington, DC: Government Printing Office.

Johnston, David C. 2003. *Perfectly Legal*. New York: Penguin Group.

Light, Paul C. 1999, 2003. *The True Size of Government*. Washington, DC: The Brookings Institution.

McKinnon, John D. 2004, April 6. Many Companies Avoided Taxes Even as Profits Soared in Boom. *Wall Street Journal*. A1, A8.

Oates, Wallace E. 1972. *Fiscal Federalism*. New York: Harcourt Brace Jovanovich. 19.

Office of Management and Budget (OMB). 2003, 2005. *Historical Tables. FY2004–FY2006 Budget of the United States Government*. Washington, DC: Government Printing Office.

Scherer, Michael. 2004. Contracts with America. *Mother Jones*. 28:3 (June), 56–61.

Shannon, John. 1984. Dealing with Deficits—Striking a New Fiscal Balance. *ACIR Intergovernmental Perspective*. 10:1, 5–9.

Singer, Peter W. 2003. *Corporate Warriors: The Rise of the Privatized Military*. Ithaca, NY: Cornell University Press. 243–44.

Sloan, John W. 1997. The Reagan Presidency, Growing Inequality, and the American Dream. *Policy Studies Journal*. 25:3 (Fall 1997), 371–86.

Soley, Lawrence. 2002. *The Corporate Threat to Free Speech in the United States: Censorship Incorporated*. New York: Monthly Review Press.

Stephens, G. Ross. 1985. New Federalism by Default, Little OPEC States, and Fiscal Darwinism. In Dennis Judd, ed., *Public Policy Across States and Communities*. JAI Press. 49–71.

——. 1989. Rich States, Poor States: An Addendum. *State and Local Government Review*. 21:2, 50–59.

——. 1996. Urban Underrepresentation in the U.S. Senate. *Urban Affairs Review*. 31:3, 404–18.

Stephens, G. Ross and Gerald W. Olson. 1975. *State Responsibility for Public Services and General Revenue Sharing*. Report to the National Science Foundation. University of Missouri–Kansas City. 2.

——. 1979. *Pass-through Federal Aid and Interlevel Finance in the American Federal System, 1957–1977*. Vol. I. Report to the National Science Foundation. University of Missouri–Kansas City. viii, xi.

Stephens, G. Ross and Karen T. Parsons. 1989. Rich States, Poor States: An Addendum. *State and Local Government Review*. 21:2, 50–59.

Stephens, G. Ross and Nelson Wikstrom. 2000. *Metropolitan Government and Governance: Theoretical Perspectives, Empirical Analysis, and the Future*. New York: Oxford University Press. 11–13, 151–155.

——. 2002. Reinventing Government and Federal Downsizing—or, Whose Ox Is Being Gored. Paper delivered to the annual conference of the Southern Political Science Association. November.

——. 2003. Republics in Miniature and Other Toy Governments. Paper delivered to the annual conference of the American Political Science Association. August.

Thurmaier, Kurt and Curtis Wood. 2002. Interlocal Agreements as Overlapping Social Networks: Picket-Fence Regionalism in Metropolitan Kansas City. *Public Administration Review*. 5 (September/October), 585–98.

——. 2005. Scope and Patterns of Metropolitan Governance in Urban America: Paper submitted to the *American Review of Public Administration*.

U.S. Advisory Commission on Intergovernmental Relations (ACIR). 1981, November. *Studies in Comparative Federalism: Australia, Canada, the United States, and West Germany*. Washington, DC: ACIR. M-130.

——. 1989. *Residential Community Associations*. Washington, DC. A-112.

——. 1993, September. *RTS: State Revenue Capacity and Effort*. Washington, DC: ACIR. M-187.

———. 1992, 1993a. *Characteristics of Federal Grant-in Aid Programs to State and Local Governments.* Washington, DC. M-182.

———. 1977. A Fiscal Note. *Intergovernmental Perspective.* 3:2, 20.

U.S. Bureau of the Census. 1961. *Historical Statistics of the United States: Colonial Times to 1957.* Washington, DC: Government Printing Office. 722–30.

———. 1953a–2003a, 2004–5. *Statistical Abstract of the United States.* Washington, DC: Government Printing Office.

———. 1980b–2004b. *Consolidated Federal Funds Reports: State and County Areas.* Washington, DC: Government Printing Office.

———. 2004c. www.census.gov/govs/estimate01.html.

———. 2004d. www.census.gov/govs/estimate02.html.

———. 1957–2002e Census of Governments, *Compendium of Government Finances.* Washington, DC: Government Printing Office.

U.S. Treasury Department. 2000–2005. www.publicdebt.treas.gov/.

Wayne, Leslie. 2002, October 13. America's for Profit Secret Army. *New York Times.*

Wheare, Kenneth C. 1964. *Federal Government.* London: Oxford University Press. 10.

Young, William H. 1962. *Ogg and Ray's American Government.* New York: Appleton-Century-Crofts, 18.

Zimmerman, Joseph F. 1994. State Mandate Relief: A Quick Look. *Intergovernmental Perspective.* 20:2, 28–30.

FEDERALISM AND INTERGOVERNMENTAL RELATIONS: THE NATIONAL POLICY PROCESS AND PUBLIC POLICY

If one were to choose a single term to characterize the national policymaking process in the 1970s, that term would probably be "fragmentation." From the rise of "subcommittee government" in Congress, to the proliferation of interest groups and political action committees in Washington, to the decline of party loyalties in the electorate and party voting in Congress, the splintering of power was a pervasive theme throughout the decade. Nowhere was such fragmentation more apparent than in the politics of federalism reform.

—Timothy Conlan, *From New Federalism to Devolution: Twenty-Five Years of Intergovernmental Reform* (1998)

This chapter centers on the actors and structures involved in the national policy process and the evolution and shaping of intergovernmental relations. Attention is devoted to the role of president, Congress, and the Supreme Court. In addition, material is provided on a paradigm of national policy-making, along with the impact of the political parties and the intergovernmental lobbies on the framing of national policies. The chapter concludes with a discussion of the rise of "Coercive Federalism" and the resultant decline of the policy autonomy of the states.

THE PRESIDENT AND THE PRESIDENCY

Presidents have long entertained an interest in federalism, intergovernmental relations, and intragovernmental relations. By the terms "federalism" and "intergovernmental relations" we are making reference, of course, to the interest of presidents in developing a viable programmatic working policy relationship between the federal government, the states, localities, and other subnational units of government; of course, by the term *"intragovernmental* relations" we are focusing on the dynamics and interaction of the president, Congress, and the federal courts in making intergovernmental policy.

Every president over the years has devoted some attention to issues involving federalism and intergovernmental relations. Indeed, President Woodrow Wilson noted, before the advent of the last century, that the relationship between the nation and the states is "the cardinal question of our constitutional system." However, whereas Wilson asserted that matters of federalism and intergovernmental relations were of first rank importance, in practice he relegated such matters to a lower priority because of the greater importance of other competing international and other national concerns. Succeeding presidents, similar to Wilson, have often spoken of the importance of federalism or intergovernmental matters, but rarely have they confronted intergovernmental matters in a comprehensive fashion.

Deil Wright (1982) has succinctly noted the various factors that have served to limit the amount of attention presidents have devoted to matters of federalism and intergovernmental relations (145–46). He notes that the most important of these limitations involves the factor of time, since other matters involving foreign affairs and domestic economic policies are of greater concern to the president. Wright reports that additional factors that served to limit the amount of time that presidents have devoted to intergovernmental relations include

1. The weakness of party allegiance and discipline
2. The localism prominent, if not predominant, in the Congress
3. The expertise and professionalism of functional specialists in IGR program fields
4. The political strength and strategic access of grant-related interest groups within the "triple alliance"
5. The comparatively modest political payoffs and pride accruing from most IGR accomplishments
6. The unexciting administrative and managerial features of IGR
7. The degree of centralization in the U.S. political system

Nevertheless, notwithstanding Wright's sage insights, we should note that presidents have utilized their position, power, and political savvy and skills to impact, and leave "their mark," on the evolution of intergovernmental relations. For example, breaking from the long past tradition of dual federalism, Franklin D. Roosevelt ushered in, during the 1930s, an era of Cooperative Federalism, which emphasized the desirability and need of the various levels of government—federal, state, and local— of working together to confront and alleviate domestic problems, utilizing a range of grant programs, technical assistance, mutual aid, and a variety of other mechanisms to realize shared policy goals.

Jane Perry Clark nicely defended in 1938 the rise of Cooperative Federalism:

> Cooperation between the federal and state governments is one solution of the difficulties caused by the governmental attempt to regulate the centripetal forces of modern

industrial life and the centrifugal elements of state interest and tradition . . . Traditional and even mythical interests cannot be swept away overnight. There is, nevertheless, need for reconciliation of those who are bewildered by the chaos of forty-nine separate governments and administrations acting in similar fields of control and those who . . . fear centralization of either authority [or] administration for both. Cooperation . . . offers means for determination of how far uniformity and a national minimum in the federal government may exist side by side with opportunities for experimentation by and within the states. (7–8)

In addition, in a more specific sense, Roosevelt encouraged Harold D. Smith, his director of the Bureau of the Budget, to participate in the formation and establishment of the Council on Intergovernmental Relations (Graves 1964, 179). Harry S. Truman established the Commission on the Organization of the U.S. Executive Branch (1947–49), more popularly known as the Hoover Commission since it was headed by former president Herbert Hoover. The charge of the commission was to recommend ways to render the executive branch of government more efficient through appropriate reorganization. In the course of its deliberations, it analyzed problems in the field of intergovernmental relations. A second Hoover Commission, with essentially the same mandate but with somewhat more of a policy focus, operated from 1953 to 1955.

Dwight D. Eisenhower, responsible for the initiation of the massive interstate highway system, in his presidential campaign in 1952 evidenced a strong interest in federalism and intergovernmental relations. At a speech presented in Des Moines, Iowa, on September 18 Eisenhower noted: "Next I want to see maintained the constitutional relationship between the Federal and State governments. My oath of office [as President] would demand that. My convictions would require it. The Federal government did not create the States in this republic. The States created the Federal Government." And further: "[I]f the States lose their meaning, our entire system of government loses its meaning. And the next step is the rise of the centralized national state in which the seeds of autocracy can take root and grow" (Graves 1964, 892).

Early on in his administration, Eisenhower demonstrated a strong interest in intergovernmental relations. In his first year in office he made a presentation at the National Governors' Conference in Seattle and emphasized the importance of the federal government and the states working together: "Unless we are partners in these things, they cannot be done. When we are partners—the Federal Government and the States—working together—there is no limit to the possibilities for progress that are open to the American people" (Graves 1964, 892). Eisenhower provided strong support for the establishment by Congress of the Commission on Intergovernmental Relations (1953–55), popularly known as the Kestnbaum Commission, which conducted the first official in-depth review of national-state-local relationships since the adoption of the Constitution.[1] Eisenhower was also responsible for proposing, at a meeting of the National Governors' Conference held in the mid 1950s, the establishment of the Federal-State Joint Action Committee (1957–59), which was charged with determining which federal programs could be transferred to the states; however, their recommendations, although relatively minor in scope, eventually became the victim of political stalemate. These developments led to the establishment in 1959 of the United States Advisory Commission on Intergovernmental Relations (ACIR), which until its demise in the 1990s was a critical resource of information on various facets of federalism and intergovernmental relations for policy-makers and scholars.

Democratic presidents in the 1960s and 1970s utilized the intergovernmental system to promote and implement their various aggressive "social justice" domestic policy agendas. In the mid-1960s, Lyndon B. Johnson in pursuit of his "Great Society" goals launched an era of "Creative Federalism," marked by a proliferation of federal grants to the states and localities, designed to attack social problems, such as poverty and urban decay. As David B. Walker (1981) has succinctly noted: "[T]he theory and practice of Creative Federalism was markedly in contrast with the practice of its Cooperative Federalism predecessor. It differed in its range of new grant programs, in its diversity of participating state and especially local units and nonprofit agencies, in its expanding federal outlays, and in its urban and city emphasis (though states still received over four-fifths of all grant funds during the Johnson years)" (104). For a variety of reasons, including the continuing and escalating war in Vietnam, Johnson's efforts eventually evolved into a skirmish and largely ended in failure. In the late 1970s, President Jimmy Carter, as part of what later became known as his "Picket-Fence or Bamboo-Fence Federalism," set forth a ambitious comprehensive "National Urban Policy" designed to revitalize and reinvigorate downtown urban areas. Carter's policy involved an expanded federal-state-local-private sector partnership, a significant enhancement of federal fiscal and programmatic assistance to urban and city areas, and expanded and new intergovernmental programs. However, because Carter's initiative failed to "target" for specific massive relief the large, old, declining urban centers, but rather ultimately involved thirty thousand to forty thousand local governments, it was not well received by local officials and the initiative failed (Wright 1982, 140).

Republican presidents, on the other hand, during the later part of the last century were committed to variants of a "New Federalism," designed to implement the devolution of powers in the intergovernmental system, by transferring political power and decision-making from the federal government to the states and localities. President Richard N. Nixon, in the late 1960s, convinced that the federal government had grown too large and that its powers were too excessive and intrusive, ushered in the term "New Federalism" in his call to return more powers and responsibilities to the states and localities. Nixon's New Federalism was part-and-parcel of his "New American Revolution" designed to streamline government, in general, and render it more effective and efficient (Hoff 2004, 1). In regard to Nixon's brand of federalism, Walker (1981) wrote:

> It was ostensibly anticentralization, anticategorical, and anti-administrative confusion. In positive terms, it supported: greater decentralization within the federal departments to their field units; a devolution of more power and greater discretion to recipient units; a streamlining of the service delivery system generally; a definite preferring of general governments and their elected officials; and some sorting out of some servicing responsibilities by government levels. (104–5)

Although Nixon was stymied by a predominately Democratic Congress in regard to many of his intergovernmental initiatives, he ultimately did realize his success of the passage by Congress in 1972 of the State and Local Fiscal Assistance Act, establishing the General Revenue Sharing (GRS) program, which, however, was ultimately terminated for the states in 1980 and for the cities in 1986. The passage of GRS was in large part due to the active and extensive lobbying of state and local officials. As Donald Haider (1974) has written: "The enactment of revenue sharing, in effect, marked the high point thus far in joint work of the government interest groups to influence their federal constituency" (75).

Nixon also proposed, in 1971, six "special revenue programs," decentralized block grants designed to consolidate 129 categorical grant programs, in the policy areas of law enforcement, urban community development, rural development, job training, education, and transportation. The total annual cost of these special revenue sharing programs, along with GRS, was estimated to be about $11.3 billion and was designed to consolidate more than one-quarter of all intergovernmental programs (Conlan 1998, 31). After a good deal of political skirmishing, Congress eventually passed the Comprehensive Employment and Training Assistance Act (CETA), which combined seventeen categorical grants, and the Community Development Block Grant Act (CDBG), which "bundled together" an array of categorical grants relating to community development. The latter was actually passed by Congress after Nixon left office and was signed by President Gerald Ford. However, Nixon's remaining proposed special revenue programs were defeated by the Congress.

Notwithstanding Nixon's stated preference for block grants and his attempt to terminate many categorical grants, during the Nixon administration federal expenditures increased about 250 percent for food provision, housing assistance, and medical care. Federal expenditures on entitlement programs doubled from $20 million in 1969 to $40 million in 1974, while spending on "means-tested" programs such as food stamps, child nutrition, Medicaid, and housing assistance grew from $3 billion dollars to $11 billion during the same time period (Conlan 1998, 81–83). Up to this point in time, the amount of funding provided by the Nixon administration to *individuals* witnessed the greatest increase in American history.

In addition, in his attempt to realize more cooperation and coordination between federal agencies, Nixon established eight Federal Regional Offices. These offices, located throughout the county, each contained a city deemed a "regional headquarters" that represented particular federal agencies. Initially, these agencies included the Department of Health, Education, and Welfare; the Office of Economic Opportunity; the Small Business Administration; the Department of Housing and Urban Development; and the Department of Labor; over time, several additional agencies were added (Hall 1989, 53). In a corollary development, eight Federal Regional Councils were established and the regional directors of the various agencies were charged with setting the formal agendas and implementing federal policy goals. Nixon's rationale for this regional system was stated as follows: "to assist state and local governments with the coordination of federal funds, develop better ways to deliver short and long-term benefits, develop integrated programs with Governors and local chief executives, assist with the quick resolution of conflicts, and evaluate programs in which two or more member agencies were participating" (Hall 1989, 54).

Finally, we should note that Nixon, responding to the strident demand of an assortment of environmental interest groups, successfully proposed and persuaded Congress to adopt the Clean Air Act (1970). This was followed by his establishment of the Environmental Protection Agency (EPA), which promulgated a number of federal air and water regulations, continuing the "onward march" of federal regulation, which had largely commenced in the mid-1960s and eventually led to the federal heavy-handed "coercive federalism," as will be documented in Chapter 6.

President Ronald Reagan, a decade later, taking up once again the mantle of "New Federalism," at the outset of his administration advocated the need of separating national and state functions in order to alleviate the "overloading" of government in Washington. As noted by John Kincaid (1990), Reagan viewed cooperative federalism as a form of collusive federalism—a cartel-like venture by liberal federal, state, and local policy activists to expand the public sector—and as such he saw cooperative federalism as a disguise of welfare statism (149–50). As nicely summarized by Kincaid, Reagan, in order to reverse this course of direction, sought to

> (1) deregulate the economy and preempt state-local authority to fill regulatory vacuums; (2) restrain government social activism by reducing direct social expenditures as well as federal subsidies for state and local governmental and nongovernmental activism—that is, defund the Left; (3) articulate a vision of dual federalism to help legitimize increased spending on defense as a traditional federal function and decreased spending on domestic programs as traditional state-local functions; (4) reduce federal regulation of social-equity programs through block grants, waivers of federal law, and fewer rules while otherwise enhancing state and local control of social programs under the assumption that state and local officials would contain and deploy them more efficiently than federal officials; and, (5) appoint persons to the U.S. Supreme Court who would lend constitutional support to these policies. (150)

The Reagan administration was successful in the early 1980s in "bundling" a variety of categorical grant programs into about twenty-five "block grants," providing more policy autonomy to the states, and it embarked upon a course of action that severely reduced the amount of federal funding provided to the states, localities, and regional organizations. In his most dramatic initiative involving intergovernmental relations, Reagan proposed a "swap" of social programs between the federal government and the states, with the national government assuming complete responsibility for Medicaid and the states taking full responsibility for the food stamp program and Aid to Families with Dependent Children (AFDC). However, this far-ranging initiative on Reagan's part failed because of the overwhelming political resistance of state officials.

Although Democratic presidents have generally pursued intergovernmental policies that have served to enhance the stature and power of government in Washington and Republican presidents have embarked upon intergovernmental policies fashioned to increase the political power and decision-making autonomy of the states and localities, Democratic President William J. Clinton departed from this paradigm in the early 1990s. Convinced the states had gained a new degree of willingness and managerial capacity, Clinton pursued an intergovernmental agenda designed to provide more responsibilities to the states. Most notably, Clinton, determined to "end welfare as we know it," led the successful effort, despite considerable and determined resistance by many of his Democratic colleagues in the Congress, to terminate AFDC, and signed, on August 12, 1996, the Personal Responsibility and Work Opportunity Reconciliation Act passed by Congress in 1995. This act converted the principal federal welfare program, that of an open-ended entitlement to individuals, to a capped block grant to the states, requiring them to develop and implement "workfare" programs designed to move individuals from welfare to work; the legislation also provided temporary assistance to needy families (TANF).

CASE STUDY 2

No Child Left Behind: Implications for Intergovernmental Relations

In 2001 the Congress passed and the president signed into law the No Child Left Behind (NCLB) Act (Pub. L. No. 107–110), of approximately seven-hundred pages. To a degree, the passage of this act was an extension of the federal effort begun under the Improving America's School Act of 1994 (Pub. L. No. 103–382). Some provisions of the NCLB Act apply to all schools, while the remainder apply to the 93 percent of school districts and 50 percent of schools that get Title I poverty aid. The purpose of the act is to raise the reading and math achievement of all students and to close the achievement gaps by race, ethnicity, poverty, disability, and limited English proficiency. NCLB allows states to develop their own assessment examinations and to define Adequately Yearly Progress (AYP), but requires that they do so in a manner that promotes real achievement toward the goal that all students by 2014 will meet established standards in English and math. However, a modification of the act by the Department of Education in early 2004 provided that the test scores of recent immigrants who do not speak English would no longer be considered in determining whether a school was meeting annual targets for academic progress. The act expressly requires that AYP include not just state assessments but also the "graduation rates" of those schools that show AYP in terms of increased test scores, taking into account students dropping out of school. A fundamental principle of NCLB is an agreement between Congress and the executive branches of the federal government, through the Department of Education, to hold the states, school districts, and individual schools accountable for improving the educational opportunities for all children, through oversight, the use of testing and the application of appropriate sanctions. Moreover, Congress posited that the nation's highest expectations in public education should be underscored with substantial federal investments in funding, critical resources, and technical assistance.

In its oversight function, the Department of Education is primarily concerned and involved with (1) accountability, (2) parental involvement, and (3) resources. In terms of *accountability*, NCLB requires that states (1) collect and report key data on student math and English achievement, disaggregated by race, ethnicity, poverty, limited English proficiency, disability, gender, and migrant status; (2) develop assessment systems that are valid, reliable, aligned with state standards, and consistent with nationally recognized professional standards; (3) hold schools accountable for demonstrating (AYP) in reading and math test scores for grades 3–8 and once at the high school level, using multiple measures that reflect real improvements in student achievement;* (4) report the qualifications of all teachers, including a comparison of teachers in high-poverty and low-poverty schools; (5) ensure that school districts must notify parents if their child attends a "persistently dangerous" school and provide parents the choice to move their child to a safer school in the district; (6) report progress in ensuring that poor and minority students are not disproportionately assigned to teachers who are inexperienced, unqualified, or out of field; and (7) ensure that schools, based on appropriate tests, provide diagnostic reports for every student.

In addition, school districts that receive Title I funds must also (1) notify parents of their right to transfer their child to another school if the current school has not made adequate yearly progress for two straight years. Low-income parents must be offered tutoring for their child if a school has not met progress goals for three years, and districts must help parents get information about the qualifications and services of tutors; (2) inform parents of children in Title I schools that they have the right to request information about the qualifications of their children's teachers; and (3) provide the parents of children with limited English skills a package of information if Title I money is spent on programs for such students. In addition to these requirements, Title I schools must also (1) provide parents timely, clear notice if their child has been taught for at least four straight weeks by a teacher who is not highly qualified; and (2) hold meetings at convenient times for parents and give parents an explanation of the school curriculum, the tests used at various levels, and the achievement levels students are expected to meet.

Further, Title I schools with one or more the six subgroups (a subgroup consisting of a minimum of about thirty students)—African American, Hispanic, white, disabled, economically disadvantaged, and limited-English proficient—failing to meet adequate yearly progress for consecutive years will

---

* President Bush proposed, in a speech given in January 2005, that annual testing in reading and mathematics be extended through the eleventh grade. However, the *New York Times* declared that Bush's proposal, because it was poorly conceived and underfinanced, was "dead on arrival in Congress." See "High School Reform, Round 1," *New York Times*, February 23, 2005, A30.

TABLE CS2.1. Moving Target: Virginia's Goals in Terms of Student Pass Standards

Year	Reading/Language Arts Pass Rate	Math Pass Rate
2001–2	60.1	58.4
2002–3	61	59
2004–5	70	70
2007–8	80	80
2010–11	90	90
2013–14	100	100

The state of Virginia's goal is to have all students pass the Standards of Learning tests by school year 2013–14. This table shows the test results for school year 2001–2 and the projected goals for the succeeding years. *Source: "Moving Target." 2003 B4.*

face sanctions. Two straight years of not meeting the standard requires that a school develop a school-improvement plan and offer parents the opportunity to transfer their children to a better performing school. Three straight years of failing to meet adequate progress mandates that a school must provide extra services, such as before-school or after-school tutoring. Four or more consecutive years of failing to meet adequate yearly progress requires a major restructuring of the school, including the replacement of staff primarily responsible for persistent underachievement and, perhaps, its transformation into a charter school.

Virginia's goal is to have 80 percent of the students pass its reading and math Standards of Learning (SOL) tests by 2007–8, according to the "pass-rates" schedule found in Table CS2.1; by 2013–14 all students are expected to pass these tests, as mandated by NCLB. While the latter goal may seem to be somewhat excessive, we should note that in the period from 1998 to 2004, public schools in Virginia have made impressive gains in the number of schools where children, in the aggregate, have met or exceed the "pass-rates" in reading and math scores. In 1998, when the tests were first administered, only 2.7 percent—or 39 of the state's 1,800 public elementary schools—met these achievement objectives; by 2004 the respective figure was 84 percent (Emblidge 2005).

With regard to *parental involvement*, NCLB requires a substantial degree of parental and public involvement, including (1) public input on the development and evaluation of federal, state, and district accountability plans; and (2) state administrative complaint procedures for parents and others who believe that the act's requirements are not being met. These requirements, in addition to the public data reporting requirements described earlier, must be promoted and strengthened by the Department of Education in order that parents and others can act with valid and comprehensive information to promote school accountability and improvement. The NCLB law requires that all states eventually adopt "written procedures" for the receipt and resolution of complaints alleging violations of the law in the administration of the law.

Finally, in regard to *resources*, NCLB requires limited but important actions regarding the provision of educational resources, including requiring (1) that all students have full and equal access to "highly qualified" teachers; (2) the provision of "scientifically based" technical assistance; and (3) that the states "supplement not supplant" federal education funds. The law mandates that all teachers in core academic subjects be "highly qualified" by 2005–6 and that states take immediate action to ensure that poor and minority students have equal access to highly qualified teachers. NCLB further requires that the states reserve funds to provide technical assistance to schools identified for improvement under the act. The act stresses that states receiving federal funds for education—somewhat over $20 billion—use these funds only to *supplement, not supplant*, state funding.

RESULTS

As a result of its various and multiple requirements, in the summer of 2003, nearly 90 percent of Florida's public schools failed to meet the requirements of NCLB. In addition, 80 percent of the schools in Idaho, 77 percent of the schools in South Carolina, and 66 percent of the schools in Alabama and New Jersey were identified as not making sufficient progress. The majority of states reported passing rates of approximately 50 percent (Young 2003, 24). A study released by the Center on Education Policy in January 2004 found that about 26,000 of the nation's 91,400 public schools were on probation because they failed to make adequate yearly progress on tests administered in the spring of 2003 (Dillon 2004a, A19). A survey conducted in 2004 found that 7 percent of the nation's public schools, because of their low "passing scores," are confronted with various consequences, ranging from school improvement plans to major restructuring (Schemo 2004, A16). The percentage of these schools in each state is found in Table CS2.2.

CRITICISMS

A basic criticism of NCLB is that it violates the concept of states' rights and allows the intrusion of the federal government into a functional and policy area that traditionally has been the province of state and local government. In January 2004 Virginia's House of Delegates passed a resolution, by a margin of 98–1, calling on Congress to exempt Virginia and other states from the law's provisions. The resolution stated that the federal law "represents the most sweeping intrusions into state and local control of education in the history of the United States, which egregiously violates the time-honored American principles of balanced federalism and respect for state and local prerogatives, especially in the crucial area of education." In similiar action, the legislature of Oklahoma followed the lead of Virginia. Other state legislatures, such as in Connecticut

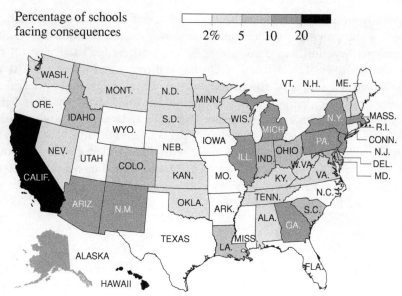

Percentage of schools facing consequences   2% 5 10 20

FIGURE CS2.1. States with many schools facing consequences under NCLB. *Source: Schemo 2004b. New York Times Graphics.*

and Idaho, passed less sweeping resolutions, urging that various modifications be made in the act (Dillon 2004b). A year later, the Attorney General of Connecticut sued the federal government over the NCLB legislation arguing that the Bush administration was being "rigid, arbitrary and capricious in its enforcement of the law" and that it was providing Connecticut insufficient funding for its implementation (Dillon 2005a).

A second criticism of NCLB is one of an intergovernmental nature, involving the implementation of the policy regulations and the funding for the act. After lavishing praise on the Bush administration in an editorial for promoting the act ("The Bush Administration Has the High Ground Here"), the *New York Times* ("Rescuing Education Reform" 2004) noted: "No Child Left Behind was the result of one of George Bush's most famous campaign promises. But the Bush administration has sadly turned out to be part of the problem [in fully implementing the Act]. The Department of Education, under the inept leadership of Rod Paige, has been painfully slow in adopting regulations on how the states can comply with the law."[†] And, further: "The administration was forced

---

† In a subsequent editorial the *New York Times* further criticized the lack of leadership of Rod Paige: "The federal Education Department failed to push the states toward doing better under the disastrous leadership of its departing secretary, Rod Paige. No matter how hard localities try, the best-designed schools in the world will still fail unless the states and the federal government finally bite the bullet on teacher training." See "Reinventing High School," *New York Times*, February 1, 2005, A22.

by Congress to accept the most crucial provision, which requires the states to hire only qualified teachers, and it has failed to enforce the provision adequately." Concerning inadequate funding, the editorial noted:

> One of the most serious complaints about the law is that the federal government is asking states for big improvements in local schools but is not providing the money to pay for such changes. The Bush administration is correct when it says that school financing went up sharply under the new law. The money for Title I, which is aimed at the poorest students, went up by nearly a third—with proportionately more of the money going to the poorest districts. But the Title I allotment is also $6 billion short of what Congress authorized when it passed the law, and the amount states are getting is certainly not adequate to meet the tough standards the law sets.

A major critic of the Bush's administration funding of the NCLB law has been Senator Edward M. Kennedy of Massachusetts, who although he was an original proponent of the law subsequently has argued that the Bush administration has failed to provide adequate funding for the implementation of the law. Borrowing a phrase from the late Senator Paul Wellstone of Minnesota, Kennedy has charged that the Bush administration has sought to fund the law with a "tin cup budget" (Schemo 2004a, A18). Further, in many states funding cutbacks for public education has further aggravated the fiscal condition of local school systems, seeking to carry out their basic responsibilities and comply with the federal law. A study issued by the Center on Education Policy in March 2005 reported that school districts in about four-fifths of the states noted that they were not receiving enough funding from the state and federal government to accomplish the goals of the NCLB law (Winter 2005). Connecticut in 2005, alleging that the NCLB law is under funded by Washington, was the first state to sue the federal government in regard to the NCLB law, charging that the law violates legislation passed by Congress during the Clinton administration that forbids Washington from requiring the states to spend their own money to carrying out federal policies (Dillon 2005a).

Third, another major criticism of the No Child Left Behind Act is that relatively few citizens are familiar with the provisions of the legislation. According to a survey conducted by Phi Delta Kappa and Gallup in June 2003, 78 percent of public school parents knew nothing or very little about the act, as advanced in Table CS2.2. In addition, 68 percent stated that they did not know enough about the act to have an opinion (Feller 2004, A2).

Further, some educators have argued that NCLB places too much emphasis on sanctions against struggling schools, rather than on developing challenging curriculum, effective teaching, and family support for student achievement. In an open letter to President Bush and Congress, the Citizens for Effective Schools, consisting of a group of educators based in Bethesda, Maryland, noted: "Time must be refocused on improving teacher's instructional knowledge and skills, administrators' capacity to lead school and community transformations, families'

TABLE CS2.2. Knowledge or Lack of It Concerning the No Child Left Behind Act, 2003[1]

How much do you know about the No Child Left Behind Act?	
A great deal	7%
A fair amount	15%
Very little	44%
Nothing at all	34%
From what you know about the act, what is your opinion?	
Very favorable	7%
Somewhat favorable	13%
Somewhat unfavorable	6%
Don't know enough to say	68%

[1] Over three-fourths of public school parents say they know very little or nothing at all about NCLB. Of those interviewed, 68 percent don't know enough to have an opinion. These figures represent 32 percent of 1,011 adults interviewed between May 28 and June 18, 2003, by a Phi Delta Kappa/Gallup poll. *Source: Feller 2004.*

capacity to provide motivation and assistance for high-level student learning, and students' concentration on academic learning at school and at home" (Wermers 2003, B3).

Fifth, educators have noted that some of the provisions of NCLB are simply not feasible. For instance, the provision of the act that allows students in low-test schools to transfer to better schools is often not workable. For example, the Chicago school system in the fall of 2003 received nearly 19,000 transfer requests; however, it only had room for 1,035, or less than 6 percent, of those students. Similarly, New Orleans in the same period could only accommodate 40 percent of the students requesting transfers (Young 2003, 25). Given the usually large geographical distance of an alternative satisfactory school, school officials in rural areas often find it virtually impossible to comply with a student transfer request. In addition, in rural schools of limited enrollment, where teachers teaching science often teach a range of subjects—such as biology, chemistry, and earth and life sciences—it is virtually impossible to recruit faculty who would be able to meet the competency requirements of the act.

Finally, an unintended consequence of NCLB is that various states have been lowering the standards of their assessment examinations. For example, the Texas State Board of Education in 2003 voted to reduce the number of questions that students must correctly answer correctly to pass it, to 20 out of 36, from 24, for third-grade reading. In the same year, Michigan lowered the percentage of students who must pass statewide tests to certify a school as making adequate progress—to 42 percent, from 75 percent of high school students on English tests. Chester E. Finn, Jr., a former assistant secretary of education, noted: "Some states are lowering the passing scores, they're redefining schools in need of improvement and they're deferring the hard task of achievement-boosting into the distant future" (Dillon 2003, A1, A25).

On February 23, 2005, the National Conference of State Legislatures released the report of its Task Force on No Child Left Behind. In its seventy-seven-page report the task force, based on public hearings conducted in six cities, praised the goal of the NCLB law of seeking to end the gap in scholastic achievement between white and minority students. However, the report reiterated the general criticisms cited here and further included a detailed inventory and discussion of the flaws of NCLB. Significantly, the report was sharply critical of the increasing role of the federal government in public education: "Under N.C.L.B., the federal government's role has become excessively intrusive in the day-to-day operations of public education. . . . This assertion of federal authority into an area historically reserved to the states has had the effect of curtailing additional state innovations and undermining many that had occurred during the past three decades" (National Conference of State Legislatures 2005). Partially responding to the criticisms contained in the report, Margaret Spellings, who succeeded Rod Paige as secretary of Education with the commencement of the second term of the Bush administration, noted that she would permit some flexibility by the states in the implementation rules of the NCLB, as long as they adhered to the basic principles of the law (Dillon 2005).

CONCLUSION

The implementation by the federal, state, and local schools of the provisions of NCLB has proved to be an enormously challenging and difficult task. The federal Department of Education has argued that the states and local schools have not always undertaken "good faith efforts" to implement the provisions of the act. In turn, the states and local schools have complained that the Department of Education has not provided sufficient funding for implementing the act and has not always provided clear and unambiguous policy implementation regulations. On the other hand, there is some evidence to believe that the NCLB law, because it requires administrators to release pupil scores by race and ethnic group, educators are working much more diligently to improve the performance of minority group students (Dillon 2005c). In regard to the difficulties of implementing NCLB, we are reminded of the erudite thoughts of Jeffrey L. Pressman and Aaron Wildavsky, as advanced in their work *Implementation* (1984), of how difficult it is to successfully implement federal policy goals in our communities.

REFERENCES

Dillon, Sam. 2003, May 22. States Are Relaxing Standards on Tests to Avoid Sanctions. *New York Times*. A1, A25.
———. 2004a, January 27. 1 in 4 Schools Fall Short Under Bush Law. *New York Times*. A19.

———. 2004b, March 8. President's Initiative to Shake Up Education Is Facing Protests in Many State Capitols. *New York Times*. A11.

———. 2005a, August 23. Connecticut Sues the U.S. Over Mandated School Testing. *New York Times*. A17.

———. 2005b, April 8. Facing State Protests, U.S. Offers More Flexibility on School Rules. *New York Times*. 2005.

———. 2005c, May 27. Under School Law, Push to Close Minority Gap. *New York Times*. A19.

Emblidge, Mark. 2005, February 13. A Decade Later: SOLs Prove Their Value with Higher Scores. *Richmond Times-Dispatch*. F1.

Feller, Ben. 2004, March 2. Parents Need to Study No Child Left Behind. *Richmond Times-Dispatch*. A2.

High School Reform, Round 1 [Editorial]. 2005, February 23. *New York Times*. A30.

Moving Target. 2003, June 14. *Richmond Times-Dispatch*. B4.

National Conference of State Legislatures. 2005. *NCSL Task Force on No Child Left Behind Report*. Washington, DC: National Conference of State Legislatures.

Pressman, Jeffrey L. and Aaron Wildavsky. 1984. *Implementation*. 3d ed. Berkeley: University of California Press.

Public School Parents Have a Lot to Learn. 2004, March 2. *Richmond Times-Dispatch*. A2.

Rescuing Education Reform [Editorial]. 2004, March 2. *New York Times*. A26.

Schemo, Diana Jean. 2004a, April 7. Kennedy Demands Full Funding for School Bill. *New York Times*. A18.

———. 2004b, August 18. Effort by Bush on Education Hits Obstacles. *New York Times*. A1, A16.

Wermers, Jason. 2003, October 16. Educators: Help, Not Punishment. *Richmond Times-Dispatch*. B3.

Winter, Greg. 2005, March 24. States Worry About Meeting Requirements of Education Law. *New York Times*. A12.

Young, Scott. 2003. The Challenges of NCLB. *State Legislatures*. 29 (December), 24–26.

THE PRESIDENT: INTRAGOVERNMENTAL AND INTERGOVERNMENTAL RELATIONS

In terms of the national policy process, the president and his aides are involved in both intragovernmental and intergovernmental relations. By the term "intragovernmental relations" we are referring to the manner in which the president and his associates interact with the legislative and judicial branches of government. At this point, we posit some observations on the intragovernmental relationship of the president with the Congress, while later on in the chapter we devote attention to the intragovernmental relationship between the president and the Supreme Court.

Intragovernmental Relations

Succinctly stating the obvious, William J. Keefe (1980) has noted that "presidential-congressional relations . . . are often unpredictable, sometimes unfathomable, and always complex" (120). In his insightful work *Separate but Equal Branches: Congress and the Presidency* (1999), Charles O. Jones has argued that "relations between Congress and the presidency depend substantially on how each judges the legitimacy and competency of the other" (105). And, further in terms of the examination of congressional-presidential relations, Jones advances:

> The two legislative bodies called Congress, separated from each other and from the executive . . . must be comprehended as in this exercise. At the most basic level, Article I reminds us that presidential-congressional relations are not relations between one person (and his appointed aides) and one body of persons organized hierarchically. Instead, the president, acting through aides, must negotiate with a variable set of congressional actors through time, through legislative stages, across issues, and for two legislative bodies. (106–7)

In a long-acknowledged sense, determinants of congressional-presidential relations include constitutional prerogatives, political party, personality, electoral margins, media expectations, and how these elements influence how congressional and presidential actors view each other. Presidential actors, of course, include those individuals in the White House Office who are assigned the responsibility of promoting the policy goals of the president in the halls of the Congress. Jones (1999) reports, reflective of this, that congressional-presidential relations are also crucially shaped by the degree to which "actors in Congress and the presidency view one another's legitimacy and competency to cope generally and to cope with specific issues" (108–9).

Utilizing this framework of analysis, with special emphasis given to the factors of legitimacy and competency, presidents overall have compiled a mixed record of success in terms of congressional-presidential relations. As advanced by Jones (1999), although Congress challenged some of the specific initiatives and programs of Presidents Franklin D. Roosevelt, Harry Truman, Dwight Eisenhower, John F. Kennedy, and Lyndon Johnson and doubted their legitimacy and competency to deal with the issues involved, Congress held overall a positive evaluation of their administration (110–11). In sharp contrast, congressional-presidential relations during the era of President Richard Nixon reached a low ebb, because Congress, as a body, perceived the Nixon administration as lacking in legitimacy and competency, bent on crippling, neutralizing, and diminishing its influence and power (Polsby 1976, 51). Aggravating this perspective, as reported by Ralph K. Huitt (1975), was the tendency of Nixon to want to "run things" without Congress (71). Although President Jimmy Carter's administration was viewed by Congress as legitimate, many in the body viewed President Carter as unequal to the task of the office. This perspective was largely because, especially in the early years of the Carter administration, of the largely inexperienced (that is, in the political ways and routines of Congress) individuals who were appointed by Carter to serve in his liaison team to the Congress (Jones 1999, 187).

Intergovernmental Relations

The Kestnbaum Commission on Intergovernmental Relations recommended the establishment and staffing of a unit in the Executive Office of the President that would devote primary attention to intergovernmental matters. President Eisenhower accepted this recommendation, and succeeding presidents have charged one or more staff members with duties centering on intergovernmental concerns.

Various individuals in the Executive Office of the President have been charged with articulating, advocating, and implementing presidential intergovernmental policies. For example, Herbert Humphrey, while serving as vice president, assumed this responsibility in the Johnson administration in the 1960s, and Spiro Agnew, also while serving as vice president, was charged with this responsibility from 1969 to 1971, during the early days of the first Nixon administration. President Jimmy Carter designated Jack Watson as his presidential assistant for intergovernmental relations, while also serving as his secretary to the Cabinet. President Ronald Reagan assigned the responsibility for intergovernmental relations to various individuals in the Office of Policy Development, who reported to the president's chief of staff.

As Wright succinctly wrote in 1982, "three common threads" pervade the roles played by presidential advisers on intergovernmental relations matters. First, their influence, impact, and effectiveness in the intergovernmental system has varied extensively because of their varying degrees of political savvy. Second, the chief function of these advisers has been to maintain close contacts and serve as "point men" for the president in dealing with state and local government interest groups. And, third, the president's adviser on intergovernmental relations has essentially carried out a political role, in which intergovernmental political, policy, and management considerations and dimensions merge (137).

Office of Management and Budget

In addition to White House staff, the president utilizes the Office of Management and Budget (OMB) to influence national program agencies and intergovernmental policies. Formerly the Bureau of the Budget (BOB), this unit, which is situated in the Executive Office of the President, was revamped and provided its new nomenclature by the Nixon administration in 1970, in order to underscore that in addition to its budget responsibilities it was charged with assorted managerial responsibilities. While the former BOB sought to be an essentially politically uncommitted institution, driven by the values of neutral competence and professionalism and intent upon providing the president with its best independent judgment, the Nixon administration "politicized" the OMB by introducing into the organization politically appointed program associate directors (PADs), responsible for the line operations of the various examining divisions. Consequently, as Hugh Heclo has underscored in his work *A Government of Strangers: Executive Politics in Washington* (1977), OMB has evolved into a forceful advocate and the "lead agency" of the president's policy priorities (78–80). Its functions include budgeting, coordinating, and managing the intergovernmental grant system and serving in a federal liaison capacity to the states and communities.

Office of Personnel Administration

As noted by Wright (1982, 156), the national government has been involved in state and local personnel administration since the passage of the Hatch Acts in 1939 and 1940, prohibiting partisan political activities by state and local employees compensated entirely or in part by federal funds; in later years these acts were made less restrictive. In 1979, the newly created Office of Personnel Management (OPM) assumed most of the operating functions of the Civil Service Commission, established in 1883, which became largely an advisory body. OPM provides to the states and localities various forms of technical assistance, involving administration, management, and recruitment activities. Over the years, presidents have utilized OPM to advance their political agenda and policy priorities. For example, in 2004, President Bush's administration, reflecting its belief in the virtue of a "culture of life" society and the utility of "faith-based" initiatives, commenced offering, through OPM, a health plan to federal employees based upon Catholic religious tenets, specifically excluding coverage for contraceptives, abortion, sterilization, and artificial insemination (Freudenheim 2004).

CONGRESS AND INTERGOVERNMENTAL RELATIONS

Congress has been involved in a number of studies involving federalism and intergovernmental relations. The Legislative Reorganization Act of 1946 charged both the Senate and House Committees on Government Operations to study intergovernmental relationships between the federal government, the states, and local governments. Responding to this charge, the Senate Committee established in 1947 a subcommittee on intergovernmental relations. Two years later, in 1949, the House Committee took similar action and established a subcommittee on intergovernmental relations. In its early years, the House Subcommittee on Intergovernmental Relations proved to be quite vigorous and constructive; however, the Senate Subcommittee was terminated when it lost its funding, and its responsibilities were assumed by the full committee. Eventually, in 1962, the Senate Subcommittee on Intergovernmental Relations was reestablished (Graves 1964, 135).

Commencing in 1955, the House Subcommittee on Intergovernmental Relations undertook a comprehensive study of federal-state-local relationships and sent a detailed questionnaire to each federal department and agency, to each state, and to a large number of cities and counties. Among other matters, state and local officials were asked whether intergovernmental programs would be improved by providing more responsibility to state and local governments and if the federal governmental supervision of these programs were satisfactory. Subsequently, the subcommittee held public hearings in Washington and in a multiple number of cities throughout the nation to which governmental and private individuals were invited to present their views on various facets of intergovernmental relations. The testimony presented at these hearings provided further support for the eventual establishment of the U.S. Advisory Commission on Intergovernmental Relations in 1959 (Graves 1964, 898–99).

During the 1960s, the Senate Subcommittee on Intergovernmental Relations, chaired by Senator Edmund S. Muskie of Maine, and the Intergovernmental Relations Subcommittee of the House Committee on Government Operations, chaired by

Representative L. H. Fountain of North Carolina, proved to be especially active and productive. These committees conducted a score of studies, held numerous public hearings, and issued a large number of reports on various aspects of federal, state, and local relations.[2]

Writing some four decades ago, Graves (1964) noted that "Congress can and does exert its influence [on programmatic federalism] in a variety of ways. If it acts in a given field, it may be assumed that it has taken over this field; this is known as the doctrine of preemption. A failure on its part to act in a given field may be interpreted to mean that, not having taken possession of the field, the States are free to act." And, "Or it may be interpreted as indicating a decision on the part of Congress that no action is necessary, or a desire that none be taken" (131). Graves further noted: "It may well be that the actions of Congress have been the most important single source of change in the character of American federalism" (134).

There are a number of ways in which actions taken by the Congress shape the nature of the intergovernmental system and exert pressure upon the states and local governments. Congress determines the amount of federal money that will be given to the state and local governments, for which programmatic purposes, and the restrictions that are placed upon the use of this aid. Congress, in most grants-in-aid legislation, "gently nudges the States, sometimes in influencing policy, sometimes in the way in which they spend their money, or in the procedures they employ in administering federally aid programs. . . . Sometimes the influence aimed at federally aided programs spills over into other State departments and programs as well" (Graves 1964, 137). Congress monitors program implementation in the state and local bureaucracies and, on occasion, notes deficiencies and recommends policy modifications.

In his perceptive paper on the theory of coercive federalism and the role of Congress in shaping federal-state-local relations, Joseph F. Zimmerman (2001) wrote:

> Congress plays three principal roles—facilitator, inhibitor, and initiator—in terms of national-state relations. As a facilitator, Congress provides direct and indirect financial assistance—exemption of municipal-bond interest from national income taxation, grants-in-aid, insurance, loans and loan guarantees, tax deductions, and tax credits—and technical assistance and training to promote subnational governmental regulation and provision of services in accordance with national standards. As an inhibitor, Congress employs its total preemption powers to nullify state regulatory laws and administrative rules, and to prohibit future enactment of such laws and promulgation of such rules. Partial preemption statutes either remove all state regulatory authority from a segment of a regulatory field or establish minimum standards.

He added:

> As an initiator, Congress plays a leadership role by enactment of partial preemption statutes establishing minimum national standards to provide the framework for new regulatory programs involving a partnership between the national and state governments, and also employs conditional grants-in-aid, and crossover and tax sanctions to encourage states to implement national regulatory policies and initiate provision of services conforming to national standards. (16)

Congress is often quite receptive to state and local governmental pleas for assistance, for a variety of reasons. First, and of primary importance, congressional receptivity to subnational interests and pressures is due to the nature of the decentralized American party system, which in an organizational sense is heavily shaped by the federal system of government. As Daniel J. Elazar (1984) has noted:

> Historically, the Democratic and Republican parties have represented two broad confederations of otherwise largely independent state party organizations that unite on the national plane, primarily to gain public office. Despite the greater public attention given the national parties, the real centers of party organization, finance, and power have been on the state and local planes. American political parties rarely have centralized power at all. Characteristically, they have done the reverse, serving as a canopy under which special and local interests are represented, with little regard for anything that can be called a party platform.

Elazar further notes:

> Moreover, party operations play a major role in producing through Congress, the basic division of functions between the federal government and state and local governments at any given moment in history, transforming the Supreme Court's well-known permissiveness with respect to the expansion of national powers into legislation that characteristically provides important roles for state and local governments. (48).

Notwithstanding Elazar's sage observations, we should note that in recent years party finance has become much more centralized.

The basic decentralized nature and disunity of the party system, along with the widespread use of the primary and single-member district system for nominating congressional candidates, renders the members of Congress particularly sensitive to the interests of their constituents and undermines, to a degree, the power and influence of House and Senate party leaders. Members of Congress are keenly aware that if there is any disagreement between party leaders in Washington and the voters in their district, the voters, given their centrality in the election process, will usually prevail. It should be further noted that in the general election the congressional party nominees usually secure most of their financial and political support from within their district; assistance from the national party organizations is usually quite limited. All of these factors result in a congressional membership that is particularly sensitive and receptive to local concerns.

Seeking to make members of Congress even more responsive to their demands, cities and counties around the nation are making increasing use of Washington lobbyists to successfully advance their goals. For instance, City of Richmond (Virginia) officials acknowledged that they were successful in getting a new $83 million federal courthouse, key to the downtown revitalization effort, constructed in the city in 2005, partly due to the lobbying efforts of the DCI Group in Washington and an Iowa law firm (Hardin 2005).

A variety of reasons have been advanced by scholars and the press for why localities are making more use of lobbyists to advance their interests in Washington.

These reasons include the increasingly competitive nature of lobbying in the Congress; strapped state budgets; the increasing number of lobbying firms in Washington seeking new business; additional demands on the complex Congressional spending process and busy Congressional staffs; and, a significant increase in Congressional spending through member-directed "earmarks," derisively described by critics as "pork" (Hardin 2005).

The decentralized primary congressional recruitment system provides additional sensitivity to state and local concerns, since most members of Congress have long resided the state or district that they represent. For instance, a study conducted by Barbara Hinckley (1988) of the personal characteristics of the members of the Ninety-sixth Congress found that more than 70 percent of the members of Congress were born in the state that they represented; two-thirds of the Senators and three-fourths of the Representatives received at least some measure of higher education in their home state; and half of the Representatives and two-thirds of the Senators held an elective office in their state prior to being elected to Congress (85–86).

In addition, the congressional committee assignment process also stimulates the localistic orientations of the members of the House and Senate, since these assignments are heavily influenced by the committee assignments that members desire, along with those assignments that will best allow them to serve their constituents effectively, and help them win reelection. (Price 1978; Rohde and Shepsle 1973). Such assignments usually involve committees studying and debating issues and fashioning public policies of significant concern to the dominant interests of their constituency.

And, importantly, members of Congress advocate and protect subnational interests through their extensive constituency service work, also known as "casework." As a result of his extensive in-depth field research conducted in the 1970s and reported in his work *Home Style: House Members in Their Districts*, Richard F. Fenno (1978) documented the increasing amount and importance of constituency service provided by members of the House of Representatives. In order to successfully deal with their increasing casework, members of Congress have assigned more of their office staff to several strategically located district offices, which facilitates the input of local perspectives into the national policy-making process. As noted by Fenno, members of the House of Representatives and the Senate are inundated with a steady flow of a variety of requests for assistance in dealing with federal agencies. As several scholars have underscored, being responsive to these requests results in political dividends at election time (Mann and Wolfinger 1980).

We should note, however, that a number of scholars have noted that state and local officials have lost some of their impact on congressional decision-making. As Kincaid (1990) has noted:

> The growing independence of presidential and congressional candidates from national, state, and local party organizations eroded the party foundations of cooperative federalism, leaving elected state and local officials feeling like "just another interest group," and disadvantaged as well because few state and local officials can deliver votes or money or great significance to presidential and congressional candidates.

Kincaid adds:

The professionalization of Congress has given members staff resources to service voters and interests, while entitlements, preemptions, and expanded authority have supplied opportunities to service constituents directly and to intervene in state and local matters, sometimes in competition with state and local officials and often on grounds of equity. (149)

INTEREST GROUPS, INTERGOVERNMENTAL LOBBIES, AND POLICY-MAKING

Since Arthur Bentley wrote his classic work *The Process of Government: A Study of Social Pressures* in 1908, along with the subsequent like-minded works of David Truman (1951), Earl Latham (1952), E. E. Schattschneider (1960), and Grant McConnell (1966), interest groups have long been recognized by scholars of American politics as playing a very important, perhaps key, role in the shaping of public policy at all levels of government. In a summary sense, an interest group may be defined as an organized collection of citizens, whether composed of private individuals and/or public officials, that seeks to influence the shaping of public policy. We should note that federalism, as a result of what Morton Grodzins (1966) famously labeled "the multiple crack" (14–15, 274–76), provides interest groups with a great many avenues and decision points for exerting influence on the public policy process. In the world of inter-governmental relations, an interest group may advance its case before municipal officials, county officials, governors, state legislators, members of Congress, judges, and bureaucrats. If one venue does not respond favorably to its demands, an interest group can seek redress in another arena.

Scholars of policy-making in Washington, such as Hugh Heclo (1977) and Harold Seidman (1975), have emphasized that the federal government consists of a number of fragmented power centers, known as "subgovernments" or "iron triangles." Rather than a set of subordinate units under the president, this interpretation of national policy-making emphasizes, of course, the importance of federal *intra-governmental* relations. As reported by Heclo, these "cracks of fragmentation are not random but run along a number of well-established functional specialties and program interests that link particular government bureaus, congressional committees, and interest groups (12–13). However, as Heclo further notes, "[W]hile academicians write about the iron triangle as if it were an immutable force, prudent political executives recognize that although they cannot stop bureaucratic sabotage, neither are they helpless against it. . . . In general, experienced political executives try to use all their means of self-help and working relations so as to reshape the iron triangles into more plastic polygons" (228). Although, to be sure, subgovernments largely operate in a "world of their own," they are receptive and responsive to executive political pressures and leadership (Aberbach and Rockman 2000).

The subgovernment concept of policy-making emphasizes that public policies typically are the result of a series of decisions made by different political actors. For example, an interest group, which has become aware of a presidential policy initiative, may lobby the White House, seeking changes in the proposal. Failing on this score, the interest group may turn to lobbying Congress as the president's proposal is discussed and revised in committee or on the floor. If legislation is eventually passed, the interest group may lobby federal officials responsible for implementing the program, along with state and local governments involved in the program.

Interest groups representing state or local officials have long been involved in lobbying Congress on behalf of various policy goals. Collectively, these groups have been identified as the "intergovernmental lobby" or in the Washington vernacular as "PIGs" (public interest groups). For instance, Jon C. Teaford notes in his work *The Rise of the States: Evolution of American State Government* (2002) that the American Association of State Highway Officials, which was organized in 1914, played a crucial role in the passage of the Federal-Aid Road Act of 1916. This legislation provided $75 million in federal highway funds, on a state matching basis, to the states over a five-year period. The Federal-Aid Road Act required each of the recipient states to establish a state highway department responsible for implementing a state highway program (34).

What is of particular note, however, is the continued proliferation over the past century, primarily because of the expansion in the number of federal grants-in-aid programs, of interest groups in Washington representing various state or local elected and administrative officials. Prior to 1900 there were relatively few intergovernmental lobbies, as labeled by Samuel H. Beer (1977), but by 1986 there were approximately one hundred of these groups functioning in Washington (Walker 1969, 894). This development is because of the general expansion of the role of the federal government, along with the desire of interest groups, for the sake of political efficiency and resolution, to often nationalize and centralize political issues (Anderson 1965, 122). The most important and influential of these groups, often referred to as the "Big Seven," include the National Governors' Association (NGA), National Conference on State Legislatures (NCSL), National League of Cities (NLC), U.S. Conference of Mayors (USCM), National Association of Counties (NACO), Council of State Governments (CSG),[3] and the International City Management Association (ICMA). It should be noted that the latter two organizations are "not self-acknowledged interest/lobbying groups" (Wright 1962, 223), but rather emphasize their research, publication, training, and service efforts. Among other policy successes, these groups played, as noted previously, a crucial role in the congressional passage, in 1971, and the several extensions, in 1976 and 1980, of the State and Local Fiscal Assistance Act, which established GRS (Wallin 1998, 39–52; Wright 1982, 120–30).[4] It should be noted that the "Big Seven" are not always united on policy goals, especially in regard to those issues that are particularly susceptible to a political division or conflict between the states and local governments.

In addition to partaking in the activities of various associations of officials or governments, state and local governments conduct their own lobbying activities. All of the states, along with most of the major cities and many of the large urban counties, maintain their own offices in Washington to promote their policy interests. Reflective of the workings of the subgovernments concept, state and local officials seek to gain a report with federal officials in order to voice complaints, gain assistance, or seek to influence decision-making in the legislative or executive branches of government. In some unique or parochial circumstances, officials of a single state or locality are of the persuasion that by acting alone they will be more successful in achieving their discrete policy goals, rather than by working through a national association.

Another category of intergovernmental lobbies of significance are the bureaucratic or program specialists, identified with in a single programmatic area, such as education, urban rehabilitation and renewal, law enforcement, and libraries. Such groups, sometimes referred to by members of the "Washington establishment" rather derisively as constituting "guilds" (Seidman 1975), include the American Library Association, the National Association of Housing and Redevelopment Officials, the American Association of State Highway Engineers, and the Association of State and Territorial Health Officers (Wright 1982, 227). These groups are highly active in developing a mutually productive working relationship, or, as noted by Thomas Anton (1989, 30–32, 67–69), a "benefit coalition," with members of Congress and political and civil service executives to support and protect their programs. As further advanced by Anton, these benefit coalitions have encouraged the emergence in the inter-governmental system of a picket-fence federalism, with its emphasis on vertical programmatic linkages.

The intergovernmental lobbies have a number of resources that serve to enhance their power and influence with administrative and legislative officials in Washington. First, governors, mayors, and other elected state and local officials are the beneficiaries of a substantial amount of political legitimacy and respect, which they have accrued as a result of being elected to office. Members of Congress and officials in the executive branch can ill afford, for obvious political reasons, to turn a "deaf ear" toward public officials who are seeking to influence some aspect of federal policy-making or who are bent upon gaining some sort of federal assistance. Second, the intergovernmental lobbies profit and gain influence because of their wide geographical dispersal and the large number of states and congressional districts in which they reside. This usually assures that individuals identified with the various intergovernmental lobbies will have political access to the decision-makers in Washington. And, third, program specialists, because of their professional and social status, along with the technical expertise that they can bring to bear on various issues, are accorded a respectful and careful hearing by congressional and administrative officials.

Notwithstanding this, some scholars have noted that organizations representing local governments had reduced access to the White House during the years of Reagan administrations (Reed 1981). This was due to the fact that Reagan administration officials, because of their belief in a revitalized dual federalism, did not regard local governments as full and equal partners in the federal system and were committed to not interfering in the internal affairs of the states. In contrast, local officials continued to enjoy substantial access to members of Congress during the Reagan years.

During the administration of President William Clinton it is generally acknowledged that state and local governmental officials enjoyed a similar level of access to the White House. Some observers note, however, that Clinton's commitment to state and local government was largely limited to policy and political support, not fiscal support. Clinton administration officials were particularly solicitous of gaining from state and local officials ideas relating to policy innovation (Walters 1994, 50). During this time frame, Congress continued to provide broad access to state and local officials; however, state and local government associations became increasingly perceived by members of Congress as simply another set of interest groups advocating their own agendas, often at the exclusion of the overall public interest (Walters 1994, 53).

To some degree the effectiveness and influence of the intergovernmental lobbies in Washington are undermined by their lack of unity and their disagreement on policy goals. Mayors of large core cities sometimes find themselves in conflict with the mayors of suburban jurisdictions and small towns. Republican conservative governors seeking more political autonomy for their states, find themselves in contention with liberal Democratic governors seeking additional fiscal assistance from Washington. State and local elected officials usually have broad policy priorities, as opposed to the narrow interests of program specialists.

SUPREME COURT: INTRAGOVERNMENTAL AND INTERGOVERNMENTAL RELATIONS

The primary role of the federal and state courts in the United States political system is to settle disputes among contesting parties. Except in the most unusual circumstances, the various courts only act upon disputes brought to them by them by the contending parties. In this regard, the federal courts, and especially the Supreme Court, tend to be actors of the "last resort" in many intergovernmental disputes. Despite the latter limitation, the Supreme Court has been a major actor—perhaps only second to the Congress—in the evolution and shaping of the intergovernmental system. As advanced by David B. Walker in 1981 (1981):

> Any notions that the federal principle and intergovernmental relations are discrete and somehow disconnected, that the judges deal with the former but exert little impact on the latter, are swept aside by the Supreme Court's record of the past two decades. Moreover, the nearly complete demise of dual federalism and the concomitant tendency to thrust nearly every type of public policy question—large or small, paramount or puny—into the intergovernmental arena was heavily conditioned (if not in some areas actually shaped) by decisions of the Supreme Court. (135)

In regard to what we noted as *intragovernmental* relations, the Supreme Court has been involved in a number of disputes involving Congress and the president, or solely the president. For instance, the Supreme Court in a series of rulings declared that much of the early "New Deal" legislation passed by Congress and signed by President Franklin D. Roosevelt was unconstitutional. This resulted in the ill-fated "court packing" plan of Roosevelt in 1937, which was designed to result in a membership on the Court that was more sympathetic of the liberal policies of Roosevelt. Although Roosevelt lost his bid to add members to the Court, subsequent developments, including the retirement of some justices from the Court, resulted in a body that was sympathetic and ruled in favor of later New Deal policies. In 1951, the Court, in its ruling of *Youngstown Sheet & Tube Company v. Sawyer*, ruled that President Harry S. Truman had exceeded the bounds of his inherent powers when he ordered his Secretary of Commerce to seize a number of steel plants in the midst of a labor crisis in that industry. The Court, in 1974, in its ruling advanced in the case of *United States v. Nixon*, ordered President Richard M. Nixon to provide to the Court the so-called "Watergate Tapes," which hastened his resignation from office. In its decision, the Court stated that there is no absolute unqualified presidential immunity from the judicial process under all circumstances, especially in regard to criminal matters. Hence, in its ruling the Court underscored that the concept of "executive privilege," which Nixon had resorted to for not turning the Watergate tapes over to the Court, should be interpreted in a limited manner. In addition, after President William Clinton had been impeached by the House of Representatives in 1998 for perjury and obstruction of justice in regard to the Monica Lewinsky affair, Supreme Court Chief Justice William H. Rehnquist presided over his trial in the Senate which eventually found him not guilty. In the extremely close and controversial presidential election in 2000 the Court, by a vote of 5 to 4, in its decision of *Bush v. Gore* (2000) ordered the termination of the recounting of ballots in Florida, effectively assuring the election of George W. Bush as President. More recently, the Court in the case of *Rasul v. Bush* (2004) held in a 6 to 3 decision that both citizens and non-citizens held in open-ended detention, in the United States and Guantanamo Bay, Cuba, are entitled to challenge their designation as "enemy combatants" before a federal judge or other "neutral decision maker."

In addition, throughout the years the Supreme Court has steadfastly asserted its independence, and that of the federal judicial system in general, of Congress. For instance, Chief Justice William H. Rehnquist, in his 2003 year-end report on the federal judiciary, sharply criticized Congress for passing a legislation that placed federal judges under special scrutiny for sentences that fall short of those called for by federal sentencing guidelines. The legislation, enacted in the spring of 1993 as a little noticed amendment to the popular Amber Alert child protection measure, asserted Rehnquist, "could appear to be an unwarranted and ill-considered effort to intimidate individual judges in the performance of their judicial duties" (Greenhouse 2004). A year later, in his 2004 year-end report on the federal judiciary, Rehnquist reiterated the need to safeguard the independence of federal judges from intrusive congressional oversight. In regard to Congress, Rehnquist noted: "There have been suggestions to impeach federal judges who issue decisions regarded by some as out of the mainstream. And there were several bills introduced in the last Congress that would limit the jurisdiction of the federal courts to decide constitutional challenges to certain kinds of governmental action" (Greenhouse 2005a, 32). In his report, Rehnquist made oblique reference to calls in Congress to deprive the federal courts of jurisdiction to hear challenges to the phrase "under God" in the Pledge of Allegiance, to the display of the Ten Commandments on government property, and to the Defense of Marriage Act. In his report, Rehnquist noted that it had been clear since early in the country's history that "a judge's *judicial* (emphasis that of the report) acts may not serve as a basis for impeachment." And, further he noted: "Any other rule would destroy judicial independence since judges would be concerned about inflaming any group that might be able to muster the votes in Congress to impeach and convict them" (Greenhouse 2005a, 32).

As Charles Wise (1998) has noted: "Throughout history, the courts have played a key role in determining the nature of the intergovernmental system in the United States. In particular, the Federal Courts have been the central arbiter in deciding between assertions of national authority and state claims to protection from federal encroachment." Further, "The Courts have been asked time and again to choose between Constitutional commands supporting the national government on the one hand and commands supporting state and local governments on the other" (95).

Through its various rulings, the Supreme Court, functioning as a sort of "referee" or "umpire," has played a major role in shaping the changing nature of our system of federalism and intergovernmental relations. As noted by Joseph F. Zimmerman (2001), a number of early Supreme Court decisions upheld and served to frame the concept of dual federalism: "A 1793 decision—*Chisholm v. Georgia*—suggested the existence of a dual federal system: The United States is sovereign as to all the powers of government actually surrendered; each State in the Union is sovereign, as to all the powers reserved." In 1819, Chief Justice John Marshall argued that Congress "is acknowledged by all to be one of enumerated powers. The principle, that it can exercise only the powers granted to it, would seem too apparent to have required to be enforced by all those arguments which its enlightened friends . . . found it necessary to urge." Zimmerman adds: "Chief Justice Roger B. Taney in 1859 declared 'the powers of the general government, and of the States, although both exist and are exercised within the same territorial limits, are very separate and distinct sovereignties acting separately and independently of each other, within their respective spheres'" (17).

Although in practice dual federalism over time became the victim of other variants of federalism,[5] the Court continued to make reference to the concept of dual federalism in a number of its rulings in the past three decades. For example, in the case of the *National League of Cities v. Usery* (1976) the Court, by a vote of 5–4, declared invalid amendments to the Fair Labor Standards Act applying minimum wage and overtime pay provisions to nonsupervisory employees of state and local governments on the ground that these amendments violated the tenth amendment and represented a threat to the "separate and independent existence" of these governments. However, it should be noted that this decision of the Court was overturned in the case of *Garcia v. San Antonio Metropolitan Transit Authority* (1985). In addition, in 1991, Justice Sandra Day O'Connor in the case of *Gregory v. Ashcroft*, in which the Court upheld the provision of the Constitution of the State of Missouri to require state judges to retire at the age of seventy, noted: "As every school child learns, our Constitution establishes a system of dual sovereignty between the States and the Federal Government." As Wise (1998) has perceptively advanced, in a series of cases involving a range of subject matters, the Court in *New York v. United States* (1992), *United States v. Alfonso Lopez, Jr.* (1995), *Seminole Tribe of Florida v. Florida* (1996), *Printz v. United States* (1997), and *City of Boerne v. P.F. Flores and United States* (1997) stressed the importance of federalism, the limits of national power, and the integrity of the states. As Wise noted: "In so doing so, the Court seems to be also reasserting its position as the protector of federalism and as the arbiter of the division of power between national and state governments" (1998, 98). In addition, continuing to rule in favor of an enhanced position of the states in the federal system, the Court in its decision of *United States v. Morrison* (2000) struck down a central portion of the Violence Against Women Act and in *Alabama v. Garrett* (2001) provided the states with immunity from suits by its employees under the Americans With Disabilities Act.

However, in a series of decisions commencing in 2003, the Court, once again, began asserting the primacy of the federal government in the intergovernmental system, at the expense of the states. In its ruling of *Nevada v. Hills* (2003) the Court upheld the right of state employees to sue under the Family and Medical Leave Act; in its decision of *Tennessee v. Lane* (2004) the Court upheld the application of the Americans With Disabilities Act to courthouse employees; and, in its ruling of *Gonzales v. Raich* (2005) the Court upheld the power of Congress to ban and prosecute the possession and use of marijuana for medical purposes, even in those states which permitted it (Greenhouse 2005b). More recently, the Court, in the case of *GDF Realty Investment v. Norton* (2005), by refusing to hear a challenge to the federal Endangered Species Act, upheld its constitutional status (Greenhouse 2005c).

Since the beginning of the nation, as Elazar has emphasized (1982), the various governments in the federal system have cooperated with each other to develop common policies and programs. However, it was not until the late 1930s that the Supreme Court, in a series of rulings, granted its *imprimatur* to the concept of cooperative federalism, which Elazar (1962) defined "to be the opposite of dual federalism which implies a division of functions between governments as well as a division of governmental structures. Although the theory of cooperative federalism assumes a division of structures, it accepts a system of sharing that ranges from formal federal-state agreements covering specific programs to informal contacts on a regular basis for the sharing of information and expertise" (305) For instance, in its ruling of *West Coast Hotel Company v. Parrish*, in 1937, the Court, by a narrow margin, upheld the validity of a State of Washington minimum wage law. On the same day, the Court, in the case of *Virginian Railway v. System Federation No. 40*, upheld the constitutionality of the Railway Labor Act, mandating that employers must bargain exclusively with a union selected by a majority of its employees. In regard to the steel industry, the Court, two weeks later, advanced a similar ruling in the case of *National Labor Relations Board v. Jones & Laughlin Steel Corporation*. The following year, in 1938, the Court, in *United States v. Carolene Products Company*, ruled constitutional the statutory regulation of commercial transactions (Zimmerman 1992, 92–93). As Zimmerman has noted: "Between 1939 and 1944, the Court rejected challenges to congressional laws fixing the price of milk and coal, minimum wage provisions of the Fair Labor Standards Act, and general price and rent controls" (93). These various rulings by the Court established the firm legal foundation for cooperative federalism.

From 1953 to 1968, the Supreme Court, known as the "Warren Court" because of its leadership under Chief Justice Earl Warren, issued a series of rulings in favor of a strongly "activist" cooperative and creative federalism. As more than a few scholars have advanced, over time this form of cooperative federalism evolved into a form of "coercive federalism." In terms of the political process, in the case of *Baker v. Carr*

(1962), involving state legislative reapportionment, the Supreme Court held that the malapportionment of legislative districts in the lower house of the Tennessee state legislature was not a "political question" beyond the Supreme Court's purview. Furthermore, it concluded that "malapportionment districts," containing an unequal number of residents, violated the equal protection clause of the fourteenth amendment and ordered the Tennessee legislature to redraw the district boundaries, in order that each district contained approximately the same number of citizens. The *Baker v. Carr* ruling ushered in a series of rulings whereby the Court eventually held that all local, state, and federal legislative districts, except, of course, the United States Senate, had to conform to the doctrine of one person, one vote, and that similar districts had to contain approximately the same number of citizens.

The "equal protection" clause in the fourteenth amendment was also utilized as the basis by the Supreme Court, led by Warren, for advancing the civil rights of African Americans. For instance, in an landmark case, the Supreme Court, in the case of *Brown v. Board of Education* (1954), ruled that the practice of segregating children on the basis of race in the public schools was inherently unconstitutional. In addition, the Court, again resorting to the equal protection clause, ruled invalid the discriminatory provision of public services in the case of *Hawkins v. Town of Shaw* (1971). In this instance, the town of Shaw, Mississippi, had clearly discriminated in the provision of public services for its African American and white residents; for example, while the streets in African American neighborhoods of the community were unpaved, unlighted, and had no curbs, sidewalks, or drains, these infrastructure improvements and public services were uniformly provided in white neighborhoods. To remedy this discrepancy, a federal Circuit of Appeals ordered the town to develop and submit a plan, for court approval, aimed at equalizing services for African American and white residents. As the previous would infer, the action of the Circuit Court of Appeals was upheld by the Supreme Court.

The various rulings of the Warren Court had a major impact upon the expansion of the rights of criminals. Repudiating the Supreme Court's 1937 decision in *Palko v. Connecticut*, in which it specifically held that the fourteenth amendment did not incorporate against the states certain guarantees contained in the first eight amendments to the United States Constitution, the Supreme Court, in *Mallory v. Hogan* (1964), embarked upon in a series of rulings a selective incorporation of various criminal provisions of the Bill of Rights into the fourteenth amendment. Undoubtedly, the most notable and wide-sweeping of these rulings involved the case of *Miranda v. Arizona* (1966), in which the Supreme Court advanced that, as noted by Zimmerman (1992): "A prosecutor may not use a statement obtained from police questioning of a person in custody as evidence unless the person has been informed that he has the right not to answer questions, that any statement he makes may be used as evidence against him, and that he has the right to have an attorney present during interrogation." Also: "The person in custody may retain an attorney or have one appointed at government expense. Furthermore, a defendant who waived these rights may at any time reinvoke them" (94).

David B. Walker (1981) has nicely summarized the major impact of the Warren Court in the shaping of federalism and intergovernmental relations:

What emerges from the Warren Court's record of the sixties is a federal judiciary determined to end racial discrimination and segregation, to carry the protection of civil liberties to the outermost bounds of the individualistic ethic, to reform totally criminal-justice procedures, to afford new and controversial protections to the accused and to the convicted, and to establish an egalitarian standard for representation in all of the nation's deliberative bodies, save for the United States Senate. With this, the federal system was transformed. National judicial power was asserted in ways and by means never before contemplated or practiced. Frequently, the Court was ordering respondents, especially subnational governmental respondents to do something, rather than simply negating what was held to be unconstitutional. Throughout, the Fourteenth Amendment became a vehicle for revising the Constitution and for transforming the federal system. Not only the First Amendment but most of the procedural guarantees of the Bill of Rights were "absorbed" within it, and even new constitutional rights were found that could be brought within its orbit. The Warren Court, then, generally seemed to come down squarely on the side of progress for individual rights, even if these decisions were harmful to the principles of federalism. (136–37)

As Zimmerman (2001) has aptly stated: "The year 1965 was a turning point in the nature of the federal system. In that year, Congress decided that water quality throughout the United States must meet minimum national standards. Subsequently, Congress came to rely heavily on its preemption powers—total and partial—to foster implementation of national policies, and it enacted more than 250 preemption statutes" (22). And, in the vast majority of those instances where a preemption statute was the subject of dispute, the Supreme Court has ruled in their constitutional favor. Preemption statutes, along with the federal techniques of direct orders (mandates), cross-cutting requirements, and cross-over sanctions, have set the stage for "coercive federalism." These techniques of coercive federalism are defined and elaborated upon in the following chapter.

The Supreme Court, along with the lower federal district and circuit courts, are major and constant participants in the shaping of intergovernmental relations. A measure of the frequency and impact of the federal courts on the workings of the intergovernmental system was documented by a 1978 survey conducted by Deil Wright of 1,400 state administrative heads (1982, 179). Over one-third (37 percent) of the agency heads acknowledged that in the past five years federal court decisions had required their agency to significantly alter their administrative procedures and policies. Almost an equal number of respondents (36 percent) acknowledged that federal court decisions had forced the alteration of some of the existing programs or the initiation of new programs at their agency. These responses clearly indicate the extent, if not the depth, of federal court impact only on a single slice of intergovernmental relations—state administrative agency operations.

SUMMARY AND CONCLUSION

As Timothy Conlan (1998) has correctly pointed out, the national policy-making process is marked by fragmentation, involving the president and other members of the executive branch, Congress, and the Supreme Court. In addition to these formal governmental actors and structures, the intergovernmental lobbies, representing the array of states and other subnational units of government, play a continuous and important role in the fashioning and implementing of intergovernmental policies. Intergovernmental lobbies include those organizations such as the National Governors' Association, the National Conference on State Legislatures, and the U.S. Conference of Mayors, which broadly represent the general policy interests of states and localities in Washington, and interest groups such as the National Association of Housing and Redevelopment Officials, and the American Association of State Highway Engineers, which represent the specific interests of program and functional specialists. It was also that all of the states and the vast majority of large cities and counties have established lobbying offices in Washington.

Presidents, because of competing national and foreign policy demands and priorities, have been limited in the amount of energy and time that they have devoted to policies relating to federalism and intergovernmental relations. Nevertheless, presidents have made their "signature mark" on the intergovernmental system. Reflecting their preference for centralizing power in Washington, Democratic presidents have sallied forth with and are immediately associated with various types of "nationalizing" federalism, including Cooperative Federalism (Franklin D. Roosevelt), Creative Federalism (Lyndon B. Johnson), and Picket-Fence, or Bamboo, Federalism (Jimmy Carter). In contrast, Republican presidents, most notably Richard M. Nixon and Ronald Reagan, intent on devolving powers and responsibilities to the states and increasing their policy autonomy, have advanced and sought the implementation of several variants of the New Federalism. In somewhat of a political anomaly, Democratic President William J. Clinton adopted the Republican stance on intergovernmental relations by favoring an increased role for the states in the federal system, especially with regard to social welfare policies.

Congress plays three principal roles—facilitator, inhibitor, and initiator—in shaping federal-state-local relations. As a facilitator, Congress provides direct and indirect financial assistance to the states and localities; as an inhibitor, Congress employs its preemption powers to nullify state regulatory laws and administrative rules and to prohibit the future enactment or such laws; and as an initiator, Congress assumes a leadership role by the enactment of partial preemption statues establishing minimum national programmatic standards. Because of the decentralized nature of the American party system and the character of the electoral system, members of Congress are particularly sensitive to the demands of the intergovernmental lobbies and constituency pressures.

As noted by such scholars as Harold Seidman (1975) and Hugh Heclo (1977), policy-making in Washington is largely carried out by, or is the function of, various policy subgovernments. Such subgovernments consist of political and career executives, appropriate members of Congress, and representatives of interest groups who collectively fashion public policy. These subgovernments constitute a "benefit coalition," as noted by Thomas Anton (1989), which seeks to protect and expand its policy accomplishments and privileges.

Functioning as a sort of "referee" or "umpire" of the intergovernmental system, the Supreme Court, along with the various federal circuit and district courts, has played a major role in sanctioning the evolving and changing character of our federal system of government. The Supreme Court, through a series of decisions, hastened the demise of Dual Federalism in the late 1930s and bestowed its legitimacy on President Franklin D. Roosevelt's Cooperative Federalism. Commencing with the tenure of the Warren Court (1953–68), the Supreme Court has generally, in its decisions, began practicing a more aggressive form of Cooperative Federalism, which scholars have labeled Coercive Federalism, resulting in less policy autonomy for the states and localities.

REFERENCES

Aberbach, Joel and Bert Rockman. 2000. *In the Web of Politics: Three Decades of the U.S. Federal Executive.* Washington, DC: Brookings Institution Press.

Anderson, Totton J. 1965. Pressure Groups and Intergovernmental Relations. *The Annals of the American Academy of Political and Social Science.* 359 (May), 116–26.

Anton, Thomas. 1989. *American Federalism and Public Policy.* New York: Random House.

Beer, Samuel H. 1977. Political Overload and Federalism. *Polity.* 10 (Fall), 5–17.

Bentley, Arthur F. 1908. *The Process of Government: A Study of Social Pressures.* Chicago: University of Chicago Press.

Choper, Jesse H. 1980. *Judicial Review and the National Policy Process.* Chicago: University of Chicago Press.

Clark, Jane Perry. 1938. *The Rise of a New Federalism: Federal-State Cooperation in the United States.* New York: Columbia University Press.

Conlan, Timothy. 1998. *From New Federalism to Devolution: Twenty-five Years of Intergovernmental Reform.* Washington, DC: Brookings Institution Press.

Elazar, Daniel J. 1984. *American Federalism: A View from the States.* 3d ed. New York: Harper & Row.

———. 1962. *The American Partnership: Intergovernmental Cooperation in the Nineteenth-Century United States.* Chicago: University of Chicago Press.

Fenno, Richard F. 1978. *Home Style: House Members in Their Districts.* Boston: Little, Brown.

Freudenheim, Milt. 2004, September 25. Federal Health Plans to Include One That Meets Catholic Tenets. *New York Times.* A1, B3.

Graves, W. Brooke. 1964. *American Intergovernmental Relations: Their Origins, Historical Development, and Current Status.* New York: Charles Scribner's Sons.

Greenhouse, Linda. 2004, January 1. Chief Justice Attacks a Law as Infringing on Judges. *New York Times.* A10.

———. 2005a, January 1. Rehnquist Resumes His Call for Judicial Independence. *New York Times.* 44.

———. 2005b, June 12. The Rehnquist Court and Its Imperiled State's Rights Legacy. *New York Times.* WK3.

———. 2005c, June 17. States Case Challenging Species Act Rebuffed. *New York Times.* A17.

Grodzins, Morton. 1966. *The American System,* ed. Daniel J. Elazar. Chicago: Rand McNally.

Haider, Donald. 1974. *When Governments Come to Washington.* New York: Macmillan.

Hall, William K. 1989. *The New Institutions of Federalism.* New York: Peter Lang.

Hardin, Peter. 2005, March 21. Deal-Making Wizards Prove Worth. *Richmond Times-Dispatch.* a1, a9.

Heclo, Hugh. 1977. *A Government of Strangers: Executive Politics in Washington.* Washington, DC: The Brookings Institution.

Hinckley, Barbara. 1988. *Stability and Change in Congress.* 4th ed. New York: Harper & Row.

Hoff, Joan. 2004. Re-evaluating Richard Nixon: His Domestic Achievements. *Nixon Era.com Library.* November 5, 2004. http://www.nixonera.com/library/domestic.asp.

Huitt, Ralph K. 1975. White House Channels to the Hill. In Harvey C. Mansfield, Sr., ed., *Congress Against the President.* New York: Praeger.

Jones, Charles O. 1999. *Separate but Equal Branches: Congress and the Presidency.* 2d ed. New York: Chatham House.

Keefe, William J. 1980. *Congress and the American People.* Englewood Cliffs, NJ: Prentice Hall.

Kincaid, John. 1990. From Cooperative to Coercive Federalism. *Annals of the American Academy of Political and Social Science.* 509 (May), 139–52.

Latham, Earl. 1952. *The Group Basis of Politics: A Study in Basing-Point Legislation.* Ithaca, NY: Cornell University Press.

Mann, Thomas E. and Raymond E. Wolfinger. 1980. Candidates and Parties in Congressional Elections. *American Political Science Review.* 74 (September), 617–32.

McConnell, Grant. 1966. *Private Power and American Democracy.* New York: Alfred A. Knopf.

Polsby, Nelson W. 1976. *Congress and the Presidency.* 3d ed. Englewood Cliffs, NJ: Prentice-Hall.

Price, David E. 1978. Policymaking in Congressional Committees: The Impact of Environmental Factors. *American Political Science Review.* 72 (June), 548–74.

Reed, B. J. 1983. The Changing Role of Local Advocacy in National Politics. *Journal of Urban Affairs.* 5 (Fall), 287–98.

Rohde, David W. and Kenneth A. Shepsle. 1973. Democratic Committee Assignments in the House of Representatives: Strategic Aspects of a Social Choice Process. *American Political Science Review.* 67 (September), 889–905.

Schattschneider, E. E. 1960. *The Semi-Sovereign People.* New York: Holt, Rinehart, and Winston.

Seidman, Harold. 1975. *Politics, Position, and Power.* London: Oxford University Press.

Teaford, Jon C. 2002. *The Rise of the States: Evolution of American State Government.* Baltimore: The Johns Hopkins University Press.

Truman, David B. 1951. *The Governmental Process: Political Interests and Public Opinion.* New York: Alfred A. Knopf.

Walker, David B. 1981. *Toward a Functioning Federalism.* Boston: Little, Brown.

Walker, Jack. 1969. The Diffusion of Innovation Among the American States. *American Political Science Review.* 63 (September), 880–99.

Wallin, Bruce A. 1998. *From Revenue Sharing to Deficit Sharing: General Revenue Sharing and Cities.* Washington, DC: Georgetown University Press.

Walters, Jonathan. 1994. Reinventing the Federal System. *Governing.* 7 (June), 49–53.

Wise, Charles. 1998. Judicial Federalism: The Resurgence of the Supreme Court's Role in the Protection of State Sovereignty. *Public Administration Review.* 58 (March/April), 95–98.

Zimmerman, Joseph F. 1992. *Contemporary American Federalism: The Growth of National Power.* Westport, CT: Praeger.

———. 2001. National-State Relations: Cooperative Federalism in the Twentieth Century. *Publius.* 31 (Spring), 15–30.

• 6 •

REGULATION IN THE
INTERGOVERNMENTAL SYSTEM

Yet success [in terms of reform objectives] sowed seeds of destruction for cooperative federalism because it placed the senior partner in a position to become the commanding partner, and it vindicated reform arguments that policy should take priority over structure and that issues of federalism should be decided by the national political process rather than by judicial readings of the federal Constitution.

—John Kincaid, "From Cooperative to
Coercive Federalism" (1990)

As Joseph F. Zimmerman (2001) has aptly written: "The year 1965 was a turning point in the nature of the federal system. In that year, Congress decided that water quality throughout the United States must meet minimum national standards. Subsequently, Congress came to rely heavily on its preemption powers—total and partial—to foster implementation of national policies, and it enacted more than 250 preemption statutes" (22). And, as John Kincaid (1990) has advanced: "Overall, federalism became less cooperative during the 1970s and 1980s. This change is demonstrated by one statistic: the number of federal preemptions more than doubled after 1969" (139). Preemption statutes, along with the federal techniques of direct orders (mandates), cross-cutting requirements, and cross-over sanctions, has set the stage for "coercive federalism." We should note that in a multiple number of decisions, bearing upon the use of these federal regulatory techniques, the U.S. Supreme Court has usually provided judicial sanctimony for the onward march of coercive federalism, or what some dubbed "regulatory federalism" (Dubnick and Gitelson 1979, 30).

This chapter commences with an overview, definition, and discussion of the various federal statutory regulatory techniques utilized by the federal government— direct orders (mandates), cross-cutting requirements, cross-over sanctions, and partial preemptions—to structure state and local operating routines and public policies.

Attention is then directed to examples of federal judicial preemption. This material is followed by an examination of the various, and somewhat common, state mandates imposed upon their political subdivisions. The concluding portion of the chapter centers on the degree to which federal and state regulation has served to alter somewhat severely the character of the intergovernmental system, resulting in the rise of coercive federalism.

OVERVIEW

Table 6.1 provides a typology of the various regulatory techniques—direct orders (mandates), cross-cutting requirements, cross-over sanctions, and partial preemptions —utilized by the federal government to structure state and local operating routines and public policies. In contrast to the various requirements that are usually attached to federal grants-in-aid programs, which may be viewed as part of a contractual agreement between two levels of government, federal regulatory techniques are mandatory in nature and may not be disregarded by a state or local government without incurring some sort of penalty. In addition to these regulatory techniques, the federal government, in a number of instances, has resorted to the use of a total preemption, usurping complete responsibility for a policy area. Prior to 1961 the federal government imposed relatively few regulations upon the state and local governments. Figure 6.1 sets forth the growth of regulatory federalism on the basis of enactments added per decade, 1931–90, which underscores the large enactment by Congress of regulatory techniques in the period from 1971 to 1990.

TABLE 6.1. A Typology of Intergovernmental Regulatory Programs

Program Type	Description	Major Policy Areas Employed
Direct orders	Mandate state or local actions under the threat of criminal or civil penalties	Public employment, environmental protection
Cross-cutting regulations	Applies to all or many federal assistance programs	Nondiscrimination, environmental protection, public employment, assistance management
Cross-over sanctions	Threaten the termination or reduction of aid provided under one or more specified programs unless requirements of another program are satisfied	Highway safety and beautification, environmental protection, health planning, handicapped education
Partial preemptions	Establish federal standards, but delegate administration to states if they adopt standards equivalent to the national ones	Environmental protection, natural resources, occupational safety and health, meat and poultry inspection

Source: U.S. Advisory Commission on Intergovernmental Relations 1984, p. 8.

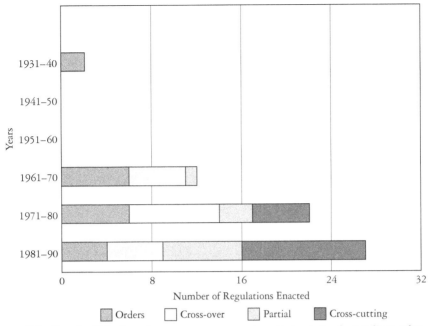

FIGURE 6.1. Growth of federal regulatory enactments—number added each decade. For direct orders, crossover sanctions, partial preemptions, and cross-cutting regulations. The total adds up to 63 by 1990. *Source: Conlan and Beam 1992.*

MANDATES

A *direct order (mandate)* is a federal regulation that must be complied with by a subnational government under the threat of a criminal or civil sanction. Presently, there are somewhat more than 200 federal mandates involving 170 federal laws, involving a broad array of state and local activities. A prominent example is the Equal Employment Opportunity Act of 1972, forbidding employee job discrimination by state and local governments on the basis of race, color, religion, sex, or national origin. This statute extended to state and local governments the requirements previously imposed on private employers commencing in 1964. In a like fashion, the Marine Protection Research and Boundary Act Amendments of 1977 prohibits cities from disposing sludge through ocean dumping.

Prior to the 1960s there were relatively few federal mandates imposed upon the state and local governments. Reflective of this, W. Brooke Graves in his seminal work *American Intergovernmental Relations: Their Origins, Historical Development, and Current Status* (1964), provides no discussion of federal mandates. However, as Paul L. Posner points out in his perceptive discourse *The Politics of Unfunded Mandates: Whither Federalism?* (1998): "[I]n the 1970s and 1980s, mandates came to be embraced by both [the Democratic and Republican] parties as an efficient tool to achieve national objectives that leaders felt compelled to promote. The shift from voluntaristic to coercive tools of federal action marked a significant departure in our federal system" (211).

Posner cites a number of important developments, commencing in the 1960s, that served to spur the enactment of federal mandates (211–15). First, he notes the emergence of a new style of policy-making at the federal level, especially in Congress. Congressional policy-making, freed to some degree from the past routines of incrementalism, became more marked by the quest for nonincremental policy reforms. Members of Congress became entrepreneurs in search of new policy ideas and profiles designed to gain media attention and political support. Echoing this sentiment, John Kincaid (1990) has advanced: "Media nationalization has focused attention on Washington and also has fostered federal activism because officials must appear to be doing something if they are to attract the media and justify their existence" (149). More often than not, these policy initiatives involved functions traditionally performed by state and local governments, such as education or law enforcement, which, hence, became susceptible to federal mandate action.

Second, Posner underscores that the federal grant system, and those interests that benefited from it, served to stimulate the enactment of mandates: "[T]he grant program served to strengthen the beneficiary coalitions and generate support from state and local bureaucracies and leaders as well. As these programs took root at the state and local level, the nation's tolerance eroded for differences among states' approaches and gaps in services to various groups, while the legitimacy of the federal role took hold." Posner adds: "Accordingly, mandates came to be seen as a logical and appropriate tool to promote greater national uniformity" (213).[1]

Third, as this might well suggest, Posner reports that the increasing political strength of the beneficiary coalitions ensured their success in convincing policy-makers to adopt more coercive policy tools such as mandates. Rather remarkably, the coalition beneficiaries realized substantial success in the adoption of additional federal mandates, along with the approval of substantial federal funds to underwrite state and local compliance, during the 1980s and early 1990s when the federal budget deficits reached peacetime highs (213).

The rapid adoption of federal mandates especially in the 1980s and early 1990s, notes Posner, was also due to the "neutralization or weakness" of actors and constraints traditionally opposed to the expansion of federal power. In particular, the Supreme Court commencing in the 1930s provided the rationale for an expanded federal role in domestic policy and, until the 1990s, generally ruled that state and local governments had to depend upon the political process to protect their jurisdictional prerogatives (215). In addition, Republicans, who have generally adhered to federalism principles, because of various political pressures and interests were forced to adopt the stance of somewhat "reluctant mandators," except in those instances where mandates were in congruence with their party objectives, such as moral policy, business preemption, and welfare (215).

Fourth, as advanced by Posner, the enactment of additional federal mandates during the last four decades was caused, on the one hand, by the political division among state and local officials and their often inability to marshal a consensus to preclude the adoption of a mandate (216). In a reverse sort of fashion, the adoption of additional mandates was assured by the fact that state and local officials discerned it to be in their interest to support the enactment of a mandate. As Posner reports: "Mandates also served a political function for state and local officials in gaining leverage—in policy struggles within their own governments, as well as in competition with other states or localities for economic development. Within their own governments, state and local officials found mandates to be a useful tool to accomplish their own policy agendas in the face of recalcitrant local political actors." (218)

Summarizing his findings, Posner concludes:

> The intergovernmental environment itself, then, came to be an important factor prompting policies' federal adoption. In an increasingly national political system, diversity among states' policies tends to be viewed, not as a cause for celebration of the strengths of our federal system, but as a reason for alarm and a rationale for centralizing policy mandates or preemptions. An infrastructure of nationalized media, interest groups, and entrepreneurial national and state political leaders combines to accelerate the diffusion and nationalization of state policy innovations in a process that has probably accelerated in recent years. (219)

Federal mandates have drawn the ire of many state and local officials. As advanced by a *New York Times* editorial published in 1980:

> Local governments are feeling put upon by Washington. Each new day seems to bring some new directive from Congress, the courts, or the bureaucrats: cities must make public buildings accessible to the handicapped, states must extend unemployment compensation to municipal and county workers, and on and on. The mandates are piling up so fast that liberal governors and mayors are enrolling in a cause once pressed only by arch-conservatives ("Fighting Federal Mandates" 1980, 20).

In a widely noted published paper, Edward I. Koch (1980), the former mayor of New York City, noted that while he was often in sympathy with the broad policy objectives of mandates, those who write them often seem to lack a sense of comprehension of the cumulative impact of mandates upon a single city, or the nation. He noted, for instance, that complying with federal (and state) mandates in New York City from 1980 through 1984 would cost $711 million in capital expenditures, $6.25 billion in money from the city's current expense budget, and $1.66 billion in lost revenue. Federal "mandate mandarins," he charged, have hung a "mandate millstone" around the necks of the nation's cities (42). The ire of state and local officials toward federal mandates has been reinforced by the often unwillingness of the federal government to provide sufficient funds to the states and localities for the implementation of mandates (Rivlin 1992, 107).

In a perceptive paper published some years ago, David R. Beam (1981) noted seven major problems associated with federal mandates (13–17). First, he reported that the preeminent problem of mandates is that they are usually very costly to implement and that state and local officials often resent being forced to pay at least part, if not all, of the costs of their implementation. Second, federal mandates have often proved to be inflexible, with federal officials prescribing rigid policies and performance standards, regardless of varying circumstances. Beam noted that this was particularly true with regard to federal mandate requirements relating to bilingual language requirements. A third problem of federal mandates, advanced Beam, is that in some instances they are inefficient. He asserted, for instance, that the federal mandate requiring that the handicapped be guaranteed access to mass public transportation does not allow local transit officials to utilize varying modes of transit to realize this objective, which might prove to be more efficient. Fourth, federal mandates have often been inconsistent, and, as Beam noted, "As a consequence, state and local officials have been faced with a confusing array of sometimes conflicting goals, standards, procedures and timetables." Further, quoting from a study completed by the U.S. Advisory Commission on Intergovernmental Relations, he concludes: "Serious problems of coordination and effective compliance clearly remain unsolved" (15). Further, federal mandates have often been marked by a quality of intrusiveness, requiring local officials to adhere to detailed organizational and procedural standards. State and local governments feel that they should be given the right when implementing a federal mandate to design their own organizational and procedural standards. Sixth, although perhaps well intended, many outside of government have charged that federal mandates have sometimes been ineffective in advancing social goals. Beam notes: "These critics doubt that the mounting paperwork and red tape, the mandated expenditures, and the federal intrusions into local decision making have reaped commensurate benefits in the quality of human life" (16). And, finally, as Beam advances, federal mandates make for a serious problem of unaccountability in our democratic process:

> [T]he complex chain of events from of events from enactment, to administrative interpretation, to adjudication, through final implementation at the state and local level (or both) diffuses policy responsibility. In one too-common scenario, Congressmen blame bureaucrats for overzealous interpretations of legislative intent; bureaucrats blame Congress for either over specificity or a lack of adequate guidance; state and local officials charge that their hands are tied by national requirements, and Washington points a finger at them for improper performance. Everyone, as often as not, blames the courts, while judges reply that they were only reading the law. (17)

In a parallel fashion, Zimmerman (1981) has advanced:

> [T]he relationship between the levels of government has become so complex and intertwined . . . that the average citizen is unable to comprehend the system or to determine who is responsible for failure to achieve goals. The lack of citizen understanding and the failure of the system to achieve Congressionally mandated goals suggests that consideration should be given to the relative advantages of alternative methods of achieving national goals. (98)

In response to the political controversy generated by federal mandates, Congress passed in 1995, although it was bitterly opposed by Democrats, the Unfunded Mandates Reform Act (PL 104–4) (Broder 1995). This bill provided that Congress was required to define the costs and consequences of mandates, but it did not prohibit Congress from imposing new mandates. The act also directed ACIR "to investigate and review the role of federal mandates in intergovernmental relations and to make recommendations to the President and Congress as to how the federal government should relate to state, local, and tribal governments." In response to the validity of its charge, the ACIR (1995) noted: "[T]he Washington tendency has been to treat as a national issue any problem that is emotional, hot, and highly visible. Often, this has meant passing a federal law that imposes costs and requirements on state and local governments without their consent and without regard for their ability to comply." And, further: "Such actions, even though they may have broad public support, are damaging to intergovernmental comity. The challenge facing the federal government is to exercise power to resolve national needs while, at the same time, honoring state and local rights to govern their own affairs and set their own budget priorities" (3).

ACIR, in conducting its study, was guided by the following concerns and issues involving mandates:

1. Does the national purpose justify federal intrusion in state or local affairs?
2. Are the costs of implementing a mandate appropriately shared among governments?
3. Is maximum flexibility given to the state and local governments in implementing a mandate?
4. Are there changes that can be made in a mandate to relieve intergovernmental tensions, while maintaining a commitment to national goals? (3)

In seeking information about whether a particular mandate satisfied the criteria of these concerns, ACIR solicited information in 1995 from state and local governments, federal agencies, and the public. Assistance was also sought from the National Governors' Association, the National Rural Development Partnership, and officials attending national and state association meetings and through a general appeal made in the magazines and newsletters of national and state groups representing state and local governments (4).

In compiling its report, ACIR was guided by the following criteria: (1) Does a mandate require state or local governments to expend substantial amounts of their own resources without regard for state and local priorities? (2) Does a mandate abridge the historic powers of state and local governments without a clear showing of national need? (3) Does a mandate impose requirements that are difficult or impossible for state and local governments to implement? (4) Are there mandates which are the subject of widespread objections by state and local officials (5)?

The ACIR acknowledged in its report that some federal mandates, such as those pertaining to civil rights, are necessary because they serve a national interest. Similarly, mandates pertaining to clean air and water are reasonable because these policies deal with problems that transcend state lines. On the other hand, ACIR noted the following common issues concerning federal mandates: (1) often detailed procedural requirements, which do not allow state and local governments to meet national goals in ways that best fit their needs and resources; (2) a lack of federal concern about state and local mandate costs; (3) the federal failure to recognize that state and local governments are accountable to the voters for their actions; (4) lawsuits by individuals against state and local governments to enforce federal mandates; (5) the inability of very small governments to meet mandate standards and timetables; and (6) the lack of a coordinated federal policy, with no federal agency empowered to make binding decisions about a mandate's requirements (6–8).

In a more specific sense, ACIR recommended that some federal mandates be terminated or modified to accommodate budgetary and administrative constraints on state and local government or revised to provide greater flexibility in implementation procedures and more participation by state and local governments in the development of mandate policies. ACIR recommended repealing the provisions in the following laws that extend coverage to state and local governments:

Fair Labor Standards Act
Family and Medical Leave Act
Occupational Safety and Health Act
Drug and Alcohol Testing of Commercial Drivers
Metric Conversion for Plans and Specifications
Medicaid: Boren Amendment
Required Use of Recycled Crumb Rubber (8–9)

Second, ACIR recommended that the following mandates, although justified in terms of the national interest, be modified to accommodate the budgetary and administrative constraints on state and local governments:

The Clean Water Act
Individuals with Disabilities Education Act
Americans with Disabilities Act (9)

And, third, the ACIR recommended that the following mandates be revised to provide greater flexibility and increased consulation between the various levels of government:

The Safe Drinking Water Act
Endangered Species Act
Davis-Bacon Related Acts (9)

Notwithstanding the passage of the Unfunded Mandates Reform Act (UMRA), Posner found a year after its enactment that it did not reduce the number of federal mandates, but made them less extensive and more narrowly written (Posner 1997, 53–71), Subsequently, some public officials have praised the effect of UMRA, declaring that it has served to fundamentally change the relationship between Washington and other levels of government. On the other hand, other officials, while lauding the UMRA, have noted that the Act has not effectively served to limit the continued intrusion of the federal government into the affairs of the state and local governments. These officials have noted that commencing at the beginning of the present century, the Bush Administration and the Congress are of the persuasion that the states and localities should be required to bear more functional and monetary responsibilities, have enacted into law a host of additional costly federal mandates, not accompanied by sufficient funding, particularly in the areas of transportation, health care, environment homeland security, public education, and election laws (Broder 2005).

CROSS-CUTTING REQUIREMENTS

Cross-cutting requirements are imposed upon grants across the board to advance various national and economic broad policy goals. Perhaps the most salient of these cross-cutting requirements is found in Title VI of the Civil Rights Act of 1964, which holds that: "No person in the United States shall, on the ground of race, color, or national origin, be excluded from participation in, be denied the benefits of, or be subjected to discrimination under any program receiving Federal financial assistance." Since 1964, cross-cutting requirements have been enacted for the protection of other disadvantaged groups, including the handicapped, elderly, and women, the latter especially in regard to education programs. There are more than sixty cross-cutting requirements that concern such matters as the environment, historic preservation, contact wage rates, access to government information, the care of experimental animals, and the treatment of human research projects. As David R. Beam (1981) has noted: "Crosscutting requirements have a pervasive impact because they apply 'horizontally' to all or most federal agencies and their assistance programs" (11).

CROSS-OVER SANCTIONS

Cross-over sanctions rely upon the congressional power of the purse and permit federal fiscal sanctions in one program area or activity to negatively impact another state and local program. Hence, the failure of a state or local government to comply with the requirements of one program can result in a reduction or termination of federal funds for another program; thus, the penalty "crosses over."

A prominent example of the use of cross-over sanctions by the federal government to achieve a policy goal involved the Highway Beautification Act of 1965. This act provided that Congress could withhold 10 per cent of a state's federal construction highway funds if it did not comply with newly expanded federal billboard requirements, designed to reduced the number of billboards situated along interstate highways. Despite the strong and bitter opposition of the outdoor advertising industry, by 1970 thirty-two states had enacted billboard control laws, while the remaining states following suit soon thereafter (ACIR 1984, 7). Another example involving the use of cross-over sanctions by the federal government is a 1984 act that required that the federal government reduce federal highway aid by up to 15 percent for any state that failed to adopt a minimum drinking age of twenty-one by 1987. In contrast, legislation proposed by Senator Hillary Clinton (D-NY) and Senator John W. Warner (R-VA) that would have required the federal government to reduce a state's highway funding by 2 to 4 percent if it failed to adopt a primary seatbelt law was defeated in the Senate in February 2004 (Hardin 2004, B4).

TOTAL PREEMPTION AND PARTIAL PREEMPTION

Over the past four decades, the federal government has promulgated an increasing number of preemption, partial preemption, and contingent preemption statutes. A study conducted by James B. Croy (1975) found that in the decade from 1964 to 1973 the federal government enacted forty-eight acts containing provisions preemptory in character (32–36). These preemptive statutes involved the following policy areas: health and safety, environmental protection and conservation, consumer protection, agricultural standards, civil rights, horse protection, and uniform time standards. Kincaid noted (1990) that more than 50 percent of the preemption statutes enacted since 1789 were enacted during two decades of the 1970s and 1980s (148). Notwithstanding his political stance of returning power to the states, President Reagan signed into law 106 preemption statutes (Zimmerman 1992, 67). Preemption statutes may be classified as total, partial, or contingent depending upon whether the Congress allows the states to exercise any regulatory power in the fields preempted. In addition to restraining the exercise of power by the states, a preemption statute may require that the state undertake a specific action or meet minimum relevant national standards.

Zimmerman reported (1992 58–60; 2005a 376) that the continued rise in the number of statutes is caused by seven major developments: (1) lobbying by industries, such as the motor vehicle industry, burdened with increasingly nonharmonious state regulatory policies; (2) influential leaders in Congress who sought higher political office and found it to their political advantage to support additional preemptions; (3) the failure of states to solve multistate problems like air and water pollution by means of interstate cooperation; (4) the perception of Congress that conditional grants-in-aid have failed to solve several critical problems, thus requiring an additional federal response; (5) effective lobbying by public interest groups, particularly those representing civil liberties and environmental issues; (6) the election of members of Congress lacking state and local government experience, and (7) the general failure of the states to enact harmonious regulatory policies.

The constitutional basis for the practice of *federal total preemption* is based upon the various provisions found in Article I, section 8, commonly known as (a) the taxing power, (b) commerce power, and (c) the necessary and proper clause. The Supreme Court also has often resorted to the supremacy clause, Article VI, section 2, in interpreting the wide-ranging preemptive powers of Congress. According to Zimmerman (1992, 63; 2005a 360), there are eighteen subtypes of complete preemption statutes, including those requiring state cooperation for their success. For instance, states have been stripped of their power to engage in the economic regulation of airline and bus companies. Nor may states establish a compulsory retirement age for their employees or regulate bankruptcies. Four total preemption statutes authorize states to enter into agreements with national agencies to perform inspections in accordance with national standards involving such matters as grain quality and weighing, hazardous and solid waste materials, and railroad safety. In several instances total preemption statutes require the states to enact statutes of a contingent nature. Thus a contingent preemption stature is applicable to a state or local government only if a specified condition(s) exists or the state fails to enact harmonious regulatory policies in a particular area by a stipulated date.

The *partial preemption* approach, which some early on dubbed the "substitution approach to federalism" (Thompson 1981, 240), removes some but not all of the political power in a regulatory area from the states and is of two general forms. The first form involves the Congress enacting a statute assuming complete responsibility for only a portion of a regulatory field. The second form is the product of Congress enacting a law and/or federal administrative agencies, as authorized by law, promulgating rules and regulations establishing national minimum standards and authorizing the states to exercise primary regulatory responsibility provided state standards are consistent with or as stringent as national standards and are enforced. Croy (1975) set forth the Water Quality Act of 1965 as an early example of the later, which he termed the "if then, if then" approach. The act was the first to establish a national policy for controlling pollution. While the statute allowed each state one year to set standards for its own interstate waters, the Secretary of Health, Education and Welfare was authorized to enforce federal standards in any state that failed to do so. As Croy noted, "[I]f a state does not issue regulations acceptable to the U.S. *then* a federal agency or department will do so, and if the state does not adopt and enforce these regulations, *then* the federal level of government will assume jurisdiction over that area" (11, emphasis added).

Zimmerman reported in 2005 that partial preemption statutes may be placed into the following eight categories: (1) minimum standards, (2) stricter state controls, (3) combined minimum standards and dual sovereignty, (4) regulatory authority transfer, (5) administrative rule preemption, (6) additional uses for a nationally controlled product, (7) franchise renewal preemption, and (8) reverse preemption (2005b, 360).[2] Some programs provide the states with an option not to participate, but if a state chooses not to do so, the national government then steps in and runs the program. A variation of this type of preemption is the mandatory partial preemption, in which the national government requires the state to act on peril of losing other funds but provides no funds to support state action. The Clean Air Act of 1990 is an example of mandatory partial preemption; the federal government set national air quality standards and required states to devise plans and pay for their implementation and enforcement.

FEDERAL PREEMPTION AND GOVERNORS

Many scholars of state government and politics have failed to note that a number of federal preemptive statutes provide various additional powers to the governors. We should note, however, that several of these preemptive statutes require action by the state legislature in order to become effective. These gubernatorial preemptive powers involve such policy areas as highways and transportation, environment, waste treatment, air and water, and motor fuel (Zimmerman 1992, 72–74).[3]

JUDICIAL PREEMPTION

Over the last four decades, the federal judiciary has been involved in various preemptive acts requiring the states and/or localities to adhere to certain policies. By and large, this preemptive action by the federal courts has been directed toward protecting the basic rights of citizens. The most salient example of this involved, following the seminal United States Supreme Court decision of *Brown* v. *Board of Education of Topeka, Kansas* (1953), the order of the Supreme Court to the states and localities to desegregate their public school systems racially. As Zimmerman (1990) points out, less well-known instances of judicial preemption involve court remedies concerning the implementation of a judicial receivership or mandating of local property tax increases (49–50). For instance, U.S. District Court Judge W. Arthur Garrity, in response to the crisis then plaguing the Boston public schools, assumed control of the Boston school system in 1974 and did not transfer control back to an elected school committee until 1985, with the provision that the school committee institute a number of reforms.[4] In 1987, U.S. District Court Judge Russell G. Clark ordered a significant increase of the property tax levy in Kansas City, Missouri, and imposed an income tax surcharge upon individuals working within the territorial boundaries of the Kansas City School District, in order to finance a racial desegregation program in the schools of the district. In addition, the Supreme Court, in 1976, ruled that the patronage dismissal of non- policy-making employees of the Cook County, Illinois, sheriff's department violated the guarantees of the of the first and fourteenth Amendments of the United States Constitution (Zimmerman 1990, 49–50).

PREEMPTION RELIEF

In the 1970s, state officials, although they did not adopt a stance of opposition to all mandates, were, in the main, critical of the use of the preemption mechanism by Congress. Indeed, many state officials described the enactment of preemptions as an instance of "federal supersession" (Croy 1975, 35). This sentiment is found in the following scholarly contribution published in 1974, authored by individuals prominently associated with the Council of State Governments:

> This is not to say that Congress is always wrong when it embarks on a preemption mission. But surely the gamut ranges beyond good sense and creditability when supersession becomes an indiscriminate habit. Regulation of everybody and everything is not necessarily the *Summum Bonum* of a legislative assembly, be it state or national. Legislative forbearance, like judicial restraint has its place in the body politic. Congress is often urged to supersede state law as a means of promoting uniform applications throughout the nation, and on occasion the need will be manifest. On the other hand, interstate cooperative devices have shown their ability to achieve necessary uniformity and coordination in many areas of public concern. A federal system of government, by definition, envisions finer intergovernmental tuning devices than a centric doctrine (Crihfield and Reeves 1974, 102).

Failing, in many instances, to prevent Congress from enacting various preemption statutes, state officials have turned to the strategy of seeking preemption relief from Congress. At base, this involves the states seeking additional funding from Congress to adequately implement mandates or, at maximum, involves the states seeking to strike from federal law all or part of a preemption statute. As Zimmerman (1992) has concluded: "Experience reveals that if the number of states petitioning for preemption relief is small—licensing new nuclear power plants is an example—the Congress may provide no relief. On the other hand, if all or a sizeable number of the States seek relief from a preemption statute or a preemption decision of the United States Supreme Court, the Congress will typically provide a degree of relief" (68). Such relief has resulted in the full or partial "rollback" of federal preemptions in the policy areas of nuclear waste, taxation, agriculture, banking, vessel source garbage, and age discrimination (68–69).

These four techniques—direct orders (mandates), cross-cutting requirements, cross-over sanctions, and total and partial preemption—are the major statutory tools utilized by the federal government for the regulation of states and localities. Sometimes the federal government has resorted to a combined use of regulatory techniques, such as in the instance of the 1970 Clean Air Act amendments. Basically, the act relies upon the technique of partial preemption to further federal policy goals; according to the legislation, states must prepare State Implementation Plans (SIPs) designed to control air pollution to satisfy federal air quality standards and must be approved by the EPA. However, if the EPA finds a SIP to be inadequate, it must disapprove the SIP. In the event that a state fails to make necessary revisions, the EPA is required to forward to the state an adequate SIP. However, the latter is not the only sanction imposed by the act, since section 176(a) prohibits both the EPA and the Department of Transportation from providing grant awards in any air quality region that has not attained primary ambient air quality standards and for which the state has failed to devise adequate transportation control plans. This, of course, represents a strong utilization of cross-over sanction technique. Furthermore, section 176(c) of the act prohibits any agency of the federal government from providing financial assistance to any activity that does not conform to a state SIP. This provision uses the cross-cutting requirement approach for strengthening SIP implementation (ACIR 1984, 7–10).

STATE MANDATES

States have imposed a wide array of mandates upon their local governments, which often reflect the need for minimum standards of service levels. Such mandates may apply to a single local government, all local governments, or a class of local governments; further, state mandates may involve the transfer of functional responsibilities from one local government to another. Local officials entertain little objection to the goals of many mandates; they may even welcome the political "cover" that mandates provide for the implementation of programs that are unpopular with some segments of their community, such as the establishment of low-income housing. Indeed, in some instances, local officials on their own volition are sometimes responsible for mandates, as in the case of Tennessee, in 1997, when county executives and county commissioners requested the state legislature to require that counties adopt certain uniform personnel policies. In addition, mandates are sometimes the result of "end runs" by local government employees, who succeed through state legislation in securing benefits that they could not gain through collective bargaining. For instance, some states require local governments to compensate police officers and firefighters with what some observers consider overly generous pension benefits (Berman 2003, 78). Zimmerman (1992) has nicely developed a typology of state mandates in which he categorized state mandates on local governments into the following types: due process, entitlement, environmental, equal treatment, ethical, good neighbor, informational, membership, personnel, record-keeping, structural, service level, and tax base (180–82).[5]

STATE MANDATE RELIEF

Localities have sought to gain some relief from state mandates, which they have been somewhat successful in achieving over the last three decades. As Berman (2003) has noted: "Over forty states have fiscal note requirements that require state agencies (in some places, commissions on intergovernmental relations) to estimate the costs that state laws or regulations will impose on localities" (79). Zimmerman (1992) reported that by 1994 half of the states would have constitutional and or statutory limitations on their ability to impose mandates on local governments. More precisely, fifteen states have constitutional provisions, fourteen states have statutory limitations, and four states had both. He noted that the most common forms of constitutional and statutory relief from state mandates are requirements for the states to (1) fund any new mandates or (2) reimburse local expenditures that result from the mandate. With regard to the latter, Pagano reported in 1990 that fourteen states require that local governments be reimbursed for the costs of state mandates, although the extent of the reimbursement varies by state. Half of the fourteen states require reimbursement by statute, the other half by the constitution (1990). The next most popular mandate relief provision is a constitutional option to allow the passage of mandates, but to allow local governments to approve or reject the mandate before it becomes legally binding. Also widely found is a statutory mandate relief provision that requires a new funding source for local governments before enabling the state to require a local action or service (Zimmerman 1994, 28). The various state mandatory relief provisions are set forth in Figure 6.2.

SUMMARY AND CONCLUSION

Responding to the socioeconomic changes in our society and the political pressures emanating from these changes, the federal government over the last four decades has imposed—through the techniques of direct orders (mandates), cross-cutting requirements, cross-over sanctions, and partial preemptions—a multitude of regulations. Since the turn of the present century, the Bush administration has issued a host of regulations pertaining to the health industry, environment, energy, worker-safety standards, and product-safety disclosure policies. By and large, these regulations have been warmly welcomed by business and industry leaders and greeted with disappointment by groups representing consumers, workers, auto and truck drivers,

State	Prohibit Unless Funded	Require Reimbursement	Local Government Must Approve	State Authorize New Funding Source	Two-Thirds Vote to Impose Mandates	Governor May Suspend Mandate	State Must Reimburse	Authorize New Local Funding Source	Prohibit Unless Funded	Delay Effective Date	Local Government Must Approve	General: Waivers/Appeals/ Fiscal Impact	Provides Specific Relief	Two-Thirds Vote of Legislature Required	Constitutional	Statutory
	Constitutional Relief					Statutory Relief									Total	
Alabama[1]			X												X	
Alaska[2]			X												X	
California		X													X	
Colorado			X						X						X	X
Connecticut										X						X
Florida	X			X	X										X	
Hawaii		X													X	
Illinois							X		X							X
Louisiana			X												X	
Maine	X	X			X		X								X	X
Massachusetts	X		X		X		X								X	X
Michigan	X	X													X	
Minnesota												X				X
Missouri	X	X													X	
Montana							X	X	X							X
Nevada							X	X								X
New Hampshire	X		X				X				X				X	X
New Mexico		X		X											X	
New York													X			X
Pennsylvania		X													X	
Rhode Island							X									X
South Carolina								X	X					X		X
South Dakota								X	X							X
Tennessee[3]	X														X	
Virginia						X						X				X
TOTALS	7	7	6	2	3	1	7	4	5	1	1	2	1	1	15	14

FIGURE 6.2. State mandate relief provisions, 1994. 1994 survey data collected by Joseph F. Zimmerman, State University of New York, Albany. [1]Alabama prohibits enforcement of a state law increasing expenditures or decreasing revenues in the current fiscal year, which ends on September 30, unless the law is approved by a governing body; [2]Alaska provides that special acts necessitating appropriations by local governments do not become effective unless ratified by the concerned voters in a referendum; [3]The Tennessee General Assembly is authorized to impose mandates on cities and counties only if the state shares the cost. *Source: U.S. Advisory Commission on Intergovernmental Relations 1994, p. 29.*

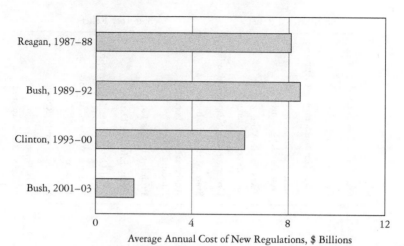

FIGURE 6.3. Calculating the average annual cost of new regulations under four presidents. The George W. Bush administration imposed lower costs on industry through regulation than any other administration since the government began keeping records in 1987. *Source: Office of Information and Regulatory Affairs, Office of Management and Budget 2004; Brinkley 2004 A1, A10.*

medical patients, and the elderly (Brinkley 2004, A1, A10). As documented by Figure 6.3, the Bush administration through regulation has imposed lower costs on business and industry than any other administration since 1987.

In turn, the states, seeking to improve their civil societies, have imposed upon their political subdivisions a wide variety of mandates. Predictably, the general practice of mandating has drawn the ire of observers of government and state and local officials. As Alan Ehrenhalt (2003), executive editor of *Governing* magazine, has sharply advanced:

> This [mandating] is the flaw in any experiment with federalism, including America's. Congress can demand that states institute new testing programs for schoolchildren, offering no money to pay for them. A federal agency can impose billions of dollars in security costs on local law enforcement officials—and postpone the question of how to pay them until another day. States can cut back drastically on their support for public health at the local level, while insisting that local authorities keep the service going just as before.

And further: "Nobody is innocent here. The feds stiff the states. The states stiff the cities and counties. Whenever one layer of government can push an unpleasant or costly responsibility down to the level below, it nearly always does so. The cities and counties would do it too—except they are on the bottom rung" (pg. 13).

All of this supports the contention that we have moved far beyond Cooperative Federalism to the new era of Coercive Federalism. As Donald F. Kettl (1983) has aptly advanced:

> Federal regulations have grown to define not only who should benefit from government programs but how states and cities must run those programs: what accounting standards they must follow, what environmental effects they must measure, who can

be hired under the programs, and how much they must be paid. These regulations have made the nation's states and cities into uncertain brides in the partnership of American federalism. The marriage has drifted between two extremes: on the one hand, generous financial grants accompanied by increasingly burdensome rules; and on the other hand, fewer rules but less money. (xv)

In a similar fashion, the states have increasingly, over the years, imposed upon their political subdivisions a host of mandatory rules and regulations. To some degree, swimming against what appears to be the inevitable tide of centralization, the states and localities have been modestly successful in gaining some relief from what state and local officials view as the onerous hand of heavy-handed regulation.

In essence, the debate over federal and state regulatory policies as they apply to other governments reflects the age-old problem of federalism: How best can our polity achieve worthy national social goals, without further eroding the policy autonomy of our state and local governments?[6] There is not an easy or ready answer to this issue. As David B. Truman (1940) so well stated in his work *Administrative Decentralization*, written almost seven decades ago, "The problem[s] of centralization/decentralization . . . are a result of the dynamic forces of a changing society and are among those problems for which a final solution has never been found" (204–5)

Further, we are faced with an equally serious problem: How can we in the face of the increasing maze and mosaic of intergovernmental relations make the democratic process intelligible and accountable to the ordinary citizenry? Similar to the query advanced in the preceding paragraph, there is no easy answer to this need as well.

For those in the academic vineyards, given the rise of Coercive Federalism there is a pressing requirement to develop a new theory of American federalism. As Zimmerman (1990) has stated:

Dual and cooperative theories of federalism continue to retain explanatory value. There are limits to the scope of congressional powers, as illustrated by Court decisions, and national-state relations are cooperative. Nevertheless, a theory of American federalism will lack great explanatory value unless it encompasses informal federal preemptions—conditional grants-in-aid, tax credits, and tax sanctions—and formal preemptions. (58)

REFERENCES

Beam, David R. 1981. Washington's Regulation of States and Localities: Origins and Issues. *Intergovernmental Perspective*. 7 (Summer), 8–18.

Berman, David R. 2003. *Local Government and the States: Autonomy, Politics, and Policy*. Armonk: M. E. Sharpe.

Brinkley, Joel. 2004, August 16. Out of Spotlight, Bush Overhauls U.S. Regulations. *New York Times*. A1, A10.

Broder, David, 2005, March 21. Mandates Remain Sometimes Unfunded. *Kansas City Star*. B5.

Bryan, Frank B. 2004. *Real Democracy: The New England Town Meeting and How It Works*. Chicago: University of Chicago Press, 2004.

Conlan, Timothy J. and David R. Beam. 1992. Federal Mandates: The Record of Reform and Future Prospects. *Intergovernmental Perspective*. 18 (Fall), 7–11, 15.

Crihfield, Brevard and H. Clyde Reeves. 1974. Intergovernmental Relations: A View from the States. *The Annals of the American Academy of Political and Social Science.* 416 (November), 99–107.

Croy, James B. 1975. Federal Suppression: The Road to Domination. *State Government.* 48 (Winter), 32–36.

Dubnick, Mel and Alan Gitelson. 1979. Intergovernmental Relations and Regulatory Policy. Paper presented at the Symposium on Regulatory Policy. Houston, Texas. November 19–20.

Ehrenhalt, Alan. 2003, April 27. Every Government's Mandate. *New York Times.* WK13.

———. Fighting Federal Mandates. 1980, August 16. *New York Times.* 20.

Graves, W. Brooke. 1964. *American Intergovernmental Relations: Their Origins, Historical Development, and Current Status.* New York: Charles Scribner's Sons.

Hardin, Peter. 2004, February 12. J. Warner, Allen Collide over Seat-Belt Legislation. *Richmond Times-Dispatch.* B1, B4.

Kettl, Donald F. 1983. *The Regulation of American Federalism.* Baton Rouge: Louisiana State University Press.

Kincaid, John. 1990. From Cooperative to Coercive Federalism. *The Annals of the American Academy of Political and Social Science.* 509 (May), 139–52.

Koch, Edward I. 1980. The Mandate Millstone. *The Public Interest.* 61 (Fall), 42–57.

Lukas, J. Anthony. 1985. *Common Ground: A Turbulent Decade in the Lives of Three American Families.* New York: Alfred A. Knopf.

Office of Management and Budget, 2004, August 14. Annual Cost of New Regulations. *New York Times.*

Pagano, Michael A. 1990. State-Local Relations in the 1990s. *Annals of the American Academy of Political and Social Science.* 509 (May), 94–105.

Posner, Paul L. 1997. Unfunded Mandates Reform Act: 1996 and Beyond. *Publius.* 27 (Spring), 53–71.

———. 1998. *The Politics of Unfunded Mandates: Whither Federalism?* Washington, DC: Georgetown University Press.

Rivlin, Alice. 1992. *Reviving the American Dream.* Washington, DC: The Brookings Institution.

Shelly, Bryan, 2004. Gold Towns and Shark Pools: The Effect of School Finance Reform on Vermont's School Boards. Paper presented at the Annual Meeting of the American Political Science Association. Chicago. September 2.

Thompson, Frank J. 1981. *Health Policy and the Bureaucracy: Politics and Administration.* Cambridge, MA: The MIT Press.

Truman, David B. 1940. *Administrative Decentralization.* Chicago: University of Chicago Press.

U.S. Advisory Commission on Intergovernmental Relations (ACIR). 1984. *Regulatory Federalism: Policy, Process Impact and Reform.* Washington, DC: The Commission.

———. 1995. *The Role of Federal Mandates in Intergovernmental Relations: Draft Report.* Washington, DC: The Commission.

Zimmerman, Joseph F. 1981. Frustrating National Policy: Partial Federal Preemption. In Jerome J. Hanus, ed., *The Nationalization of State Government.* Lexington, MA: Lexington Books, D.C. Heath and Company. 75–104.

———. 1990. Regulating Intergovernmental Relations in the 1990s. *The Annals of the American Academy of Political and Social Science.* 509 (May), 48–59.

———. 1992. *Contemporary American Federalism: The Growth of National Power.* New York: Praeger.

———. 1994. State Mandate Relief: A Quick Look. *Intergovernmental Perspective.* 20 (Spring), 28–30.

———. 2001. National-State Relations: Cooperative Federalism in the Twentieth Century. *Publius.* 31 (Spring), 15–30.

Zimmerman, Joseph F. 2005a. Congressional Preemption: Removal of State Regulatory Powers. *PS: Political Science and Politics,* 38 (July), 359–362.

Zimmerman, Joseph F. 2005b. The Nature and Political Significance of Preemption. *PS: Political Science and Politics.* 38 (July) 359–362.

• 7 •

THE RESURGENT STATES IN THE
INTERGOVERNMENTAL SYSTEM:
COOPERATION AND CONFLICT

The blossoming of state governments in the 1980s—their transformation from weak links in the federal chain to viable and progressive
political units—resulted from a number of actions and circumstances.
In turn, the resurgence of state governments has generated a number
of positive outcomes. During the 1990s, states and localities honed
their capacity and became proactive rather than reactive. They
squarely faced hard choices and creatively crafted new directions.

—Ann O'M. Bowman and Richard C. Kearney,
State and Local Government (2002)

Over the years, scholars of federalism and intergovernmental relations have inordinately focused their research and scholarly efforts on the national government and
its *vertical* relationship with the states; to a significantly lesser degree some scholars
have examined the *vertical* relationship of the state government to their political
subdivisions, including cities, towns, and counties. Conversely, relatively few scholars
have centered their research and scholarship efforts on the states and the *horizontal*
aspects of American federalism, involving interstate relations or the relationships
between local governments.

This chapter focuses on the resurgence of the states and interstate relations. At
the outset, attention is devoted to the various ways in which the states have increased
their administrative and political capacity, and the consequences of this development.
This introductory material is followed by a discussion of how the United States
Constitution has established the constitutional framework of interstate relations.
Attention is then given to material concerning the ways in which states cooperate
with each other. The discussion of interstate cooperation also incorporates material
involving the diffusion of policy innovations throughout the states. The fourth section
of this chapter focuses on the major causes of interstate conflict and the methods and
structures utilized by the states for resolving this conflict. The chapter concludes with

a summary overview of interstate relations and a discussion of the future of the states in the intergovernmental system.

THE RESURGENCE OF THE STATES

For much of the political history of the United States, state governments were considered by most scholars to be hopelessly deficient and, in some instances, downright corrupt—the "weak links" in the American system of federalism (Teaford 2002, 1–2). As noted by Ann O'M. Bowman and Richard C. Kearney (2002): "[S]tates and their local governments in the 1950s and 1960s were havens of traditionalism and inactivity. Many states were characterized by unrepresentative legislatures, glad-handing governors, and a hodgepodge court system. Public policy tended to reflect the interests of the elite; delivery of services was frequently inefficient and ineffective" (6). An extremely critical portrait of state legislatures entitled *The Sometime Governments: A Critical Study of the 50 American State Legislatures*, issued in 1971 by the Citizens Conference on State Legislatures, called for the substantial reform of these bodies. Indeed, even former governors voiced strong criticism of state government and, as noted by Terry Sanford (1967), the former governor of North Carolina, in his work *The Storm over the States*, the states "lost their confidence, and the people their faith in the states" (21). Even the noted political scientist Luther Gulick (1933) added to this chorus of dismay by declaring: "It is a matter of brutal record. The American State is finished. I do not predict that the States will go, but affirm that they have gone" (420).

However, commencing in the mid-1960s, stimulated by the United States Supreme Court decision of *Baker v. Carr* (1962), the states have significantly improved their political and managerial capacity and became capable of creating and implementing "an explosion of innovations and initiatives" (Herbers 1987, 28).[1] States have modernized their constitutions; during the past three decades, more than three-quarters of the states have ratified new constitutions or substantially amended their existing document. In reality, it should be pointed out, states started their reorganization in the 1950s with the activities of "little Hoover Commissions" modeled after the Truman-appointed commissions at the federal level headed by former President Herbert Hoover. Modernized constitutions and statutory changes have strengthened the powers of governors by increasing their appointment and removal powers and by providing for longer terms of office, consecutive succession, larger and more competent staffs, enhanced budget authority, and the authority to reorganize the executive branch. State bureaucracies are staffed by more professional administrators and the bureaucracy better reflects and is more representative of the larger public. Annual, rather than biennial, sessions; more streamlined rules and procedures; additional trained and competent staff; and higher salaries have resulted in making reapportioned state legislatures more professional, capable, and effective. State judicial systems have also been reformed; examples include the establishment of unified court systems, the retention of court administrators, and the establishment of additional layers of courts. Reflective of their newfound capacity and resurgent status, states have become a much stronger lobbying force in Washington.

As a result of their increased capacity, states have been the beneficiaries of a number of important developments. They have diversified and improved their revenue systems, resulting in larger sources of revenue; expanded the scope of their operations, assuming a range of additional functions; experienced the faster diffusion, or spread, of new programs and policy innovations; and benefited from additional interjurisdictional cooperation. However, as might be expected, the resurgence of the states has resulted in a measure of increased national-state conflict.

CASE STUDY 3

Welfare to Work

Prior to the 1930s there was little government involvement in public welfare, and that which existed was primarily a local government responsibility. States were not involved at all until the 1920s and then in only a very minor way. Federal funding was virtually nonexistent until the New Deal programs of the 1930s when major grants were given to the states for welfare programs along with significant federal direct expenditures for welfare (U.S. Bureau of the Census 1961, 725–730). Since then, most welfare services have been delivered by state and local governments with federal grants-in-aid paying much of the cost. While federal welfare grants-in-aid have gone to state governments, in the 1930s these funds were generally passed-through to local governments who administered the services involved. Nationally, in 1932, local governments delivered 83 percent of the state-local package of welfare services; by 2002, states administered 86 percent (see Figure CS3.1). It should be noted, however, because large states like New York and California tend to be more decentralized, that the average state actually delivered 93 percent of this service.

For decades, aid to families with dependent children, known as AFDC, was a major part of the U.S. public welfare effort. AFDC was a federal entitlement program long criticized by conservative politicians. The system provided welfare aid to families in poverty, many of which were headed by single mothers. The political rhetoric criticized the fact that work requirements were not a part of the AFDC program and that the federal entitlement was synonymous with lifelong dependency and a lack of responsibility on the part of recipients. AFDC was criticized as being full of freeloaders, women who had extra children to increase the dole, and families that had been on welfare for three generations. There were some instances of this, but they were not typical. Other images were that welfare recipients were drug addicts, simply lazy, or scam artists who had found a way to rip off the government and were living it up at taxpayer expense.

The overwhelming majority of recipients used welfare as a temporary transitional program until they could get back to work or were disabled and could not work. There was always an undercurrent of racism inferring that this was a

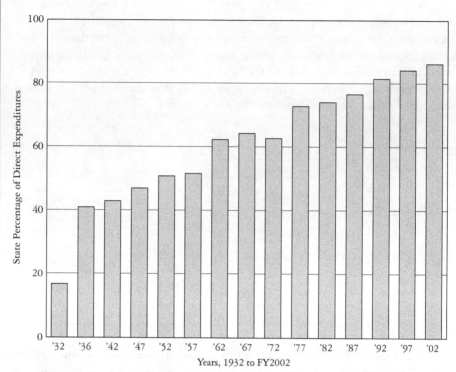

FIGURE CS3.1. State share of state and local expenditures for public welfare, 1931–FY2002. This is the national average of direct expenditures for public welfare. The state portion is much higher for the average state. For FY2002 the national average is 86 percent; for the average state it is 93 percent. Large states tend to have more decentralized service delivery. *Sources: U.S. Bureau of the Census 1961; Census of Governments 1962–2002.*

program for minorities when most welfare recipients were actually Caucasian. Starting with Ronald Reagan's criticism of big government and because of mounting criticisms over the years, some warranted and some not, consensus grew that the welfare system, particularly AFDC, distributed money for nothing without end. AFDC was also criticized as an open-ended entitlement with no set limits on the amount of money to be spent.

In his 1992 television ads, then governor of Arkansas and presidential candidate William Jefferson Clinton said,

> For so long government has failed us, and one of the worst failures had been welfare. I have a plan to end welfare as we know it—to break the cycle of dependency. We'll provide education, job training, and child care, but then those who are able to work must go to work. . . . It's time to make welfare what it should be—a second chance, not a way of life. (Cabe 2002)

The Democratically controlled Congress of 1993–94 did little to reform the welfare system and it was not at that time a high priority of President Clinton.

After the Republicans took over in 1995 they passed and President Clinton signed the legislation known as the Personal Responsibility and Work Opportunity Reconciliation Act (PRWOA) of 1996, more commonly called the "Welfare to Work" program. Many congressional Democrats opposed this legislation.

PRWOA ended the federally controlled open-ended entitlement of the AFDC program that had existed for several decades. In its place was a time-limited cash assistance program to the states supported by federal block grants, called Temporary Assistance for Needy Families (TANF). States were free to spend the money in any way as long as they met the objectives of the TANF grants. As listed by the Department of Health and Human Services (HHS), the objectives of the TANF grants were several: (1) to reduce dependency by promoting job preparation, (2) to promote transfer from welfare to work, (3) to provide assistance to needy families so children could be cared for in their homes, (4) to promote marriage and reduce out-of-wedlock pregnancies, and (5) to encourage the formation and maintenance of two-parent families. The legislation also contained restrictions as well—anyone who had been convicted of a drug-related felony was ineligible for life. Moreover, eligibility included only families with a child or an expectant mother, and there was a twenty-four-month limit on benefits for most recipients.

State response to TANF was quite good during the early years and came much faster than expected. Many used the savings from the administration of AFDC caseloads to provide work support programs. There were increases in job rates and reductions in out-of-wedlock births, but whether or not this is the result of federal legislation is debatable. The fact that a lot of money went into child care, allowing single mothers to work, may have had something to do with these changes—two-thirds of those on TANF are single mothers.

Welfare to Work legislation was fortunate in terms of timing. It was enacted at a time when the economy was expanding, 1996–2000, which means it was easier to shift recipients from welfare to work at that time. It would not be quite as easy after 2001. Most states responded rather rapidly to these changes through the period of economic expansion. The AFDC system provided aid to 1.7 percent of the population in 1960, which then increased to 5.2 percent by 1975 and remained in the 4.5–5.3 percent range over the next twenty years until the mid 1990s. With the enactment of Welfare to Work legislation, the proportion on welfare dropped to 1.8 percent by 2002 (U.S. Bureau of the Census 2003, 8, 371) (see Figure CS3.2).

While the Welfare to Work legislation has received considerable public and media attention, the work support system critical to the success of this legislation has not. The work support system for those at the bottom of the income scale involves other federal and several state programs, including minimum wage, child tax credits, Earned Income Tax Credits, food stamps, Medicaid and health insurance, child care, state income supplement programs, and child support enforcement. These work support programs are at least as important as

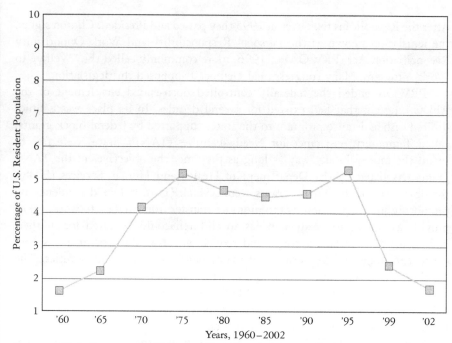

FIGURE CS3.2. Percentage of U.S. population on welfare, 1960–2002. *Sources:* Statistical Abstract of the United States, *2003, pp. 8, 371; Cabe 2002.*

the TANF block grant given the roles they play in helping low-income families maintain some minimum living standard (Sawhill and Haskins 2002).

During the early years of Welfare to Work legislation, it appeared to be quite successful. Since that time, however, there have been problems. First, with the downturn in the economy in 2001 and later it was not so easy to move families from welfare to work. Some who had been successful found themselves unemployed with no benefits. The minimum wage of $5.15 per hour has not been increased between 1997 and 2005, a period in which consumer prices have increased between 19 and 20 percent, meaning that the purchasing power of the dollar received by minimum wage workers has declined significantly (U.S. Bureau of the Census 2003, 476). Not helping this situation is the enactment of hundreds of increases in regressive sales and excise taxes, fees, and service charges by local and state governments that fall heavily on those at the bottom of the income scale.

The economic setbacks of 2001 and 2002 meant that state revenues were down, and a number of states have been reducing many of the supplemental work programs that supported TANF and the concept of Welfare to Work up to that time. Most states exhausted their surpluses built up during the 1990s and have had to struggle financially since then. Starting with the budgets for FY2005 and FY2006, the federal government is cutting back on federal grants-in-aid to state and local governments as well as other federal domestic programs (OMB 2004, 2005). Given the fact of federal cutbacks, when they materialize, states are also likely to reduce their work support programs. In fact, judging by proposed FY2006 budgets in several states, it appears that this is already occurring. If nothing else this indicates the interrelationship between actions at the national and state levels.

The verdict is still out as to whether or not in the long run Welfare to Work gets families off the dole and to work or simply shoves them off welfare without putting them to work. A report by the Joyce Foundation (2005) found that while welfare recipients have gone to work "most have taken jobs that pay low wages, are part-time, or don't last." Hurting the ability of states to provide supplemental work support programs have been lowered revenue expectations, higher unemployment rates as jobs have been outsourced, and massive increases in the cost of health care. A lot will depend on the direction the economy takes in the years after 2005. TANF must now be renewed every two years, and President Bush's FY2006 budget and proposals for renewal for the 109th Congress will shift more of the responsibility for funding to the states, primarily through cuts to child care. Many states are ill equipped financially to pick up the slack (Waller 2004). Child care has been an important component of TANF. In any case, it appears from the federal budget proposal for FY2006 that the ultimate result is that the federal government will renege on its financial support for this program, the states' financial responsibility will be increased, and, ultimately, more of the needy will be pushed off of welfare.

REFERENCES

Cabe, Delia K. 2002, Autumn. Welfare to Work. *Kennedy School of Government Bulletin.* www.ksg.harvard.edu/ksgpress/bulletin/autumn2002/features/welfare.html.

Census of Governments. 1962–2002. Washington, DC: Government Printing Office.

Joyce Foundation. 2005, January 28. *Welfare to Work: What Have We Learned.* www.joycefdn.org/welrept.

Office of Management and Budget (OMB). 2004, 2005. *FY2005 and FY2006 Budget of the United State Government.* Washington, DC: Government Printing Office.

Sawhill, Isabel V. and Ron Haskins. 2002, March. *Welfare Reform and the Work Support System.* Washington, DC: The Brookings Institution. www.brookings.edu/es/research/projects/wrb/publications.

Statistical Abstract of the United States. 2003. Washington, DC: Government Printing Office.

U.S. Bureau of the Census. 1961. *Historical Statistics of the United States: Colonial Times to 1957.* Washington, DC: Government Printing Office. 725–30.

———. 2003. *Statistical Abstract of the United States.* Washington, DC: Government Printing Office. 8, 371, 476.

Waller, Margy. 2004. Whither Welfare Reform and Working Families? The Federal Debate and the States. Speech to the Association of Capitol Reporters and Editors. Washington, DC. November 14. www.brookings.edu/views/speeches/waller/20041114.htm.

However, as a result of the economic recession of the early 2000s, the proactive and forward momentum of the states was somewhat derailed. A report prepared by the National Governors Association and the National Association of State Budget Officers found that in 2003 thirty-seven states had chopped a total of $14.5 billion off their budgets, most cutting services across the board, half laying off workers, and ten reducing fiscal assistance to municipalities. In order to meet their revenue shortfalls, governors in twenty-nine states proposed a total of $17.5 billion in new taxes and various fees. Ten governors sought an increase sales taxes, eight argued for higher income taxes, fourteen supported raising the tax on cigarettes, and six fought for raising alcohol taxes (Wilgoren 2003). In somewhat of a more positive light, a report issued by the National Conference of State Legislatures (NCSL) toward the end of 2003 ("Study Finds Improvement in Finances for States" 2003), along with a subsequent report issued by the NCSL the following year (Dao 2004b), noted that due to the overall improving economy and the resultant increase in income and sales tax revenues, the fiscal condition of the states had moderately improved.

THE CONSTITUTIONAL FRAMEWORK OF INTERSTATE RELATIONS

To a significant extent, the United States Constitution provides in Article IV the legal framework for the conduct of interstate relations, as it contains provisions relative to full faith and credit, interstate citizenship, and interstate rendition of fugitives from justice. The fourteenth amendment also affects interstate citizenship. It should be noted that in a series of cases the United States Supreme Court has interpreted in a relative, rather than an absolute, sense the following provisions and requirements of the Constitution relating to relations between the states.

Privileges and Immunities

Article IV, section 2, of the Constitution states: "The citizens of each State shall be entitled to all privileges and immunities of the citizens in the several States." And, further: "No state shall make or enforce any law which shall abridge the privileges and immunities of the citizens of the United States." The federal courts have interpreted the privileges and immunities clause to provide that a state may not discriminate against nonresidents regarding fundamental rights. These rights include access to the state for the purpose of making a living, access to the courts, and freedom from discriminatory taxation, as in the instance of a tax that must be paid only be nonresidents.

Notwithstanding this clause, the states often treat nonresidents differently in a number of respects. For instance, nonresident college students usually have to pay higher tuition to attend state universities and colleges. In addition, hunting and fishing licenses are invariably more costly for nonresidents. More expensive fees imposed upon nonresidents are justified on the grounds that state residents pay taxes to support these facilities and programs, and, therefore, nonresidents, who have not paid these taxes, should be required to pay a reasonable surcharge for certain services. In addition, the states generally require a professional who is licensed to practice in another state to obtain a new license in order to practice in his or her new state of residence.

Full Faith and Credit

Article IV, section 1, of the Constitution provides that "Full Faith and Credit shall be given in each state to the public acts, records, and judicial proceedings of every other State." According to this provision, a legal ruling of a state generally must be recognized and enforced by the other states. However, the Full Faith and Credit clause has not always been interpreted in an absolute sense by the United States Supreme Court, particularly in regard to family law. For example, the Court, in its decision of *Haddock v. Haddock* (1906), ruled that the State of New York did not have to recognize a divorce obtained by a former resident, Mr. Haddock, in the State of Connecticut. However, the Court ruled that because the former Mrs. Haddock was neither notified of the divorce suit nor represented at the proceeding, the divorce was not binding in her home state of New York. However, the Court also ruled that the states have the power to regulate the marital status of their residents, and therefore, Mr. Haddock's divorce was valid in Connecticut, his state of residence. Similarly, in the case of *Williams v. North Carolina* (1945), as wryly noted by Joseph P. Zimmerman, "the Supreme Court upheld the decision of the Supreme Court of North Carolina that the state did not have to recognize a Nevada divorce because the parties had not established residence in Nevada. As a result of this decision, a couple may be considered legally divorced in one state and legally married in another state. In the latter state, one or both parties could be charged with bigamy upon remarriage in that State" (Zimmerman 1992, 148).

We should point out that the wider impact of these decisions was limited by the general tendency of the states to voluntarily recognize the divorce decrees granted by other states. However, under the doctrine of the *divisible divorce*, a state may honor that portion of a divorce decree that terminates a marriage, without recognizing those portions of the decree that deal with property settlements, child custody, child support, and alimony. Consequently, states have often been hesitant and less willing to enforce another state's ruling in these areas.

Interstate Rendition (Extradition)

Although the Full Faith and Credit clause, Article IV, section 2, does not apply to criminal laws, the Constitution provides that a person charged with a crime in one state and found in another shall be delivered up on the demand of the governor of the state from which he has fled, so that he may be tried by the state in which he crime was committed. This process is called rendition—although it is sometimes referred to as extradition. Although the provision is clear and to the point, and was reinforced by an act of Congress in 1793, neither the rendition clause nor the legislation includes any enforcement language. Nevertheless, for many years the Supreme Court underscored that governors had a constitutional duty to hand over fugitives from other states, but that the federal courts had no authority to enforce that obligation. Indeed, in some high-profile cases in the past century, governors have refused to return a fugitive to a state from which he had fled. For instance, in 1977, Governor Edmund S. Brown, Jr., refused to return Dennis Banks, an American Indian activist, to South Dakota because the governor feared for his safety in South Dakota. And, in 1985 Governor Bill Clinton of Arkansas refused a New York rendition request on the ground that the nineteen-year-old woman would be subject to a severe penalty—a minimum of fifteen years to life jail sentence—under a law designed to punish career drug dealers (Zimmerman 1992, 153).

As a general rule of thumb, and for a variety of reasons, governors usually quickly agree to extradite a criminal to the state from which he or she has fled. No governor desires to secure for his or her state the reputation of being "soft on criminals" or a "safe haven" for criminals. In addition, a governor who refused to return a fugitive may risk losing the cooperation of officials in other states when he is seeking the return of a criminal. Further, it should be noted that the rendition clause was supplemented in 1934 by congressional legislation that made the crossing of a state line by a fugitive, to avoid prosecution or confinement, a federal crime. The law stipulates that fugitives should be tried in the federal court district in which the original crime was committed, a practice that makes them readily available to state officials concerned about the original offense.

Interstate Travel

While the Constitution does not explicitly mention a right to travel, the courts have held that it can be inferred from a variety of provisions in the Constitution—the ability of the national government to fill offices and raise an army, the conduct of interstate commerce, and the right of citizens to petition the government all imply the right to travel throughout the states. Based on the premise of the right to travel, the Supreme Court has struck down state laws that required a year of residence before an individual became eligible for welfare assistance (*Shapiro v. Thompson*, 1969), gained the right to vote (*Dunn v. Blumstein*, 1972), or was entitled to free medical care for the poor (*Memorial Hospital v. Maricopa County*, 1974). In the aggregate, these decisions facilitated the ability of mobile citizens to participate in the electoral process and reduced the risk of individuals being left outside the social "safety net" simply because they moved to a new residence in another state.

Interstate Compacts

The Constitution provides for the utilization of compacts, or agreements, between or among the states. Article I, section 10, states in part: "No State shall, without the consent of Congress, . . . enter into agreement or compact with another state." W. Brooke Graves (1964) noted in his classic text *American Intergovernmental Relations: Their Origins, Historical Development, and Current Status*: "The application of this clause was originally restricted largely to political agreements, the settlement of boundary disputes, and the apportionment of water, but not to important policy matters." Further:

> The first successful modern compact was that which established the Port of New
> York Authority [currently the Port Authority of New York and New Jersey] in

1921. . . . Since then, the compact device has been adapted to an ever-increasing list of problems, including oil and gas conservation, river basin development, marine fisheries, parks and forests, education and—of special significance in connection with the Port Authority—metropolitan area problems. (580)

The popularity among state officials for utilizing compacts for responding to challenges and problems is still evident. In January 2004 officials in North Carolina and Virginia began giving serious consideration to establishing the Virginia–North Carolina Interstate High-Speed Rail Compact to serve as a vehicle for receiving federal funds to improve rail transportation in the two states (Jones 2004).

The requirement for the congressional consent of a compact has not been very strictly defined (or applied), and the federal courts have been called upon to interpret this requirement in a number of instances. In practice, congressional approval in the past has been granted in advance, after a compact has been approved by the relevant states, or approval can be implied from legislation passed by Congress. We should note that explicit congressional approval apparently is required only for compacts that affect "a power delegated to the national government" or "the political balance of the federal system" (Wright 1982, 332). For other compacts, the absence of objection by Congress is generally regarded as a form of implicit consent.

COOPERATION AMONG THE STATES

A prominent feature of cooperative federalism in the United States is that of cooperation between and among the states. State officials often consult and work with their counterparts in other states, particularly when working in similar functional areas. A substantial amount of interstate cooperation between officials is informal in nature; indeed, Zimmerman (2002) reports, "Informal, verbal cooperation is considerably more common than formal cooperation and may be ad hoc or continuing in nature" (42). An example of informal cooperation includes the instance of a state official who personally meets or contacts, through the phone, fax, or e-mail, a colleague in a neighboring state for advice on how to deal with a policy problem or consults a well-regarded reference work, such as the *Book of the States*, to determine the degree to which his or her state compares with other states in policy areas like education, mass transportation, or environmental protection. Informal cooperation also takes place when state officials exchange information with their counterparts in other states regarding future activities that might impact another state, such as the construction or major repair of an existing highway. Another example of informal cooperation is that of state officials conversing about common problems at a professional meeting or banding together to speak with a collective voice to the federal government on a national policy issue.

In an especially insightful study conducted in the 1970s, Deil S. Wright and his colleagues (1982) found that a significant proportion of top-level state administrators had frequent horizontal contacts, either face-to-face or over the phone, with their counterparts in other states. More than one-fourth (27 percent) had daily or weekly contacts. Another third (35 percent) were in touch on a monthly basis. Contacts with heads of dissimilar agencies were noticeably, but not surprisingly, fewer. Importantly, commenting upon the latter, Wright and his colleagues perceptively noted: "[I]t is mildly surprising to find that more than one-fourth (28%) of the administrators [had] contacts with dissimilar agencies at least monthly. This frequency of contact suggests that state agency heads' interstate relationships transcend to some degree the narrow, single-function focus that fits the picket fence federalism pattern. . . . About 15% of the agency heads had at least monthly contacts with staff persons from the governor's office in other states" (338–39). Further, Wright and his colleagues found that officials in other states were an important source of new ideas for state administrators.

To be certain, there are some inherent limitations involving informal cooperation between and among the states. Without a formal agreement, conflict may take place over the exact meaning of an informal understanding, resulting in misunderstandings between the states. And, an informal agreement entered into by a governor or a department head may not be respected by his successor.

Administrative Agreements

States routinely enter into administrative agreements with other states, and in some instances with Canadian provinces or Mexican states (Zimmerman 2002, 42). In contrast to interstate compacts, administrative agreements are easier to initiate, negotiate, and amend, and involve virtually all governmental functions. Such functions most prominently include criminal justice, welfare fraud, education, air pollution, fisheries, river management, recycling, waste management, transportation, taxation, and state lotteries (Zimmerman, 2002, 42–47). The governors of Georgia, North Carolina, and Tennessee signed the "Southern Air Principles" in 2001, which directed the environmental agencies of their states to work together to develop a regional plan to address air pollution problems in the Southern Appalachian Mountains (Henderson 2001). The advent of multistate prescription drug purchasing pools is another illustration of interstate administrative agreements. Maine, New Hampshire, and Vermont created the first coalition in 2001; within months, other states were exploring the benefits of collaborative action (Bowman 2003). In December 2003 Maryland and Virginia entered into an agreement leading to the establishment of the Mid-Atlantic Regional Spaceport, to facilitate governmental, academic, and commercial space endeavors ("Virginia and Maryland to Join in Space Effort" 2003). More recently, the states of New Hampshire, Vermont, and Rhode Island, established the New England Compact Assessment Program through an administrative agreement in 2004 as a common system for measuring student assessment in this functional area more efficiently (Zimmerman 2005). As Zimmerman (2002) notes: "Credit for promoting multistage administrative agreements must be given to associations of state administrative officials, Congress and federal-government administrators. The associations draft interstate administrative agreements and hold periodic meetings that enable state officials to become acquainted on a personal basis with their counterparts in other states, thereby facilitating interstate cooperation." Further: "In addition, Congress has enacted statutes creating interstate administrative bodies and has provided funding for interstate cooperative activities. And a significant number of federal government administrators work closely with their state counterparts and encourage interstate cooperation" (47).

Multistate Legal Action

As Ann O'M. Bowman (2004) has reported, another vehicle of interstate cooperation is the willingness of states to enter into lawsuits with other states; it offers a means by which states can assert and protect their role in the federal system. The organization facilitating multistate legal action is the National Association of Attorneys General (NAAG), an entity composed of the chief legal counsels of the states and territories. During the period from 1992 to 1999, states, on the average, were a party to a multistate legal action on twenty-five occasions. Two high-profile examples of this approach during the 1990s involved the state-initiated lawsuits against the tobacco industry and against the Microsoft Corporation. In the tobacco case, although a few states acted independently and reached their own settlements with tobacco companies, most litigating states relied on joint action. Eventually state attorneys generals were able to broker a national agreement with the tobacco industry (Derthick 2005). In the Microsoft case, twenty states filed an antitrust lawsuit in 1988, alleging illegal anticompetitive, anticonsumer actions by the corporation (Bowman 2003). More recently (2004), the states of New York, New Jersey, Pennsylvania, and Connecticut commenced joint legal action designed to force the Allegheny Energy Company to install antipollution equipment in five coal-fired generating plants (DePalma 2004). In the same year a much larger group of states, consisting of California, Connecticut, Iowa, New Jersey, New York, Rhode Island, Vermont, and Wisconsin, along with New York City, initiated legal action against a number of energy producers, including American Electric Power, Cinergy, the Southern Company, the Tennessee Valley Authority, and Xcel Energy, seeking "substantial cuts" in the amount of carbon dioxide emitted from their plants (Revkin 2004).

Interstate Compacts: Developments[2]

As noted earlier, the Constitution provides for the states to enter into legally binding compacts with each other and the federal government. Interstate compacts may be bilateral, multilateral, sectional, or national in terms of membership; presently there are 26 types of compacts, including those of a federal-state nature, classified by subject matter ranging from advisory to taxation (Zimmerman 2002, 40). Prior to 1920, only 34 compacts were entered into by the states and were primarily employed for resolving boundary disputes. During this period, because of their limited focus, compacts were enacted on an average of about one every four years. We should note that there was a substantial increase in the number of compacts adopted by the states since 1920, particularly during the period from 1940 to 1970, when somewhat over 100 new compacts were adopted. During this time frame new compacts were being adopted at a rate of somewhat over four each year. However, this rate of adoption declined to about two per year in the 1970s and has continued at this pace (Wright 1982, 330; Zimmerman 1992, 142). Because some compacts have been rendered defunct, there are presently 155 compacts, 57 between two states (Bowman 2004, 36).

As reported by Bowman (2004), the states vary in terms of the number of compacts of which they are a member; the average rate of compact membership for the states is 25.4. Nine states—New York, Vermont, Maine, New Mexico, Pennsylvania, New Jersey, Virginia, Colorado, and Maryland—are parties to twenty-nine or more compacts, while, at the lowest end of the scale, eight states—Hawaii, Wisconsin, Alaska, South Dakota, Iowa, Michigan, North Dakota, and Nevada—are parties to twenty-one or fewer compacts. The remaining states are members of twenty-two to twenty-eight compacts.

Since 1920 compacts have been utilized by the states for a much wider range of policy issues, including bridge construction, economic development, crime and parole, child support and placement, higher education, law enforcement, health, parks, and water. Several compacts have been entered by all the states—for example, the Interstate Compact on the Placement of Children, which has established procedures for the placement of children across state lines, and the Uniform Interstate Compact on Juveniles. In addition, forty-seven states have become members of the Interstate Compact on Adult Offender Supervision (Bowman 2004). Further, the Compact on Mental Health was created to provide care for the mentally retarded and to provide the basis for other agreements in the field of mental health. Several states have entered into regional compacts to help prevent and combat forest fires. Compacts are currently utilized by the states to study problems, resolve disputes, coordinate regulatory policies, and deliver public services.

A second development in the utilization of compacts, particularly since World War II, is the increasing establishment of regional multistate compacts. A prominent example of the use of multistate compacts involves public higher education. These bodies include the Southern Regional Education Compact (1949), the Western Regional Educational Compact (1953), and the New England Higher Education Compact (1955). The broad purpose of these regional compacts is to promote regional cooperation between the institutions of higher education situated in the member states and provide varied educational opportunities, particularly those of a technical and professional nature, to the residents of the region in the most cost-effective manner, regardless of the state in which they are citizens. In addition, Governor George E. Pataki of New York proposed in July 2003 the development of a ten-state New England and Mid-Atlantic interstate compact, involving the states of New York, Connecticut, New Jersey, Vermont, New Hampshire, Delaware, Maine, Pennsylvania, Massachusetts, and Rhode Island, aimed at reducing carbon dioxide emissions from power plants (Johnson 2003).

Finally, another noteworthy development involving the use of compacts is the limited number of compacts established that involve both a number of states and the national government as equal partners. An excellent example of such a body is the Delaware River Basin Commission. Although these types of compacts have created some concern about the appropriate scope of national and state powers, the combined participation of the two levels of government has served a useful role in improving communication and coordinating the activities of the federal and respective state governments.

Uniform State Laws

One of the virtues of federalism is the ability of the states to provide different policies to accommodate the particularistic needs or preferences of the citizens residing in various parts of the country. Unfortunately, these variations in state laws sometimes pose substantial problems for the members of the legal profession, who must deal with a variety of conflicting precedents and rulings in the various states. Businesses that operate in more than one state are similarly burdened by variations in state laws; not being aware of which practices are required, allowed, or forbidden in the various states can be a daunting task.

In response to these problems, the National Conference of Commissioners on Uniform State Laws (NCCUSL) was founded in 1892. The conference meets on an annual basis and is attended by three commissioners, all lawyers, appointed by the governor of each state. The conference drafts model legislation on selected subjects for which greater uniformity throughout the states is beneficial. Recognizing that its proposed legislation must be acceptable to a wide variety of states, the conference seeks to avoid subjects that are too controversial. Many of the proposed laws of the conference have been widely adopted by the states; for example, in the 1990s twenty-two new uniform proposed laws were finalized by the NCCUSL and the states, on the average, adopted 7.7 of them (Bowman 2004). The Negotiable Instruments and the Warehouse Receipts Act, the first "model act," has been adopted by all of the states and the four territories. The Uniform Commercial Code, adopted by all of the states except Louisiana, governs the transfer of checks and the sale of all goods valued in excess of $500 (Zimmerman 1992, 160).

The Diffusion of Policy Innovations Throughout the States

One of the distinct advantages of federalism is its ability to provide a variety of state arenas in which new programs policies can be created and tested and, if successful, adopted by other states. In this sense, United States Supreme Court Justice Louis Brandeis noted that states serve as "laboratories of democracy." For instance, during the first part of the twentieth century, Wisconsin was a leader in adopting new and innovative social policies, which eventually were adopted by other states. More recently (2003), Maine has been lauded for adopting a plan to provide universal access to affordable health insurance (Goodman 2003). Federalism stimulates policy innovation and, through the process of policy diffusion, cooperation between and among the states in rendering government more effective in dealing with common challenges. Research on policy innovation and diffusion in and among the states has focused on (1) the kinds of states that generally have been classified as policy innovators and (2) the manner in which new ideas are spread through the process of policy diffusion—from one state to another.

In a seminal analysis of state policy innovation, Jack Walker (1969) studied the rapidity with which states adopted eighty-eight different programs in a variety of policy areas, including air pollution control, child labor standards, conservation, direct primary; highways, nurse licensing, schools for the deaf, taxation, and welfare.

TABLE 7.1. Composite Innovation Scores for the American States

New York	.656	Nebraska	.425
Massachusetts	.629	Kentucky	.421
California	.604	Vermont	.414
New Jersey	.585	Iowa	.413
Michigan	.578	Alabama	.406
Connecticut	.568	Florida	.397
Pennsylvania	.560	Arkansas	.394
Oregon	.544	Idaho	.394
Colorado	.538	Tennessee	.389
Wisconsin	.532	West Virginia	.386
Ohio	.528	Arizona	.384
Minnesota	.525	Georgia	.381
Illinois	.521	Montana	.378
Washington	.510	Missouri	.377
Rhode Island	.503	Delaware	.376
Maryland	.482	New Mexico	.375
New Hampshire	.482	Oklahoma	.368
Indiana	.464	South Dakota	.363
Louisiana	.459	Texas	.362
Maine	.455	South Carolina	.347
Virginia	.451	Wyoming	.346
Utah	.447	Nevada	.323
North Dakota	.444	Mississippi	.298
North Carolina	.430		
Kansas	.426		

Source: Walker 1969, p. 883.

Walker found, on the basis of calculating "innovation scores," that some states, during the period from 1870 to 1966, were usually among the first to engage in policy innovation, while others tended to be laggards in this regard. Walker labeled those states that were leaders in policy innovation "pioneers." Specifically, Walker found, as underscored in Table 7.1, that New York, Massachusetts, and California were leaders in policy innovation, while Wyoming, Nevada, and Mississippi proved to be far more cautious in adopting new policies and programs. He also reported that innovative states tend to be those that have ample resources, which is understandable in view of the fact that officials holding office in a relatively poor resource state are reluctant to assume additional costly responsibilities. As a rule of thumb, Walker noted, policymakers in poor states have been hesitant to devote scarce resources to a program until it has been successfully implemented in a fairly large number of states (890–91). While serving on a Missouri Governor's Council on Local Government Law (1968), one of the authors proposed an agency to oversee local government such as the Ontario (Canada) Municipal Board or the Minnesota Municipal Board. Another council member, a long-serving state senator, responded with, "Ross you know better than to suggest that. You know that if the other forty-nine states do it, then Missouri *might* consider it."

Walker also found that innovative states tend to have large populations and are heavily urbanized and industrialized. He noted that large populations make a wide variety of demands, which serves to stimulate officials to be policy innovators; in addition, states with larger populations are able to support state bureaucracies with greater managerial capacity, specialization, and expertise. Such bureaucracies, Walker advanced, are more likely to have information on new programs and the required skills to engage in policy innovation. Walker's analysis found that urbanized and industrialized states are generally quicker to engage in policy innovation, since urbanization and industrialization both bring about a sense and recognition of citizen interdependence to which governmental responses are required. In a related vein, Walker found that states with legislatures that provided urban areas with equitable representation were quicker to adopt new programs (883–87).

We should be cognizant that Walker's analysis of policy innovation and diffusion concerns the states' average response to new programs. Individual states, although largely not generally considered a pioneer in policy innovation, have proved to be leaders in a particular policy area. For example, Mississippi, which Walker found to be dilatory in adopting new programs, was the first state to adopt a general sales tax. This finding underscores the fact that when a state, whether a pioneer in policy innovation or not, faces a crisis it will usually adopt a new policy to deal with the crisis. In other instances, a new policy or program may gain ready acceptance throughout all the states because it is politically popular, even among those states that are usually slow to implement new policies (883).

Walker's analysis found that a group of states, that is, "national pioneers," tended to lead in terms of policy innovation. These pioneering states, which were scattered around the country, seek guidance from each another in regard to the implementation of new policies and programs. The remaining states, which he labeled the "non-pioneers," usually look to the most innovative state or states in their respective regions for new policies. Not until the pioneer state for a particular region implements a new program are the adjacent states likely to adopt it.

In his research, Walker reported that three significant changes in the diffusion of innovations throughout the states took place in the last century. First, the length of time that innovations took to spread across the country significantly declined. Specifically, in the period from 1870 to 1899 an innovation required an average of fifty-two years from the time it was adopted in the first state until it was finally implemented in the last state; by the years 1900–29 this timeframe had been reduced to approximately forty years; the corresponding figure for the years 1930–66 was about twenty-six years. Walker noted that in the more recent time period the rapidity of policy innovation was much more rapid among states that were generally less innovative (895).

A second change in the diffusion of innovations involved a shift in the ranks of state national pioneers and non-pioneers. Some states that were early pioneers in the past century became more cautious in regard to policy innovation, while, over time, a number of states that were initially slow to make policy changes joined the ranks of states that were more innovative. This shift is accounted for by a number of factors. States that early on were policy innovators found themselves burdened with an accumulation of commitments and expenses that make further innovation prohibitive. Conversely, states that were dilatory in adopting new policies eventually experienced considerable public pressure to adopt more innovative policies. In other instances, the shifting nature of state pioneer leaders and followers was accounted for by public problems, changes in the economy of the states, or the enhanced skill levels of state administrative officials.

A third change in the diffusion of innovations throughout the states in the past century involved the blurring, but not total elimination, of regional patterns. While regional clusterings did persist, they became less distinctive over the past century. This finding suggests that state officials, who became more professionalized, became more receptive to seek beyond their respective regions policy solutions for dealing with problems.

The increasing rapidity with which innovations have spread across the county and the blurring of regional patterns, as Walker and others have reported, is the result of several important changes in the federal system. The first of these changes involved the establishment of an increasing number of national associations of state officials. While there were only five national associations of state officials prior to 1900, by 1986 there were over one hundred associations of state and/or local officials (Walker 1969, 894–95; Penne and Verduin 1986). The most prominent of these associations include the Council of State Governments (1935), National Conference on Uniform State Laws (1892), National Governors' Association (1908), National Conference on State Legislatures (1948), Conference of Chief Justices (1949), National Association of Attorneys General (1907), National Association of State Budget Officers (1945), and National Association of State Purchasing Officials (1947). Among other activities, these associations hold national annual meetings and disseminate information on methods and programs for dealing with policy problems. For instance, the major focus of the ninety-sixth annual meeting of the National Governors' Association, held in Seattle in 2004, involved the various challenges posed by the increasing number of the elderly, especially in regard to the rapidly escalating costs of Medicare ("Governors' Meeting Turns to Aging of America" 2004). Through these strategies, state officials and administrators, the latter who have become increasing educated, mobile, and professionalized, a trend that Wright and his colleagues documented as early as the 1970s (Wright 1982, 245–46, 342–44), quickly learn of new programs and, hence, become less dependent on regional leaders for innovative policy information.

Second, the federal grant system has served to stimulate innovation, not only by subsidizing activities but also by requiring the states (and local governments) to fulfill certain structural and programmatic requirements as a prerequisite for receiving grant money. These prerequisites have included upgrading and professionalizing state civil service systems. States that tend to be innovative have regarded the grants as a method for financing routine services, freeing funds for innovation in other policy areas.

Factors Stimulating Interstate Cooperation

Increasing cooperation between the states has been stimulated by a variety of factors. First, the growth of interstate cooperation since the 1930s may be viewed as a parallel development associated and intrinsically linked with the emergence of President Franklin D. Roosevelt's "cooperative federalism." Cooperative federalism, with its emphasis on the need and value of governments working together to respond to challenges, has served as a strong theoretical paradigm and working model for interstate cooperation.

Second, interstate cooperation has been stimulated by the emergence of a wide range of challenges and policy issues that do not respect state boundaries. These challenges and problems, which include air and water pollution, homeland security, crime, mass transportation, the enforcement of child support awards, and conflicts relating to the relocation of children of divorced parents (Eaton 2004), require a cooperative state response, involving several or a multitude of states. The increasing growth and utilization of interstate compacts, as reported previously in this chapter, is a reflection of this cooperative action. Simply stated, the rise of shared concerns and problems between and among the states has served as a strong catalyst for cooperative action by the states. Additionally, the increase in urban and suburban state populations of 120 million over the second half of the twentieth century placed pressure on both state and local governments in terms of providing additional services to these new residents.

In addition, the increase in interstate cooperation reflects the changing nature of state political systems and the political culture of the states. Research underscores that states that are more involved in cooperative actions with other states generally have a more liberal or moderate political parties, more professionalized legislatures and legal systems, and higher state-local taxes relative to state income. An increasing number of states share these characteristics. In general, therefore, states involved in more cooperative activity with other states have a political culture and a set of governmental and political institutions—executive, legislative, and judicial—that are strongly supportive of interstate cooperation.

Finally, the extent to which a state involves itself in interstate cooperation is, obviously, a function of the degree to which neighboring states are cooperative. In part, this reflects the fact that state officials often seek from adjacent states guidance in dealing with challenges. As a truism, states that are receptive to cooperative efforts will spur more interstate cooperation, while states that adopt a negative stance will discourage further attempts at cooperation.

Interstate Competition and Conflict

Graves (1964) reminds readers that at the outset of the establishment of the United States, a considerable amount of tension and conflict existed between the states. For example, North Carolina and Virginia were strong trade rivals, and Maryland and Virginia were involved in several bitter disputes regarding the control of shell fisheries and the regulation of navigation in the Chesapeake Bay (581). Modern-day sources of tension and conflict between the states are varied. A base source of interstate conflict involves the lack of communication between state officials regarding the adoption of a new policy or program. For example, state officials, without prior consultation with their regional counterparts, may make a policy decision, such as the construction of a new road or industrial site, that might negatively impact neighboring states. Obviously, prior consultation with the officials in adjacent states could have enabled them to adopt program modifications, reducing these negative effects.

Second, another source of conflict between the states, more of a decided historical import, but still occasionally newsworthy, involves boundary disputes. Especially in the latter part of the 1700s and the early 1800s, ambiguous land grants from the Crown, survey errors, and natural changes in the courses of boundary rivers were responsible for several boundary controversies. For instance, commencing in 1799 in the decision of *New York v. Connecticut*, the United States Supreme Court adjudicated a number of boundary disputes between Connecticut and New York. More recently, the Court has adjudicated boundary river disputes between New Mexico and Texas (*New Mexico v. Texas*, 1927), California and Nevada (*California v. Nevada*, 1980), Ohio and Kentucky (*Ohio v. Kentucky*, 1980), South Dakota and Nebraska (*South Dakota v. Nebraska*, 1982), Louisiana and Mississippi (*Louisiana v. Mississippi*, 1984), Georgia and South Carolina (*Georgia v. South Carolina*, 1990), and Illinois and Kentucky (*Illinois v. Kentucky*, 1991). In contrast, some state boundary disputes have been settled by negotiations between the states, resulting in a mutually agreed-upon interstate agreement, as in the instance of a boundary dispute between Maine and New Hampshire in the 1970s and North Carolina and South Carolina in the early 1980s (Zimmerman 1992, 136–37). Although boundary disputes between the states have become less common in recent years, a satellite-imaging map made in 2004 to reassess property in North Stonington, Connecticut, cast doubt on the precision of nineteenth-century land surveys allocating land to Connecticut and Rhode Island and engendered a local property tax battle on the state line of the two states in 2004 (Yardley 2004).

A third source of perennial conflict between the states, especially those states located in the West, has involved disputes regarding the use and control of water (El-Ashry and Gibbons 1986; Zimmerman 1996, 25–27). The most lasting water dispute involved the Colorado River, which originates in Rocky Mountains north and west of Denver, Colorado, and flows through Utah to constitute the Arizona boundary line with Nevada and California. In 1952, Arizona sued California for diverting an excessive amount of water from the Colorado River. At the time, the San Diego and Los Angeles metropolitan areas were consuming more water from the Colorado River than the six other states with access to the river water combined. Eleven years later, the Court, in *Arizona v. California* (1963), settled the dispute by concurring in general with the claims of Arizona when there is normal water flow, but ruling that the United States Secretary of Interior has the power to allocate the water whenever the flow of water declines below normal. Utilizing the latter power, the federal government in October 2003 "brokered" an agreement among the seven states concerning the distribution of river water during times of drought conditions (Murphy 2003). In a somewhat unusual case, the Court, in *Oklahoma v. New Mexico* (1991), resolved a dispute over an interpretation of the Canadian River Compact entered into by New Mexico, Oklahoma, and Texas in 1951. The dispute focused on the amount of water that New Mexico could store in a reservoir under the terms of the contract. The Court ruled that the compact limit only applied to stored water, and not the physical reservoir capacity (Zimmerman 1992, 138). More recently, in a somewhat high-profile case involving the control of water, *Virginia v. Maryland* (2003), Virginia argued that Maryland did not have the right to control, or dictate the conditions, concerning the use of the Potomac River by Virginia localities. In contrast, Maryland stressed that it enjoyed the right to control the use of the river since it was given ownership of the Potomac River "from shore to shore" by a charter signed by King Charles I in 1632 and therefore had "sovereign authority" over the river (Hardin 2003a). Ultimately, the Supreme Court ruled in favor of Virginia in regard to the controversy (Hardin 2003b).

Fourth, another source of interstate conflict involves the competition between the states for new business investment. In what has been referred to as a "zero-sum" game, the states continually and vigorously compete with each other for new economic development and investment, seeking to attract additional firms to the state or encouraging businesses already situated in the state to remain and increase their investment, by enlarging their facilities and thereby generating additional employment opportunities and tax revenues. Governors take special pride in noting studies that praise the favorable business climate of their states. Governor Mark R. Warner of Virginia, before a group of business executives in December 2003, noted that both *Plant Sites & Parks* magazine and the recently released *Pollina Corporate Top 10 Pro-Business States*, by Ronald R. Pollina, cited Virginia as having the best business environment among the states (Rayner 2003). In addition, governors note with public pleasure when an existing firm in their state decides to expand their operations. Warner stated in December 2003 relative to the expansion of the Wachovia Securities firm in the Richmond metropolitan area: "After many years of banking jobs and financial jobs going South, we are now seeing bank jobs and financial jobs returning here to Richmond. . . . We have stretched the extra mile to have a top-flight securities firm keep its headquarters here. It's the kind of long-term economic growth we want in our city" (Hazard 2003).

As this would imply, states often are often involved in "bidding wars" with one another to attract a particular new business firm, with the winning state usually offering the most attractive package in terms of taxation and other inducements. States (and local governments) offer to potential businesses infrastructure improvements, various tax abatements, lower income taxes, outright payments, training grants, and wage subsidies (Zimmerman 1996, 146–47). It is estimated that as a result of these incentives, the states and local governments lose about $30–50 billion a year in tax revenue (Uchitelle 2003). In their quest to attract new commercial investment, states will routinely enlist the efforts of the state and local Chambers of Commerce, public-private economic growth partnerships, other business leaders, and developers. Enhanced economic investment in the state is based on the premise that such investment will lead to job creation and larger tax revenues because of the increase of property and sales tax revenues derived from new employees. However, not all economic subsidies by the states to lure new investment have proved to be profitable, and some governors have questioned their long-run utility (Uchitelle 2003). Dick Netzer (1991), a well-respected and noted economist, has noted in reference to state subsides for business, "[T]he empirical evidence on what works in economic development is thin or unpersuasive" (234).

It should also be said that states in seeking to promote their own economic self-interest will enact economic public polices, notwithstanding strong moral censure and opposition by a determined segment of their citizenry. Perhaps the best example of this has been the enactment of gambling legislation by the majority of the states. Seeking to stem the flow of "gambling dollars" to adjoining states, legislators in Maryland and Pennsylvania commenced in the spring of 2004 the process of considering adopting legalized gambling for their states as a method for holding or reducing state and local taxes (Dao 2004a). Although the issue was still pending in Maryland in 2004, Governor Edward G. Rendell of Pennsylvania, was eventually successful in 2004 in convincing the legislature of his state to enact a bill authorizing gambling in his state, on the basis that "gambling revenues" would to used to reduce local property taxes. In his successful effort, Governor Rendell "had to overcome stiff opposition from conservatives, religious groups, and government watch-dog organizations who argued that gambling would increase corruption, crime, and social problems like gambling addiction and bankruptcy" (Dao 2004c).

In addition, states now compete with one another in the international arena for new economic opportunities, which reflects the rapid rise of the multinational global economy. Governors and their economic development staffs spend a significant amount of time overseas, in Africa, Asia, Europe, and Latin America, conversing with political and business leaders promoting the virtues and benefits of trading with and investing in their state. For example, at the Paris Air Show in June 2005, Alabama, Florida, Maryland, South Carolina, and New Mexico each set up booths providing elaborate and well crafted literature for business executives in the aerospace industry. This literature was designed to encourage firms to invest and operate in their states or to expand their investment. In many instances these executives were wined and dined in the various elegant restaurants of Paris. Governor Warner during his administration (2001–5) centered a major amount of his foreign investment efforts on Mexico. As a result of the successful initiatives of various governors, the German automobile manufacturer Bavarian Motor Works (BMW) builds cars in South Carolina, Nissan Motors (Japan) manufacturers vehicles in Tennessee and Mississippi, Daimler-Chrysler (Germany) produces Mercedes-Benz vehicles in South Carolina, Toyota Motors (Japan) operates large vehicle assembly plants in California and Kentucky, and Honda Motors (Japan) has for several decades manufactured automobiles in Ohio.

Further, Joseph F. Zimmerman in his insightful work *Interstate Economic Relations* (2004) underscores the manner in which the states, bent on protecting their own economic well-being, have erected various barriers to interstate trade. He notes that the states have routinely imposed discriminatory taxes on firms headquartered in other states. In a similar discriminatory fashion, reports Zimmerman, the states have utilized their police powers, designed to protect the public health and well-being, to erect trade barriers, protecting their own business firms and farmers from interstate competition. In addition, he notes that the states have used their proprietary powers to favor their states' business firms in the awarding of state contracts for the purchase of goods and raw materials. Further, the states that gained the power to regulate the sale of alcoholic beverages in their state with the passage of the twenty-first amendment to the Constitution in many instances, like Michigan and New York, passed legislation requiring out-of-state sellers of alcoholic beverages to sell only to licensed wholesalers. The latter then market wine and other drinks to retailers who, in turn, sell it to individual customers. Obviously, this "three-tier" distribution system, which perhaps is in conflict with the commerce clause of the United States Constitution, precludes individuals in New York State, like in about half the states, from directly purchasing alcoholic beverages over the Internet from producers outside of the state (Tedeschi 2004). However, the U.S. Supreme Court in its closely divided decision in *Granholm v. Heald* (2005) declared that such discriminatory laws violated the commerce clause of the Constitution. The Cour declared that states had to decide as a policy matter whether to permit direct shipment by all wineries without reference to their business location or to prohibit it for all wineries (Greenhouse 2005).

In addition, the varied economic structures and social policies of the states have proved to be another source of competition and conflict. For example, although increasing energy prices are beneficial to the economies of Louisiana, Oklahoma, and Texas, they serve as a retarding element on the economies of energy-importing states, such as Maine and Massachusetts. States that tax products, such as minerals or manufactured goods, which they exported to other states may incur their latent or overt hostility. A state with higher welfare benefits, such as Wisconsin, may some-what resent the fact that it attracts from neighboring states, such as Illinois, so-called high-cost welfare-dependent citizens.

Sixth, negative spillover effects, especially in regard to water and air pollution, are another source of interstate conflict. A state that allows pollutants to be deposited into rivers will incur the hostility of affected downstream states. In a parallel fashion, a state that fails to adopt adequate measures to curb air pollution will be criticized harshly by affected neighboring states. A state may be reluctant to sacrifice resources devoted to other programs to remedy the problem of air or water pollution when the negative effects are largely borne by neighboring states; in turn, the negatively affected neighboring states are sometimes unwilling or unable to make resources available for alleviating a problem that originated in another state.

Seventh, interstate conflicts may be the direct result of national policies that impact the states in a different manner. For example, federal policy regarding the use of public lands has sometimes produced tension between Western states, where the federal government has extensive landholdings, and Eastern states, where relatively little land is owned by the federal government. Given this situation, the Western states are obviously much more directly impacted by national land policies and have sometimes expressed resentment over federal policies inordinately shaped by national legislators from outside of their region.

Finally, interstate conflict may be attributed to symbolic politics and political "grandstanding" by public officials. For instance, a governor may engender a highly publicized "feud" with the governor of another state, in part, seeking to enhance or strengthen his political profile and projecting his role as a defender of the interests of his state. For example, the *Richmond Times-Dispatch* reported on July 4, 2004, "Virginia Governor Mark R. Warner has joined attempts by state Civil War enthusiasts to reclaim a Confederate flag lost at the Battle of Gettysburg and now held in Minnesota. Warner plans to raise the subject of the return of the 28th Virginia

Infantry Regiment's battle flag with Minnesota Governor Tim Pawlenty at the National Governors' Association meeting in Seattle later this month" The article continued: "People have fought over the flag for more than 140 years, and neither Virginia nor Minnesota shows any sign of relinquishing its interest. . . . But Minnesota still doesn't plan to relinquish the flag. . . . 'He's [Pawlenty's] certainly willing to hear him out and discuss the issue, but as far as we're concerned nothing has changed,' said Daniel Wolter, a spokesman for Pawlenty, a Republican" ("Warner Joins Flag Property Debate" 2004). Unfortunately, political maneuvering of this sort may result in lasting political conflict between the states, with dire consequences for interstate cooperation.

On a lighter note, in the 1960s the governor of Florida was chiding the governor of Alabama about the many Alabama residents who were moving to Florida. The governor of Alabama responded with, "That just raises the IQ level on both sides of the state line."

Strategies for Dealing with Interstate Conflict

A number of strategies are utilized to deal with interstate conflict. At the outset of a dispute, the contending states may seek to resolve their differences through some form of diplomacy. In this regard, state officials engage in phone calls, exchange e-mails or letters, or meet face-to-face. Through these alternatives, officials can exchange information, clarify misunderstandings, and better appreciate each other's point of view. Negotiations between state officials concerning a problem may ultimately result in the creation of an administrative agreement or interstate compact involving certain services or the operation of a facility.

If the states are unable to resolve a dispute on their own they may turn to the federal government for assistance. In the past, Congress has enacted legislation to resolve interstate conflicts or address issues that the states have been unable to resolve on their own. For example, the inability of the states to successfully deal with the problem of air pollution ultimately led to congressional action (Jones 1976).

Controversies between and among states may also be the subject of federal litigation; this reflects the fact that resolving disputes between states are a part of the original jurisdiction of the Supreme Court, as set forth by Article III, section 2. As Zimmerman (2006) has reported in his insightful recent work titled *Interstate Disputes: The Supreme Court's Original Jurisdiction* most of the interstate disputes resolved by the Court have involved boundary lines, financial matters, and water allocation, diversion, and pollution. In this work, Zimmerman underscores the role and importance of "Special Masters" appointed by the Court to gather data and testimony on interstate disputes before the body. It should be noted that the Court has sometimes declined to provide a "full hearing" for a case it deemed insufficiently important and sought to encourage the contending states to resolve their differences through negotiation and by entering into an interstate compact. Further, the Court has taken the position that a dispute must be between states, and not between a state and the citizens in another state.

If a state refuses to abide by a Supreme Court decision, various courses of action may follow. First, state resistance to a Court ruling may pave the way for further negotiations, with state officials seeking to come to a settlement acceptable to all concerned. Second, Congress may enact further legislation designed to encourage the compliance of a state or to defuse the issue. Third, the matter in dispute might become subject to further litigation. In this regard, one is reminded of the lasting dispute between Virginia and West Virginia over debts Virginia incurred during the Civil War before the two states were separated. Discussions involving this matter commenced in 1865, and, after protracted negotiations, Virginia in 1906 filed suit against West Virginia in the Supreme Court for a determination of the amount due. The dispute was not resolved conclusively until 1919, when the West Virginia legislature met in a special session and enacted a law providing for the payment ordered by the Court (Zimmerman 1992, 138–39). Finally, state resistance to a Court ruling may result in action by the executive branch, as in the instance when President Dwight Eisenhower sent federal troops to Little Rock, Arkansas, in 1955 to enforce the decision of the Court to racially integrate the high school of that community.

Interstate Regional Organizations

Most state boundaries were established prior to 1900, and social, economic, and technological changes since that date have brought about a variety of problems that cover distinct regions of the nation. The latter has resulted in various political pressures to create regional organizations that can serve a geographical area, without resulting in the excessive centralization that a national program would entail.

Many different regional organizations have been created over the years, with widely varying degrees of success. Many of these organizations have provided the states with a direct role, while the remaining of these entities have been subject to indirect state influence. Among the most notable of these regional organizations are the Tennessee Valley Authority, Delaware River Basin Commission, and Appalachian Regional Commission.

As a federally chartered government corporation, the Tennessee Valley Authority was created during the era of the Great Depression (Selznick 1949). The TVA is a public corporation with responsibility for water projects, such as flood control and navigation improvements; power generation; and fertilizer manufacturing. Its congressional proponents argued that the TVA would stimulate economic growth in the Tennessee River Valley, improve agricultural production and land use, and harness the Tennessee River.

The TVA does not provide the states in the region with any official role in its operations, but in practice the states do influence many of its decisions. In part, this occurs because the organization of the TVA was deliberately structured to be somewhat insulated from national government control. In order to facilitate the latter, its directors are appointed to staggered, nine-year terms; it has its own personnel system; and it is authorized to retain and spend revenues from its operations, such as the sale of electricity. In addition, since its creation the TVA has emphasized in its decision-making structure its "Grass Roots Doctrine" (Selznick 1949) of consulting with state and local governments, private citizens, and interest groups in the region. This doctrine was adopted by the TVA to reduce the risk of antagonism of state officials toward the body, making them more supportive of the TVA and its programs. In addition, the TVA makes payments in lieu of taxes to local governments in its jurisdiction. While much of the progress accomplished in Tennessee Valley region, in terms of economic growth, flood control, and rural electrification, would have occurred without the TVA, the rate of change probably would have been slower (Derthick and Bombardier 1974, 41–42).

The Delaware River Basin Commission is the product of a compact entered into by Delaware, New Jersey, New York, and Pennsylvania, along with the national government (Derthick and Bombardier 1974, chap. 3). The stimulus for the creation of the body was the interstate conflicts over the use of water from the river and problems of flooding. Proponents were of the persuasion that the commission could assist in resolving the conflicts and provide a coordinated program to develop and protect the river's water resources. Unfortunately, the commission has not accomplished as much as its advocates had predicted, in part because it cannot, because of its compact status, embark upon a course of action unless it has the unanimous support of its members. Moreover, the commission has no independent sources of revenue, which further limits its ability to act. Finally, national government agencies have often ignored the commission and proceeded with their agenda, disregarding the recommendations of the agency (Lord and Kenney 1993, 20–22).

The Appalachian Regional Commission (ARC) was established in 1965 by the Appalachian Regional Redevelopment Act and is considered "the original and prototypic interstate agency for regional economic development." Subsequently, from 1965 through 1972 seven other regional commissions were established in various parts of the United States (Wright 1982, 333–34). The ARC, which consists of a federal co-chair, designated by the president, and state representatives from the thirteen member states who elect a co-chair from their ranks, has evolved as the coordinator/administrator for special federal aid programs to Appalachia. The commission's region includes all of West Virginia and parts of Alabama, Georgia, Kentucky, Maryland, Mississippi, New York, North Carolina, Ohio, Pennsylvania, South Carolina, Tennessee, and Virginia. Additional counties in Kentucky, Tennessee, Ohio, and Virginia are currently (2004) seeking to be included in the geographical boundaries of the commission. The ARC has devoted considerable time and effort to lobbying Congress for more federal benefits for Appalachia. The commission was granted $66 million in federal funds for 2004, which was used for a wide variety of purposes, including constructing water and sewer lines, improving health care, funding business start-ups, creating telecommunications links, promoting tourism, constructing industrial parks, and building roads (Bowman 2003).

SUMMARY AND CONCLUSION

After long being the target of criticism by scholars for being inefficient, uneconomical, and unrepresentative of the larger body politic, state governments over the past four decades, as a result of constitutional, legislative, executive, and judicial modernization, have enhanced their political and administrative capacity. This has allowed them to become far more proactive, diversifying and enhancing their sources of revenues and assuming a much greater range of functional activity. As a result, states have enhanced their role and position in the intergovernmental system. We should note, however, that as a result of the economic recession of the early 2000s, the proactive and forward momentum of the states was somewhat derailed.

Horizontal relationships among the states are an important aspect of American federalism and intergovernmental relations. While the Constitution provides a basic legal framework for interstate relations, the limited number of relevant constitutional provisions and the vagueness of those provisions provide states with a considerable amount of latitude and maneuverability in interacting with each other.

Interstate cooperation takes many forms, ranging from informal discussions to administrative agreements, interstate compacts, uniform state laws, multistate adjudication, and the diffusion of policy ideas. Innovative program and policy states tend to be wealthy, urbanized, industrialized, and large in terms of population. Cooperation between states is stimulated by common problems, positive orientations toward the uses of governmental powers, and cooperative neighbors. In contrast, state officials are concerned with problems relating to excessive entanglement in interstate agreements, fears of creating uncontrollable centers of power, and the difficulty of reaching consensus, which serves to limit cooperation.

Conflict between the states comes from a variety of sources. For example, a state may take action, or fail to take action, that adversely affects the residents of other states. Conflict between the states is also the result of their perennial competition for new industries and economic investment; other sources of interstate conflict include boundary disputes, water disputes, differing economic and social structures, and political "grandstanding" by state officials. Interstate conflict is usually resolved through informal negotiations, administrative agreements, interstate compacts, litigation, or legislation enacted by Congress.

Because some policy challenges are regional in scope, and not of a national orientation, a number of regional organizations have been established over the years to respond to these problems. Among the most prominent of these organizations are the Tennessee Valley Authority, Delaware River Basin Commission, and Appalachian Regional Commission. However, most of the regional organizations that have been established have enjoyed only a modest record of success, simply because many national and state officials lack sufficient confidence in them, failing therefore to entrust these organizations with substantial legal and financial power.

Given the current political popularity of the concept of "devolution of powers" and the enhanced administrative and political capcity of the states, we can reasonably expect the role of state government to become increasingly important and for states to enjoy an increasingly enlarged position in the intergovernmental system.

REFERENCES

Bowman, Ann O'M. 2003. Interstate Equilibrium: Competition and Cooperation in the U.S. Federal System. Paper presented at the Annual Meeting of the American Political Science Association. Philadelphia. August 28–31.

———. 2004. Trends and Issues in Interstate Cooperation. *The Book of the States: 2004 Edition.* Lexington, KY: The Council of State Governments. 34–40.

Bowman, Ann O'M. and Richard C. Kearney. 1986. *The Resurgence of the States.* Englewood, Cliffs, NJ: Prentice-Hall.

———. 2002. *State and Local Government.* 5th ed. Boston: Houghton-Mifflin.

Bowman, Rex. 2003, December 21. Counties Line Up for a Piece of Appalachia. *Richmond Times-Dispatch.* B1, B4.

Citizens Conference on State Legislatures. 1971. *The Sometime Governments: A Critical Study of the 50 American Legislatures.* Kansas City, MO: Citizens Conference on State Legislatures.

Dao, James. 2004a, March 3. Two States Trying to Keep Gambling Money at Home. *New York Times.* A16.

———. 2004b, April 4. States' Tax Receipts Rise, Leading to Some Surpluses. *New York Times.* A14.

———. 2004c, July 7. Bill to Allow Slot Machines Is Passed in Pennsylvania. *New York Times.* A9.

DePalma, Anthony. 2004, May 21. 4 Northeast States Join Against Pollution. *New York Times.* A25.

Derthick, Martha A. 2005. *Up in Smoke: From Legislation to Litigation in Tobacco Politics.* 2nd ed. Washington, DC: CQ Press.

Derthick, Martha A. and Gary Bombardier. 1974. *Between State and Nation.* Washington, DC: Brookings.

Eaton, Leslie. 2004, August 8. Divorced Parents Move, and Custody Gets Trickier. *New York Times.* A1, A23.

El-Ashry, Mohammed T. and Diana Gibbons. 1986. *Troubled Waters: New Policies for Managing Water in the American West.* Washington, DC: Water Resources Institute.

Goodman, Ellen. 2003, July 7. Maine Takes Leadership Role in Health Care. *Richmond Times-Dispatch.* A9.

Governors' Meeting Turns to Aging of America. 2004, July 19. *Richmond Times-Dispatch.* A2.

Graves, W. Brooke. 1964. *American Intergovernmental Relations: Their Origins, Historical Development, and Current Status.* New York: Charles Scribner's Sons.

Green, Linda. 2005, May 17. Court Lifts Ban on Wine Shipping. *New York Times.* A19.

Gulick, Luther. 1933. Reorganization of the State. *Civil Engineering.* August, 420–21.

Hardin, Peter. 2003a, October 8. Va v. Md as River Dispute Goes to Court. *Richmond Times-Dispatch.* B2.

———. 2003b, December 10. Ruling a Victory for Va. *Richmond Times-Dispatch.* B1, B4.

Hazard, Carol. 2003, December 20. Wachovia Deal: 1,000-Plus Jobs. *Richmond Times-Dispatch.* A1, A15.

Herbers, John. 1987. The New Federalism: Unplanned, Innovative, and Here to Stay. *Governing.* 1 (October), 28–37.

Johnson, Kirk. 2003, July 25. 10 States Plan United Talks on Emissions. *New York Times.* A20.

Jones, Charles. 1976. Regulating the Environment. In Herbert Jacob and Kenneth Vines, eds., *Politics in the American States.* 3rd ed. Boston: Little Brown. 388–427.

Jones, Chip. 2004, January 14. States Hitch Efforts for Rail Funds. *Richmond Times-Dispatch.* C6.

Lord, William and Douglas Kenney. 1993. Resolving Interstate Water Conflicts: The Compact Approach. *Intergovernmental Perspective.* 19, 19–25.

Murphy, Dean E1. 2003, December 12. Nevada and Part of California May Face Water Shortages. *New York Times.* A29.

Netzer, Dick. 1991. An Evaluation of Interjurisdictional Competition Through Economic Development Incentives. In Daphne A. Kenyon and John Kincaid, eds., *Competition Among State and Local Governments.* Washington, DC: The Urban Institute Press. 221–45.

Penne, R. Leo and Paul Verduin. 1986. *State Government Associations: A Reconnaissance.* Washington, DC: National League of Cities.

Rayner, Bob. 2003, December 11. State Is Good for Business. *Richmond Times-Dispatch.* C1.

Reeves, Mavis Mann. 1990. The States as Polities: Reformed, Reinvigorated, Resourceful. *The Annals of the American Academy of Political and Social Science.* 509 (May), 83–93.

Revkin, Andrew C. 2004, July 21. New York City and 8 States Plan to Sue Power Plants. *New York Times.* A15.

Sanford, Terry. 1967. *The Storm over the States.* New York: McGraw-Hill.

Selznick, Philip. 1949. *TVA and the Grass Roots.* Berkeley: University of California Press.

Study Finds Improvement in Finances for States. 2003, November 11. *New York Times.* A20.

Teaford, Jon C. 2002. *The Rise of the States: Evolution of American State Government.* Baltimore: Johns Hopkins University Press.

Tedeschi, Bob. 2004, November 29. Justices to Hear Arguments on Interstate Wine Sales. *New York Times.* C2.

Uchitelle, Louis. 2003, October 10. States Pay for Jobs, but It Doesn't Always Pay Off. *New York Times.* A1, A17.

Virginia and Maryland to Join in Space Effort. 2003, December 4. *Richmond Times-Dispatch.* B2.

Walker, Jack. 1969. The Diffusion of Innovations Among the American States. *American Political Science Review.* 63 (September), 880–99.

Warner Joins Flag Property Debate. 2004, July 4. *Richmond Times-Dispatch.* B9.

Wayne, Leslie. 2005, June 17. Think Locally, Flirt Globally: U.S. States Chat up Aircraft Makers. *New York Times.* C6.

Wilgoren, Jodi. 2003, June 27. As Deadline Nears, 9 States Are Stalled in Budget Discord. *New York Times.* A1, A21.

Wright, Deil S. 1982. *Understanding Intergovernmental Relations.* 2nd ed. Monterey, Ca: Brooks/Cole.

Yardley, William. 2004, April 3. Border Dispute Affects Death and Taxes. *New York Times.* A12.

Zimmerman, Joseph F. 1992. *Contemporary American Federalism.* New York: Praeger.

——. 1996, *Interstate Relations: The Neglected Dimensions of Federalism.* Westport: Praeger, 146–147.

——. 2002. Trends in Interstate Relations: Political and Administrative Cooperation. *The Book of the States: 2002 Edition.* Lexington, KY: The Council of State Governments. 40–47.

——. 2004. *Interstate Economic Relations.* Albany: State University of New York Press.

——. 2005. Interstate Relations Trends. *The Book of the States.* Lexington, KY: Council of State Governments. 36–41.

——. 2006. *Interstate Disputes: The Supreme Court's Original Jurisdiction.* Albany: State University of New York Press.

• 8 •

STATE-LOCAL RELATIONS

Municipal corporations owe their origin to, and and derive their powers and rights wholly from, the legislature. It breathes into them the breath of life, without which they cannot exist. As it creates, so may it destroy. If it may destroy, it may abridge and control.

—Judge John F. Dillon, *City of Clinton v. Cedar Rapids & Missouri Railroad Company* (1868)

No mention is made of local government in the United States Constitution, and, as Daniel J. Elazar (1961) has clearly stated, the states, in a broad and sweeping sense, provide the legal framework for the existence and operation of their local governments. As noted by Elazar:

> The State government is the source and central authority for all the local governments within boundaries, even for those special districts created by the State virtually at the behest of the Federal Government. It has very definite powers of coercion [over these] creatures of the State, "home rule" notwithstanding. The legislature serves as the constituent assembly for local governments, creating and defining them, limiting or extending their powers, even delimiting the possible forms of government they may adopt.

Further:

> In order to amend the local "constitution," it is often necessary to go to the State capitol—unless the legislature has already provided for options which can be exercised locally, as in the choice of forms of municipal governments. The State even functions as a local legislature and executive in a wide variety of fields, sometimes retaining exclusive powers and sometimes sharing them with the city council or county board. (24–35)

Thus, local governments, inclusive of cities, towns, townships, counties, school districts, and special districts, are considered to be products or "legal creatures" of the states, and the only powers they can exercise are those provided by the state. As Joseph F. Zimmerman (1992) notes in his work *Contemporary American Federalism: The Growth of National Power*, while cities and towns are identified as municipal corporations,

188

counties and special districts are classified as quasi-municipal corporations (164). Local governments are established as a result of state action and are under the control of the state. Nevertheless, in our federal system of government, marked by a complex array of intergovernmental relationships, local governments have been able to maintain a degree of autonomy and a sphere of freedom of action.

This chapter, at the outset, sets forth an analysis of the constitutional and legal relationship between the states and their local governments. This is followed by a discussion of the various ways by which the states provide assistance to their local governments, along with the various techniques by which the states maintain their supervision and control over local governments. Attention is given to the role of municipalities and their statewide associations, local employee professional and union organizations, and other groups in the state policy-making process, in their attempt to achieve policy goals. Note is made of the phenomenon of state centralization and its consequences for state-local relations. The chapter concludes with an analysis of the sources of current state-local political and operational tensions and a discussion of the future of state-local relations.

THE CONSTITUTIONAL AND LEGAL SETTING

Although the legal context of state-local relations varies somewhat from state to state, some general observations may be advanced concerning the relationship between the states and their cities, counties, school districts, towns, and townships.[1] Since the United States Constitution makes no mention of local governments and because the state constitutions provide that local governments derive their authority from the state rather than from the populace, the legal setting of state-local relations is framed by state policies. As Joseph F. Zimmerman (2004) has noted: "Constitutional provisions, statutes, state administrative rules and regulations, and court decisions determine the nature of the legal relationships between a state and its political subdivisions" (29).

A general framework for state-local relations was provided by Justice John F. Dillon, an Iowa judge presiding largely in the latter part of the nineteenth century, who in a number of court rulings, as well as in his seminal and influential work *Commentaries on the Law of Municipal Corporations* (1911), formulated and advanced what has become known as Dillon's Rule. Concerning the relationship of state-local relations, Dillon's Rule notes that municipalities, cities, towns, and townships are "creatures" of and established by the state. Dillon advanced in one of his often-quoted court decisions: "Municipal corporations owe their origin to, and derive their powers and rights wholly from, the legislature. It breathes into them the breath of life, without which they cannot exist. As it creates, so may it destroy. If it may destroy, it may also abridge and control" (*City of Clinton v. Cedar Rapids and Missouri Railroad Company*, 24 Iowa 455, 1868). Dillon noted that a municipality may exercise only those powers explicitly granted to it by the state, those powers clearly implied in the explicitly granted powers, or those powers that are essential to meeting the declared objectives and responsibilities of the local government. If there is any doubt concerning whether a municipality has the right to exercise a particular power, the issue is resolved in its disfavor.

In terms of state-local relations, a number of negative ramifications flow from Dillon's Rule. First, a local government can become involved in a contentious and costly legal dispute concerning whether it has the right to exercise a certain power. This may well serve to preclude a locality from addressing and formulating a policy designed to deal with a serious problem. A second consequence of Dillon's Rule is that because it has framed local powers in such a limited fashion, it has resulted in the expansion of the role, or scope, of the states and the national government. Third, since local officials may be uncertain of whether they have the right to exercise a power they may, particularly in states situated in New England and the South, seek the passage of "special legislation" in the state legislature in order to exercise such a power. This routine serves to significantly enhance the workload of the state legislature and also may well produce some measure of resentment among local officials. W. Brooke Graves (1964) in his seminal work *American Intergovernmental Relations* noted in his highly critical assessment of this practice:

> Under this system, municipalities have to go to the legislature for authority to pave a street, raise the salary of an official, or even to install a hydrant. Such a system is vicious; the members of the legislature are permitted to make political capital by handling matters in which they have little competence and no real interest, at the expense of valuable legislative time which might otherwise be used constructively. At the same time, local units are denied the opportunity to decide questions purely local in character. Many of the States have brought this problem under control, and the remainder should do so without delay. (706)

It should be noted that since Graves penned this advice four decades ago, a total of forty-one states have passed constitutional amendments that forbid the practice of "special legislation" (Zimmerman 2004, 28).

MUNICIPAL CHARTERS

The authority of cities and towns is based on and derived from a municipal charter, granted to a community by the state. The municipal charter constitutes the fundamental law of the city, and, in this sense, it is somewhat analogous to a state constitution or the constitution of the United States. The municipal charter sets forth the boundaries of a community, its form and structure of government, the powers it may exercise, authorized programmatic activities and responsibilities, sources of revenues, along with a variety of other general and specific provisions.

The states have provided to their cities and towns a variety of municipal charters. The special act charter approach, of long-standing duration, requires that the state legislature draft an individualized charter for each city and town. The advantage of the special act charter approach is that it has a measure of flexibility, recognizes that the needs and goals of all municipalities may not be similar, and allows the state legislature to fashion and provide a charter to meet the particular needs of a locality.

However, over the years, many of the states have abolished granting special act charters.

A number of shortcomings have been associated with the special act charter approach. First, from the perspective of local officials, a major limitation of the special act charter approach is that the framing and writing of a special act charter is largely done by members of the state legislature, and not by city officials. As a result, state legislators, perhaps because of arbitrary political reasons, may provide one community with a very restrictive charter, while granting another community a far less restrictive charter, providing for the latter a substantial amount of policy autonomy. Another criticism of the special act approach is that it serves to maximize state control over local government, since the legislature may grant or withhold from a community its quest to gain additional powers. A third, often voiced, criticism of the special act charter approach it that it usually creates a large amount of charter revision work for the state legislature, particularly in states like Virginia, which continue to structure their state-local relationship according to the tenets of Dillon's Rule, leaving legislators less time for dealing with statewide concerns and issues.

Partly as a result of the problems associated with the special act approach, some states began to adopt a system of general act charters. Under this scenario, a similar charter is bestowed upon all of the municipalities in the state, thereby freeing the members of the state legislature from the time-consuming burden of drafting an individual charter for each city. Unfortunately, the general act charter approach is not free of reproach, since it provides little flexibility for accommodating the different needs and requirements of individual cities. For instance, the general act approach may force a city to accept a responsibility it does not need or desire, while another city may lack the authority to deal with a special pressing problem.

The classified charter system combines the flexibility of the special act charter with the fairness of the general act charter approach. The classified charter approach provides that the cities of a state are divided into classes, usually according to population size. For instance, in some states cities containing at least one million residents are designated "Class A" cities, while communities ranging in population from 500,000 to 999,999 are labeled as "Class B" cities. An appropriate charter has been drafted for each class of city. The classified charter approach provides some recognition of the fact that cities of differing population size are confronted with somewhat unique challenges and are required to fashion different public policy responses.

Several criticisms have been advanced by scholars in regard to the system of classified charters. They have noted that cities of the same population class, and therefore granted the same charter, may well be faced with unique challenges and public policy needs. In addition, the intended fairness of the classified charter approach may be undermined if the state legislature has developed classes of charters that include only one city, thereby facilitating some measure of political favoritism or retribution. Finally, as scholars have noted, the classified charter approach may also result in unwanted and disruptive changes in a city charter when the population of a city no longer conforms to its prior population classification (Zimmerman 1992, 171).

Efforts to provide cities more choice over the adoption of their charter has resulted in the optional charter approach. Under this scenario, cities are free to choose from a range of appropriate charters, often providing for a variety of forms of local governmental structure. Cities that are of the same size but have different challenges or needs can select the charter and form of government that is most appropriate for their community.

HOME RULE

The chartering system of home rule maximizes local flexibility and minimizes the interference of the state and has long been advocated by municipal reformers. Graves (1964) has said the following regarding home rule: "Home rule may be defined as the power of local self government. Communities have the right to select their own form of governmental organization and either draft their own charter or select one to their liking under an optional charter plan." Further, "Home rule may be granted by constitutional provision, by legislative act, or by a constitutional provision which become effective only upon legislative implementation" (700). Iowa was the first state to adopt statutory home rule in 1858, while Missouri was the first state to adopt constitutional home rule in 1875; by 1915 fifteen states had granted constitutional home rule to their municipalities (Graves 1964, 701, 703–4). Currently, in sixteen states municipalities enjoy constitutional home rule, while the vast majority of the balance of the states provide their municipalities with statutory home rule (Zimmerman 2004, 28). It should be noted that some of these states restrict the granting of home rule to cities above a certain population limit and, conversely, deny home rule to communities below a certain population size. However, it should be noted that only twenty-eight states provide home rule to municipalities that grant cities broad functional authority. And, further, it should be stressed that the doctrine and granting of home rule does not prevent home-rule states from enacting legislation in an area of paramount and substantial state concern (Zimmerman 2004, 28). Although the home-rule concept was originally limited to cities, by 1964 home rule had been extended to counties in a number of states, including California, Maryland, Minnesota, Ohio, West Virginia, and Wisconsin (Graves 1964, 709). This figure increased to twenty-four states by 1991 (Benton 2002, 9) and to thirty-seven states by 2005. However, as David R. Berman (2003) has noted, only about one out of every ten counties eligible to adopt a home-rule charter has done so (74). The reluctance of many county officials to seek a home-rule charter is largely because of their concern over what the impact of home-rule status would be on their powers and responsibilities.

Under the home-rule approach, city leaders, usually with the advice of municipal governmental consultants, draft a charter for their community and submit it to the voters for their approval. The home-rule approach serves to increase local autonomy and flexibility, thereby allowing city leaders to draft a charter to meet the particular needs of their community and revise it when necessary. Revisions of the charter do not usually require city officials to gain the approval of the state legislature; however, it should be noted that the ambiguity of some home-rule charters has been the source of a good deal of litigation. In his assessment of home rule, Graves (1964) reported:

[T]he concept has . . . served a number of useful purposes. It has provided for variations in the structure of local government. It has helped state legislatures by relieving them of most of the local bills that were a great burden to their predecessors and that still are a burden in many non-home-rule jurisdictions. It has sometimes provided a satisfactory solution to the jurisdictional problems which plague many urban centers. Home-rule has frequently created a favorable climate for the growth of metropolitan government, encouraging citizen participation and a certain amount of self-reliance in the solution of local problems. (704)

One the other hand, some scholars have expressed some measure of concern about the concept and reality of home rule. For instance, Daniel J. Barron, Gerald E. Frug, and Rick T. Su have reported in their study *Dispelling the Myth of Home Rule: Local Power in Greater Boston* (2004), based upon an analysis of the Home Rule Amendment of the Massachusetts state constitution and interviews conducted with officials in more than half of the cities and towns in the Boston metropolitan region, that the localities lack home rule in the local autonomy sense of the term. They note that this is because localities are limited in regard to their authority over taxing and borrowing, enjoy only limited land use powers, are saddled with an array of unfunded mandates, and have no protection against conflicting general state legislation.

In addition, scholars have argued that home rule may encourage individual localities to pursue their own parochial interests, without regard for well-being of neighboring localities or the region in which they are situated. Rather paradoxically, Barron, Frug, and Su (2004) have noted that the perception of local officials in the Boston region that home rule is important has frustrated attempts to achieve a greater sense of regionalism (71–89). Further, scholars have noted that the concept of home rule, along with its companion notion of local autonomy, may serve to preclude needed state involvement in local affairs, particularly in regard to economic development, crime, and other social problems. Finally, Zimmerman (1972) has reported that in some politically active communities home rule may result at election time in a continuing onslaught of proposals to change the city charter, a situation that may prove frustrating to the voters and undermine local governmental stability (1992, 173).

Approximately half of the states following the legislative supremacy approach have put into effect some form of devolution of powers for at least some of their local governments. For example, the New York Constitution devolves upon local governments ten specific powers in addition to matters involving "property, affairs or government" (Zimmerman 2004, 28). Devolution, with or without home rule, grants local government the authority to utilize those powers not denied to them by the state. It facilitates the ability of local officials to respond more rapidly to challenges than if they had to seek a grant of authority from the state before acting on particular problems.

COUNTY GOVERNMENT

County governments exist in every state except Connecticut and Rhode Island. In the latter states, and throughout New England, county governments have functioned as distinctly weak governmental entities, with largely only judicial responsibilities. The origins of the county government in the United States may be traced back to their establishment in Virginia in 1634. The historical prominence and role of county government has varied considerably according to region. Whereas county government has long been a major provider of services in the South, its counterpart in the Northeast, as the aforementioned would imply, has usually played a decidedly secondary role to municipalities.

Unlike municipalities, counties are considered to be formal extensions, or "arms," of the state government. An Ohio court decision handed down in 1857 succinctly noted the difference between a municipality (city) and a county:

> A municipal corporation proper is created mainly for the interest, advantage, and convenience of the locality and its people; a county organization is created almost exclusively with a view to the policy of the State at-large, for purposes of political organization and civil administration, in matters of finance, of education, of provision for the poor, of military organization, of the means of travel and transport, and especially for the general administration of justice. With scarcely an exception, all the powers and functions of the county organization have a direct and exclusive reference to the general administration of that policy.

Further:

> Counties are local subdivisions of a State, created by the sovereign power of a State, of its own sovereign will, without the particular solicitation, consent, or concurrent action of the people who inhabit them. The former organization (municipal corporation) is asked for, or at least assented to by the people it embraces; the latter is superimposed by a sovereign and paramount authority. (*Commissioners of Hamilton County v. Mighels*, 7 Ohio St. 109 at 118, 1857)

The structure of county government varies considerably. The traditional form of county government is marked by a board of commissioners, usually consisting of three to five members, who exercise both executive and legislative powers. Another traditional form of county government has been the supervisor form, in which the mayors of the cities and villages and the principle trustee of the townships act as the county board. In contrast, the county executive form is characterized by an elected county executive who is responsible for the administration and operation of the county government and a board of commissioners who make public policy. In addition, counties are making increasing use of the county manager form or plan of government, consisting of an elected board of commissioners (supervisors) who, in turn, retain a professional manager to administer the county government.

The service role of the county government varies significantly according to the state and geographical setting in which it is located. For instance, in Maine and Massachusetts counties are largely limited to providing judicial functions, whereas in Maryland counties are the principle providers of local services. In Virginia, where counties statewide are uniquely geographically distinct from cities, county governments, especially suburban units situated in large metropolitan areas, provide the usual broad range of municipal-type services. Whereas counties situated in rural areas throughout the nation have usually delivered a limited number of services most often limited to water and sewer services and fire protection, counties in metropolitan areas are rapidly assuming more municipal-like service responsibilities (Benton 2002).

SPECIAL DISTRICTS

In addition to municipalities and counties, special districts, sometimes referred to as authorities, are an important type of local government; throughout the last half of the past century they have proved to be the most rapidly increasing form of government. Special districts, usually autonomous units of government, are created by the state legislature or by local action to provide one or a limited number of services. Although autonomous, special districts often interact in a variety of governing, financial, and services ways with other units of local government. School districts, considered by scholars as a distinct form of special district government, remain, by far, the most numerous type of special districts, although there was a substantial absolute decline in the number of these units throughout the last half of the past century. Nonschool special districts, which are either unifunctional or multifunctional in character, are involved in the provision of fire protection, water supply, sewerage, housing and community development, drainage and flood control, soil and water conservation, economic development, and a wide variety of other services (Stephens and Wikstrom 1998, 133). Special districts raise their revenues either through the imposition of a service charge, property taxes, or sales taxes. Due to the legal, political, and fiscal restraints associated with municipal and county governments, and the usual inability to realize radical metropolitan reform, special districts have been increasingly established in metropolitan areas since they provide a more flexible organizational approach for providing services to the public. In this regard, special districts often transcend municipal and county boundaries and provide services, like mass transportation, on a regional basis; conversely, it should be noted that municipal and county governments have established special districts within the boundaries of their communities, largely for the purpose of spurring economic development in distressed areas. Districts are sometimes used to tap tax sources not available to other local governments.

STATE IMPACTS SHAPING LOCAL GOVERNMENT

In addition to the incorporation of municipalities (cities and towns) and establishing counties, states impact the structure, development, and operation of local government in a variety of ways. For instance, practically all states, following the lead of Indiana, which adopted the first intergovernmental statute in 1851, have passed legislation providing the legal framework for local governments to engage in local intergovernmental functional cooperation (Zimmerman 2004, 30). Although this type of cooperation involves a wide variety of functions, the most salient example involves the widespread use of fire and police mutual assistance aid agreements, which are especially prevalent in metropolitan areas. Intergovernmental agreements are popular with local officials because they allow a local government to obtain and provide a service it could not otherwise provide, lower the cost of a service through economies of scale, and provide a higher quality of service (Zimmerman 2004, 30). In a similar vein, twenty states explicitly allow, either through a constitutional or statutory provision, a local government to voluntarily transfer a functional responsibility to another local government or the state government because of lack of equipment, facilities, personnel, fiscal restraints, or the desire to eliminate the duplication of services (Zimmerman 2004, 31). Finally, most states provide the legal basis for local governments to become members of a regional organization, such as a council of governments or a regional planning commission, designed to facilitate and promote regional cooperation and areawide policies and services.

In addition, state laws provide the legal basis for far more drastic ways of reshaping the nature of local government. For example, the strategy of annexation provides a method for a city to include within its boundaries additional unincorporated territory. Through annexation, many cities, including Boston, Massachusetts, and Richmond, Virginia, substantially increased their territorial boundaries in the nineteenth century. In the twentieth century a host of cities, most prominently in Texas (including Dallas, El Paso, Fort Worth, Houston, and San Antonio), along with Oklahoma City, Atlanta, and Kansas City, Missouri, significantly enlarged their territorial boundaries through the annexation process. However, annexation by cities has become increasing more difficult and uncommon during the present times, since practically all core cities are surrounded by incorporated suburban entities.

The states usually provide the legal framework for the consolidation of two (or possibly more) units of local government. For example, in the past century, most of the local governments of the metropolitan areas of Baton Rouge, Louisiana; Nashville, Tennessee; Jacksonville, Florida; and Indianapolis, Indiana have been restructured into a system of city-county consolidation. As a result of this restructuring, most of the local municipal services in the Nashville metropolitan area were transferred to the government of Davidson County (Stephens and Wikstrom 2000, 68–87). A corollary example of metropolitan governmental reform took place in the Miami-Dade County, Florida, metropolitan area in the mid-1950s when the State of Florida provided the legal basis for the establishment of a federative, or two-level, type of metropolitan governmental structure (Stephens and Wikstrom 2000, 88–95). However, the goal of annexation, city-county consolidation, and federative metropolitan government, especially in large metropolitan areas, has proved increasingly difficult for current-day reformers to achieve.

MECHANISMS OF STATE ASSISTANCE AND INFLUENCE

Without doubt, the most important mechanism that the state has for influencing the political behavior of local officials involves financial assistance, including general assistance, shared taxes, in lieu payments, block grants, grants-in-aid for particular projects or services, and categorical grant aid. Sales, income, and gasoline taxes are among the state taxes that are most often shared with localities. As noted by Michael A. Pagano (1990), state constitutional and statutory restrictions on the taxing and spending authority of local governments, excluding restrictions on local sales and income taxes, exist in forty-three states. Only Connecticut, Georgia, Maine, New Hampshire, South Carolina, Vermont, and Wisconsin do not limit local government expenditures or taxes. Hawaii and Tennessee impose only a full-disclosure rule. Further, as Pagano advanced, the six generic state limits on local government and tax and expenditure powers are revenue rollbacks, full disclosure, limits on assessment, the property tax rate, property tax revenues, and general expenditures (97). Local governments have become increasingly dependent upon state fiscal assistance, and this fiscal aid has served, to a limited extent in a few states, to moderate financial disparities between communities. State fiscal aid to communities for local public education primarily has been provided through block grants. Over the years, state financial assistance to communities, in the form of categorical grants, largely has been used toward the costs of social services, roads and highways, general support for local government, and special capital projects. State assistance, sometimes involving federal Community Development Block Grant (CBDG) funding, to local communities or large companies, in the form of project grants or cash incentives, has been largely used to defray the costs of the construction of new public infrastructure, such as water and sewer lines, water treatment plants, roads, and new or improved railroad access. For instance, Virginia's Commonwealth Transportation Board in January 2004 provided grants of a varying amount to three localities to improve their access to railroad service (Bacque 2004, B2). Grants provided to local governments by the state require careful monitoring by state officials to assure that the funds involved are appropriately spent according to state guidelines.

In addition, as reported by Zimmerman (2004), a number of states have established municipal bond banks and municipal investment pools for the benefit of their smaller communities (32). Following the lead of Vermont (1970), eight additional states have established a municipal bond bank that permits small localities to borrow funds at a favorable rate of interest. Twenty-nine state legislatures have created municipal investment pools, which allows smaller communities to benefit from the professional management of short-term investments, resulting in greater liquidity, lower administrative costs, and a higher return.

States also shape the activities of local governments through the practice and use of state mandates. State mandates are implemented in the form of statutes, executive orders, and administrative regulations and often result in unfunded costs for local governments by requiring that localities establish new programs or meet higher performance standards. States impose many more mandates on their local governments than does the federal government. However, it should be noted that some of the most expensive mandates are federal mandates that states have passed on to localities. In this sense, local governments, being at the end of the path of "one-way federalism" or what some have labeled "shift-and-shaft federalism," wind up paying many of the costs of government (Gold and Ritchie 1992). Because of their legal and political superiority over local governments, states often mandate, or order, local units to adhere to a wide variety of mandates involving the environment, equal treatment, ethics, information policies, personnel, record-keeping, governmental structure, and minimal service levels (Zimmerman 1992, 181).[2]

Relevant studies document that the states make widespread use of mandates. For instance, research reported by the U.S. Advisory Commission on Intergovernmental Relations (ACIR) (1982) found that the typical state in the 1980s imposed thirty-five different mandates on local governments, requiring some measure of spending by the effected governments. The study found that North Carolina had the fewest mandates, totaling somewhat more than 250, while California had the most mandates, with well over 1,400 (162–65). Berman reported in 2003 that Kansas has imposed about 941 mandates on its local governments, but has a compelling interest in the adoption and enforcement of only about 100 (Berman 2003, 77).

State mandates have proved to be a considerable source a source of irritation to local officials. Lawrence J. Grossback (2002), reporting on a study conducted by the Minnesota Office of the Legislative Auditor in 2000, noted that somewhat over 70 percent of the city, county, and township administrators surveyed felt that state "mandates made their jobs either somewhat or considerably more difficult" (188). According to the study, about 40 percent of the local Minnesota administrators were of the persuasion that state mandates, even if fully funded by the state, were not appropriate in the local policy areas of economic development, general governmental administration, and recreation, and that existing mandates in the policy areas of economic development and general governmental administration were viewed by administrators as either "unreasonable" or "very unreasonable" (189–90). In addition, local officials resent being ordered to pursue a particular course of action that they feel is inappropriate for their community. For instance, in the fall of 2003, the town officials of Chautauqua, New York, argued that the state code concerning the size of windows in residential dwellings imposed on communities was too restrictive, and especially placed an undue burden on their Amish residents (Foderaro 2003, A12). Further hostility on the part of local officials to state mandates, as found in the study reported on by Grossback (2002), is because of their belief that mandate compliance may be very expensive, with little or none of the costs covered by the state. Orders from the state capital may not be accompanied by funds to cover the costs (189). As a result of these concerns, fifteen states have amended their constitution and sixteen states have enacted legislation designed to restrict the power of the state legislature and administrative agencies to mandate costs upon their local governments (Zimmerman 2004, 31).

On the other hand, a reasonable defense may be made for state-imposed mandates on local governments. Mandates often reflect the recognition of the need for minimum standards of service levels (Berman 2003, 78) and provide a way for needed state policy uniformity, as in the instance of common road or highway signs, or elementary and secondary educational standards. Mandates can also promote and ensure coordination between various nonprofit and profit agencies, local governments, and regional organizations involved in the same functional and policy areas. In addition, we should bear in mind that although local officials often criticize mandates, they frequently approve of the policy thrust of mandates. In the world of local politics, mandates often serve as a form of "political cover" for local officials who sympathize with and implement a mandate, despite broad community hostility.

In addition to mandates, the policy autonomy of local governments has been eroded further by the state practice of enacting preemptions, which result in their dominance of certain policy areas and serve to prevent local governments from undertaking a wide range of regulatory activities. For example, thirty-three states presently prohibit local governments from adopting rent control measures. States have largely preempted the policy field regarding use of tobacco through the passage of statewide clean-indoor-air legislation. Largely as a result of the political pressures of the National Rifle Association (NRA), forty states currently prohibit local gun-control ordinances, and a majority of the states deny local authority to regulate who can carry concealed weapons. And finally, in many states local employee groups have been successful in securing state action in eliminating local residency requirements for municipal workers (Berman 2003, 83–86).

In addition to the use of mandates and preemptions, states have other methods and techniques for holding accountable, monitoring, and regulating the activities of local governmental officials. The most basic of these techniques involves that of either formal or informal consultation between state and local officials, which serves to facilitate communication between the two levels of government. Such communication may well provide an arena, or setting, for negotiation between officials over an important policy matter or administrative procedure. Officials may confer by telephone, cell phone, or e-mail or in face-to-face meetings. Although consultation is useful and plays an important role in facilitating state and local governmental cooperation, it is often too irregular to provide state officials with a dependable source of information regarding local activities or a reliable means to resolve serious administrative or policy disagreements.

All states have established minimum service standards and methods of enforcement to ensure cooperation and compliance by their local governments. The establishment of minimum state standards ensures adequate local performance and, at the same time, frees local units from the restrictive effects of a rigid uniformity. Local authorities are often encouraged to exceed the minimum service level within the limits of their resources and the citizen preferences of their community. All states have adopted minimum standards in regard to, for instance, public education, health, welfare, and the operation of waste disposal sites. If an operation of a locality fails to comply with minimum state standards, the state may order the cessation of operations. A case in point, in March 2004, Virginia's Department of Environmental Quality ordered Page County to close down its landfill operation because it took in too much trash and endangered the environment (Springston 2004, B1).

States provide a wide range of advice and technical assistance and training to local governments, which serve to influence the behavior and practices of local governmental officials. Such advice and technical assistance is provided on a large variety of matters, including law enforcement, fire-fighting, road construction, accounting techniques, personnel systems, water treatment methods, and economic development. Robert Agranoff and Michael McGuire (1998) found in their survey of the chief administrators of cities and counties located in either Illinois, Indiana, Michigan, Ohio, or Wisconsin with a population in excess of 2,500 and in cities and counties with less than 2,500 residents but with a professional manager that the states, along with a variety of nongovernmental entities, played the key role in assisting local communities in their economic development efforts (150–64). States provide law enforcement training and expertise for local police officials, especially in regard to laboratory analysis and forensic techniques. State advice and technical assistance is especially useful and valuable to small towns and rural counties, since these governmental entities have only a limited amount of managerial capacity and expertise.

States also utilize the practice of requiring their localities to submit to the state periodic reports on specific activities, especially in regard to financial matters. These reports enable state officials to monitor local programs and the success of policy implementation, in accordance with state guidelines. More often than not, however, these reports are not always carefully prepared by local officials since they are aware that state officials do not always provide them with a careful reading and review. As a result, report inaccuracies and omissions may remain unquestioned, and annual changes in report formats and standards can result in problems of comparability over time.

States also conduct inspections and investigations to gather information on local governmental services and activities. State inspections are generally carried out on a routine basis. Such inspections might involve the condition of streets, school buses, or water treatment plants. Although state inspections are usually conducted on a regular and routine basis, occasionally these inspections may be carried out on an unpredicted basis. Surprise inspections by the state may result in a more realistic assessment of local governmental services and activities, but such inspections risk the possibility of antagonizing local officials and straining state-local relations. More intensive state investigations of a municipal government usually involve nonroutine matters, such as a financial crisis, purported corruption, or the cessation or breakdown of an essential service.

States require that a local government must secure state approval before undertaking a range of actions. For example, Virginia requires that a local government must gain the approval of the state before commencing the construction of a major road. Such reviews by the state provide a future guide, or precedent, for localities concerning the sort of actions they can undertake.

In extreme situations, states have the authority to remove a local official and designate her or his replacement. Generally this removal power by the state is exercised with considerable caution and is only resorted to in extreme cases involving personal gross misconduct, corruption, incompetence, or financial mismanagement. A highly unusual problem is required for the state to exercise its removal power, as in the instance of the serious allegations involving corruption and misconduct ascribed to Mayor James Walker of New York City, who in 1932 was the subject of a hearing conducted by Governor Franklin Roosevelt. The information provided at the hearing could well have resulted in Walker's removal from office, but he resigned before the completion of the hearing.

The most extreme method involving state control of their local governments is that of the state assuming direct control, review powers, or the responsibility of a local government or a local governmental program. As Berman (2003) has noted: "State takeovers of financially distressed, general-purpose local governments (municipalities and counties) and 'academically bankrupt' school districts have been the most noticeable in recent years" (113). Direct state control of a local government or a particular program is a course of action followed by the state in regard to extraordinary circumstances, such as widespread corruption, impending or actual financial collapse, or a major disruption in vital services. For instance, at the beginning of the twentieth century, the State of Texas assumed full control and all of the responsibilities of the City of Galveston, which had fallen into bankruptcy after being severely damaged by a hurricane. In a parallel more recent action, the State of Massachusetts in 1991 took full control of the City of Chelsea, after it had been placed in receivership (Berman 2003, 119). In less sweeping action, in 1975 when New York City was facing bankruptcy the state legislature enacted a number of laws to assist the city. Among other actions, it established the state-controlled Emergency Financial Control Board and the Municipal Assistance Corporation to solve the city's fiscal problems. The board controlled the city's financial transactions, and the corporation issued bonds and notes and utilized the proceeds to pay off the city's maturing notes (Zimmerman 1992, 180). Although the Board is still in existence the word "Emergency" has been deleted from its title. Zimmerman (2004) reports that in response to their deteriorating financial position the New York legislature established similar boards for the cities of Yonkers (1978), Troy (1995), and Buffalo (2003); however, the improving financial health of Yonkers and Troy resulted in the dissolution of their respective state-imposed control boards (31). New Jersey officials in 1989 assumed direct control and responsibility of the public schools of Jersey City after concluding that the school administration was plagued by political patronage in hiring, corruption, and excessive union demands (Berman 2003, 123). Some years later, the State of Connecticut assumed direct operational responsibility of Hartford's public schools, due to their poor performance under local control. Eventually, Jersey City and Hartford regained operational responsibility of their public schools.

The use of direct state control is limited by a number of factors, not the least of which is its conflict with the American tradition of strong local autonomy and control (Syed 1966). On this score, one is reminded of the magnificent work of Robert C. Wood written a half-century ago titled *Suburbia: Its People & Their Politics* (1958), in which he characterized suburbanites as dwelling in "republics in miniature" and being fiercely protective of their local political autonomy. Local electorates may well resent state intrusion into their community affairs, unless the need is clearly demonstrated; and, since these same voters play a role in choosing governors and state legislators, state officials are mindful of their concerns. Local officials throughout the state would react with strong displeasure if state officials were to assume direct control of a local program without a compelling state interest and justification. State officials usually hesitate to become involved in a quagmire of complex local problems; assuming direct control may prove embarrassing if the situation does not improve. However, when a genuine crisis exists, state officials risk considerable criticism if they do not act, and much of that criticism will come from citizens in the affected locality.

INTERGOVERNMENTAL LOBBYING AND
STATE POLICY-MAKING

Local officials along with their statewide associations lobby the state legislature to achieve policy goals. According to Zimmerman (1992), most of this lobbying is directed toward increased funding for localities and to defeat legislation mandating actions by political subdivisions (179). In every state there is at least one statewide association of local officials, while in a number of the states there are several of these types of organizations. For instance, in Virginia, as noted in Chapter 3, the Virginia Municipal League (VML) represents cites, towns, and urban counties in the state policy-making process, while the Virginia Association of Counties (VACO) lobbies on behalf of the interests of counties. As Berman (2003) has astutely noted: "[T]he key to success [for local governmental associations] may well be in getting their members engaged, especially lining up mayors or other top elected officials to make vital, politician-to-politician contacts with state legislators." Further: "Pursuing their objectives, local lobbyists working for associations of local officials cultivate ties with legislators, meeting with them individually between as well as during legislative sessions to discuss their concerns and to inform them about local issues" (39).

The Virginia Municipal League (2003) set forth a wide variety of policy goals in its "Legislative Program" for the 2003 legislative session of the Virginia General Assembly (state legislature). These policy goals included, but were not limited to, support for tax restructuring, increased funding for public education, full funding of many state mandates, and transportation funding. Additional policy goals sought by the league included increased state funding for land conservation, the continued use of nonpartisan local elections, and photo–red light traffic enforcement (4–7).

In addition to being represented in the state policy process by statewide associations, most of the larger cities and counties in the states have their own lobbyist who represents and advocates their interests in the state legislature. This is simply because larger localities often have their own unique interests or policy goals. For example, the legislative goals of Henrico County, Virginia, a large Richmond suburban county containing a population of somewhat in excess of 270,000 residents, in the 2004 session of the General Assembly included, among other items, increased state funding for public education, human services, mental health, and an array of other services; full funding of all federal and state mandates; and the right to impose road impact fees. Additional goals sought by Henrico County included that of denying the state the ability of imposing a fee on the disposal of waste in local landfills or on the provision of water or wastewater services by localities and continued state support for public and private partnerships designed to spur economic development (Henrico County 2004, 2–4).

In the mid 1990s, William DeSoto (1995) conducted a study, utilizing a mail survey, concerning the political interaction of municipal governments, with a minimum population of at least sixty thousand residents, with their state government (188–94). He reported that a majority, precisely 52 percent, of the municipalities, in addition to belonging to a league of municipalities, designated a staff person or retained a contract lobbyist to represent their interests in the state political arena. DeSoto noted that the three major broad areas of concern to municipalities involved taxation and revenue, the environment, and crime. In addition, matters relating to education and labor relations were also of significant concern to municipalities (191). As reported by DeSoto, state officials more likely perceived local municipalities as "special interests," rather than as "valued governmental partners" in the state governmental process (192). The study found that the governor's office is somewhat more receptive to the interests of municipalities than the state legislature, while the state courts were viewed as the least receptive (193).

In addition, lobbyists representing municipal employees and community interests are heavily engaged in the state legislative process. Among the most active and influential local employee associations are those representing public schoolteachers, predominately the National Education Association (Loftus 1994, 129). Various professional organizations, unions, and other employee organizations lobby for the interests of other local employees. These entities not only lobby for higher tangible benefits for their members, including compensation and better working conditions, but also seek to impact state policies setting the educational and training standards for those who wish to engage in their profession. Among the most active and salient of these organizations are those representing employees engaged in law enforcement and fire-fighting. Community interests that are heavily represented in the state legislative process include lawyers, bankers, doctors, real estate, and developers (Thomas and Hrebenar 1999, 117–18).

STATE CENTRALIZATION

As reported by one of the authors three decades ago in a published paper entitled "State Centralization and the Erosion of Local Autonomy," a major development in state-local relations over the past century has been the trend of greater state centralization, reflecting the enhanced position of state government relative to their local units, as documented in Figure 8.1 (Stephens 1974, 44–76, and updates). In support of his contention, Stephens noted that he devised a composite index of state centralization utilizing the following three components that reflect the relative distribution of power between the state and local governments: (1) financial responsibility, or which level pays for goods and services; (2) determination of the level that delivers each of fifteen major functional activities; and (3) distribution of public personnel between levels modified by the relative labor intensity of different services rendered by state and local governments. These ratings were placed on a continuum from 0 to 100 and segmented into the following five categories: decentralized, local services, balanced, state services, and centralized (Stephens 46, 54–55).[3] Utilizing the same methodology as he employed in his initial investigation, Stephens found in a more recent inquiry a general trend toward greater state centralization over the period from 1902 to 2002. As documented in Table 8.1 by 2002 a total of twenty-seven states were classified by Stephens as either "centralized" or "state services"–oriented; in contrast, only two states were classified as "local services"–oriented, and none were found to "decentralized."

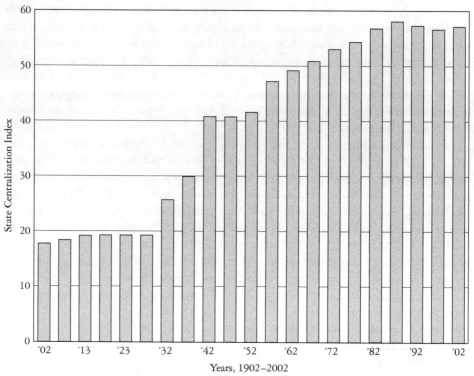

FIGURE 8.1. State centralization for the average state, 1902–2002. Uses Stephens' typology for classifying states in terms of state versus local activity in relation to financial responsibility, service delivery, and personnel, with the latter adjusted for state differences in labor versus cash and capital inputs. *Source: Stephens, 1974, pp. 44–76 and later updates.*

TABLE 8.1. State Centralization for Selected Years, 1902–2002

Classification of State Role	1902	1913	1932	1942	1957	1969	1977	1986	1995	2002
Centralized, 60.0 or higher	—	—	—	1	4	6	9	20	17	14
State services, 55.0–59.9	—	—	—	5	5	9	12	14	14	13
Balanced, 45.0–54.9	—	3	1	12	20	24	25	15	18	21
Local services, 40.0–44.9	—	—	3	7	8	6	4	1	1	2
Decentralized, 39.9 or less	45	45	44	23	13	5	—	—	—	—
TOTALS	45	48	48	48	50[1]	50	50	50	50	50
Average state rating	17.8	19.3	29.3	41.7	47.1	51.6	54.2	58.4	58.0	57.0

[1] Both Alaska and Hawaii are included even though they had not quite achieved statehood by 1957. Actually, all of the increase in the role of state governments between 1913 and 1932 occurred between 1927 and 1932.

Table 8.2 provides data for the level of state centralization for each of the states in 2002. These data are particularly noteworthy in a number of respects. First and most strikingly, despite the fact that each of the states in the New England region—Vermont, Rhode Island, Maine, Connecticut, Massachusetts, and New Hampshire—have been noted for their strong attachment to local government, they are, in fact,

TABLE 8.2. State Centralization Indices, 2002

States	Adj. State Personnel Index	Service Delivery Index	Financial Responsibility Index	State Centralization Index
HI	77.92	89	79.54	82.15
DE	64.3	71.5	78.76	71.52
VT	62.34	70.5	80.4	71.08
AK	67.54	67.5	76.92	70.65
WV	62.01	62.5	80.27	68.26
RI	63.51	64.5	72.9	66.97
ME	60.82	63.5	72.72	65.68
AR	57.99	60	78.07	65.35
CT	59.37	66	70.57	65.31
MT	59.74	61	74.01	64.92
NM	57.65	59	78.01	64.89
KY	59.77	56	72.95	62.91
MA	52.12	63.5	67.13	60.92
NH	51.57	64.5	66.07	60.71
ND	58.11	50.5	70.41	59.67
NJ	50.88	62	65.64	59.51
UT	54.21	59.5	64.76	59.49
SC	56.1	54	67.97	59.36
MD	50.82	62.5	64.49	59.27
OK	54.74	54	69.08	59.27
MS	53.72	51.5	70.06	58.43
SD	52.98	58	64.17	58.38
ID	50.59	54.5	69.65	58.25
OR	49.82	56	66.51	57.44
LA	51.15	53	66.16	56.77
PA	49.34	53.5	64.46	55.77
IA	48.8	53	64.5	55.43
VA	45.04	57	61.62	54.55
OH	46.95	51	64.82	54.26
MO	47.73	52	61.43	53.72
WI	43.87	54	63.21	53.69
KS	45.58	52	63.27	53.62
WY	45.5	51	64.26	53.59
MI	43.35	50	67.17	53.51
NC	45.67	50	62.89	52.85
WA	46.75	49	61.48	52.41
MN	45.47	46	65.58	52.35
AL	48.72	46	61.93	52.22
IL	41.24	57.5	54.68	51.14
IN	43.11	45.5	59.36	49.32
CA	38.07	47.5	61.78	49.12
TX	41.27	50.5	53.98	48.58
GA	40.93	46.5	57.22	48.22
NY	40.53	47.5	56.35	48.13
NE	38.8	51	49.6	46.47
TN	42.45	43	53.34	46.26
CO	39.29	45.5	51.42	45.4
AZ	35.61	45.2	54.85	45.22
FL	38.04	44	52.72	44.92
NV	35.2	39	54.06	42.75
Average State	50.34	55.23	65.46	57.01

highly centralized in terms of their mode of operation. Second, states that are the most centralized—Hawaii, Delaware, Vermont, and Arkansas—are scattered about the United States, rather than sharing any regional similarity. And, third, the eleven states that are the most decentralized—Indiana, California, Texas, Georgia, New York, Nebraska, Tennessee, Colorado, Arizona, Florida, and Nevada—likewise share no regional similarity.

While the states in the past were often referred to as the "fallen arch" in the federal system, throughout the past century states have generally demonstrated, as supported by the cited data, an increasing resourcefulness and vitality compared to local governments. For example, at the beginning of the last century local government was the dominant financial partner in the federal system, raising and spending more money, in the aggregate, than the national and state governments combined. In addition, local government retained more personnel than the total employed by the national and state governments. However, as Stephens (1974) advanced: "The assertion made here is that the states are increasingly providing more direct service, exercising greater control over basic public policy, accepting greater financial responsibility, and through the use of state and federal aids becoming more viable than their local counterparts" (48).

The dominant labor and financial position of local governments at the turn of the last century appeared even more dramatic when compared to the states. At that point in time, local employment, revenues, and expenditures exceeded their state counterparts by a margin of about five to one, and local governments internally raised almost all of their own revenue (Stephens 1974, 49). In sum, local governments, notwithstanding their constitutionally weak position, were marked by a position of considerable financial strength and independence.

The stature of local governments relative to the states has changed dramatically since the early 1900s. The most dramatic change has taken place with regard to the raising of revenues; to wit, the local share of state-local revenues has fallen from 83 percent in 1902 to well under 50 percent in recent years. Although the local share of state-local expenditures has declined less substantially, the states nevertheless tripled their share by 1990. All of this underscores the fact that local governments have generally become increasingly dependent upon other levels of government, particularly the states, for financial assistance. While local governments received approximately 6 percent of their revenues from the state and federal governments levels in 1902, this figure rose to approximately 40 percent by 1979–1980, with state financial assistance providing 31 percent of all local revenues. We should note, however, that in the last decade of the past century, the trend toward increased state centralization had somewhat stabilized, and we can speculate that because of the present deterioration of state finances there may well have occurred a reversal of state centralization commencing in 2000 (Stephens 2004). On this score it is of interest that by 1990 local reliance on external financial assistance aid had declined to 33 percent of all local revenues, with the states providing approximately 30 percent of this total. A less dramatic, yet parallel, change in the position of the states in relation to their local governments involves the local share of state-local employment; this figure declined from 86 percent in 1901 to 71 percent in 1989 (ACIR 1992, 90).

Somewhat reflecting the increase of state centralization and the enhanced role of the states in local affairs has been the establishment of state executive and legislative departments (agencies) of community affairs. Graves (1964) reported that Pennsylvania established the first executive agency on the community affairs—the Bureau of Municipal Affairs, Department of Internal Affairs—in 1915 and the first legislative agency of this type—the Local Government Commission—in 1935 (713). As of the late 1950s only about a dozen states had established executive and legislative agencies on local affairs, while this was true of all states by 1980. Thirty-five of the executive agencies enjoy cabinet-level status, nine are situated in other departments, while the remainder are found in the office of the governor. These agencies serve as a contact point in state government for local officials and help to formulate and implement intergovernmental policies. In a somewhat corollary fashion, in the quest to improve state-local relations twenty-nine states have created state-local commissions or state advisory commissions on intergovernmental relations designed to promote cooperation and formal linkages between state and local governments (Pagano 1990, 103).

CAUSES AND EFFECTS OF STATE CENTRALIZATION

A number of broad causes account for the general increase in state centralization. First, state residents have become more mobile, are more socially and economically interdependent, and voice similar political demands. As the states have experienced greater urbanization and industrialization, decisions made in a community often affect the inhabitants of another jurisdiction, stimulating demands for state intervention. Second, the lack of resourcefulness and vitality of many local governments in adequately responding to community challenges and needs has been the stimulus for state intervention, resulting in further state centralization. County governments, especially those situated in rural areas, have generally lagged behind city governments in developing expert personnel, administrative coherence, and sufficient management capacity to provide economical, competent performance. On this point, Graves (1964) noted, "Local units which had to be small in the early days are today too small to operate efficiently in some areas or even to function at all in others. The conditions of modern life virtually compel government to function in larger units, if it is to be effective" (705). Third, for the most part, the decentralized and fragmented nature of local government in metropolitan areas has rendered such units incapable of coping with areawide problems, often requiring intervention by the state and the establishment of special districts. Fourth, the relative inelastic nature of local governmental financial resources has made it more difficult for local governments to raise revenues as opposed to the states, which are the usual beneficiaries of more broadly based sales and income taxes. Local governments always have been in an inferior position to the states in the competition for revenues. In general, larger local governments have been better able to diversify their revenue sources.

In addition to the reasons cited here, state centralization has been brought about by the growth of the national grant system. Many of the state grants provided to local governments are financed, directly or indirectly, by federal grants forwarded to the states. In addition, federal grants to the states provides funding for the state provision of community services. Seen in this light, the national grant system, which facilitates federal power relative to the states, also serves to enhance state power over local governments.

Further, technological changes have also played a role in the trend toward greater state centralization. The replacement of dirt roads by concrete and asphalt highways and expressways, and the general inability of local governments to finance this transition, required the intervention of the state. State support and involvement became a prerequisite for the development of sophisticated police crime laboratories, modern schools, and adequate health care facilities, which were beyond the financial capability of most localities.

Finally, the increase of state centralization reflects, in some instances, the operation and utility of the "scope of conflict" political concept elaborated upon by E. E. Schattschneider in his seminal work *The Semisovereign People* (1960). To wit, individuals and interest groups who are dissatisfied with the decisions of local governments often "target" the state capital to achieve their policy objectives. For instance, parents and educators dissatisfied with the lack of uniform local public school quality have pressured the state government to adopt statewide standards for all local school systems. Needless to say, once the state government becomes involved in a program it becomes reluctant to withdraw its involvement; more particularly, state officials are often reluctant to relinquish their influence over a program. In a parallel sort of fashion, local officials often appreciate and become increasingly dependent upon state assistance, and program clienteles may fear that state withdrawal will mean a loss of services.

Numerous consequences result from increasing state centralization, although the import of these consequences varies to some degree among the states. First and foremost, increasing state centralization has resulted in a proliferation of the establishment of state agencies over the past four decades. Utilizing what they described as an agency-level approach to understanding change in the administrative functions of state government, Stephen S. Jenks and Deil S. Wright (1993) reported on the continued increase in the number of state agencies from 1959 to 1989 (76–86). Their aggregate findings are set forth in Table 8.3. For example, they noted that state agencies established in all of the states by 1959, which they labeled "first generation agencies," were associated with functions historically and traditionally associated with state government. These basic functions included corrections, education, health, higher education, highways, mental health, motor vehicles, revenue (tax collection), unemployment insurance, welfare, and workmen's compensation. Other agencies included adjutant general, agriculture, attorney general, banking, civil defense, fishing, insurance, parks, parole, secretary of state, treasurer, and vocational education.

As noted by Jenks and Wright, a significant number of state agencies were established in at least three-quarters of the states in the 1960s, and especially in the 1970s, because of a variety of national, state, and state-local factors. "Second-generation agencies" established in the 1960s included, for example, agencies involved with the functions of administration, air quality, criminal justice planning, economic development, and natural resources. A much larger number of "third-generation agencies"

TABLE 8.3. Presence and Proliferation of State Administrative Agencies, 1950s to Early 1990s

---

A. *First-Generation Agencies—1950s (agencies present in thirty-eight or more states since 1959)*

1. Adjutant General	18. Geology	36. Public Utility Regulation
2. Aeronautics	19. Health	37. Purchasing
3. Aging	20. Higher Education	38. Revenue
4. Agriculture	21. Highways	39. Secretary of State
5. Alcoholic Beverage Control	22. Insurance	40. Securities (Regulation)
6. Attorney General	23. Labor	41. Soil Conservation
7. Banking	24. Labor Arbitration & Mediation	42. Solid Waste (Sanitation)
8. Budgeting	25. Law Enforcement	43. Tourism (Advertising)
9. Child Welfare	26. Library	44. Treasurer
10. Corrections	27. Mining	45. Unemployment Insurance
11. Education	28. Mental Health	46. Veterans Affairs
12. Emergency Management (Civil Defense)	29. Motor Vehicles	47. Vocational Education
13. Employment Services	30. Oil & Gas	48. Water Quality
14. Fire Marshal	31. Parks & Recreation	49. Water Resources
15. Fish and Game	32. Parole	50. Welfare
16. Food (Inspection/Purity)	33. Personnel	51. Workmen's Compensation
17. Forestry	34. Planning	
	35. Post Audit	

B. *Second-Generation Agencies—1960s (additional agencies present in thirty-eight or more states since 1969)*

1. Administration	5. Comptroller	9. Federal-State Relations
2. Air Quality	6. Court Administration	10. Highway Safety
3. Commerce	7. Criminal Justice Planning	11. Juvenile Rehabilitation
4. Community Affairs	8. Economic Development	12. Natural Resources

C. *Third-Generation Agencies—1970s (additional agencies present in thirty-eight or more states since 1979)*

1. Alcohol and Drug Abuse	10. Exceptional Children	20. Public Lands
2. Archives	11. Finance	21. Railroad
3. Arts Council	12. Historic Preservation	22. Savings & Loan
4. Child Abuse	13. Housing Finance	23. Social Services
5. Civil Rights	14. Human Resources	24. State-Local Relations
6. Consumer Affairs (Consumer Protection)	15. International Trade	25. Telecommunication
7. Energy	16. Manpower	26. Transpotation
8. Environment	17. Mass Transit	27. Veterinarian
9. Ethics	18. Medicaid	28. Vocational Rehabilitation
	19. Occupational Health and Safety	29. Women's Commissions

D. *Fourth-Generation Agencies—1980s (additional agencies present in thirty-eight or more states in 1989)*

1. Emergency Medical Services	3. Ground Water Management	6. Training & Development
2. Equal Employment Opportunity	4. Hazardous Waste	7. Underground Storage Tanks
	5. Small and Minority Business	8. Horse Racing

E. *Emergent Agencies—1990s (other agencies present in twenty-five or more states, but fewer than thirty-eight, in 1989)*

1. Coastal Zone Management	4. Mining Reclamation	7. Public Defender
2. Licensing (Occupations)	5. Ombudsman	8. Victim Compensation
3. Lotteries	6. Public Broadcasting Systems	

Source: Jenks and Wright 1993.

were created by at least three-quarters of the states in the 1970s and constituted the "administrative foundation stones" for the resurgence of state government in the 1980s. These agencies are responsible for a wide range of functional activity involving, for example, child abuse, consumer affairs, historic preservation, international trade, mass transit, Medicaid, and vocational rehabilitation. Concerning the vast proliferation of state agencies in the 1970s Jenks and Wright advanced: "It was a watershed decade in the sense that the cumulative effect of agency creation and proliferation reached its most extensive point. In this respect the states had created a broad and new reservoir of administrative entities that was perhaps unprecedented in any previous decade" (81).

In contrast, the number of "fourth-generation agencies" established in at least three-quarters of the states in the 1980s and the number of additional "emergent agencies" created in a *minimum of twenty-five states* in 1980s was decidedly much fewer than during the decade of the 1970s. The limited number of fourth-generation agencies created is most prominently associated with the broad functional areas of individual human resources and environmental resources. Jenks and Wright, commenting upon the relative scarcity of agencies created in the 1980s, noted: "If any general theme runs through the 1980s in terms of agency creation, however, it is one of relative quiescence. From an administrative organization standpoint, the states appeared more reactive and consolidative in the 1980s." (82) The limited number of emergent agencies, as defined earlier, created in the 1980s were most prominently involved with lotteries, public broadcasting, and victim compensation.

Summarizing their findings, Jenks and Wright noted: "We have . . . documented what most of us already suspected—that state government has experienced considerable growth in new functions and activities over the past three decades [1959–1989]. Further this growth has encompassed a broad range of policy areas some of which include responsibilities that many people would have thought more likely to be limited to national (e.g., international trade) or local (e.g., mass transit) jurisdictions" (83).

In addition to stimulating the creation of many state agencies, state centralization has stimulated, in many instances, increased levels of community services. State financial assistance has enabled localities to provide services that they could not otherwise afford, and state supervision and technical assistance has enabled local officials to improve the quality of services. State involvement in the provision of local services has served to a very limited extent to equalize service levels and distribute costs and benefits more equitably. While state grants and subventions have helped most local governments, seldom has state financial aid been given to local governments on a redistributive basis, that is, giving more money to poorer local units. The exceptions include some state aid to education and Wisconsin's redistribution of half of the state's income tax.

Finally, increasing state centralization has enhanced the importance and scope of the state policy process, at the expense of the local political arena. As perceived by local officials, state centralization has increased the range of local policy decisions that are subject to state influence, review, or control. The wider realm of local decisions subject to state influence led one of the authors to advance that in a sense local governments may be characterized as somewhat "counterfeit polities," noting, "Our localities are increasingly dependent upon larger governments for money, for resolution of basic policy issues, for reallocation of resources, and even for the delivery of many public goods and services" (Stephens 1974, 74).

Although mindful of the phenomenon of state centralization, we should note that local political autonomy has not completely withered away. Home rule, the long-standing political influence of localities in the state political process, the strong American tradition of local political control, and the often hesitancy of state officials to become involved community political conflicts have served to retain a significant measure of local discretion and control.

Local officials have successfully maintained a measure of local autonomy through a variety of strategies, including organizing their own intergovernmental lobbies, as previously noted, to influence state government decisions. In addition, they have implemented more diverse sources of revenues, including user fees and service charges. Further, local governments in a number of states have won legal standing to sue their respective state governments, a development of considerable implications, as noted by Michael E. Libonati (1988): "In the first place, state courts have begun to undo the unitary theory of sovereignty whereby localities are presumed not to have interests adverse to those of the state that created them." Further: "[L]ocal governments are viewed not as mere servants of the state but as potential protagonists in the ongoing process by which state legislative claims to omnipotence are checked and balanced by judicial review" (116) And, finally, the large volume and range of local government activity, combined with the multiple responsibilities of state governments, ensures, from a practical point of view, that a significant amount of local activity cannot be effectively controlled or monitored by the states.

STATE-LOCAL TENSIONS

Graves (1964) has succinctly noted the underlying basis for the tensions between the states and their localities: "The field of State-local relations reproduces in miniature, in fact, a great many of the same problems encountered in the field of Federal-State relations. The psychology of the two situations is closely parallel. Just as they protest against what they regard as the centralizing tendencies of the Federal government and talk loudly about States' rights, so the representatives of local units protest against State centralization and talk quite loudly about home-rule" (705). Reiterating this sentiment some four decades later, David R. Berman (2003) wrote: "Because of what one might call the forces of localism—local officials and their organizations among them—state-local relations may be said to resemble those between the federal government and the sovereignty-sharing states" (1).

As has been widely acknowledged, relations between state and local governments are not uniformly satisfactory. A survey of state associations of counties conducted in the 1980s, found that 45 percent of the respondents felt local government officials did not trust state officials, while only 26 percent responded that local officials trusted state officials (Pagano 1990, 103). The officials of large cities, in particular, often do not enjoy a harmonious relationship with their respective state governments, since they feel that the state is often unresponsive to the needs and problems of their community. For instance, only after a long and arduous struggle in the state legislature were the residents of Richmond, Virginia, provided the ability to directly elect their mayor (Stallsmith and Whitley 2004, A1). A survey conducted of the chief administrative officers in over six hundred cities in the early 1970s reported that 55 percent of the officers employed in large cities (500,000 or more residents) believed that state officials were only seldom or occasionally sympathetic or helpful in regard to the problems of their community; officials in smaller communities generally had a more favorable view of state officials (Harmon 1970, 170). In addition, as reported by Grossback (2002), local administrators in Minnesota perceive that state legislatures and state agencies do a poor job in seeking local governmental input into the fashioning of state mandates (190).

A number of factors account for tension between the states and their localities. Especially in the past, many state legislative and administrative officials were of the Jeffersonian persuasion and mindset that the good and moral community is found in small towns and rural areas, as opposed to the environment of large cities, marked by corruption and a lack of adherence of the citizens to traditional moral values.[4] This cultural prejudice and underlying political hostility toward large cities is still present, although less overt, in the halls of many state capitals.

Second, state-local tensions are also a product of contending interest groups seeking the political arena that is most likely to achieve their policy goals. Interest groups that are politically strongest at the state level, such as state chambers of commerce, will, of course, prefer state policy decisions, a situation likely to provoke conflict with interest groups that have more local political influence, such as a varied array of environmental groups. In sum, state-local governmental tensions are often a product of, or stimulated by, the dynamics of state-local interest group activity.

Third, political tensions between a state and the largest city within the state have often been caused by the political rivalry between the governor and the mayor. Many times this has accounted for the tension between New York City and New York State and between Chicago and Illinois. When the governor and the mayor have belonged to the same party, they have struggled for control of the state party; when they identified with different parties, partisan rhetoric and quarreling have been the norm. Partisan and political quarrelling serves, obviously, to undermine harmonious state-local relations.

Fourth, another factor stimulating conflict between the states and localities centers on finances. Many local officials feel that the states impose excessive restrictions on local governmental financial powers and authority. It is common for the states to provide local governments with only limited grants of authority, requiring, at times, for local officials to seek additional financial powers from the state, which may or may not be granted. From the perspective of local officials, state restrictions on local financial powers, which are found in virtually all states, render local governments less able to raise their own revenues and borrow needed funds. In a parallel fashion, local officials often believe that their state legislature is not doing enough to ease the financial burdens on their governments. In a rare display of public political ire, a group of local officials in New York vowed to defeat members of the state legislature who did not take more seriously the need to reduce the Medicaid costs of local governments (Baker 2004, A18). And finally, as Pagano (1990) has reported: "Where mandates and state preemptions are not accompanied by sufficient funds to carry out the function, the state-local partnership comes under severe strain" (103).

Fifth, state-local tensions may be the result of state-local differences concerning the nature of a specific policy or service and the priorities to be enhanced in the delivery of a service. For instance, Jocelyn M. Johnston (1998) has noted that the effort by the State of Kansas in the 1990s to promote greater equal opportunity and equity in public education for all students, through revised school financing legislation, resulted in a severe diminishment of local control over local schools (26–41).

Finally, tensions between the states and particularly their large cities are caused by the not infrequent tendency of state officials to interact with local officials in a parental-like fashion (Berman 2003, 14). This tendency has been particularly stimulated when state officials have sought to supervise the activities of local bureaucrats; the latter often believe that they have greater expertise and knowledge than their state counterparts. This practice of state officials has often proved to be a strong irritant to local officials, who complain about being treated like children. Fortunately, the long-term increasing professionalism of state administrators, as reported by Deil Wright, has served to ameliorate this problem (1982, 245–46, 343).

In extreme situations, as Graves (1964) has reported, tensions between the state and a locality have resulted in calls for succession. For instance, Mayor Fernando Wood suggested in 1861 that New York City, for a variety of reasons, should secede from New York State, a plea that was reiterated by the president of the City Council nearly a century later. Following in the footsteps of his earlier elected colleagues, in the early 1970s, Mayor John V. Lindsay (1977) called on the federal government to charter several "national cities" so that his city, which had a budget larger than the State of New York, and other large cities throughout the country could escape the "servitude" imposed by state governments. Over the years, proposals for the secession of Philadelphia from Pennsylvania and Chicago from Illinois were advanced by several of their respective mayors (Graves 1964, 710–12).

State-local conflict should not negate the fact, as noted earlier, that there is a substantial amount of state-local cooperation. The states provide their localities with a wide range of administrative and technical assistance. State fiscal aid to localities provides, on the average, about 30 percent of all local revenue. We should also note that many states have provided their localities with broader discretion in the raising of their own revenues, especially in terms of specialized taxes and user fees. More often than commonly realized, relationships between state and local functional specialists, such as law enforcement officers and physical and social planners, are usually cordial and cooperative.

SUMMARY AND CONCLUSION

Over the years, Dillon's Rule has served as the major legal framework for structuring state-local relations. Dillon's Rule states that local governments enjoy only those powers and functions expressly granted to them, those clearly implied from granted powers or essential to executing their responsibilities. As a result, local governments have often lacked sufficient authority to deal with community problems. However, with the emergence of constitutional and statutory home rule and, more recently, the devolution to local governments of broad grants of authority in many states, local officials presently enjoy more power and discretion to act without prior state approval.

States shape the structure and policies of local government through policies regarding voluntary intergovernmental cooperation, incorporation, annexation, consolidation, and urban federation. Because of relatively liberal state municipal incorporation laws and, conversely, state statutes that have made annexation and, especially, consolidation and urban federation more difficult, most American metropolitan areas contain numerous local governments. In a parallel fashion, states impact the operation of local governments in a variety of ways, including providing advice and technical assistance, distributing grants, issuing mandates, and, in rare instances, assuming direct control of local governments.

The state share of state-local revenue raising, spending, and personnel increased significantly throughout the past century. That development, which we have labeled the phenomenon of state centralization, was stimulated by growing mobility and interdependence of the population; the administrative, fiscal, and political weakness of local governments; and fiscal assistance provided by the federal government. There is some empirical evidence to support the belief that because of the economic recession at the beginning of the present century, the movement toward greater state centralization has been somewhat stabilized. Among other effects, state centralization has led to the proliferation and establishment of many additional state agencies over the past four decades.

Although state-local relations are usually marked by widespread cooperation, especially in a functional sense, conflict does take place, especially between the states and their large cities. Some conflict is a result of our deeply imbedded historical and cultural suspicions of large cities, but other tensions are caused by financial issues, political rivalries, state restrictions on local decision-making, and the scope of conflict strategy. The array of political, legal, financial, and administrative relationships between the states and their local governments provides many opportunities and strategies for shifting policy disputes between the various levels of government.

For a number of reasons, it is reasonable to assume that the interaction between the states and their localities will become even more intensively pervasive in the future. The continuing political popularity of devolving functional responsibility from the federal government to the states will undeniably result in a closer working relationship between the states and their localities. Because of the rise of the financially dependent city (Kantor 1988), local governments have become, and will continue to remain (perhaps even to a greater extent for core cities), strongly dependent upon state fiscal assistance. In order to respond successfully to an array of increasing economic and social problems, such as the rising crime rate and organized gangs and the specter of terrorism, states and their localities will be required to develop closer and more significant ongoing working relationships. And, finally, enhanced state, regional, and local cooperation and efforts will be required to cope with the consequences of demographic metropolitan trends and metropolitan problems and to provide adequate opportunities and services for all of our urban citizens.

REFERENCES

Agranoff, Robert and Michael McGuire. 1998. The Intergovernmental Context of Local Economic Development. *State and Local Government Review*. 30 (Fall), 150–64.

Bacque, Peter. 2004, January 19. 3 Localities Get Railroad-Service Grants. *Richmond Times-Dispatch*. B2.

Baker, Al. 2004, January 12. Fed Up with Albany, County Officials Take Aim at a Most Elusive Target: Incumbents. *New York Times*. A18.

Barron, David J., Gerald F. Frug, and Rick T. Su. 2004. *Dispelling the Myth of Home Rule: Local Power in Greater Boston*. Cambridge, MA: Rappaport Institute for Greater Boston, John F. Kennedy School of Government, Harvard University.

Benton, J. Edwin. 2002. *Counties as Service Delivery Agents: Changing Expectations and Roles*. Westport, CT: Praeger.

Berman, David R. 2003. *Local Government and the States: Autonomy, Politics, and Policy*. Armonk, NY: M. E. Sharpe.

City of Clinton v. Cedar Rapids and the Missouri Railroad Company. 24 Iowa 455 (1868).

Commissioners of Hamilton County v. Mighels. 7 Ohio St. 109 at 118 (1857).

DeSoto, William. 1995. Cities in State Politics: Views of Mayors and Managers. *State and Local Government Review*. 27 (Fall), 188–94.

Dillon, John F. 1911. *Commentaries on the Law of Municipal Corporations*. Boston: Little, Brown.

Elazar, Daniel J. 1961. Local Government in Intergovernmental Perspective. In Lois M. Pelekoudas, ed., *Illinois Local Government*. Urbana: Institute of Government and Public Affairs, University of Illinois. 24–25.

Foderaro, Lisa W. 2003, November 15. No Wiggle Room in This Window War. *New York Times*. A12.

Gold, Steven D. and Sarah Ritchie. 1992. State Policies Affecting Cities and Counties in 1991: Shifting Federalism. *Public Budgeting and Finance* (Spring), 23–46.

Graves, W. Brooke. 1964. *American Intergovernmental Relations: Their Origins, Historical Development, and Current Status*. New York: Charles Scribner's Sons.

Grossback, Lawrence J. 2002. The Problem of State-Imposed Mandates: Lessons from Minnesota's Local Governments. *State and Local Government Review*. 34 (Fall), 183–97.

Harmon, B. Douglas. 1970. The Block Grant: Readings from a First Experiment. *Public Administration Review*. 30 (March/April), 141–42.

Henrico County, Virginia. 2004. *Legislative Program*. Henrico County, VA: Henrico County.

Jenks, Stephen S. and Deil S. Wright. 1993. An Agency-Level Approach to Change in the Administrative Functions of American State Governments. *State and Local Government Review*. 25 (Spring), 78–86.

Johnston, Jocelyn M. 1998. Changing State-Local Fiscal Relations and School Finance in Kansas: Pursuing Equity. *State and Local Government Review*. 30 (Winter), 26–41.

Kantor, Paul. 1988. *The Dependent City: The Changing Political Economy of Urban America*. Glenview, IL: Scott, Foresman.

Libonati, Michael E. 1988. Intergovernmental Relations in State Constitutional Law: A Historical Overview. *The Annals of the American Academy of Political and Social Science*. 496 (March 1988), 116, cited in Michael A. Pagano, "State-Local Relations in the 1990s." *The Annals of the American Academy of Political and Social Science*. 509 (May), pp. 94–105.

Lindsay, John V. (1977). Remarks by Mayor John V. Lindsay, reprinted in Robert L. Morlan, ed., *Capitol, Courthouse, and City Hall*. 5th ed. Boston: Houghton-Mifflin.

Loftus, Tom. 1994. *The Art of Legislative Politics.* Washington, DC: CQ Press.

Pagano, Michael A. 1990. State-Local Relations in the 1990s. *The Annals of the American Academy of Political and Social Science.* 509 (May), 94–105.

Schattschneider, E. E. 1960. *The Semisovereign People.* New York: Holt, Rinehart, and Winston.

Springston, Rex. 2004, March 11. State Closing Page Landfill. *Richmond Times-Dispatch.* B1.

Stallsmith, Pamela and Tyler Whitley. 2004, March 13. Strong Mayor Bill Approved. *Richmond Times Dispatch.* A1.

Stephens, G. Ross. 1974. State Centralization and the Erosion of Local Autonomy. *Journal of Politics.* 36 (February), 44–76.

——. 2004. Working Memorandum.

Stephens, G. Ross and Nelson Wikstrom. 1998. Trends in Special Districts. *State and Local Government Review.* 30 (Spring), 129–38.

——. 2000. *Metropolitan Government and Governance: Theoretical Perspectives, Empirical Analysis, and the Future.* New York: Oxford University Press.

Syed, Anwar. 1966. *The Political Theory of Local Government.* New York: Random House.

Thomas, Clive S. and Ronald J. Hrebenar. 1999. Interest Groups in the States. In Virginia Gray, Russell L. Hanson, and Herbert Jacob, eds., *Politics in the American States: A Comparative Analysis.* 7th ed. Washington, DC: CQ Press. 113–43.

U.S. Advisory Commission on Intergovernmental Relations (ACIR). 1982. *State and Local Roles in the Federal System.* Washington, DC: The Commission.

——. 1992. *Significant Features of Fiscal Federalism.* Washington, DC: The Commission.

Virginia Municipal League. 2003. *Legislative Program.* Richmond, VA: The League.

Wood, Robert C. 1958. *Suburbia: Its People & Their Politics.* Boston: Houghton Mifflin.

Wright, Deil. 1982. *Understanding Intergovernmental Relations.* 2nd ed. Monterey, CA: Brooks/Cole.

Zimmerman, Joseph F. 1992. *Contemporary American Federalism: The Growth of National Power.* Westport, CT: Praeger.

——. 2004. Trends in State-Local Relations. In *The Book of the States 2004.* Vol. 36. Lexington, KY: The Council of State Governments. 28–33.

LOCAL GOVERNMENTS IN THE AMERICAN INTERGOVERNMENTAL SYSTEM

It is widely alleged that local government in the United States is unequal to the challenges confronting it. Its inadequacies are said to be many: apathy, inaction, organizational backwardness, legal and financial impotence, short-sightedness, parochialism, corruption, and the cardinal defect of excessive fragmentation. With the emergence of the metropolitan problem, reformers have urged metropolitan integration and consolidation, both of which have been slow in materializing. There are still too many units of local government.

—Anwar Syed, *The Political Theory of Local Government* (1966)

The situation referred to by Professor Syed has hardly changed in the past four decades since these words were penned—if anything the situation of local government is even more complex and diffuse than it was in the 1960s. As was emphasized earlier, the United States has, in all probability, the most complex system of local government of any federal system that exists today—or in the past. In fact, it has many systems of local government that are similar in some cases, but vary widely across the range of the fifty states.

LOCAL GOVERNMENTS

Simply looking at the national totals for the types of local government in the fifty states and other statelike entities, as shown in Figure 2.1, does not give one any sense of the differences that exist in the way the fifty states structure their systems of local government in the United States. It does, however, illustrate the overall complexity of local organizational structure for the nation as a whole. Moreover, the characteristics of local communities have changed radically as we have layered 361 metropolitan and 573 micropolitan (smaller urbanized) areas, containing 91 percent of the population, on top of the existing systems of local government—systems that were largely established during the seventeenth, eighteenth, and nineteen centuries. Only Alaska and Hawaii have had the opportunity to establish their basic system of local government during the latter part of the twentieth century.

Few textbooks on state and local government ever analyze the differences that exist in state systems of local government (SSLGs) from one state to the next. All too often textbook authors simply list the national totals for different types of local government as tabulated by the Census Bureau. The names of types of local governments are similar in different states, but their authority and what they do are highly disparate. Roles played by townships vary from providing virtually all services of local government to places where they are only historic boundary lines or survey townships without a civil government. Similar statements can be made for county governments and municipalities. Special districts can range from those that spend a few hundred dollars per year for a single service to those that spend several billion dollars for multiple services (Stephens 2003; Stephens and Wikstrom 1998, 2000, 128–48). In addition to the local special district governments listed by the Census Bureau as separate or "independent" from other local units, there are some three thousand *types* of semi-independent districts, authorities, and government corporations mostly serving local areas—even though some are listed under the aegis of the state government (see Case Study 4, Semi-Independent State and Local Agencies). The public education function can be organized as separate school district governments or may be provided by the state, or by townships, counties, and municipalities. Kindergarten through high school public education is a state-level service provided in Hawaii.

CASE STUDY 4

Semi-Independent State and Local Agencies: Special Districts, Authorities, and Government Corporations

We should not always visualize individual local governments, whether they be counties, municipalities, or townships, as monolithic or integrated organizations. County government was once described as a "collection of officials and agencies that just happen to occupy the same county courthouse." This type of situation applies to many local governments, particularly larger local entities. Within local governments, and even among types of local governments, power is often scattered among officials and agencies.

The 2002 *Census of Governments* (GC02(1)-1) lists 35,052 special district governments and authorities that meet the Census criteria for being considered a separate local unit, not a part of some other existing local government or the state. In order to be classified as a separate unit of local government, rather than a dependency of another local government, it must exist as an organized entity, have governmental character, and exhibit substantial autonomy. This means they have officers who are elected or appointed by other state or local public officials, have considerable fiscal and administrative independence, have the ability to levy taxes or service charges, can sue and be sued, can issue bonds, are able let contracts or be a party to contracts, and so on.

There are, however, many special districts and special authorities that are not counted as separate local governments as they do not fully meet the Census criteria for being considered a separate local government—they are partly separate from the county, municipality, or township in which they are situated. Volume I of the 2002 *Census* does not, as of this point in time, list the thousands of *types* of semi-independent special districts and authorities that have been tabulated for earlier years. Both those classed as independent and those that do not fully meet the Census criteria go by a variety of other names, including areas, trusts, commissions, boards, and corporations. The 1997 *Census* (GC97(1)-1) listed 3,086 such entities. Some, perhaps half, are single units, whereas others may consist of a few such entities, perhaps dozens, or even a hundred or more. Some 1,002 *types* are listed as subunits of the state with 2,084 *types* shown as subunits of local governments. In fact, most of those listed as subunits of state government serve local areas or regions of the state. Some serve the area of more than one local or state government (see Table CS4.1).

Roscoe C. Martin (1957, 1965) is but one of the many scholars over the years who have decried the rapid proliferation of special district governments. But the numbers of these semi-independent agencies (districts? authorities? corporations? whatever?) have risen at an even faster rate—up 154 percent compared to 84 percent for special districts deemed to be independent of other local governments and the state between 1962 and 1997. The 1962 Census listed 1,221 such semi-independent agencies, 288 state and 933 local (GC62(1)-1). Over this thirty-five-year period, those listed as state-created have increased faster than local. The total number increased from an average of 24 per state to 62. The average number per million residents per state doubled, increasing from 10.6 to 20.5, this during a time period when the U.S. population increased 47 percent. If past trends apply, there may be as many as 3,500 of these *types* of semi-independent agencies in 2002—numbering in the tens of thousands—perhaps more than the number listed as independent special districts and authorities. As of 2002, the average state is likely to have 70 of these types of semi-independent agencies.

These semi-independent agencies make our overall system of local government even more atomistic and diffuse than most scholars recognize (see Table CS4.1). In 1962 there was a rather high simple correlation of the total number of semi-independent agencies per state and resident population of +.679, but by 1997 this had dropped to +.474. Interestingly, the correlation between resident population and the number of these types of semi-independent entities per million state population is almost identical and negative for 1962 and 1997, at −.576 and −.579, respectively, indicating that small states tend to have a larger number of these semi-independent agencies per unit of population.

TABLE CS4.1. Types of Semi-Independent Subordinate State and Local Agencies: Special Districts, Authorities, and Corporations, 1962 and 1997

States	State Agencies	Local Agencies	1962 Total	State Agencies	Local Agencies	1997 Total	No. of Units per Million Residents
AL	11	16	27	57	66	123	27.7
AK	8	4	12	12	7	19	30.3
AZ	5	12	17	16	30	46	8.9
AR	0	10	10	14	36	50	18.7
CA	19	55	74	25	95	120	3.5
CO	3	21	24	19	56	75	17.4
CT	3	11	14	20	43	63	18.5
DE	3	6	9	11	10	21	26.8
FL	7	35	42	28	44	72	4.5
GA	10	33	43	28	89	117	14.3
HI	1	4	5	16	4	20	16.5
ID	8	14	22	10	23	33	25.5
IL	9	9	18	32	24	56	4.5
IN	8	22	30	27	61	88	14.5
IA	0	18	18	13	25	38	12.9
KS	2	35	37	7	40	47	17.5
KY	7	20	27	31	52	83	20.5
LA	19	26	45	61	131	192	42.9
ME	10	17	27	19	27	46	36.1
MD	6	26	32	26	66	92	17.4
MA	9	26	35	28	47	75	11.8
MI	7	28	35	21	67	88	8.9
MN	0	12	12	16	40	56	11.4
MS	0	13	13	16	55	71	24.9
MO	3	7	10	17	26	43	7.9
MT	3	19	22	5	42	47	52.1
NE	1	21	22	25	47	72	42.1
NV	4	17	21	10	31	41	20.5
NH	4	10	14	13	18	31	25.1
NJ	10	19	29	36	57	93	11.1
NM	7	16	23	23	26	49	26.9
NY	22	42	64	56	102	158	8.3
NC	5	28	33	16	50	66	8.2
ND	2	10	12	8	21	29	45.2
OH	7	18	25	19	44	63	5.5
OK	13	19	32	20	18	38	11.1
OR	4	27	31	8	28	36	10.5
PA	12	16	28	19	18	37	3.1
RI	8	10	18	8	27	45	42.9
SC	11	21	32	20	43	63	15.7
SD	5	11	16	10	15	25	33.1
TN	2	22	24	19	39	58	10.2
TX	1	14	15	13	46	59	2.8
UT	3	11	14	11	30	41	18.4
VT	2	10	12	16	10	26	42.7
VA	9	27	36	27	54	81	11.4
WA	3	21	24	10	42	52	8.8
WV	3	14	17	22	55	77	42.6
WI	5	16	21	8	30	38	7.1
WY	4	14	18	10	27	37	74.9
TOTALS	284	933	1,217	1,002	2,084	3,086	20.5[1]

[1] Average per state.

Recognition that these semi-independent entities exist further indicates that many activities of local government are at least partly disconnected from the rest of the local government. We might ask, who controls these agencies and for what purposes? It raises many serious questions about the disparate characteristics of local government and whether it is possible to have any semblance of a democratic response to the needs of local residents.

While local governments have, of necessity, adapted to the changes from a rural to an urban society where the bulk of the population lives in metropolitan and micropolitan areas over the last ten or eleven decades, many states have been slow to reconsider how local government is organized to fit this new environment—or how the amorphous character of local governments affects its ability to respond to the needs of residents. This fragmentation of the local polity often means that the need for service is not coincident with the ability to pay for public services. The piling of agency on agency along with multiple layers of local governments often means that local governments are unable to respond democratically.

As a post script to this case study, data have just become available from the 2002 *Census of Governments* (2002) concerning the number of types of these of these subordinate agencies in the fifty states and the District of Columbia. There are now 3,458 in the fifty state and 12 in the District for a total of 3,470. The number under the aegis of the state is 1,149 while those classed as local number 2,321 counting 12 in the District. This represents an increase of more than 12 percent over the most recent five-year period making local governments even more amorphous.

REFERENCES

Martin, Roscoe C. 1957. *Grass Roots*. Tuscaloosa, AL. University of Alabama Press.
——. 1965. *The Cities in the Federal System*. New York: Atherton Press.
U.S. Bureau of the Census. 1962, 1997, 2002. *Census of Governments*. Governmental Organization. Vol. 1, no. 1. Washington, DC: Government Printing Office.
——. 1963, 2003. *Statistical Abstract of the United States*. Washington, DC: Government Printing Office.

All too often textbook authors and others assume that what they have in their own state is similar to that in other states, when in reality wide divergences exist in the roles played by the same type of local government and how they are structured in different states. No two states have exactly the same organizational structure. At times there are even important intrastate differences among the same type of local unit. Unfortunately, members of Congress, those in the executive branch, and sometimes the courts of the federal government, make similar assumptions when crafting legislation or making decisions affecting local governments in the fifty states.

State-local systems of government range from the simple to the complex, from rather highly centralized to much less centralized, even though state-local systems have become generally more centralized over the course of the twentieth century. State systems of local government generally have become more complicated over the course of the last several decades—with more governments as well as more private activity relative to public services with various mixtures of public and private activity.

Moreover, as a general trend, we have moved from what Henry J. Schmandt and John Goldbach (1969) called the "political city" (using "city" as a generic term for local government) down the path to the "dependent city". The political city is where local governments make the basic policy decisions, are largely in charge of the delivery of services, and have their own revenue sources available to pay the bill. The dependent city is where more services are delivered by higher levels of government; many, if not most, of the decisions affecting local government are made by higher levels of government or other institutions because they pay an important segment of the cost; larger governments issue regulations that limit local action; or decisions are made by elements of the private sector for private gain—by contractors or RCAs, the latter being a kind of private government providing services usually associated with local government (Stephens and Wikstrom 2000, 11–14). Today larger governments, particularly states but also the national government, are directly providing more of the services received by residents, although the federal government has been downsizing its domestic service activity over the last decade.

Over the last half-century, the Governments Division of the Census Bureau has collected data on local governments in the United States every five years, although the amount of detailed information included has been declining over the last decade. This is called the *Census of Governments*, with 2002 the latest year. Much of what we know about the characteristics of local government in the fifty states derives from these and other Census publications.

STATE SYSTEMS OF LOCAL GOVERNMENT

There are five basic types of state systems of local government (SSLGs); thirteen states combine elements of two of the five. The first two apply only to a single state; that for Hawaii has some similarities to the system in the Commonwealth of Puerto Rico.

State-County Type

Hawaii is our simplest and most centralized state-local system, with three county governments and one city-county (Honolulu/Oahu), plus one local area (island) administered by the state government. There is very little difference between the roles played by the one city-county and the other county governments except the form of organization. The three counties raise and spend slightly more money per capita than Honolulu. Using Stephens's state centralization indices,[1] Hawaii receives a rating of 82.2 on scale where 100.0 would be a completely state system with no local government activity. In addition, there are fifteen very minor special district governments, fourteen of which are soil and water conservation districts. The Hawaiian state government provides a number of services, like public education, that in other states are delivered at the local government level.

If Puerto Rico were a state rather than a commonwealth, it would probably be placed in this category. There are seventy-six local governments called municipios (municipalities). They are area-type units like New England towns (townships) or counties in Hawaii and on average are more the size of New England towns. The state-local system in Puerto Rico is even more centralized than that in Hawaii.

State-Municipal Type

Alaska is the lone example of this arrangement; along with Delaware and Vermont, Alaska is among our most centralized states—all three get a rating in the 71–72 range in terms of state centralization. In 2002 Alaska had 12 counties, called boroughs; 4 city-counties; 145 municipalities; and 14 special districts—13 of which are housing and community development authorities. With the exception of the city-counties, most municipalities are quite small. There are also 11 "census areas" covering large parts of the state where local services are provided by the state government. The state has 9 semi-independent districts or corporations, some of which provide services to these census areas lacking local governments. Public education is provided by 53 cities and counties and by the state in the census areas. Nearly three-fifths of the land area of the state has no civil local government (Census GC02(1)-1) 2000).

Southern Type

In the Southern system, counties and large cities or city-counties are the important governments in terms of raising revenue and delivering local government services. Most, if not all, counties should be classed as at least quasi-municipal corporations in view of the citylike services they provide. In its purest form, the southern system applies to four states: Maryland, Virginia, North Carolina, and Tennessee. Public education is provided exclusively or almost exclusively by counties, city-counties, or large cities. While all have special districts, there are no minor civil subdivisions such as townships. It should, however, be noted that Virginia has about 150 "towns" that operate as minor municipalities within the counties in which they are located.

New England Town

The New England town type of local government is really two types—southern New England and northern New England. In most of New England, towns, which the Census calls townships, are the principle form of local government. What the Census calls municipalities are towns that have changed their name and form of organization. For the overwhelming majority, both towns and municipalities are area-type units that are unable to annex territory. There are a few small boroughs that are urban-type areas that exist within and are separate from the town, but this is the only exception. The number of boroughs has been on the decline since the mid-twentieth century.

In southern New England, nearly all local government services are provided by the town government, including public education. There are a few school districts, but these are largely consolidated schools for more rural areas where the participating towns retain financial control and must individually raise and appropriate the funds for their operation.[2] These school districts probably should not be considered as separate local governments—they are more like a contractual arrangement between two or more towns. Counties as civil governments do not exist in Connecticut and Rhode Island and are rather unimportant in the rest of New England. For the other four New England states, counties largely perform only judicial functions. Counties in Rhode Island have never been more than judicial districts. As defined herein, southern New England towns raise and spend about 90 percent of local revenue in the three states, with special districts accounting for another 8 or 9 percent (in this accounting New England municipalities are considered towns).

The situation with respect to towns and municipalities is the same in New Hampshire and Vermont, with the exception that schools are provided by separate school district governments that largely conform to town boundaries. Maine uses similar separate coterminus school district governments for some towns and dependent school systems for other towns. The town meeting form of government still exists, particularly in the more rural parts of New England. Counties as civil governments are largely limited to the judicial function and are likewise relatively unimportant in the overall scheme of local government in northern New England as well.

Conventional System

This is called the conventional system because it exists in one form or another in half the states. It exhibits a variety of types of local government with both discrete and overlying jurisdiction—counties, municipalities, school districts, special districts, and, in some cases, townships. Most K–12 public education is provided by school district governments. School districts and special districts often have boundaries that are not coterminus with other local governments. In many cases there are several layers of local government—counties overlying municipalities, overlying of at least one and often multiple school districts, and commonly several layers of special districts, particularly in metropolitan areas. Eleven of these states have civil township governments to include in the mix and add to the layers. In most cases civil townships cover the entire state or the entire state outside municipal boundaries, although in Missouri and Nebraska they exist, respectively, in only 20 and 30 percent of the counties. For the most part townships in these states provide few services, usually minor roads and a volunteer fire department or a cemetery. In Wisconsin townships, called towns, have been able to increase services by creating coterminus township special districts. Minnesota and Michigan have classified townships into two categories, one of which has the authority of a minor municipality such as a village or fourth-class city. Townships do not exist in fourteen of the twenty-five states in this category. With so many types and layers of local government, local intergovernmental relations can become critical to the basic functioning of local government.

Combined Systems

Mid-Atlantic states—New Jersey, New York, and Pennsylvania—combine townships with the authority of municipalities, as in New England, with the conventional system of local government. Ten states combine the Southern system with the use of separate, usually coterminus, school district governments (Arizona, Florida, Georgia, Kentucky, Louisiana, Mississippi, Nevada, South Carolina, Utah, and West Virginia). Only South Carolina has mostly noncoterminus school districts.

"TOY GOVERNMENTS"

Most of the comparable detailed information about the finances and personnel of local governments comes from the Governments Division of the Census Bureau, which has been collecting and publishing less and less information over the last decade. Much of the detailed information disseminated concerns local governments with a population of over 25,000. In 2002, only an estimated 6 percent of all local governments had more than 25,000 residents, and only 4 percent of special districts are classified as large using different criteria. Two-thirds of all municipalities and three-fourths of townships have fewer than 2,500 residents. In fact, half of all municipalities and townships have fewer than 1,000 residents (Census 2002, GC02(1)-1).

The predominant characteristic of local governments in the United States is that they are mostly quite small. This is emphasized by the fact that in 1997, 30 percent of all local governments operated without so much as a paid half-time employee.[3] These entities are referred to as having zero full-time equivalent employees (zero FTE) by the Census. The authors like to refer to them as toy governments or "republics in miniature". The 26,313 zero FTE units included 3,860 municipalities, 7,296 townships, 14,951 special districts, but only 205 school districts and one county government. These benighted local entities are somewhat concentrated in the Midwest and Plains states. In 1997 the numbers ranged from 7 in Alaska and 9 each in Rhode Island and Hawaii to 2,133 in Kansas (see Table 9.1).

While the number of zero FTE units has generally declined over the years that the Census has been tracking them, from 30,913 in 1977 to 26,313 twenty years later, there was a large increase in 1982. This seems to have been a result of the economic recession being experienced at that time. Midwestern townships and special districts have the highest percentages of zero FTE units at 56 and 43 percent, respectively.

In Delaware 76 percent of all local governments operate without so much as a 0.5 FTE employee, but Delaware is a small, rather highly centralized state. Twenty of its 57 municipalities are zero FTE, as are 236 of its 257 special districts. All 236 are "ditch districts," which most states would call drainage districts. Other states with very large percentages of zero FTE local governments include Minnesota, 51 percent; Kansas, 54 percent; South Dakota, 65.5 percent; and North Dakota, 71.5 percent (see Appendix Table 9.1).[4] For these states townships and special districts make up the bulk of the zero FTE units, although all have significant numbers of zero FTE municipalities.

Most of these minuscule entities use a variety of methods to provide what appears to be rather minimal services to their residents—contracting out is one of the more important ways they cope, along with the use of volunteer personnel. Some employ workers on a very part-time basis, a few hours a week. Current and earlier research by

TABLE 9.1. Zero FTE Local Governments in the United States, 1977–1997, and Preliminary 2002

Types of Governments	1977	1982	1987	1992	1997[1]	2002[2]
Total units	30,913	35,881	29,454	29,522	26,313	30,183
Counties	2	5	6	3	1	0
Municipalities	4,424	4,072	3,916	3,737	3,860	3,713
Towns and townships	8,673	9,734	7,467	7,678	7,296	7,091
New England towns	173	154	135	128	116	89
Mid-Atlantic townships	280	279	189	192	184	181
Midwest townships	8,220	9,301	7,143	7,358	6,996	6,821
Special districts	17,534	21,737	17,800	17,787	14,951	19,252
School districts	280	333	265	317	205	127
Percent of Units with Zero FTE Personnel						
Total units	38.7	43.9	35.4	34.8	30.1	34.5
Counties	0.1	0.2	0.2	0.1	0.03	0.0
Municipalities	23.8	21.3	20.4	19.4	19.9	19.2
Towns and townships	51.6	58.2	44.7	46.1	43.9	43.0
New England towns	12.1	10.8	9.5	9.0	8.2	6.3
Mid-Atlantic townships	10.3	10.3	6.9	7.0	6.8	6.7
Midwest townships	64.8	73.9	56.9	61.4	56.0	55.1
Special districts	67.5	77.4	60.3	56.4	43.1	54.9
School districts	1.8	2.2	1.8	2.2	1.5	0.9

Source: U.S. Bureau of the Census 1977–2002.

[1] The figures for 1962 for units with zero FTE personnel mentioned in the narrative are estimates based on the characteristics of different types of units and services delivered projected back in time for special districts, townships, and municipalities. The school districts shown are nonoperating districts.

[2] Data for 2002 have just become available, but the detailed information used herein is not yet available. The new data show a significant increase in the number of zero FTE local governments to 30,183 for 2002. As shown have, there were very modest declines in the number of zero FTE townships and municipalities; zero FTE school districts declined to 127, and there were no longer any zero FTE county governments. On the other hand, the most recent five-year period witnessed a rather massive increase in zero FTE special districts.

the authors indicates that the use of FTE personnel and FTE personnel per unit of population are very important measures of activity on the part of local governments in terms of the provision of public services. In a previous book we analyzed each type of local government by state in terms of per capita own source revenues, per capita own expenditures, and FTE personnel per unit of population for a combined index of activity, but personnel turned out to be the critical variable (Stephens and Wikstrom 2000, 129–42).

Zero FTE Townships

In an earlier article, Stephens (1989) developed a rather elaborate index of township activity for the twenty township states that included the previously mentioned variables of personnel, per capita own source revenue, and per capita expenditures, but added township legal status and the number and types of major and minor services delivered for 1982. Much later it was determined that the correlation between this 1982 index and 1982 FTE personnel per unit of population (twpFTE/pop) approached unity at r = +.969. In fact, the correlation between twpFTE/pop for 1997 and the

TABLE 9.2. Township Activity Levels as Measured by Fulltime Equivalent (FTE) Personnel per 10,000 Residents, 1997

(1)	CT	286.2	(4)	VT	47.9	(6)	IN	6.6
	MA	252.4		NY	41.2		IL	6.2
	RI	242.0					KS	6.1
			(5)	PA	28.0		NE	6.0
(2)	ME	161.5		MI	23.4		MO	5.9
				WI	22.5		MN	5.8
(3)	NJ	85.3		OH	16.9		ND	4.7
	NH	73.0					SD	3.1

more elaborate 1982 activity index was almost unity at $r = +.995$ (Stephens and Wikstrom 2003). Corroborating this, there is a high negative correlation, a curvilinear relationship, between the 1982 township index and the percent of each state's townships that are zero FTE [$r = -.584$; but if $Y = a + b(1/X)$, $r = +.925$].

Using township FTE per ten thousand residents (twpFTE/pop), there are six levels of township activity, not just the two used by the Census Bureau where they separate out the townships in the Northeastern states and the Midwest. Townships in the twenty township states range from being the primary form of local government to those where townships are insignificant. There are, of course, other states where townships are only section-line or historic areas, not civil governments (see Table 9.2).

Zero FTE Municipalities

As with townships, for the fifty states FTE per ten thousand municipal residents (muniFTE/pop) is a good measure of municipal activity if we delete the four states where city-counties are a significant part of the mix (Alaska, Maryland, New York, and Virginia), $r = +.892$. Again, this is using the indices developed by Stephens and Wikstrom (2000) for comparison. Six states have no municipalities with zero FTE personnel (Hawaii, Maine, Massachusetts, Nevada, New Hampshire, and Rhode Island). There appears to be little relationship of these zero FTE units to characteristics other than regional location. Together, states in the Midwest, the tier from North Dakota to Texas, plus three adjoining states (Arkansas, Kentucky, and Pennsylvania) comprise four-fifths of all zero FTE municipalities (see Table 9.3).

Municipalities are proportedly for the purpose of providing urban-type services. Could it be that municipalities in these states are often created for other purposes, for example, to thwart annexation to an adjacent municipality? This could also mean some states have rather loose requirements for incorporation or perhaps these municipalities plan to contract out for all of the services they are supposed to deliver, as was done in Lakewood, California. Perhaps in a few cases these are communities that have lost population and ceased to exist as municipal governments, but still have to be taken off the books.

North Dakota Municipalities and Townships

Using North Dakota as an example of a state with a large number of zero FTE municipalities and townships, 200 of its 363 municipalities have zero FTE personnel. The

TABLE 9.3. Number of Municipalities with Zero FTE Employees by State, 1997

States	Number of Zero FTE Municipalities in Each State	States	Number of Zero FTE Municipalities in Each State
HI, ME, MA, NV, NH, RI	0	UT	50
AZ	1	SC	53
CA, CT	3	WI	61
NJ, NM	4	AL	71
AK, WY	6	NC	79
WA	7	GA	90
VT	10	AR	112
MT	19	IN, SD	114
DE	20	KY	132
FL	22	OH	172
OR	23	KS	178
MD, VA	30	TX	179
WV	37	NE, OK	186
CO, MS	38	ND	200
NY	39	PA	224
MI	40	IL	290
ID, LA	44	IA	309
TN	47	MO	333

median population for these zero FTE governments is 87. Given the fact that municipalities in North Dakota have a minimum of five elected officials, this would indicate that 1 out of every 12 or 13 adults is an elected official. They receive almost the same per capita state aid as municipalities with employees, but spend twice as much per capita for highways and police (Stephens and Wikstrom 2003).[5]

The situation for North Dakota townships is even worse. Ninety-seven percent, 1,306 out of 1,341, are classed as having zero FTE personnel. Over 80 percent have fewer than 100 residents. The median population for zero FTE townships in 1997 was 58, meaning that 1 out of every 8 or 9 adults was a township elected official. These are truly "republics in miniature". Thomas Jefferson would be pleased. Total expenditures averaged about $200 per resident. If capital outlay and administrative costs are allocated functionally, about 70 percent of the money was spent on roads. The case of North Dakota seems to mean that these republics in miniature aren't doing much anyway—or maybe are incapable of doing very much. One could even question whether they are actually capable of performing the road function. How can it be economic or even administratively or politically viable to have services like roads and police devolved to such minuscule political entities? The situation with reference to zero FTE local governments is similar in Kansas, Minnesota, and South Dakota.

Zero FTE Special Districts

The actual use of special-purpose governments goes back to colonial times to the 1,600s in what is now the United States. They were usually created for the purpose of providing goods and services that were at the time beyond the capability of the limited resources of the then local governments. These special-purpose governments were often established to construct transportation facilities such as roads, bridges, canals, and harbors (Foster 1997, 15).

Having grown from less than 8,300 in 1942 to 35,052 by 2002, special districts have been the fastest growing type of local government in terms of numbers, personnel, and finances over the last six decades. Ninety-two percent perform only a single service. Of the 34,683 districts extant in 1997, 14,951, or 43 percent, were classified as zero FTE units. There were over 3,000 special districts in California and Illinois, nearly 2,200 in Texas, in excess of 1,900 in Pennsylvania, and about 1,500 each in Kansas and Missouri. At the other end of the scale, Alaska has 14 and Hawaii 15, while the average state has nearly 700. In earlier publications it was reported that 93 percent of the variation in the use of special district governments in 1987 and 1992 is explained just by two variables—the level of activity on the part of other local governments (negative) and the degree of state centralization (negative). This indicates that special districts are used to fill in the service gaps in states where the state government and other local governments are less active (Stephens and Wikstrom 1998, 2000, 129–133). (See Table 9.4.)

Two-thirds of the variation in the number of zero FTE special districts ($R_{1.234}$ = .827) among the fifty states is explained by three variables: (1) number of districts added between 1962 and 1997 (positive), (2) state resident population (positive), and (3) the degree of state centralization (negative). Indeed, the degree of state centralization is significantly and negatively related to (1) the total number of districts in each state, (2) the 1962–97 increase in the number of districts, (3) total state population, (4) special district activity as measured by a composite index of per capita district own source revenue and per capita direct expenditures, and (5) the number of zero FTE districts per state.

As with townships and municipalities, on a state by state basis, there is a quite significant relationship between the 1997 special district FTE per ten thousand residents (sdFTE/pop) and the special district activity index developed by Stephens and Wikstrom (2000, 131) for 1992. The simple correlation is +.821, but if outliers Michigan and Alabama are deleted the correlation is +.842. It should be pointed out that statewide population is used, as no district population tallies are available for a district-by-district comparison.

It is not just the proliferation of special districts that makes for voter confusion about services and responsibility; aggravating the situation is the fact that only about half of the membership of district governing boards are elected. The remainder are either appointed by other local officials, serve *ex officio* as a result of some other elected or appointed position, or gain office by some even more circuitous route. When one of the authors lived in Ohio in the late 1950s, he discovered that the governing board of the Miami Conservancy District was really appointed by the officials of a major national private corporation. Even when members of special district governing boards are elected, voter turnout is far lower than that for other, usually also low turnout, local elections. In addition, special districts can have property qualifications for voting and, by a 1973 decision of the U.S. Supreme court, they do not need to abide by the "one person, one vote" requirements that apply to other local governments (Stephens and Wikstrom 1998; Burns 1994).

TABLE 9.4. Single-Function Special Districts with Zero FTE, by Function, 1997

Function	Total Number of Districts	Number of Districts with Zero FTE	Percentage of Districts with Zero FTE
Natural Resource Districts			
Drainage and flood control	3,369	2,132	63.7
Soil and water conservation	2,499	998	39.9
Other natural resources	1,165	475	37.6
Subtotal[1]	7,033	3,605	51.3
Other Single-Function Districts			
Fire protection	5,601	3,242	57.9
Housing and community development	3,469	476	13.7
Water supply	3,409	1,385	40.6
Sewerage	2,004	899	44.9
Cemeteries	1,655	1,053	63.6
Libraries	1,496	136	9.1
Parks and recreation	1,253	474	37.8
Hospitals	763	198	26.0
Education	755	742	98.3
Highways	721	400	55.5
Health	686	197	28.6
Solid waste management	482	105	21.8
Air transportation	476	232	48.7
Gas and electric utilities	470	40	8.5
Industrial development and mortgage credit	215	105	51.2
Other transportation	207	50	24.2
Welfare	59	10	16.9
Other and unallocable	1,260	426	33.8
Subtotal, single-function	31,964	13,780	43.1
Multifunction Districts			
Sewerage and water supply	1,384	584	42.2
Natural resources and water supply	117	42	35.9
Other multifunction	1,217	545	44.8
Subtotal multifunction	2,718	1,171	43.1
TOTAL, all districts[2]	34,682	14,951	43.1

[1] There appears to be some misclassification by the Census within the natural resource category.
[2] The one district in the District of Columbia is not included.

A Proliferation of Special Districts

In 1997, nineteen counties in the United States had from 100 (Fairfield County, CT) to 445 (Harris County, TX) special district governments. California has eight such counties; Illinois three; Texas two; and one each in Colorado, Connecticut, Nebraska, New Mexico, New York, and Pennsylvania. Harris County (Houston), Texas, is a rather extreme example, where 280 of these districts are classed as having zero FTE personnel. In fact, there were 421 zero FTE districts in the six-county primary metropolitan statistical area (PMSA) and 448 in the eight-county consolidated metropolitan statistical area (CMSA).

Nearly 89 percent of the zero 280 FTE districts in Harris County are utility districts that provide sewage, water services, or both. The same statement applies to over 80 percent of the 448 zero FTE districts in the eight-county CMSA (see Appendix Table 9.2). Similar percentages apply to the total number of districts with and without full-time employees in Harris County and the CMSA. Most of these utility districts were created by developers in the 1960s and 1970s to serve residential areas being built by private contractors (Foster 1997, 1–12).

In the year 2000, Harris County had 3.4 million residents with 1.5 million living outside the central city. Suburban Harris County is served by more than two dozen municipalities and over four hundred utility districts providing sewage and water services, most of which operate without a single full-time employee. It is almost inconceivable that such an arrangement for the delivery of public utilities could be viable, economically or otherwise, particularly for critical services like sewage and water.

Looking back, it appears that one of the best measures of local government activity across the entire range of local government in terms of services performed is full-time equivalent personnel per unit of population. This measure works quite well for townships and municipalities, when certain anomalies like city-counties are set aside. For special districts FTE per unit of population also seems to work fairly well using data based on state population. It is our hypothesis that this same measure would work quite well for special district governments if population data could be obtained for individual special district governments.

As stated previously, is not always accurate to visualize general-purpose local governments, whether they be counties, municipalities, or townships, as monolithic or integrated organizations. This is particularly true for counties and larger local governments. For many individual local governments, political power is often scattered among officials and agencies. As Case Study 4 points out, there are thousands, perhaps tens of thousands, of semi-independent special districts, authorities, and government corporations that do not quite meet the Census criteria for being considered a separate unit of local government. Moreover, this is not the full measure of intragovernmental independence as within many larger local governments, as the regular departments and agencies often lack coordination with other agencies within their own municipality or county government.

As a kind of postscript to this discussion, the Census Bureau has recently (2005) published the 2002 *Compendium of Public Employment*. It reveals that the number of zero FTE local governments increased to 30,183 by that date, represents a 15 percent increase in five years, and they now constitute 34.5 percent of all local governments in the fifty states. This increase in toy governments is undoubtedly partly the result of the economic downturn in 2002.

The number of zero FTE units declined for all types of local governments except special districts and authorities—all of the increase was accounted for by a 29 percent rise in the number of zero FTE special districts from 14,951 to 19,252 over the five years in question, some 55 percent of the total number. Zero FTE municipalities declined from 3,860 to 3,713; the number of such townships went from 7,296 to 7,091; school districts dropped from 205 to 127; and there are no longer any zero FTE county governments. Interestingly, there was very little change in the numbers of zero FTE townships in the six states that account for three-fourths of such entities—North and South Dakota, Minnesota, Kansas, Nebraska, and Missouri. Half of all of the increase in special district governments occurred in the eleven states that had over five hundred such units in 1997 (Census 2002, GC02(3)-2, 248–54). The nation is still saddled with huge numbers of toy governments, or, if you prefer, "republics in miniature"—if that is what they are.

GOVERNING METROPOLITAN AREAS

Will the city disappear or will the whole planet turn into a vast urban hive?—which would be another mode of disappearance. . . . Is there still a choice between Necropolis and Utopia?

—Lewis Mumford, *The City in History* (1961)

In 1900, less than 40 percent of the population lived in urban places of more than 2,500 residents; less than 19 percent resided in places of over 50,000. Over 60 percent of the population was classified as rural (Census 1953, 26). It wasn't until later that the Census Bureau decided to collect information for metropolitan areas, which we now call metropolitan statistical areas (MSAs).

By 2005, 81 percent, or 239.3 of the 295.5 million residents of the United States, live in the nation's 261 MSAs and 18 consolidated metropolitan statistical areas (CMSAs), not counting the 6 MSAs in Puerto Rico. A MSA must have (1) a core incorporated place of at least 50,000 population or (2) an urbanized area of at least 50,000 population and a total of 100,000 residents (75,000 for New England). In addition to the county or counties containing the core city or urbanized area, the MSA may include outlying counties that meet certain criteria such as commuting to work, population density, and percent urban. Most residents of metropolitan areas now live in the suburban and fringe portions rather than the core city or core urbanized part of the nation's MSAs. As of 2005, a little over 56 million reside outside MSAs. A CMSA is simply an aggregation of adjacent, regionally related MSAs.

Recently, the Census started collecting data on 573 "micropolitan" statistical areas (microMSAs), which are smaller urbanized areas that have a core city or urbanized area of at least 10,000 residents. These microMSAs range in size from about 12,000 residents, as is the case of the Pecos, Texas, area, to Torrington, Connecticut, which has a population of nearly 188,000. About 30 million people live in these microMSAs. This leaves only something like 26 million, or less than 9 percent of the 2005 U.S. population, living in the even more rural parts of the nation beyond the metropolitan and micropolitan areas as of the year 2005 (Census 2003, 9, 28, 919–40; Census 2004–5, 901–22).

No MSA in the United States is governed by a single local government, although two come close—Anchorage, Alaska, has the city-county government and three special districts, and the Honolulu-Oahu, Hawaii, city-county government, with four small soil and water conservation districts. Both Alaska and Hawaii became states in 1959 and were not saddled with a system of local government left over from previous centuries, some even from colonial times. Honolulu is not affected by urban sprawl beyond its boundaries—when you get beyond the city-county boundary, you get wet.

If there is such a thing, the average MSA has a little over one hundred local governments located in two counties, with some forty municipalities and/or townships and over sixty school and special district governments. In larger MSAs the numbers can go up to several hundred, in some cases over one thousand, local governments. In 2002 the numbers of governments even within single county areas ran to several hundred in larger metropolitan areas, as in the cases of Los Angeles County, with 347; Harris County (Houston), with 487; or Cook County (Chicago), with 539 (Census 2002, GC02(1)-1).

Much of the proliferation of local governments has taken place in the attempt to use a rather antiquated system of local government to secure needed services as the urbanized population and density increased rather dramatically over the course of the twentieth century. Most of the overall state systems of local government were devised for rural communities that are no longer rural. As population has been layered on top of these governments, many new suburban municipalities have been organized, and dozens of special-purpose governments have been created, it is hard to know what is "local"—or, is local merely a small part of a larger construct in terms of social, economic, and political characteristics?

In these terms, what is local government? What is local self-government? Can there be local government, much less local self-government, given the layered multiplicity of minor legal governmental entities that exist in the nation's 922 metropolitan and micropolitan urbanized areas? Is local self-government merely a myth held over from previous generations while the real task of governance has gone by default to the semi-public institutions and private for-profit and nonprofit corporations—corporations that deliver many of the services at taxpayer expense, services that were once the prerogative of government? It appears that private corporations through their monied influence over elections at all levels of government exercise a high degree of control over public policy. Has our federal system become so atomistic and diffuse that it no longer responds to the wishes and needs of the general public? Does the shell of government that remains respond only to the corporate elites with their oligopolistic control of the mass media (Soley 2002) and the electoral process?

Over sixty years ago, Charles Merriam wrote in his preface to Victor Jones's book on *Metropolitan Government* (1942, ix) that "the adequate organization of metropolitan areas is one of the great unsolved problems of modern politics." It is still a major unsolved problem in the overwhelming majority of states and localities. The root of the problem goes back to the overall structure of the federal government, which in turn set the pattern for the organization of most state governments—a system of divided powers and checks-and-balances. The system was set up *not to work*—at least, not to work very well. A system in which the different branches of government "check-and-balance" other branches of government. A system "to protect life, liberty, and *property*." A system where the executive, each house of the legislature, and the judiciary are selected by different electorates and processes. Sometimes many different government agencies are established so that they can act in a manner independent from the rest of the government.

In the states, there are similar, sometimes even more restrictive, checks-and-balances and divisions-of-power between the legislative, executive, and judicial branches of government. At the state level the executive branch is even more electorally divided, as states usually separately elect not only a governor and lieutenant governor, but also an attorney general, a secretary of state, and a treasurer. Some states elect other administrative officials such as insurance commissioner, agriculture commissioner, or state auditor and governing boards or commissions like state boards of education and even one called the Railroad Commission (primarily concerned with oil and natural gas in Texas) (CSG 2003).

This is a system where in some cases rather limited special interests can gain control over the public policy that directly affects their own particular activity. A system where often it is much easier to prevent concerted action by government for general public purposes than it is for the government to act in the interests of selected groups—be that action at the national, the state, or the community level—a system designed for deadlock unless, as in a few instances, the same political party gains control over the entire system. If policy decisions are not made in the interest of the general public, they will inevitably be made by economic interests operating in the absence of political power.

All of this means it is very hard to reform local government as conditions change—or to reform any government for that matter, be it federal, state, or local. Existing local governments are the political power base of the state electoral process, and most state and local officials are reluctant, even hostile, to changes that affect their own power base, however limited their authority actually is. And, in most states, that power base is the system of local government that evolved in the rural communities of the seventeenth, eighteenth and nineteenth centuries. Just as states and state officials actively lobby the federal government, local governments and local officials do the same relative to both the state and the national levels of government.

Starting in the nineteenth and carrying through the twentieth century, there were many attempts to reorganize local governments to conform more appropriately to the needs and geography or ecology of the urban phenomenon. Most failed. The few that succeeded were often then engulfed with further expansion of the urbanized area. This occurred in both New York and St. Louis after their urbanized areas were integrated during the nineteenth century. Often the successes were for what many consider halfway measures—for one or a very limited number of services or for only a portion of the urbanized area. Over the years, the integration of local government in metropolitan areas has been promoted by both scholars and "good government" reformers, like the National Municipal League.

Although they posit a contrary view to the metropolitan governmental reform approach to local government in metropolitan areas, Vincent Ostrom, Charles Tiebout, and Robert Warren (1961) give a useful summary of that approach to the need for local governmental reorganization:

This view assumes that the multiplicity of political units in a metropolitan area is essentially a pathological phenomenon. The diagnosis asserts that there are "too many governments" and not enough government. The symptoms are described as "duplication of functions" and "overlapping jurisdictions". Autonomous units of government, acting in their own behalf, are considered incapable of resolving the diverse problems of the wider metropolitan community. . . . The political topography of the metropolis is called a "crazy quilt pattern" and its organization said to be "organized chaos." The prescription is reorganization into larger units—to provide "a general metropolitan framework" for gathering up various functions of government. (831–842)

What Ostrom, Tiebout, and Warren do not say is that this "crazy quilt pattern" usually dissects the metropolis in such a manner that some, often many, local governments lack the resources to provide the basic services that are the responsibility of local government. They must either obtain subsidies or go without. Nor does it mention the economic or governmental inefficiencies generated by units that are so small they cannot achieve economies-of-scale for different governmental activities. Too many cooks may not only spoil the broth, but they may prevent it from ever being assembled in the pot.

The successes at reform were often in terms of the integration of what Oliver P. Williams (1967) called "system maintaining services," services that must be integrated for a larger urban area in order for the system to continue to function. These are services like transportation, communications, sewage systems, water systems where water is a critical commodity, or perhaps fire protection where there is a high risk of conflagration. These are services that must be maintained at some level of integration and efficiency so there won't be a collapse in the delivery of a vital service. As Scott Greer noted in 1962, "[T]two subterfuges have been widely adopted: the special district and outside subsidy." The actual system maintaining service or services needed can differ from one urban area to the next. System-maintaining services are often integrated using a variety of techniques, including federal and/or state subsidy of local services, federal or state assumption of the services in question, federal or state regulation of service delivery, formal and informal interlocal agreements and cooperation, special district governments serving larger areas, or delivery by a private company of an integrated service. Integration of services may not be complete, but only what is necessary for the system to function at some minimum level of effectiveness. In relatively few cases does one ever get more radical reforms such as city-county consolidation, and then often only in the face of some major fiscal or service crisis.

Williams posits a continuum of services that range from those necessary to maintain the system to what he labels "lifestyle" services (see Figure 9.1). System-maintaining, neutral, and lifestyle services can vary from one urban area to the next. It is, however, quite rare to achieve urban integration of lifestyle type services. The political giblets of the metropolis, the municipalities, townships, and school districts, have control over most of the services that affect the lifestyle of residents: services such as education, housing and occupancy regulations, zoning and subdivision regulations, and even local police protection. Services that relate to lifestyle are probably fairly consistent from place to place. As Williams noted in 1967, "It is central to the argument of this paper that socio-spacial units (cities and towns) resist integration of what I

Public Education, Zoning and Land-Use Policies, Housing, Subdivision Regulations, Local Police Protection	Water (if in plentiful supply)	Pollution Control, Water (if critical), Other Transportation, Communications, Fire Protection (with high risk of conflagration)
Lifestyle-Maintaining Services	Neutral Services	System-Maintaining Services

FIGURE 9.1. Williams's (1947) continuum of lifestyle versus system-maintaining services. Lifestyle services are those that are seldom integrated for large urban areas, whereas system-maintaining services are often integrated using a variety of techniques and devices.

have called lifestyle services, but accept, and at times encourage, integration of system-maintenance services. More accurately, this is the response when issues are perceived correctly" (309). With reference to lifestyle services particularly, it should be remembered that local officials are an important, some would say critical, channel of communication to larger governments, the state and the nation, and are themselves an important interest group in terms of public policy.

Between the late 1940s and the mid 1950s there was considerable consolidation of school district governments in the United States, promoted by states with the purpose of providing a better, more equitable system for the delivery of public education. As if to underline Williams's thesis, St. Louis County, Missouri, school districts provide a good example of what can happen when state governments attempt to consolidate local lifestyle type services. Between 1948 and 1956, the consolidation of school districts in St. Louis County resulted in the decline from eighty-six to twenty-nine districts, but this change resulted in almost no equalization of district financial resources—the rich districts consolidated with the rich districts, the middle-class districts consolidated with the middle-class districts, and the poor districts consolidated with the poor districts, with the exception of the poor little racially black Kinloch district, which was entirely left out of the process (Metropolitan St. Louis Survey 1957, 56–67).

In a contrary vein to the advocates of metropolitan governmental reform are those who, like Ostrom, Tiebout, and Warren, think the political fragmentation of our urban areas is a good thing. They base their approach on the writings of James Madison and Alexander Hamilton in *The Federalist* Papers and those of Alexis de Tocqueville. *Public choice* advocates argue that the multiple communities in a metropolitan area allow the public a choice in terms of lifestyle as well where to live, work, and carry on other activities. To some degree they are correct. They suggest that the polycentric character of government in the metropolis is far less chaotic than suggested by those who would overhaul local government in our metropolitan areas; that it works through cooperative, contractual, and even competitive interaction; that it really operates as a kind of "intergovernmental system." They are right—it works, but at what level of performance?[6]

Public choice advocates base their stand on the principles of local self-government and a laissez-faire approach to economics based one three assumptions—(1) individual behavior should be the unit for analysis, (2) individuals are motivated by rationality and self-interest, and (3) individuals adopt strategies to realize their public and private goals. The multiplicity of local governments allows for a broad range of individual choice and participation in the decisions of local government and its administration. The degree to which these assumptions apply differs markedly among individuals and communities. Lots of small communities allows for choice in terms of lifestyle and on what and how local governments spend their money, therefore self-determination in terms of public policy at a very local level. Citizens as consumers can pick a community that suits their needs and preferences for lifestyle and public goods—*if individually they have the financial resources that enable them to do so.*

One thing is certain, however—current systems for organizing government in our over nine hundred metropolitan and micropolitan areas are often highly inefficient and often ineffective and uneconomic in terms of the delivery of a large number of public services, however responsive they might be to the wishes of selected small aggregations of voters. Often all sorts of devices must be resorted to in order to obtain the necessary public services, including the use of volunteers, hiring part-time help, contracting-out for services, obtaining state and/or federal aid, creating add-on ad hoc special districts, and so on, to going without needed public services. These mini-polities and republics-in-miniature are often incapable of obtaining the expertise necessary to administer public services in the interest of their citizens in a highly technological society—even when they hire contractors. The goals of private contractors, like maximizing profit, may well be quite opposed to that of delivering effective public services to the residents. If local governments are without the necessary expertise they may be incapable of judging whether or not they are getting their money's worth or whether the service is being delivered in an effective manner so as to meet the needs of the community.

While areas outside of MSAs (with 573 micropolitan areas can we still call them rural?) are the locale of three out of every four zero FTE municipalities, seven of eight zero FTE townships, and two of every three zero FTE special district governments, the density of zero FTE special districts in MSAs is three times that of non-MSA areas—layered on top of counties, municipalities, school districts, and, in some cases townships. Zero FTE local governments are about evenly divided between central and suburban county areas. Special districts account for much of the proliferation of local governments over the last five or six decades.

INTRALOCAL AND INTRAMETROPOLITAN COOPERATION

In order to work at all, a system of local government as diffuse and amorphous as the one in the United States must have considerable interlocal and intrametropolitan cooperation on some policy issues and service delivery arrangements. Among the most common are those formal and informal agreements among police and fire departments, particularly in urban areas. With reference to cooperation among fire departments, there is often a high degree of cooperation in rural areas where there is a high risk of conflagration, as in normally arid or forested environments. With reference to emergency services, there are commonly agreements among local governments in terms of communications and how these can be handled expeditiously. Often there are interlocal agreements for the provision of utility services, particularly with relation to water supply. In fact, these interlocal agreements are usually in terms of what Oliver P. Williams (1967) called "system-maintaining" services.

Kurt Thurmaier and Curtis Wood (2002) found overlying and overlapping social networks of local public officials concerned with interlocal agreements in the Kansas City metropolitan area. They explored interlocal agreements as a network phenomena and found service-oriented policy networks that produce a kind of picket-fence regionalism of interlocal agreement participation in the metropolitan area. These networks vary somewhat depending on the particular service involved. The major network functions list for the Kansas City area include roads, utilities, other public works, planning, law enforcement, recreation, support facilities, and public health. The important actors appear to be city and county managers and assistant managers, augmented by functional specialists, with the Mid-America Regional Council (MARC, the local regional council, see later) acting as broker. Interestingly, most local governments do not have an inventory of their own formal and informal agreements with other local governments.

One of these authors (Thurmaier or Woods) submitted an article to the *American Review of Public Administration* (2005) outlining an amazing number of 1,805 interlocal agreements involving some twenty-eight different services among forty-six municipalities in the Kansas City metropolitan area. This means the average municipality was involved in 39 such agreements. The most common agreements concerned public health, 93; fire protection, 99; police, 101; emergency preparedness, 107; and ambulance services, 109. Seventy percent, 1,257, involved system-maintenance type services. While some 548 agreements are classified by the author as involving lifestyle type services, it is not known whether these agreements involve municipalities with disparate or similar socioeconomic status. We strongly suspect that it was the latter.

Writing in 1962, political sociologist Scott Greer noted that coordination among local governments in a metropolitan area often takes place at the municipal level with voluntary consultation among local governments as well as contractual arrangements. He noted that such an arrangement has all of the weaknesses of a confederation and does not allow for the integration of many major services of local government. It can't overcome the maldistribution of taxable resources. He called the special district an expedient solution to problems of jurisdictional fragmentation given its access to taxes and borrowing powers beyond those granted municipalities. By outside subsidy he meant federal and state grants-in-aid and shared revenues. But these "solutions" also have consequences as well as side-effects. Special districts further fragment the local polity and can make local fiscal policy even more irrational. Grant policies are not always directed toward the basic need for services. They have, however, provided a patch on a system that might not otherwise continued to function at some minimum level of effectiveness.

Councils of Government

One mechanism that has to a degree fostered interlocal cooperation is the Regional Council, more often referred to as Council of Governments (COGs). These are voluntary associations of local governments, usually located in metropolitan areas, but there are some in micropolitan areas and more rural parts of the nation. As a voluntary association of locally elected officials they are designed to promote discussion and intergovernmental cooperation among its members concerning common and regional problems and to engage in regional planning on a multijurisdictional basis. The fact that these voluntary organizations involve elected officials from the important local governments was a definite advance over the earlier metropolitan planning commissions that were promoted by federal planning grants. In the 1960s and 1970s the conversion of regional planning commissions made up of citizens to regional councils with elected officials as members was strongly supported by federal grant legislation.

COGs are not a local government and do not have the power to levy taxes or service charges, pass ordinances, or regulate local governments. They are usually organized as a nonprofit corporation. Their revenue comes from fees assessed their members along with federal and state grants where such funding is available. Most have a professional staff that supports the activities of the council.

COGs have existed since the 1930s, but their number increased greatly in the 1960s and 1970s when federal funding became available and reached a peak of about 660 in 1980, just before federal funding was reduced—about 500 are still operating (Wikstrom 1977, 2005). Typically, they are the only group involved in interjurisdictional planning for their region. They have been criticized for not dealing with the more serious socioeconomic problems of their areas, but as voluntary organizations they do not have the authority to make such decisions. They have also been charged as "marching and chowder" societies dividing up federal grant monies.

On the other hand, over the last two decades COGs have characteristically been almost the only agencies involved in regional planning. They have disseminated the results of regional planning efforts; in some cases they have established joint purchasing programs and helped in terms of other interlocal agreements. They provide a forum where interlocal and regional issues are discussed and sometimes resolved. COGs have helped promote cooperation and cooperative agreements among local governments. Kenneth Bickers and Robert Stein (2003) conclude that the existence of interlocal agreements in the metropolitan areas they studied provides an infrastructure for new federal grant awards that might not otherwise be sought or obtained by area governments. Councils have fostered some incremental programmatic and organizational change, particularly with reference to system-maintaining services. In addition, they have served as a conduit for communication between local governments, the state, and various federal agencies and programs. COGs have provided a forum where interlocal problems and issues can be aired. The fact that COGs have not disappeared when federal grants were significantly reduced in the 1980s and 1990s is a testament to their useful role in the region (Wikstrom 1977, 2005). And, as Thurmaier and Wood point out for the Kansas City area, the Mid-America Regional Council functions as a broker for interlocal agreements.

The Lakewood Plan Approach

Named for Lakewood, California, this approach is where a municipality or township contracts with a county or other local government for some or nearly all of the services it provides residents. Right after World War II, the recently incorporated City of Lakewood contracted with Los Angeles County for all of the services it provided. Los Angeles County provides about 60 contractual services to municipalities within its jurisdiction involving some 1,600 contracts. Similar intergovernmental contracting has been reported in a number of metropolitan areas, including Detroit, Michigan; and the Quad Cities metropolitan area in Iowa and Illinois; and Philadelphia, Pennsylvania. In St. Louis County, Missouri (outside St. Louis City), and Johnson County, Kansas, in the Kansas City Metropolitan area, some of the smaller municipalities contract with adjacent municipalities for police and other services. Scores of studies in the 1950s and 1960s reported use of intergovernmental contracts (Wikstom 2002).

COMMENT

State and local governments, but particularly local governments, have become a multidimensional maze of political jurisdictions with a similar complex of private, both profit and nonprofit but largely for-profit, service providers. Additionally, the structure of local government is politically associated with the policies of the state level and is often directly related to the actions and inaction of state government. The system does not work very well. It is amazing it works at all! As a system, it is rife with political, jurisdictional, and economic inefficiencies. Many of these state systems provide hundreds of thousands of access points where those intent on perverting it for private gain, or other nefarious activities, can enter and bend it toward their goals. These access points also allow the redefinition of corruption of what was once illegal, such as changing a government institution that was once for a public purpose so it can become the private fiefdom of an individual or a corporation, or perhaps a power base for some special interest. In these terms we may in the eyes of some have a very corrupt system.

The future of metropolitan governance, as well as the future of local government, is dependent upon the action or inaction of state governments. With reference to way local governments are organized and administered, states to a considerable degree have largely ignored the problems experienced with changing demographics. How states handle the problems of local government is critical to the future of local self-government and perhaps to the ability of local governments to provide the basic public services. What good is local self-government if it is incapable of establishing and carrying out local public policy in the interest of its citizens?

So far, all that many states have provided is a patchwork system that is not only costly, but also highly inefficient and for some local areas incapable of providing basic public services. Over the last fifty or sixty years states have assumed more activities that were once the prerogative of local government, but is that enough? Up to now, most state systems of local government been held together (1) by patchwork additions to local government, (2) by federal and state aid, (3) by states taking on additional service responsibilities, (4) to a more limited degree by federal assumption of state or local activity, and (5) by the ability of local governments to interact and mitigate some of the more critical problems. But will these formal and informal interactions be sufficient to keep the system functioning as the nation becomes even more populous and urbanized or when states and the federal government download increased responsibility for public services? Can we be as sanguine about the future as Scott Greer was a half century ago when he said, "The metropolitan community is continuously improvised; its evolution is organic, not rational; change is crescive, not revolutionary; problems are solved by trial and error, rather than by fiat" (148).

Is there a point beyond which the structural clutter makes it impossible to govern, much less govern democratically, responsibly, efficiently, effectively, or economically? As a nation, can we afford the clutter? Given the current rush by federal and some state policy-makers to downsize government, how capable are our state systems of local government in responding to problems and the needs of their citizens as they arise? Short of a needed major overhaul, at minimum, many state governments need to get their act together and deal with the way local governments are organized. Our systems of local government have yet to collapse. Perhaps that is what it will take before anything major is done to force states reorganize their systems of local government. *It's still a jungle out there!*

Appendix 9.1

RANKING OF LOCAL GOVERNMENTS WITH ZERO FULLTIME EQUIVALENT (FTE) EMPLOYEES BY STATE, 1997

State	State Zero FTE Totals	Counties	Municipalities	Townships	Special Districts	School Districts	Percentage of Local Units with Zero FTE
AK	7		6		1		4
RI	9				9		7.6
HI	9				9		47.4
VA	46		30		16		9.5
LA	56		44		11	1	12
NV	66				66		32.2
MA	67			1	61	5	7.8
NH	77			14	54	9	13.4
ME	103			59	42	2	12.4
NJ	117		4	1	94	18	8.2
SC	126		53		73		17.6
WV	129		37		92		18.3
AL	138	1	71		66		12.2
AZ	141		1		133	7	22.1
NC	150		79		71		15.8
TN	157		47		110		16.7
FL	163		22		141		15.1
CT	165		3		162		28.3
MS	165		38		125	2	17.6
VT	167		10	42	50	65	24.2
MD	198		30		168		47.1
GA	208		90		117	1	15.6
DE	256		20		236		76.2

State	State Zero FTE Totals	Counties	Municipalities	Townships	Special Districts	School Districts	Percentage of Local Units with Zero FTE
UT	262		50		212		38.4
WY	283		6		277		43.3
KY	284		132		152		20.8
OK	316		186		127	3	17.6
MT	351		19		324	8	20.7
MI	363		40	271	46	6	13.1
NM	398		4		394		45.2
AR	401		112		286	3	26.5
ID	405		44		361		35.3
OH	444		172	144	125	3	12.3
OR	475		23		450	2	31.8
WA	525		7		518		29
IA	605		309		295	1	32.2
CO	658		38		618	2	35.2
NY	720		39	4	674	3	21.1
WI	734		61	274	395	4	24
TX	1,074		179		891	4	22.9
MO	1,132		333	202	595	2	33.1
CA	1,134		3		1,116	15	24.6
SD	1,185		114	929	137	5	65.5
NE	1,218		186	369	647	16	42.1
PA	1,237		224	179	830	4	24.4
IN	1,526		114	688	723	1	47.7
MN	1,786		212	1,499	73	2	51
IL	1,969		290	235	1,437	7	28.8
ND	1,975		200	1,306	466	3	71.6
KS	2,133		178	1,079	875	1	54
TOTAL	26,313	1	3,860	7,296	14,591	205	30.1

Appendix 9.2

SPECIAL DISTRICTS WITH ZERO FULL-TIME EQUIVALENT EMPLOYEES (FTE=0) IN THE HOUSTON, TEXAS, CMSA, PMSA,[1] 1997

Function	CMSA Total	PMSA Total	Number of Zero FTE Districts in PMSA by County							
			Harris	Ft. Bend	Montgomery	Liberty	Waller	Chambers	Galveston-Texas City	Brazoria
Drainage and flood control	4	1	–	–	1	–	–	–	–	3
Soil and water	2	1	–	–	1	–	–	–	–	1
Other natural resource	10	10	1	8	–	1	–	–	–	–
Fire protection	15	15	7	6	7	–	–	–	–	–
Housing and Community Development	1	1	1	–	–	–	–	–	–	–
Housing finance	1	1	–	–	1	–	–	–	–	–
Sewerage	2	2	1	–	1	–	–	–	–	–
Water supply	26	24	15	6	2	–	–	1	2	–
Other, unallocable	2	2	1	1	–	–	–	–	–	–
Natural resources and water supply	3	3	1	1	–	1	–	–	–	–
Sewerage and water	277	256	158	70	28	–	–	–	7	14
Other multifunction[2]	105	105	95	2	7	–	1	–	–	–
Zero FTE district totals	448	421	280	89	48	2	1	1	9	18
Districts with one or more FTE	293	248	165	22	45	10	2	4	30	15
Special district totals	741	669	445	111	93	12	3	5	39	33
Percentage of zero FTE districts	60.0	62.9	62.9	80.2	51.6	16.7	33.3	20.0	23.1	54.5
1997 population (in thousands)	4,320.0	3,851.7	3,158.1	321.1	258.1	63.9	26.8	23.5	243.0	225.4
Other Multifunction Zero FTE Districts										
Municipal utility districts	84	84	77	1	6	–	–	–	–	–
Public utility districts	6	6	5	–	1	–	–	–	–	–
Utility districts	6	6	6	–	–	–	–	–	–	–
Water conservation improvement	7	7	5	1	–	–	1	–	–	–
Tattor Road Municipal District	1	1	1	–	–	–	–	–	–	–
Timberlake Improvement District	1	1	1	–	–	–	–	–	–	–

Source: U.S. Bureau of the Census, 1997 Census of Governments, Government Organization, GC97(1)-1; Finances of Special Districts, GC97(4)-2, Washington, DC: Government Printing Office; www.William.K.Koerber@census.gov, FTE=0 Special Districts.xls.
[1] CMSA, Consolidated Metropolitan Statistical Area; PMSA, Primary Metropolitan Statistical Area.
[2] At least 96 of the 105 zero FTE "Other Multifunction" districts are utility districts of some kind; see subtable.

REFERENCES

Bickers, Kenneth N. and Robert M. Stein. 2003. Inter-local Cooperation and the Distribution of Federal Grant Awards. Paper delivered to the Annual Meeting of the American Political Science Association. Philadelphia.

Council of State Governments (CSG). 2003. *The Book of the States*. Lexington, KY: Council of State Governments.

Foster, Kathryn A. 1997. *The Political Economy of Special-Purpose Government*. Washington, DC: Georgetown University Press. 1–12, 15.

Greer, Scott. 1962. *Governing the Metropolis*. New York: John Wiley and Sons. 130–34, 149.

Jones, Victor. 1942. *Metropolitan Government*. Chicago: University of Chicago Press. ix.

Martin, Roscoe C. 1957. *Grass Roots*. Place: University of Alabama Press. University, Alabama.

———. 1965. *The Cities in the Federal System*. New York: Atherton Press.

Metropolitan St. Louis Survey. 1957. *Background for Action: First Report of the Metropolitan St. Louis Survey*. St. Louis, MO: Washington University and St. Louis University. 56–67.

Mumford, Lewis. 1961. *The City in History: Its Origins, Its Transformations, and Its Prospects*. New York: Harcourt, Brace, and World. 3.

Ostrom, Vincent, Charles M. Toebout, and Robert Warren. 1961. The Organization of Government in Metropolitan Areas: A Theoretical Inquiry. *American Political Science Review*. 60:4 (December), 831–42.

Schmandt, Henry J. and John Goldbach. 1969. The Urban Paradox. In Henry J. Schmandt and John Warner, eds., *The Quality of Urban Life*. Urban Affairs Annual Review. Beverly Hills, CA: Sage Publications. 473–98.

Soley, Lawrence. 2002. *Censorship, INC. The Corporate Threat to Free Speech in the United States*. New York: Monthly Review Press. 219–47.

Syed, Anwar. 1966. *The Political Theory of Local Government*. New York: Random House. 3.

Stephens, G. Ross. 1989. The Least Glorious, Most Local, Most Trivial, Homely, Provincial, and Most Ignored Form of Local Government. *Urban Affairs Quarterly*. 24:4, 501–12.

———. 2003. Special District Governments. In *Encyclopedia of Public Administration and Public Policy*. New York: Marcel Dekker. 2003.

Stephens, G. Ross and Nelson Wikstrom. 1998. Trends in Special Districts. *State and Local Government Review*. 30:2, 128–38.

———. 2000. *Metropolitan Government and Governance: Theoretical Perspectives, Empirical Analysis, and the Future*. New York: Oxford University Press. 11–14, 133–48.

———. 2003. Republics in Miniature and Other "Toy Governments." Paper delivered to the annual conference of the American Political Science Association. Philadelphia. September 2003.

Thurmaier, Kurt and Curtis Wood. 2002. Interlocal Agreements as Overlapping Social Networks: Picket-Fence Regionalism in Metropolitan Kansas City. *Public Administration Review*. 5 (September/October), 585–98.

U.S. Bureau of the Census. 1953. *Statistical Abstract of the United States*. Washington, DC: Government Printing Office. 26.

———. 2000, August. *County and City Data Book*. Washington, DC: Government Printing Office. C-2.

———. 2003, 2004–5. *Statistical Abstract of the United States*. Washington, DC: Government Printing Office. 9, 28, 919–40.

———. 1952–2002. *Census of Governments*. Government Organization. Vol. 1. Washington, DC: Government Printing Office. GC62(1)-1, GC97(1)-1, GC02(1)-1.

———. 1962–2002. *Census of Governments*. Compendium of Public Employment. Washington, DC: Government Printing Office. Vol. 3, no. 2. GC62(3)-2 to GC02(3)-2.

Williams, Oliver P. 1967. Life-style and Political Decentralization in Metropolitan Areas. *Southwestern Social Science Quarterly*. 48:3 (December), 299–310.

Wikstrom, Nelson. 1977. *Councils of Governments: A Study of Political Incrementalism.* Chicago: Nelson-Hall, 1977.

———. 2002. The City in the Regional Mosaic. In H. George Fredrickson and John Nalbandian, eds, *The Future of Local Government Administration.* Washington, DC: The International City/County Management Association. 21–38.

———. 2005. Councils of Governments. In *Encyclopedia of American Federalism.* Westport, CT: Greenwood Press. 2005.

· 10 ·

INTERGOVERNMENTAL RELATIONS:
PRESENT AND FUTURE

The American federal system has served the people well for nearly 200 years. It has great elements of strength. It has survived crises in the past and will, in all probability, survive others in the future. But there is no assurance that it will always continue to do so unless statesmanlike solutions are found—and found quickly—to meet new problems arising out of an almost completely different set of social and economic conditions under which it must operate now and in the future.

—W. Brooke Graves, *American Intergovernmental Relations* (1964)

As we have underscored throughout this volume, the one *constant* in the federal system as it has evolved in the United States is *change*:

- *Change* in the *roles* played by federal, state, and local governments, as well as in the various branches and agencies that constitute each level
- *Change* in the *power relationships* between levels
- *Change* in the *numbers* of governments
- *Change* in the *mechanisms* through which different levels, governments, and agencies at the same level relate and interact
- *Change* in the *basic documents and the interpretation* of the meaning of these basic documents that are supposed to outline the *authority and jurisdiction* of different governments and different levels of government
- *Change* in the *roles* played by government versus the private sector

We also would like to emphasize that these changes in the intergovernmental system have both initiated and partly been brought about by the *changing socioeconomic structure* of the nation.

As the intergovernmental system has evolved over time, scholars have bestowed different labels on the system reflective of these changes: Dual Federalism,

Cooperative Federalism, Creative Federalism, New Federalism, Picket-Fence Federalism, Prefectorial Federalism, Coercive or Regulatory Federalism, different constructs of a New Federalism, Privatized Federalism, and New Federalism *by default*. Samuel H. Beer (1978) has noted that it was the Americans at their Constitutional Convention in 1787 who, taking advantage of "the new science of politics," in a practical and applied sense invented federalism. He noted that the preceding permutations of federalism each are sequential versions of what he labeled "Representational Federalism" (1, 12, 13).

Some scholars over the years have argued that the American experiment in federalism represented simply a "way station" on the road from confederation to a centralized or unitary system, with all of the important powers of government concentrated at the national level. To this date in time, the American system has not progressed that far, although certain powers have become much more centralized. In a contrary vein, as a result of the extreme complexity and atomistic character of our federal system, there is the foreboding possibility of governmental deadlock or arteriosclerosis.

FRAGMENTED FEDERALISM AND INTERGOVERNMENTAL RELATIONS

Simplistic "layer-cake" or "marble-cake" models of the federal system cannot accurately commence to describe or portray the fragmented American federal system in regards to manner in which it functions—or *fails to adequately function*—in the United States. Elazar (1987) noted almost two decades ago that the intellectual models of federalism have tended to lag behind actual developments in intergovernmental relations (225). Given the multitudinous and multifarious discrete and overlying political, legal, and public and private administrative jurisdictions in the American federal system, it is somewhat miraculous that it can work at all, much less accomplish what it sets out to realize in terms of policy goals. Using a term that once was utilized popularly by scholars to portray the governmental structure of metropolitan areas, we can well describe our federal system as consisting of a "crazy-quilt" tapestry of governments, stitched together in a somewhat haphazard incremental fashion. Or, perhaps given the multifarious array of relationships in our present intergovernmental system it may be useful to view our federal system, as argued by Joseph P. Zimmerman (2004), in a kaleidoscopic fashion. Given all of this, where do the concepts of democracy and public accountability fit into the scheme of our federal system? And, more precisely, how does the public know which governmental unit to praise when praise is due and, conversely, how to correctly sort out the supposed culprits when policies or services go awry?

CASE STUDY 5

System Failure: The Response to Hurricane Katrina

On Friday, August 26, 2005, Hurricane Katrina passed into the Gulf of Mexico, presenting a significant weather threat to the coastal areas of Alabama, Mississippi, and Louisiana, along with New Orleans—the major city in the region. On the same day, Louisiana Governor Kathleen B. Blanco declared a "state of emergency" for her state and requested federal assistance. This request was followed by her plea the next day for the federal government to declare an emergency for her state and assist in helping to save lives and property. In response, President George W. Bush declared a state of emergency in Louisiana and authorized the Federal Emergency Management Agency (FEMA), an agency of the Department of Homeland Security (DHS), to provide aid. On the same day, New Orleans Mayor C. Ray Nagin announced a state of emergency for his community and issued a voluntary evacuation order. The next day—Sunday, August 28—Mayor Nagin, fearing growing concerns about gas leaks, fires, toxic water, and diseases, ordered a mandatory evacuation of all citizens from the city.

On Monday, August 29, Hurricane Katrina made landfall. Its wind and rain caused widespread destruction along the Gulf Coast and claimed over 1,100 lives, mostly in Louisiana (885) and Mississippi (219) (Time Warner 2005 3), though this may not be the final tally. A number of major levees breached in New Orleans, and large parts of the city, especially the poorer sections, were flooded. Responding, in part, to Governor Blanco's second plea for assistance, President Bush declared Louisiana to be a major disaster area, releasing federal funds to supplement local and state aid. President Bush met with Governor Blanco and Mayor Nagin on Friday, September 2, but was unable to persuade the governor to relinquish her control of the Louisiana National Guard. President Bush, largely for political reasons, refrained from being more aggressive in seeking federal control of the National Guard troops (Lipton, Schmitt, and Shanker 2005).

Meanwhile, due to the flooded conditions of their neighborhoods, large numbers of the citizens of New Orleans—along with a substantial number of tourists—sought shelter in the Superdome, which housed about 20,000 people on August 31 and September 1. By this time, the supply of food and water was exhausted and toilet facilities were largely inoperative. Adding to the complexities, violence and lawlessness broke out in the Superdome, the Convention Center, and numerous other parts of the city (a large number of individuals had fled to the Convention Center for shelter). However, among FEMA, state, and local governmental authorities there was no clear plan or agreement concerning which level of government would provide the necessary number of buses to evacuate the citizens who had fled to the Superdome and Convention Center. Eventually, the Louisiana National Guard reported on Saturday, September 3 that it had successfully evacuated all individuals from the two public facilities. The following Monday, September 5, that National Guard reported that it had restored order and "secured" New Orleans.

Complicating the governmental response to the disaster was the lack of an adequate system and flow of communications between local, regional, and national FEMA officials, and between FEMA officials and the state officials of Alabama, Mississippi, and Louisiana. Michael D. Brown, the Director of FEMA, has been severely criticized for not fully comprehending the magnitude of the disaster or immediately developing a comprehensive response plan. For instance, Brown readily acknowledged that he was not aware that 20,000 individuals were at the Convention Center until twenty-four hours after news reports of them were broadcast (Lichtblau 2005, A20). FEMA was largely blamed for failing to develop an overall command-and-control structure for dealing with the disaster and for having a myriad of organizational problems—resulting, for example, in leaving thousands of people stranded for an extended period of time at the Superdome and Convention Center, without food, water, security, or medical assistance. In addition, largely because of the ineptness of FEMA, evacuees safe from immediate danger confronted long delays in finding adequate assistance and navigating a maze of federal and local programs. Officials and citizens complained that FEMA's computers were repeatedly "crashing," further adding to the communications problem.

Local officials complained bitterly about FEMA's overall performance, or lack thereof. For instance, Mayor Laura Miller of Dallas, where about 1,500 evacuees had been transported to, stated:

> "Where is FEMA national? We keep being told that help is coming and so far we're not getting the help. So we will do what the government can't do. We will take the 1,500 people sleeping on cots and air mattresses and move them into apartments with beds and furniture and sheets and towels. There is so much chaos and dysfunction going on with the federal government that Dallas can't wait any longer for federal help." (Stevenson and Kornblut 2005, A1, A14).

Early in the relief effort, Louisiana officials complained about the slow pace at which FEMA was moving evacuees living in shelters to longer-term and more comfortable housing arrangements.

In response to the crisis, President Bush (on his third trip to the region), speaking from historic Jackson Square in New Orleans, issued a televised address to the nation on the evening of Thursday, September 16. He said:

> "The work that has begun in the Gulf Coast region will be one of the largest reconstruction efforts the world has ever seen. . . . And tonight I also offer this pledge of the American people: Throughout the area hit by the hurricane, we will do what it takes, we will stay as long as it takes to help citizens rebuild their communities and their lives."

In implementing his pledge, Bush created a Gulf Opportunity Zone—a government enterprise that he said would provide help on taxes, housing, education, and training for the victims of the hurricane. In addition, Bush noted that he would ask Congress to pass an Urban Homesteading Act, designed to provide building sites on federal land through a lottery to low-income citizens, free of charge. In return, residents would pledge to build on the lots, with either a mortgage or help from a charitable organization like Habitat for Humanity. In his address, Bush took special note of the division between rich and poor in the United States, and especially the plight of the many African-Americans who reside in an environment of desperate poverty (Bumiller and Sanger, A1).

Initially, about $10.5 billion was allocated to the relief effort, with a supplemental appropriation of $51.8 billion, with most of the funds—$50 billion—directed to FEMA for recovery efforts including shelter, food, and medical care. The balance of the funds were provided to the Defense Department ($1.4 billion) for military deployment and the Army Corps of Engineers ($400 million) for repairs to levees, pumps, and clearing channels. Informed observers noted however, that the total costs of reconstruction and the resettlement of residents could well total two or three times this amount (Hulse 2005a, A22). Some conservative Republicans in Congress voiced their strong concern about the extent of funding advanced by Bush (Hulse 2005b, A1).

Due to his inept performance, Brown was relieved on September 9 by the Bush administration from his oversight of the post-storm relief effort and replaced with Vice Admiral Thad W. Allen of the Coast Guard, known for his communication skills and steady resolve (Shanker 2005). The following Monday, September 12, Brown—under intense political pressure from both Democrats and Republicans, and viewed as a political liability by the White House—resigned his post as director of FEMA. He was replaced on an acting basis by R. David Paulison, who in strong contrast to Brown has pursued a long-time career in emergency assistance and disaster relief (Kornblut 2005, A23).

Members of Congress were quick to react to the failed response of the government, particularly FEMA, to the disaster. Senator Susan Collins, Chair of the Senate Homeland Security Committee, expressed her strong dismay at the inadequacy of the local, state, and federal response and noted: "If our system did such a poor job when there was no enemy how would the federal, state, and local governments have coped with a terrorist attack that provided no advance warning and that was intent on causing as much death and destruction as possible?" (Longman and Chan 2005, A1). On September 12, Collins began to hold public hearings on the inadequate response of the federal government to the disaster. Senator Bill Frist, the Senate majority leader, along with the Speaker of he House of Representatives, J. Dennis Hastert, announced on September 7 the establishment of a joint House-Senate inquiry into the failures surrounding the response to Hurricane Katrina by the Bush administration. The members of the panel were charged with providing a report to Congress by

February 15, 2006. Many leading Congressional Democrats, including Senator Harry Reid, the Senate Democratic leader, and Senator Hillary Rodham Clinton, opposed this initiative, along with Representative Nancy Pelosi, the House Democratic leader. They stressed the need for an independent panel, such as was established after the tragedy of September 11, 2001. At minimum, many Democrats in Congress stated that such a panel should include an equal number of Democrats and Republicans, in order to ensure a fair and impartial inquiry. In addition, some Democratic members of Congress suggested that FEMA should be severed from the Department of Homeland Security, arguing that FEMA's effectiveness was diminished by being placed under the broader organizational umbrella (Hulse 2005c, A20).

CONCLUDING COMMENTS

Our overview of the inept performance of the government—particularly FEMA—to the Katrina disaster provides us with a number of lessons. First, given the complexity of the federal system, with its numerous federal, state, and local agencies, developing a comprehensive plan of responsible relief is undermined by the very nature of the fragmented intergovernmental system. In the instance of the Katrina disaster, this difficulty was further magnified by the uncertain and confused response of FEMA officials, who failed to quickly develop an appreciation of the magnitude of the disaster and to put in place a central and coordinated command structure.

Second, President Bush's management style, often described by observers as haphazard and reactive, also significantly contributed to the inadequate response of the federal government to the disaster. As William Kristol noted in regard to the operational style of Bush: "He is a strong president . . . but he has never really focused on the importance of good execution. I think that is true in many parts of his presidency." David Ignatius (2005, A25) elaborating in the *Washington Post* about Kristol's comments, wrote:

> "What accounts for this management failure? Experts cite a number of factors. First, this White House lacks a strong, substantive chief of staff who could act as a kind of deputy president, riding herd on the Cabinet agencies. Bush's chief, Andrew Card, is good at organizing the President's schedule, but he hasn't played the broader, make-the-trains-run role of many of his predecessors . . . Another problem is Bush's own style. As a key adviser once told me, this President isn't interested in hitting singles and doubles; he wants home runs. This approach almost guarantees that the administration won't do well at crisis prevention—which succeeds best when nothing dramatic happens at all, thanks to good planning."

Third, the initial lackluster and confused response of FEMA was partly due to the Bush administration's penchant for staffing the agency (along with other components of the federal government) with individuals known for their strident conservative political beliefs and personal political loyalty, rather than demonstrated competence. For instance, Michael D. Brown, the former director of FEMA, had little experience in disaster relief before assuming his position. In addition, FEMA has been accused of engaging in wasteful spending practices, funding many projects of little real value or significance ("FEMA Spending a Disaster?" 2005, A1, A6). The departure of Brown from FEMA does not guarantee the future success of FEMA; for, as noted by an editorial in the *New York Times* (2005, September 16, A26): "An administration staffed on many levels by people who distrust big government is now faced with handling an unprecedented task: housing hundreds of thousands of homeless people, making sure their children are educated over the short term, and eventually getting them a start on a new life. There is no way to meet the challenge without a focused federal effort."

In addition, the U.S. Army Corps of Engineers may be criticized for not allocating a larger share of its funding to more adequately strengthen the levees of New Orleans largely because of intense pressure for pork-barrel projects in Congress. As the *New York Times* (2005, September 13, A28) expressed in an editorial: "There has been much grumbling that Congress and the Bush administration denied the Army Corps of Engineers the money that was required to fortify New Orleans against a hurricane like Katrina. These complaints need to be pursued. Flood control is mainly a federal obligation and the agency most responsible for it must have enough money to do the job right." And, as it further advanced: "But there is another question worth asking: has the Army Corps made wise use of the money it has? Louisiana has received about $1.9 billion over the past four years for corps civil works projects, more than any other state. Although much of this has been spent to protect New Orleans, a lot has been spent on unrelated water projects—a new and unnecessary lock in the New Orleans Industrial Canal, for instance, and dredging little-used waterways like the Red River—mainly to serve the barge industry and other commercial interests" (*New York Times*, September 13, 2005, A28).

And finally, because of the inept performance of the federal government in regard to the challenge of Katrina, many Americans have lost some degree of confidence in the ability of their government to protect them from the onslaught of a natural disaster. The Pew Research Center for People and the Press found that somewhat more than 60 percent of the respondents judged the federal government's response to the disaster to be fair or poor (Stevenson 2005, A23).

Federal, state, and local officials have been criticizing each other for their response to hurricane Katrina, and there is certainly enough blame to go around. Michael Brown claims FEMA has been gutted by several years of budget cuts by the DHS (McCaffrey 2005, September 28, A1). And this seems to be the case. FEMA was layered-under when some twenty-two agencies were consolidated into the DHS, which has focused on the threat of terrorism rather than the possibility of major natural disasters like Katrina. Brown went on to say that FEMA was overwhelmed by the massive storm and its response was complicated by state and local officials: "My biggest mistake was not recognizing by Saturday (August 27) that Louisiana was dysfunctional."

All three levels of government have been negligent in their preparation for and execution of emergency procedures for a category four or five hurricane. The federal government was very slow in its response to a forecast category five hurricane, and it is the only level with the necessary resources to cope. The Bush administration was not slow, however, in throwing out no-bid procurement contracts to their favorite corporations, like Halliburton and Bechtel (Stephens 2005, B8). In fact, the news from National Public Radio (September 29, 2005) indicated that FEMA has let dozens of no-bid contracts with few controls over contract performance and cost in the aftermath of Katrina.

Over time, all three levels of government have been negligent in the maintenance and upgrading of the necessary infrastructure given the resources they had at their disposal. However, most state and local governments along the Gulf coast lack the financial resources needed to properly upgrade their infrastructure for such a disaster. Even if public officials at all levels had done their best, given the fragmented and amorphous governmental characteristics of our federal system, it is doubtful that the outcome for a disaster of this magnitude would have been much better. To have satisfactorily coped with this disaster would have required the coordination and direction of officials from a dozen federal agencies, three states, and hundreds of local governments, not to mention the officials and governments of surrounding states that were affected by refugees from the states directly in the path of Katrina.

REFERENCES

Bumiller, Elisabeth, and David E. Sanger. 2005, September 16. Bush Pledges Federal Role in Rebuilding Gulf Coast, *New York Times*. A1, A19.

FEMA Spending a Disaster?, 2005, September 18. *Richmond Times-Dispatch*. A1, A6.

Hulse, Carl. 2005a, September 8. Bipartisan Inquiry Proposed as Bush Seeks $51.8 Billion More For Relief, *New York Times*. A22.

Hulse, Carl. 2005b, September 16. G.O.P. Split Over Big Plans for Storm Spending, *New York Times*. A1, A19.

Hulse, Carl. 2005c, September 9. Democratic Leaders Reject G.O.P. Storm Inquiry Plan, *New York Times*. A20.

Ignatius, David. 2005, September 7. A CEO's Weakness, *Washington Post*. A25.

Kornblut, Anne E. 2005, September 13. Pick as Acting FEMA Leader Has Disaster Relief Experience, *New York Times*. A23.

Kornblut, Anne E. and Carl Hulse. 2005, September 9. Bush Promises to Seek Answers to Failures of Hurricane Relief, *New York Times*. A17, A22.

Lichtblau, Eric. 2005, September 8. Chertoff Draws Fire on Briefing, *New York Times*. A20.

Lipton, Eric, Eric Schmitt, and Thom Shanker. 2005, September 9. Political Issues Snarled Plans for Troop Aid, *New York Times*. A1, A20.

Longman, Jere and Sewell Chan. 2005. Flooding Recedes in New Orleans; U.S. Inquiry is Set, *New York Times*. A1, A21.

McCaffrey, Shannon. 2005, September 28. Don't Blame FEMA, Says Ex-Director. *Kansas City Star*. A1, A10.

New York Times. 2005a, September 16. Editorial. Mr. Bush in New Orleans, *New York Times*. A26.

New York Times. 2005b, September 13. Editorial. Katrina's Message on the Corps, *New York Times*. A28.

Shanker, Thom. 2005, September 10. The Recovery Chief: Commander Accustomed to Scrutiny and Crises, *New York Times*. A14.

Stephens, G. Ross. 2005, September 21. Hurricane Contracts. *Kansas City Star*. B8.

Stevenson, Richard W. 2005, September 13. After Days of Criticism, Emergency Director Resigns, *New York Times*. A23.

Stevenson, Richard W. and Anne E. Kornblut. 2005, September 10. Director of FEMA Stripped of Role as Relief Leader, *New York Times*. A1, A14.

Time Warner Cable News Network. 2005, September 28. The Latest on Rita and Katrina. http://edition.cnn.com/2005/US/09/27/news.update.tues/. 3.

In addition to structure, in a somewhat ironic sense, the very dynamics, or currents, of federalism involving national and state regulation and intergovernmental cooperation have further served to undermine democracy and accountability. The rise of Coercive Federalism, with its "toolbox" of mandates, cross-cutting regulations, preemption, and partial preemption, has effectively served, in more than a few functional areas, to divorce between the levels of government the functions of policy-making and policy implementation. The potpourri of federal and state categorical grants, surely benevolent in their intent, has served to make even more confusing for the common citizen the determination of to what extent each level of government is providing the funding for a particular service. With reference to the latter, the long-cherished principle that the level of government that provides the service is to fund the service has been, in many cases, effectively cast asunder.

FISCAL FEDERALISM

The most important development in fiscal federalism during the first half of the twentieth century was the greatly increased reliance of the federal government on progressive income tax revenue, as a result of the adoption of the sixteenth amendment in 1913. As a result of the latter development, the federal government was able to significantly expand its role in the governmental sector, as well as in the larger society. We should note that the federal government is a much better collector of revenue than the states or localities because it is much more difficult for individuals to avoid or evade the payment of federal taxes. During the same time frame, state and local governments largely abandoned their reliance on revenues derived from the property tax and began to rely more on general and selective sales tax revenues, charges for services, and to a somewhat lesser degree on income taxes. The major change in the financing of the federal system over the last five decades concerns the alterations that have taken place in terms of who pays federal, state, and local taxes and who benefits from public sector policies.

In contrast to other federal systems around the world, there have been few concerted attempts by the federal and state governments in the United States to equalize or place a minimum floor under the revenue resources of poorer state and local governments. The few exceptions include the State and Local Fiscal Assistance Act of 1971, popularly known as General Revenue Sharing (GRS), which was completely phased out during the Reagan administration; Wisconsin's sharing of half of the state income tax in a redistributive manner with its local governments; and the redistribution of additional local nonresidential property tax revenue in the Minneapolis–St. Paul metropolitan area. State and local governments, seeking a greater variety and diversity of revenue sources, utilize a host of revenue-raising devices to meet their funding needs, including property taxes, general sales taxes, assessments, fees, fines, service charges, special taxes and fees on telephones and cell phones, departure taxes at airports, per diem and special excise taxes on hotels and car rentals, and revenues raised from gambling and lotteries. In Rhode Island, South Dakota, Louisiana, Oregon, and Nevada, taxes from casinos, slot machines at race-tracks, and lotteries make up more than 10 percent of all state revenues. In Rhode Island gambling revenue has surpassed the corporate income tax to become the state's third largest source of revenue after the personal income and sales taxes (Butterfield 2005, A1). In addition, local governments have made wide use of special taxing dis-tricts to make infrastructure improvements to accommodate new business investment.

In addition, the use of progressivity in personal and corporate income taxes steadily declined rather preciously over the last half of the twentieth century, while flat-rate payroll taxes increased markedly. At the outset of the twenty-first century, tax relief for large corporations and the very wealthy accelerated during the presidency of George W. Bush, with major reductions for taxpayers in the $200,000 to $1,000,000 plus tax brackets inserted into the FY2006 federal budget (Krugman 2005), along with the move to permanently eliminate federal inheritance and estate taxes. At the same time, state and local governments have been increasing their reliance on more regressive revenue sources, adopting new or increasing general and selective sales taxes, franchise taxes, special fees, and service charges. These developments have resulted in an overall federal + state + local revenue structure that has evolved from one in which the top 1 percent of taxpayers paid four times the percentage of their income in taxes compared to the bottom 50 percent of income earners, to a structure obligating the bottom 50 percent to pay a higher percentage of their income in taxes than those at the very top—from a progressive to a regressive revenue structure. And the average voter hasn't a clue as to what has transpired (Bartels 2005).

At this point in time, stimulated by the very large budget deficit resulting from the 2001 economic recession, wars in Afghanistan and Iraq, and tax cuts for corpora-tions and the wealthy, the Bush administration is considering "tax reform." By tax reform the Bush administration is apparently seeking to implement a flat-rate income tax, where all income groups pay the same percentage of personal income in taxes, or a national general sales or value-added tax. If such proposals were to be enacted, it could result in the average taxpayer paying at least twice the percentage of his or her income in taxes compared to the very wealthy. Changes made in the federal + state + local revenue structure over the last half-century, along with those of the early twenty-first century, amount to a massive redistribution of wealth from the poor and the middle classes to the corporate rich.

PRIVATIZED FEDERALISM

Further, the rise of political conservatism to its dominant status, along with the increasing importance of privatization of our public sector, further serves to fractionate and render more bewildering our system of intergovernmental relations. It obscures what is really happening from the general public. Scholars, most prominently E. S. Savas (1982, 1987, 2000) and a score of others, have argued that the federal, state, and local levels of government by contracting with the private sector can provide services more efficiently and economically, by realizing and taking advantage of reduced costs, improved service, increased management flexibility, specialized expertise, and decreased public monopoly inefficiencies. Empirical studies have found that this may be the case for selected services, but not for others.[1] Indeed, the use by government of a for-profit vendor to provide a service may ultimately prove to be unsatisfactory and may even result in human tragedy. For instance, the *New York Times* in a three-part series published in February and March 2005 reported that a for-profit vendor who was awarded a contract by a number of local governments in New York to provide health services for jail inmates carried out its responsibilities in such an unsatisfactory manner that it allegedly contributed to the death of a number of inmates.[2] Donald Kettl (1993) reminds us that for any government to realize the benefits of "privatization" it must invest in the appropriate public management capacity, inclusive of personnel with contract-management experience, policy expertise, negotiation, bargaining and mediation skills, oversight and program audit capabilities, along with the necessary communication and political skills to manage programs with third parties in a complex political environment. Unfortunately, many local governments are not large enough or wealthy enough to aquire these skills. Although in-depth studies focusing on the attitude of the public toward privatization are relatively scarce. Lyke Thompson and Richard C. Elling (2000), in a survey of Michigan residents, reported that the vast majority largely opposed the privatization of fourteen services. Specifically, they noted: "A majority of respondents support having for-profit, private firms handle garbage collection and janitorial services, and over 40 percent support this approach in the case of clerical services, street cleaning, and snow removal. . . . By contrast, large majorities favor public delivery of more coercive services, such as maximum and minimum security prisons, enforcement of building regulations, and police and fire protection" (341). Whatever may be the merits of "privatization," the increasing adoption of market approaches by all levels of government, especially by the federal government, for doing what was formerly the "business of government" has further complicated the issue of democracy, public accountability, and the development of social capital and the vitality of a civil society in our intergovernmental system (Box 1999).

Given the intergovernmental scheme of things, we are troubled by the increasing number and role of nonprofit organizations in providing services, and what appears to be declining public confidence, often irregular operating practices, and violation of the norm of conflict of interest. Nonprofit organizations have become so prominent in our society that they have been labeled by Jennifer R. Wolch (1990) as constituting "the shadow state." In 1992, the number of 501(c)(3) nonprofit organizations numbered about 1.03 million, increasing to approximately 1.27 million by 1998 (Eikenberry and Kluver 2004). Many nonprofits are created to avoid taxes and/or to push a political agenda. They are often not really charitable organizations re performing charity for the poor. In a survey released in September 2004 a scant 15 percent of the survey respondents state they had a "great deal" of confidence in charities and only 14 percent believed that charities spent their funds wisely (Strom 2004a). Nonprofit organizations in Nebraska, Georgia, and Minnesota have been cited as having engaged in irregular financial practices and violating conflict-of-interest norms (Storm 2004b).[3]

We should also like to note that because of the declining amount of federal funds available to nonprofit organizations and their increasing "professionalization," nonprofit organizations have become increasing more concerned with issues relating to their organizational maintenance, rather than serving as a significant creator of social capital (Hinds 2003). As reported by Hinds (2000): "The focus on organizational maintenance [by nonprofit organizations] has led to a devaluing of people's involvement in organizations. This devaluation has led to a diminished level in the quality and quantity of opportunities for people to be active participants in non-profits, which in turn has led to diminished opportunities for people to form relationships with other people in their communities." (8)

Ralph M. Kramer noted in his work *Voluntary Agencies in the Welfare State* (1981) that traditionally nonprofit agencies have served to enhance civil society through their role as value guardians, service providers and advocates, and builders of social capital. However, as Angela M. Eikenberry and Jodie Drapal (2004) report, the increasing adoption by nonprofit organizations of marketing trends involving commercial revenue generation, contract competition, the influence of new and emerging donors, and social entrepreneurship have severely compromised the ability of these organizations to promote the democratic ideals of fairness and justice and to serve in their civil society roles as value guardians, service providers and advocates, and builders of social capital (138). Certainly, these developments bode ill for the delivery of services in the intergovernmental system, especially in terms of democracy and public accountability.

THE INTERGOVERNMENTAL SYSTEM AND PUBLIC POLICY CHALLENGES

While obviously mindful of the fact that our federal system has been defended on the basis that it serves to mitigate national political conflict and ensures the government in Washington will not become "overloaded," we are concerned that the extreme dissection of the body politic into many parts, sometimes in a state of cooperation with each other while on other occasions engaged in brutal conflict, may often prevent it from assembling a coherent political mass to seek and implement policies that would serve to benefit the overall public interest. The system provides hundreds of thousands or perhaps millions of access points, borrowing from the sage observations of Morton Grodzins and E. E. Schattschneider, where small, determined, well-financed groups or individuals can, over long periods of time, work their private will and interests on the body politic—perhaps without the average citizen even knowing the true state of affairs. Often policy decision centers, government agencies, and even local governments are captured by special interests in such an inclusive manner that they do the bidding of these interests, rather than pursuing the interests of the majority of citizens.

Medicaid

Our system of federalism and intergovernmental relations is faced with a number of severe challenges, in addition to those that are the focus of the case studies contained in this volume—homeland security, education, welfare, and atomistic governments. Perhaps the most serious of these challenges is that of ensuring an adequate permanent intergovernmental system of financing for Medicaid. An editorial in the *New York Times* noted:

> Everyone seems to be howling about the cost of Medicaid, and no wonder. Spending on the health care program for the poor has been exploding, up from $200 billion in 2000 to more than $300 billion at last count. State governments, which share the costs with the federal government, were hit with the bill just as the economic downturn hit their revenues. And, the Bush administration, awash in red ink, wants to cut costs. ("Medicaid in the Cross Hairs" 2005, A22)

Medicaid provides health services for about fifty million low income and disabled recipients, with the number of individuals involved in the program increasing by a third between 2000 and 2005 (Lyman 2005). Medicaid pays for one-third of all births, covers more than one-fourth of all children, and finances care for two-thirds of all nursing home residents (Pear 2005). Medicaid costs during the same time frame rose 63 percent to somewhat more than $300 billion annually. Although in an aggregate sense Medicaid costs constituted 21 percent of state budgets—although it was a larger share of the budget in some states, as underscored by Table 10.1—in 2005, as opposed to only 12 percent of state budgets in 1990, twenty-three states in 2003 exceeded their Medicaid budget, as shown in Figure 10.1 (Lyman 2005). As a result of the increased cost of Medicaid, it appears that nearly all other services, from education to transportation, have suffered declining shares of state expenditures.

Responding to the escalating costs of Medicaid, President Bush proposed in the early part of 2005 to cut $60 billion—about 2 percent—from projected Medicaid spending in the period from 2005 to 2015 (Pear 2005). Bush suggested that the federal government should provide the states with fixed sums of funding, or block grants, instead of basing Medicaid payments on actual health costs and enrollment, or caseload size. Governors, responding in a unified fashion at their winter 2005 meeting

TABLE 10.1. Change in State Expenditures for Medicaid and Other Services as Percentage of Total, 1990–2003

	1990	2002
Medicaid	12	21
K-12 education	23	22
Higher education	12	11
Transportation	10	8
Corrections and welfare	8	6
All other	36	32

Source: "Medicaid Cost" 2005, A22.

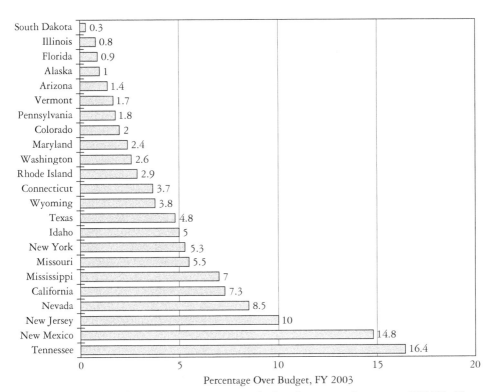

FIGURE 10.1. Medicaid costs as a percentage over budget for twenty-three states, FY2003. These 23 states were over budget for a total of $5.2 billion in FY2003, a year of budget shortfall for most states. *Sources: Rick Lyman, New York Times, February 23, 2005 and National Association of State Budget Officers.*

of the National Governors Association, assailed the proposed Bush initiative, stating that they needed every federal dollar they can receive to support the Medicaid program in their respective states. Governors, while agreeing that the Medicaid program was in financial trouble, stated their fear that Congress, in an effort to reduce the federal deficit, might limit federal Medicaid spending without relieving the states of any of their legal or financial obligations. Instead of federal budget cuts, the governors stressed that they wanted more freedom to manage and reconfigure their Medicaid programs, a position that drew some support from President Bush (Peer 2005).

In a number of states, governors are in the process of restructuring (usually by lowering their contribution to) their Medicaid programs. In his annual address to the New York State Legislature on January 5, 2005, Governor George E. Pataki noted: "I will propose Medicaid reforms that will reduce costs and also protect county property taxpayers, while ensuring the quality of health care we all deserve." Pataki's initiative was received sympathetically by members of the legislature, given the rapidly escalating costs of the Medicaid program in the state, which provides health coverage to three million individuals at an annual cost of $44 billion, representing 44 percent of the state's budget (Hernandez and Baker 2005a). In his proposed budget, Pataki suggested that the state should institute a $1 billion cut in Medicaid costs, place a cap on local Medicaid costs, and have the state pick up a larger share of these costs over time (Hernandez and Baker 2005b). In a somewhat similar cost-cutting spirit, Governor Phil Bradesen of Tennessee at the same time suggested eliminating 323,000 individuals from TennCare, a somewhat more expansive version of the traditional Medicaid program, while Governor Jeb Bush of Florida, in a more far-reaching proposal, argued for "privatizing" the Medicaid program in his state. Under his proposal, the state's 2.1 million Medicaid recipients would be allotted funding to purchase their own health care coverage from managed care organizations and other private medical networks (Lyman 2005).

Infrastructure and Core Cities

Another major challenge confronting our intergovernmental system is the continuing infrastructure problems (involving deteriorating water and sewer systems, roads, and bridges) and fiscal stress confronting many of our older core "dependent" cities. Nor are these problems limited to core cities; older suburban areas face similar difficulties. These challenges are rendered even more ominous by the proposal of President Bush to terminate the Community Development Block Grant (CDBG) program and to substantially reduce federal housing subsidies in urban areas (Chen 2004). Although a number of our cities, such as Boston, Cleveland, and New York, have enjoyed somewhat of a renaissance from the dire "urban crisis"[4] decade of the 1960s, many cities remain faced with considerable fiscal and service challenges. Among these cities is Detroit, which lost more than half of its population since 1950 and presently has 911,000 residents and is confronted with a $389 million revenue shortfall and the threat or receivership. Words that are used to describe the condition of the city are "cataclysmic," "debilitating," "monumental," "dire," and "grave." Among the basic causes of Detroit's woes is a stagnant economy with an unemployment rate of 14 percent, far higher than the rate for the state of Michigan and the nation. Detroit's efforts to attract new commercial development and investment is hampered by the nature of its tax structure, which relies more heavily on earnings taxes than revenues derived from property taxes that finance most other cities. It is estimated that Detroit's tax burden is 5.5 times that of the average Michigan municipality. A second cause for

Detroit's dire condition is due to the continuing and increasing flight of the middle class to the surrounding suburbs, along with the consequent decline in the number of children enrolled in its public schools. The school system has witnessed a loss of 33,000 students in public school enrollment from 1998 to 2005. The remaining students enrolled in the city's schools tend to be the most difficult and expensive to educate. One in seven Detroit students is enrolled in special education classes and 72 percent reside in homes that qualify them for free lunches, up from 61 percent in 2001. In addition, the fiscal crisis of Detroit has been aggravated by its receipt of less state funding. Detroit received 3.5 percent less in state funding in 2003, along with a reduction in state funding of 3 percent in 2004. Fourth, Detroit must compensate a municipal workforce of about the same size as a decade ago—approximately 18,000— which results in 1.4 employees for every 1,000 residents, far higher than the 1.0 median for major cities. Detroit spends more per capita on policing ($377 per capita, compared with a median of $221), garbage collection ($100 per capita, versus Chicago's $62 and Milwaukee's $52), and a similar range of other public services (Wilgoren 2005).

Even smaller cities, such as Camden (New Jersey), Petersburg (Virginia), and Schenectady (New York) are confronting, for a variety of well-known reasons, the usual litany of urban ills. Similar to Detroit, Schenectady, with a population of about sixty thousand, has witnessed a major decline in its economic sector and a movement of a good share of its more affluent citizens to the surrounding suburbs. In a manner comparable to Detroit, Schenectady has experienced some measure of mismanagement of city funds, with money intended for capital projects, like roads and buildings, being used to cover operating expenses. Finally, Schenectady, like many of its companion cities around the nation, is the recipient of less state funding than in the past; it received 15 percent less money from the state in 2005 than it received in 1989. In a broad-brush fashion, the State of New York has been criticized for not developing a more comprehensive and effective approach for revitalizing cities in the state like Schenectady (Polgreen 2003, A18).

Environment

A third major problem confronting the intergovernmental system concerns the need for a comprehensive public policy, involving all levels of government, for enhancing the quality of our environment. A report prepared and released by researchers at Columbia and Yale in 2005, involving an index of environmental sustainability, ranked the United States 45th of the 146 counties studied. The study scored nations on their success at such tasks as maintaining or improving air and water quality, maximizing biodiversity, and cooperating with other countries on environmental problems. The report was based on seventy-five specific measures, including the rate at which children die from respiratory diseases, fertility rates, water quality, over-fishing, emission of heat-trapping gases, and the export of sodium dioxide, a crucial component of acid rain. The top ten counties in the overall rankings in descending order were Finland, Norway, Uruguay, Sweden, Iceland, Canada, Switzerland, Guyana, Argentina, and Austria (Barringer 2005). In regard to the problem of acid rain, some political leaders have accused the Bush administration of utilizing state initiatives as a cover for its own inaction. For instance, Governor Gary Locke of Washington noted: "The states are taking action for one simple reason: because the federal government is not. For the White House to say it is looking for leadership from the states is just an excuse to delay and procrastinate. We are limited in what the states can do. We need a national policy to address global warming" (Revkin and Lee 2003, A22).

In a sharply worded thirty-eight-page report released on February 18, 2005, the Union of Concerned Scientists, a group of distinguished scientists, accused the Bush administration, in regard to environmental, health, biomedical research, and nuclear weaponry policies, of repeatedly censoring and suppressing reports by its own scientists, stocking advisory committees with unqualified political appointees, disbanding government panels that provided unwanted advice, and refusing to seek any independent scientific expertise in a number of instances. More specifically, the report noted that the Bush administration has misrepresented scientific consensus on global warming, censored at least one report on climate change, manipulated scientific findings on the emissions of mercury from power plants, and suppressed information on the use of condoms. The report also charged that the Bush administration allowed industries with conflicts of interest to influence technical advisory committees, disbanded for political reasons a panel on arms control, and subjected other prospective members of scientific panels to a political litmus test. A spokesman for the Bush administration denied the allegations contained in the report and stated that it simply did not make a good case for the charge of the suppression of good scientific advice by the administration (Glanz 2004).

Unacceptable levels of air pollution, as defined by the Environmental Protection Administration (EPA), still plague a substantial portion of the United States. The EPA reported in April 2004, on the basis of new tighter ozone exposure rules that went into effect that month, that about five hundred urban and rural counties, housing about 160 million residents, were in violation of federal clean air standards (Lee 2004a). A second EPA report issued in December 2004 noted that about a third of all Americans reside in counties that do not meet the standards for microscopic particles of pollution that cause thousands of premature deaths every year. The District of Columbia and the 225 counties, located in twenty states, contain a total of ninety-five million residents. In response to the problem, the Bush administration suggested a modification of "Clean Air Interstate Rule" that would lower emissions from coal-fire power plants, and the "Clean Skies Initiative," which is designed to lower emissions levels nationwide (Janofsky 2004).

However, and rather ironically, the EPA made rule changes in the Clean Air Act in August 2003, which went into effect the following December. These rule changes involved the modernization of power plants, oil refineries, and industrial boilers. Under the less stringent new rules adopted by the EPA, any renovation project of a facility that added less than 20 percent of the power generating unit's value was exempt from adding additional pollution control equipment, even if the project resulted in increased emissions. As a result of the new rules, the EPA terminated investigations into fifty power plants for past violations of the Clean Air Act (Drew and Oppel 2003, 1).

Officials in many states, especially in the Northeast, viewed with strong disfavor the new rule changes by the EPA. In a report released by the General Accounting Office (GAO) in December 2004, officials in twenty-seven states noted that the changes would increase emissions, while officials from five states stated that it would decrease them. Officials from the twelve states reported either that emissions would remain the same or were unsure what the impact would be. The remaining states failed to respond to the survey. State officials in twenty-nine states indicated that the changes' main benefits would be to give the utility industry increased flexibility (Lee 2004a). In an interesting example involving the transfer of policy conflict in the intergovernmental system from the federal to the state level, the states of Connecticut, New Jersey, and New York, along with a number of environmental groups, initiated litigation designed to force the power companies in their states to make billions of dollars of pollution-control improvements (Oppel and Drew 2003).

It should be noted that the Bush administration, citing budget concerns, has proposed the creation of new Superfund toxic waste sites at a much slower rate than during of the Clinton administration. The Superfund program was established in 1980 to help clean up toxic waste sites. For instance, in 2003 the Bush administration nominated fourteen sites to the Superfund program, along with nine sites the previous year. In contrast, the Clinton administration added about thirty-four to forty-five sites each year (see Figure 10.2). Adding to the decline of funds available for

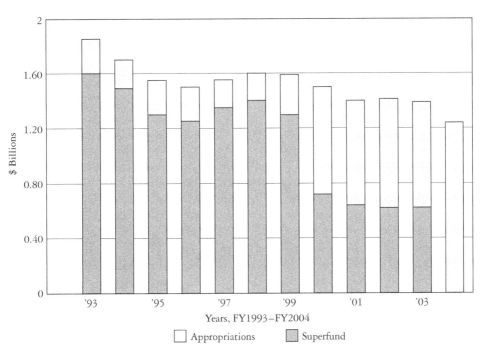

FIGURE 10.2. Appropriations from Superfund and general revenue, FY1993–FY2004. The Superfund trust fund is completely depleted, with all money coming from appropriations after FY2003. *Sources: Lee, 2004 A23; EPA General Accounting Office.*

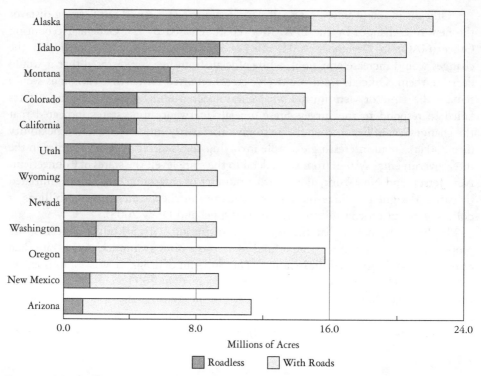

FIGURE 10.3. Roadless areas in and total areas of national forests in Western states in millions of acres, 2004. *Sources: Barringer 2004, A1, A14; National Forest Service.*

the clean up of toxic waste funds is that the revenues derived from a trust, largely financed by taxes on some chemical and oil companies, have been depleted (Lee 2004c).

Finally, we should note in regard to environmental policy, the Bush administration proposed in July 2004 the termination the Clinton-era so-called roadless rule that placed nearly eighty million acres of national forest largely off limits to logging, mining, or other forms of development. As is documented in Figure 10.3, the termination of this rule would have its greatest impact on the forests of Alaska and eleven Western states. In its place, the Bush administration argued that governors should have greater policy authority to seek additional or fewer strictures on road construction in federal forests and that the termination of the rule would be a way to sidestep the existing tangle of litigation regarding constructing roads through national forests. The termination of the rule, the Bush administration argued, would facilitate as a stimulus to local participation and federal flexibility in determining the use of national forests.[5] A variety of environmental groups voiced their strong displeasure of the proposal of the administration (Barringer 2004).

The *New York Times*, in reaction to the Bush administration proposal, published a scathing critical editorial entitled "Surrender in the Forests," in which it stated in part:

The Bush administration has taken apart so many environmental regulations that one more rollback should not surprise us. Even so, it boggles the mind that the White House should choose an election year to dismantle one of the most important and popular land preservation initiatives of the last 30 years—a Clinton administration rule that placed 58.5 million acres of the national forests off limits to new road building and development.

Further:

There are no compelling reasons to repudiate that rule and no obvious beneficiaries beside a few disgruntled Western governors and the timber, oil and gas interests that have long regarded the national forests as profit centers. It's not even a case of election-year pandering to Western voters; indeed, early returns suggest that most Westerners below the rank of governor do not like the Bush proposal at all. Especially aggrieved is the so-called hook and bullet crowd—anglers and hunters who, though overwhelmingly Republican, have become increasingly disenchanted with the administration's timid and in some cases careless policies on wetlands, mercury pollution and oil and gas exploration on sensitive public lands.

The various policy challenges we have elaborated upon—financing Medicaid, responding to the declining infrastructure and overall condition of some of our most distressed core cities, and ensuring the quality of our environment—have each served to place "downward pressure" on intergovernmental systems. In each instance, federal governmental policy decisions have placed new responsibilities on the states and their local governments. Threatened cutbacks in federal funding for Medicaid have placed additional financial pressures upon the states, the decline in federal funding assistance for core cities has aggravated their infrastructure problems and overall condition of their finances, and the adoption of new policies and rules by the federal government may well have the long-term effect of undermining the quality of our environment.

In addition, the intergovernmental system is confronted with a host of social issues, on which the populace is deeply divided, as underscored in the splendid work of John Kenneth White entitled *The Values Divide: American Politics and Culture in Transition* (2003). To a significant degree, discussion and political debate center on whether these issues should be subject to and resolved by a national uniform policy, or whether each state should be able to determine its own set of policies. In addition to the perennial issue of abortion rights, these issues include allowing gay couples to marry, as in Massachusetts (Belluck 2004),[6] or allowing states to adopt a constitutional amendment forbidding same-sex marriages, as has taken place in eighteen states (Tanner 2005); the right of individuals to use marijuana for medical purposes (Greenhouse 2004a); and the role of Congress and the federal and state courts in matters of the life and death of the seriously ill. As is commonly recognized, the latter issue was brought to the attention of the public and triggered considerable political debate with the case of Terri Schiavo in the early months of 2005 (Nagourney 2005). Additional social issues that have provoked considerable controversy, and in some instances litigation, include the appropriate role of the federal and state governments in regard to the rights of the disabled as set forth by the Americans With Disabilities Act (Greenhouse 2004), the purchase of drugs in Canada (Davey 2003), the apprehension of illegal immigrants (Swarns 2004), and Native American tribal recognition and rights (Belluck 2003; Fuchs and Stowe 2004). As Christopher Caldwell (2004) wrote in the *New York Times Sunday Magazine:* "By (the) consensus of the adversaries, divisive (social) issues are being argued in ever widening jurisdictions." And further: "Many gay-marriage advocates claim that same-sex marriage should remain a local issue. They argue that once one state recognizes gay marriage, there is little danger that the Constitution's full-faith-and-credit clause will compel other states to follow suit. But this is little more than the signature debating trick of our time: trying to advance one's own effort to enforce national standards in the guise of modest localism" (11, 12).

THE INTERGOVERNMENTAL SYSTEM AND THE FAUX MIDDLE CLASS

Commencing with the writings of Aristotle, it has long been argued by political theorists that one of the basic prerequisites of a stable democratic system is the presence of a large middle class. From the mid twentieth century until the 1980s, the United States had a large, quite prosperous, and growing middle class, who dwelled, as Lizabeth Cohen (2004) has noted, in "A Consumers' Republic." Since the 1970s much has changed on this score, in large part because of fiscal developments that have taken place in our intergovernmental system. To be sure, we still have large numbers of people with all of the accoutrements of a middle-class lifestyle. Over two-thirds of the population own their own home, stocked with automobiles, television sets, DVD players, cell phones, computers, and so on, but as far as owning these things outright, it is a different matter. Much, if not most, of the recent economic expansion in the United States has been based on the expansion of consumer and mortgage credit and by having more persons gainfully employed full-time in each family. And as Daniel Elazar (1990) has pointedly stated, in this mass consumer culture we have tended to judge all things by consumer standards and we have lost our sense of responsibility to each other and to the larger polity:

> Americans are beginning to sense the failure of consumerism, namely, the redefinition of people primarily as consumers and their institutions primarily as vehicles for the satisfaction of consumer wants. At the very least, the redefinition of government as a service-delivery mechanism and citizens as consumers leads to an unmanageable acceleration of public demands. It also leads to the evaluation of all institutions by a set of standards that, being human institutions, they are bound not to meet. Not the least of these problems of the consumer model is the abandonment of the principle that people have responsibilities as well as rights, and that they have obligations to each other, if not to the polity in the abstract, which, when neglected, imperil democracy by undermining its very foundation. (20–21)

As home ownership has increased, the equity in homes has tended to decline. Students graduating from college are often saddled with huge debts for student loans as the cost of higher education has been increasingly shifted from the state to the students at our publicly supported colleges and universities. As manufacturing has declined as a portion of our economy, manufacturing jobs have been outsourced to low-wage countries, with lower-paying service jobs taking their place. Seventy percent of the economy is based on consumption, so effectively lowering the income of a large number of residents is bound to have long-term consequences (CEA 2004–5, 208). Further, there is a very real question of how much flexibility remains for the further expansion of credit to stimulate the economy as the federal government over the period since the year CY2000 has increasingly used debt to finance its operations and wars and as federal, state, and local revenues have been downloaded on low- and middle-income families over the last two or three decades.

The average family has to work harder and longer just to maintain its economic position and lifestyle and to pay for their mortgages, credit card debt, student loans, and health care. Between 1950 and 2002, the number of persons per household has declined from 3.52 to 2.58; at the same time the number of employed workers per household has increased (Abstract 1969, 35; 2003, 60). Over the last quarter-century, the United States has experienced a massive redistribution of income from the poor and middle classes to the corporate elite using the federal tax structure and the combined revenue systems of federal, state, and local governments (Krugman 1994, 23–29; Phillips 1990). We have become a nation of *credit indentured servants*, indentured servants who devote their lifetime seeking to pay off these debts to the Fortune 500 and the other multinational corporations. Except for the first five years of the George W. Bush administration, the changes in the distribution of income have come about very gradually over the last half-century, but since CY2000, these changes have markedly accelerated. The average person in the faux middle class has yet to realize they have been sold into *credit* bondage and will spend his or her lifetime paying off accumulated debt, from the cradle to the grave.

The redistribution of income using the federal-state-local revenue structure and personal and public debt are not the only problems bearing down on the average citizen. Another major challenge involves that of providing health care to all of our citizens; in this sense, ensuring adequate health care represents another real threat to the faux middle class (Krugman 1994, 73–83). The United States spends the highest percentage of its GDP on health care of any developed nation. The United States has the highest per capita cost of health care with the lowest performance of any developed nation, as measured by various health statistics. Moreover, between 1980 and 2001, the cost of health care as a percentage of GDP has recently increased by 60 percent. Given an 88 percent increase in the constant dollar GDP this translates into a 200 percent rise in the cost of health care during the period when constant dollar family income increased only 20 percent (Census 2003, *Abstract*, 510, 690, 848–52; CEA 2003, 284).

Current government estimates of the number of people without health insurance are in the range of forty-four to forty-five million and increasing, but that is only one aspect of the problem. As health costs rise, increasingly employers, such as General Motors as well as many others, are seeking to reduce health care benefits to their employees and retirees, with much more of the cost being passed on to their recipients. Health care costs are rising at double-digit rates, while income is not. The federal budget for FY2006 is reducing public support for Medicaid (for children) and

FIGURE 10.4

Source: Toles © 2005 The Washington Post. Reprinted with permission of Universal Press Syndicate. All rights reserved.

Medicare (for the elderly), and many state governments are following suit by reducing Medicaid coverage. The federal budget for FY2006 also proposes cuts in health benefits for veterans, although Congress may well defeat that initiative. Personal bankruptcies rose 122 percent between 1980 and 2002, with half of recent filings attributed to the cost of health care (Census *Abstract*, 2003, 114; Frosch, 2005, 11–14).

Given the rate at which the national debt is rising, it is unlikely that this situation will improve. Because of tax cuts and wars in Afghanistan and Iraq, the national debt increased $596 billion in FY2004, up $1.8 trillion during President Bush's first four years in office. It is likely to be much higher for FY2005, FY2006, and FY2007. The FY2006 federal budget proposal by OMB released in February 2005 stated that the deficit for FY2004 was $412 billion (they don't read their own Treasury reports!) and projects deficits for FY2005 and FY2006 of $427 billion and $390 billion, respectively (page 343). Yet the same document notes that the national debt for FY2005 and FY2006 will increase $676 and $677 billion, respectively (page 367). If Social Security funds were taken off the table and placed in a locked box, the real increase in the national debt would be somewhere in the order of $800 to $900 billion. In the long run, this means higher interest rates will be needed simply to finance the national debt. Personal and public debts are not the only consideration; there is also the problem of the balance-of-payments deficits or monies we owe to other countries through our imbalance in international trade (Krugman 1994, 43–58). These debts amounted to nearly $500 billion in CY 2003, increased to $618 billion in CY2004, and are running at about $700 billion in early CY2005. Recent spikes in the price of oil are accelerating the balance of payments deficits as well as the national debt and increasing inflation. In the long run all of this debt could have a deleterious effect on the stock markets. The United States used to manufacture its own products, but now it seems we largely export raw materials and import finished products as our corporations have outsourced manufacturing jobs to other countries.

But there is another "fly in the ointment" for the nation and the faux middle class. Over the last six decades, the United States dollar has been the standard medium of exchange for international trade. Countries like China, Japan, Saudi Arabia, and others, as well as private investors, have been willing to fund our debt. During the last four or five years the dollar has plummeted against the euro, as of 2004 down nearly one-third since the Clinton administration, making the dollar a much less desirable medium for international investment and exchange (Krugman 2004, 111–21). Some

FIGURE 10.5

Source: Toles © 2005 The Washington Post. Reprinted with permission of Universal Press Syndicate. All rights reserved.

nations are beginning to consider switching from the dollar to the euro, which could further depress the value of the dollar and increase interest rates and inflation. With these massive increases in debt, interest payments will be piled on top of interest payments. These higher interest rates translate into high rates for not only government borrowing, but also higher interest rates for businesses, consumer credit, and mortgages, which, in turn, could result in a huge drag on our credit-based consumer economy. Where will this leave our debt-ridden, tax paying faux middle class?

THE FUTURE OF FEDERALISM AND INTERGOVERNMENTAL RELATIONS

A federal system can have certain advantages over that of a polity, which is highly centralized or a confederation, but much depends on how power is distributed between levels, whether the functions of government are appropriately positioned, and whether each level and each constituent government has the resources to provide the basic level of public services required. With any large and geographically diverse federal system, there are public services needed in some states and some localities that are unnecessary elsewhere in the nation or services that are needed at different levels of intensity in different parts of the federal system. Moreover, some services can be more effectively or efficiently provided at the state or local levels if the financial resources are available.

As Arthur Maass underscored almost fifty years ago in his seminal edited work *Area and Power: A Theory of Local Government* (1959), in federal systems there is a continuous debate concerning which government and which level of government should occupy a particular territorial expanse and/or perform a particular activity. A federation, if it chooses to do so, can equalize or provide some minimum level of resources to poorer states so they can perform their assigned activities. The United States has never done this is in any systematic manner, although other developed federal systems have. Moreover, there is the problem of economies of scale. Different government activities achieve an optimum level of performance at different points along the scale of population size in terms of economic, social, service, administrative, and/or political efficiency. Efficiency and effectiveness for a particular service can vary according to the criteria.

A democratic federal system does provide places where the political party or parties out of power at the national level can maintain themselves for a return to power at the national level—provided those in power at the national level do not attain too much power and obliterate the opposition at the lower levels of government. This type of power position at the federal level appears to be the objective of the Republican Party in 2005–6. There is, however, another problem with democratic systems. Once the representatives of the people realize how much their votes are really worth, they sometimes sell out, usually to the highest bidder, the economic elite. In the United States we now have the best Congress and the best president that money can buy—and they have been bought. According to Lord Action (1834–1902), "Power tends to corrupt, absolute power tends to corrupt absolutely."

The ad hoc evolution of the American federal system leaves a great deal to be desired. The multidimensional maze of federal, state, and local political and administrative jurisdictions with a similar complex of private for-profit and nonprofit service providers—but mostly for-profit service providers—makes the federal system so amorphous, its amazing it works at all. Often it doesn't, at least not in the public interest. The system is rife with access points for legal, extralegal, and illegal corruption where private interests can capture a government agency, a regulatory board, a critical legislative committee, or even an entire government. While these statements apply to all levels of government, it is most noticeable at the local level of government and most hidden at the national level, although it is becoming more apparent to those paying attention. In terms of the public, the federal system appears to have a severe case of arteriosclerosis.

Certain developments have in small ways helped to ameliorate or mitigate but not solve the problems faced by local governments. The system has been held together (1) by a patchwork of additions to local government, particularly by the creation of special district governments; (2) by federal aid to state and local governments and state aid to local government, although federal aid is currently declining during the 2003–6 period; (3) by the states taking on more fiscal and service responsibility, but this could change as federal aid diminishes; (4) to a more limited degree by the federal government taking on some service responsibility and more fiscal responsibility, until recently when there has been some retrenchment; and (5) by the ability of local governments to interact and lessen the impact of a few of the more critical problems.

The question is: Is there some point when the structural clutter of the federal system makes it impossible to govern, much less govern democratically, responsibly, efficiently, effectively, or economically? Given the fact that state and local governments provide the bulk of the domestic public services received by their residents, what will happen given the current rush of federal and state policy-makers to downsize and privatize government? How capable are our states and our state systems of local government in responding to the problems and needs of their citizens?

ROAD TO REFORM

At this point, we would like to set forth a suggested agenda of reform that we believe would serve to render the intergovernmental system a bit more democratic and responsible, as well as efficient, effective, and economical. At base, given the expansive rise and scope of "privatized federalism" in our intergovernmental system we believe that all governments—federal, state, and local—should provide on an annual basis information, through the Internet, concerning their use and costs of private for-profit and nonprofit vendors for the provision of services. In addition, where feasible, we believe that the state and local governments should conduct a widely publicized public hearing on any proposal to contract with a profit or nonprofit entity for the delivery of a service before granting its formal acceptance. These measures, we believe, would serve to at least partially remedy the "black hole" of knowledge that the public and, indeed, scholars face in regard to the ever-increasing role of privatized federalism in our intergovernmental system. In a more specific sense, we believe that:

1. The federal government should reestablish and appropriately fund the United States Advisory Commission on Intergovernmental Relations (ACIR).

2. The Congress should establish a subcommittee on Intergovernmental Relations as part of the House of Representative's Committee on Government Reform and the Senate's Committee on Governmental Affairs.

3. The federal government should adequately fund the Governments Division of the Census Bureau so that it could again collect and publish all of the data that were once available to policy-makers and scholars concerning federal, state, and local government activities.

4. The federal government needs to consider folding many of the hundreds of categorical grants-in-aid into a truly redistributive federal general-purpose grant that places a floor under the revenue-raising capability of our poorer state-local systems using something like the state-local tax and revenue capacity indices developed by the U.S. Advisory Commission on Intergovernmental Relations, 1993.

5. The federal government should rescind all tax cuts that have been enacted since 2000 with reference to the individual income tax, dividends, capital gains, and estate and inheritance taxes.

6. Completely revise and reinstitute a progressive federal corporate income tax with provisions that include taxation of the earnings of both domestic and foreign corporations within the jurisdiction of the United States preventing them from taking their profits offshore.

7. Consider the revision of laws relating to not-for-profit and nonprofit corporations preventing their use as tax dodges and funding sources for political activities.

Further, we believe that the *state governments* should undertake appropriate structural and financial reforms to coordinate, or mesh, their physical and social planning and economic development efforts more closely with local governments, regional planning agencies, and public-private economic development entities. In addition, short of a badly needed overhaul of their state systems of local government, states need to develop a well-considered and comprehensive approach for dealing with the structural clutter of their local governments:

1. States should remedy the sometimes very lax procedures for incorporating special districts.

2. They should provide the means whereby local governments that are no longer viable or effective service providers can be readily consolidated with other local units or be disincorporated.

3. They must ensure that new local governments are created for a valid public purpose, rather than for unregulated private gain.

4. Where special districts are used primarily as a funding device, the state government, counties, and other large governments should be given the latitude to establish subordinate service areas with sufficient revenue authority, rather than create another local government; or, these new service areas should be annexed to an existing service provider.

5. The functional activities of like special districts should be coordinated with each other and with general purpose local governments.

6. Provisions should exist for the annexation of territory to existing special districts, in some instances, rather than the creation of additional units of local government.

7. Township states situated in the Plains or the Midwest should provide procedures for the consolidation of very small township governments or for the assumption of their activities by their county governments.

8. Periodically, perhaps every ten years, states should comprehensively reevaluate their systems of local government.

9. Ideally, TIFs should be eliminated, since these entities tend to shift the tax burden for new development to existing taxpayers, property owners, and residents and in some instances provide a distinct advantage to tax wealthy state and local governments.

10. States should provide "bonus grants" to their local governments to promote and facilitate semi-regional and regional functional cooperation where appropriate.

11. States need to develop some kind of general-purpose redistributive grant system to provide a basic level of revenue resource to their poorer local governments.

With reference to *local governments*, we suggest that the following reforms are in order:

1. All general and special-purpose local governments with the necessary resources should designate an administrative official to monitor vertical and horizontal intergovernmental developments and promote intergovernmental cooperation.

2. All local governments should provide their regional planning agency with a copy of any federal or state grant application for appropriate review and comment.

3. All special district governments and authorities should provide their regional planning agency with an annual report of their activities and performance.

4. Where it is not currently taking place, local and regional COGs should facilitate the adoption of interlocal regulatory and service agreements.

We are of the persuasion that the adoption of these reforms would tend to make our intergovernmental system a bit more democratic, responsible, efficient, effective, and economical. Even so, it is unlikely that much will be done along these lines and the system will continue to deteriorate.

WHITHER THE FUTURE OF FEDERALISM
AND INTERGOVERNMENTAL RELATIONS?

To be sure, given the complexity, currents, and dynamics of federalism in the United States it is somewhat hazardous to predict the future of intergovernmental relations as we move on through the twenty-first century. However, if the past is at least partially a guide in terms of extrapolating the future, we believe that the following intergovernmental trends will be evident: First, although many federal, state, and local officials will publicly pay homage to the virtues of the "devolution revolution," the federal and state governments will continue to practice their heavy hand of regulation, resulting in a sort of "paradoxical federalism," one with major cross-currents. Second, given the financial constraints of both the federal and many state governments, conflict over program funding will continue to escalate. Third, Congress will rely less upon conditional grants-in-aids for achieving its national goals, but will make occasional use of its "tool box" of regulatory devices on behalf of advancing social causes. Fourth, Congress will continue to make use of its broad powers of total and partial preemption to restrain state action, or to induce the state administration and funding of national programs, as part of an acknowledged leadership-feedback model of decision-making. Fifth, pressures will continue to mount on the federal government for the reimbursement of added costs imposed on state and local governments by federal mandates, but the continuing and increasing federal deficit will render Congress largely unresponsive to these demands for reimbursement. Some political interests would like to see the federal government divested of all social programs like Social Security. Sixth, the United States Supreme Court will continue to referee national-state conflicts involving a host of policy disputes, including extremely volatile social issues. Seventh, a good deal of political rhetoric will continue to be voiced by some public officials and conservative public policy "think tanks" promoting the virtue of downsizing government and privatizing services. Eighth, there will be continuing erosion of the position of the middle class as the tax structure is downloaded, higher-paying jobs are outsourced, and the health care crisis continues. And, finally, the intergovernmental system will continue to be very bewildering, complex, and kaleidoscopic, rendering it difficult for the ordinary citizen, and even the attentive public, to pinpoint responsibility and hold national, state, and local public officials fully accountable for their responsibilities, actions, and broad policy decisions.

In conclusion, we should like to note the sage thoughts of Deil S. Wright, a long-time scholar of federalism, contained in his recent paper entitled "Federalism and Intergovernmental Relations: Traumas, Tensions, and Trends" (2003). In his paper Wright correctly notes: "The history of federalism in the United States has been one of shifting patterns and fluctuating balances between two contrasting themes. On one side of the relationship ledger are patterns of conflict, contentiousness, and cleavages. The other side of the balance sheet reflects the themes of cooperation, collaboration, and coordination" (5). At the present time, Wright notes, the federal initiatives particularly centered on homeland security and elementary and secondary education, accompanied by a host of federal mandates, serve to provoke a considerable amount of federal-state tension. As he notes: "The demands placed on state [and local] officials in confronting these issues are daunting. State policymakers must deal with resource(s) restrictions, make decisions under conditions of increased complexity and greater uncertainty, cope creatively with extraordinary difficult problems, and build reform/reinvention capabilities" (11). However, Wright argues that by public officials forcefully responding to these problems and practicing the art of "contingent collaboration" they will gain the trust, confidence, and assurance of the citizens. All of this suggests that we should maintain some modicum of hope for the future of our intergovernmental system. But maybe not too much. Deil Wright is an optimist.

REFERENCES

Associated Press. 2003, August 19. Majority Against Gay Marriages, Poll Says. *Richmond Times-Dispatch*. A2.

Barringer, Felicity. 2004, July 13. Bush Seeks Shift in Logging Rules. *New York Times*. A1, A14.

——. 2005, January 24. Nations Ranked as Protectors of the Environment. *New York Times*. A9.

Bartels, Larry M. 2005. Homer Gets a Tax Cut: Inequality and Public Policy in the American Mind. *Perspectives on Politics*. 3: 1 (March), 15–31.

Beer, Samuel H. 1978. Federalism, Nationalism, and Democracy in America. *American Political Science Review*. 72 (March), 9–21.

Belluck, Pam. 2003, December 30. Tribe Loses Suit on Tax-Free Tobacco. *New York Times*. A12.

——. 2004, February 5. Massachusetts Gives New Push to Gay Marriage. *New York Times*. A23.

Box, Richard C. 1998. *Citizen Governance: Leading American Communities into the 21st Century*. Thousand Oaks, CA: Sage Publications.

Butterfield, Fox. 2005, March 31. Gambling Grows, States Depend on Their Cut. *New York Times*. A1, A24.

Caldwell, Christopher. 2004, April 18. No Politics Are Local. *New York Times Sunday Magazine*. 11–12.

Chen, David W. 2004, February 20. Bush Housing Aid Proposal Stirs Anxiety in New York. *New York Times*. A24.

Cohen, Lizabeth. 2004. *A Consumers' Republic: The Politics of Mass Consumption in Postwar America*. New York: Vintage Books.

Council of Economic Advisors (CEA). 2005. *Economic Report of the President*. Washington, DC: Government Printing Office. 208.

Davey, Monica. 2003, September 16. Illinois Considers Buying Drugs in Canada. *New York Times*. A17.

Drew, Christopher and Richard A. Oppel Jr. 2003, November 11. Lawyers at E.P.A. Say It Will Drop Pollution Cases. *New York Times*. A1, A25.

Eikenberry, Angela M. and Jodie Drapal Kluver. 2004. The Marketization of the Nonprofit Sector. *Public Administration Review*. 64 (March/April), 132–40.

Elazar, Daniel J. 1987. *Exploring Federalism*. Tuscaloosa: University of Alabama Press.

——. 1990. Opening the Third Century of American Federalism. *Annals of the American Academy of Political and Social Science*. 509 (May), 11–21.

Frosch, Dan. 2005, February 21. When Getting Sick Means Going Broke: Your Money or Your Life. *The Nation*. 11–14.

Fuchs, Marek and Stacy Stowe. 2004, January 31. Connecticut Faces Showdown over a Tribe's Recognition. *New York Times*. A14.

Glanz, James. 2004, February 19. Scientists Say Administration Distorts Facts. *New York Times*. A21.

Greenhouse, Linda. 2004a, November 30. States' Rights Defense Falters in Medical Marijuana Case. *New York Times*. A18.

———. 2004b, January 14. Dispute Heard on States' Duties Under Disabilities Act. *New York Times.* A17.

Hernandez, Raymond and Al Baker. 2005a, January 9. Bush's Medicaid Proposals Could Lead to Overhaul of New York's Program. *New York Times.* 24.

———. 2005b, January 15. Pataki said to Favor $1 Billion Cut in New York Medicaid. *New York Times.*

Hinds, Mark. 2003. Building Community May Mean Rebuilding Non-profits. *PA Times.* 26 (July), 8.

Janofsky, Michael. 2004, December 18. Many Counties Failing Fine-Particle Air Rules. *New York Times.* A10.

Kettl, Donald F. 1993. *Sharing Power: Public Governance and Private Markets.* Washington, DC: Brookings Institution.

Koontz, Tomas M. 2002. *Federalism in the Forests: National Versus State Natural Resource Policy.* Washington, DC: Georgetown University Press.

Kramer, Ralph M. 1981. *Voluntary Agencies in the Welfare State.* Berkeley: University of California Press.

Krugman, Paul. 1994. *The Age of Diminished Expectations.* Cambridge, MA: MIT Press.

———. 2005, February 11. Bush's Class-War Budget. *New York Times.* www.newyorktimes.com/2005/02/11/opinion/11krugman.html.

Lee, Jennifer 8. 2004a, April 13. Clear Skies No More for Millions in the U.S. *New York Times.* A16.

———. 2004b, March 2. Most States Expect Pollution to Rise if Regulations Change and Slows Superfund Program. *New York Times.* A23.

———. 2004c, March 2. Drop in Budget Slows Superfund Program. *New York Times.* A23.

Lyman, Rick. 2005, January 23. Florida Offers a Bold Stroke to Fight Medicaid Costs. *New York Times.* 18.

Maass, Arthur, ed. 1959. *Area and Power: A Theory of Local Government.* Glencoe, IL: The Free Press.

Medicaid Cost. 2005, January 23. *New York Times.*

Medicaid in the Cross Hairs [editorial]. 2005, March 14. *New York Times.* A22.

Nagourney, Adam. 2005, March 23. G.O.P. Right is Splintered on Schiavo Intervention. *New York Times.* A14.

Office of Management and Budget (OMB). 2005. *Budget of the United States Government: Fiscal Year 2006.* Washington, DC: Government Printing Office. 343, 367.

Oppel, Richard A. Jr. and Christopher Drew. 2003, November 9. States Planning Their Own Suits on Power Plants. *New York Times.* 1, 24.

Pear, Robert. 2005, February 27. Governors Prepare to Fight Medicaid Cuts. *New York Times.* 19.

Phillips, Kevin. 1990. *The Politics of Rich and Poor: Wealth and the American Electorate in the Reagan Aftermath.* New York: Random House.

Polgreen, Lydia. 2003, December 23. As Schenectady Rusts, Experts Fear Policy Inertia. *New York Times.* A1, A18.

Revkin, Andrew C. and Jennifer S. Lee. 2003, December 11. Administration Attacked for Leaving Climate Policy to States. *New York Times.* A22.

Savas, E. S. 1982. *Privatizing the Public Sector.* Chatham, NJ: Chatham House.

———. 1987. *Privatization: The Key to Better Government.* Chatham, NJ: Chatham House.

———. 2000. *Privatization and Public-Private Partnerships.* Chatham, NJ: Chatham House.

Strom, Stephanie. 2004a, September 13. Public Confidence in Charities Stays Flat. *New York Times.* A18.

———. 2004b, January 9. Battle in Omaha Charitable Group Reflects Issues Raised in Corporate Scandals. *New York Times.* A11.

Surrender in the Forests [editorial]. 2004, July 18. *New York Times.* 12WK.

Swarns, Rachel L. 2004, April 12. Local Officers Join Search for Illegal Immigrants. *New York Times.* A12.

Tanner, Robert. 2005, April 10. Gay Marriage Splits States. *Richmond Times-Dispatch.* A2.

Thompson, Lyke and Richard C. Elling. 2000. Mapping Patterns of Support for Privatization in the Mass Public. *Public Administration Review.* 60 (July/August), 338–48.

Van Slyke, David M. 2003. The Mythology of Privatization in Contracting for Social Services. *Public Administration Review* 63 (May/June), 296–313.

von Zielbauer, Paul. 2005a, February 27. As Health Care in Jails Goes Private, 10 Days Can Be a Death Sentence. *New York Times.* 1, 26–28.

———. 2005b, February 28. Inside City's Jails, Missed Signals Open Way to Season of Suicides. *New York Times.* A1, A18–19.

———. Paul 2005c, March 1. A Spotty Record of Health Care at Juvenile Sites in New York. *New York Times.* A1, A20.

United States Advisory Commission on Intergovernmental Relations (ACIR). 1993. *RTS: State Revenue Capacity and Effort.* Washington, DC: ACIR.

United States Bureau of the Census. 1969, 2003. *1969 Statistical Abstract of the United States.* Washington, DC: Government Printing Office. 35; 2003 *Abstract*, 60, 114, 510, 690, 842–52.

White, John Kenneth. 2003. *The Values Divide: American Politics and Culture in Transition.* New York: Chatham House Publishers/Seven Bridges Press.

Wilgoren, Jodi. 2005, February 2. Shrinking, Detroit Faces Fiscal Nightmare. *New York Times.* A12.

Wright, Deil S. 2003. Federalism and Intergovernmental Relations: Traumas, Tensions, and Trends. Paper presented at the 64th National Conference of the American Society for Public Administration. Washington, DC. March 15–18.

Zimmerman, Joseph P. 2004. The United States Federal System: A Kaleidoscopic View. Paper prepared for presentation at a research seminar, Rothermere American Institute, Oxford University. Oxford, England. November 23.

Notes

PREFACE

1. "Micropolitan areas" are smaller urban areas that do not meet the criteria for being considered as one or a part of the 361 "metropolitan statistical areas." They have an urbanized core of at least 10,000 residents as defined by the Office of Management and Budget for the 2000 Census. In fact, the 573 micropolitan statistical areas range in size from 12,000 to 171,000 residents. *Statistical Abstract of the United States* (Washington, DC: Government Printing Office, 2004–05), pp. 901–22.

1 THE UNITED STATES AS A FEDERAL SYSTEM: THEORETICAL INSIGHTS AND EXPERIENCE

1. This disparity in terms of representation continues into the twenty-first century.
2. Daniel Elazar in *The American Partnership* (1962) outlines nineteenth-century cooperative federal intergovernmental relations in terms of the development of canals and railroads, public education, land-grant universities, and the establishment of the banking system, many of which involved land grants. Currently, the extent and use of federal grants is outlined annually in the Census Bureau's *Consolidated Federal Funds Reports* to Congress.
3. From www.usahistory.info/New England.
4. From www.usinfo.state.gov/infousa/facts/democ/4.
5. For much more detail covering colonial government and the period up to the adoption of the Constitution, see Ogg and Ray 1948.
6. These indices measure the relative role of the three levels of government using a composite index of three subindices that measure service delivery, financial responsibility for public services, and personnel adjusted for labor versus cash and capital inputs of different public services (Stephens 1974 and later updates; Stephens and Wikstrom 2003a).
7. These are really index numbers using Stephens's indices of state centralization vis-à-vis local government as indicated in endnote number 6.
8. The sources of this material are too many to be listed in parentheses in the paragraph. They include publications of the Census Bureau, www.census.gov/govs/estimate/01s100us.html; the 2002 *Statistical Abstract*; the 1961 *Historical Statistics of the United States, Colonial Times to 1957*; the 2002 *Economic Report of the President*; and OMB, *Historical Tables*, Budget of the United States Government, Fiscal Year 2004.

2 FEDERALISM AND INTERGOVERNMENTAL RELATIONS: CONCEPTS, MODELS, AND THE AMERICAN SYSTEM

1. These numbers are based on a projection of the increased numbers of local governments, since the Governments Division of the Census Bureau no longer publishes Vol. 1, no. 2 of the *Census of Governments, Popularly Elected Officials*.

2. This came out in a meeting of a small group of researchers with Nelson Rockefeller, Wilbur Mills, and John Connally in 1974. The meeting was arranged by the National Science Foundation. G. Ross Stephens was a part of the group doing research on the impact of GRS in 1975.
3. This is really a gross summary as the process is much more complex and involved concerning the FDIC and FSLIC (Stephens and Wikstrom 2000).
4. From wysiwyg//39http//www.whitehouse.gov/wtt/EOP/OVP/initiatives_bottom.html.

3 CONTEMPORARY AMERICAN FEDERALISM AND INTERGOVERNMENTAL RELATIONS: COOPERATION AND CONFLICT

1. Our use of the term "the web of intergovernmental relations" is a paraphrasing of the title of Robert MacIver's important work *The Web of Government* (New York: Macmillan, 1947).
2. We have drawn the concept of social capital from the recent influential work of Robert D. Putnam, *Bowling Alone: The Collapse and Revival of the American Community* (New York: Simon & Schuster, 2000). Regarding the role of regional organizations in promoting social capital among and between officials in the metropolis, see the insightful paper by Richard C. Feiock and Hyung-Jun Park, "Social Capital and the Formation of Regional Partnerships," presented at the Annual Meeting of The American Political Science Association, Philadelphia, August 27–30, 2003.

4 FISCAL FEDERALISM

1. From www.census.gov/govs/03sl.html.
2. A recent check of these data for 2002 indicated this is still the case, if not moreso, as the Senate has increased the percentage that small states, no matter how small, receive from federal grants-in-aid from 0.5 percent of the total allocation to 0.75 percent. This greatly enhances the per capita amounts the smallest states receive from federal aid.
3. One particularly egregious example comes to mind. In the 1990s General Electric was criticized for not paying any corporate income tax on a net profit of over $2 billion. They self-righteously responded that they had paid $13 million in corporate taxes. That's six-tenths of 1 percent. They didn't say whether the corporate taxes they paid were federal or state.
4. The constant dollar figures used in this chapter are the result of correlating chain-type price indices and implicit price deflators (used by the Council of Economic Advisors in their *Economic Report of the President*, 1991, 2002, 2003) for such things as gross domestic product, personal consumption, and federal and state/local finances.
5. Before 1957 and the enforcement of *Brown vs. Topeka, 1954*, K–12 education was a state function in North Carolina. State legislators thought they could thwart desegregation by devolving education to counties and large municipalities, so it is now locally provided, but heavily subsidized by the state government.
6. From www.census.gov/govs/0200us.html. As of this time (May 2004), detailed information concerning state aid by state is not available from the Census. It is becoming increasingly difficult to get information concerning government from the Governments Division of the Census Bureau because of budget and staff reductions.
7. The regression-line index is a simplified measure of the slope of the regression line. This is a calculated straight-line index. The AGI categories used are the same as the Tax Foundation uses to show that high-income taxpayers are overly burdened by the federal individual income tax (www.taxfoundation.org). They use the top 1 percent, the next 4 percent, the next 5 percent, the next 15 percent, the next 25 percent, and the bottom 50 percent of tax returns to show the bottom 50 percent doesn't pay as much as those at the top. This is the way the progressive income tax is supposed to work. We use the years 1950 and 2000 because we have already calculated 1950 for our earlier book and because 2000 is the latest year for which these data

are available at this writing (Stephens and Wikstrom 2000, 151–55). The levels of income in these categories, as would be expected, are exponential in the amounts of AGI, but for this index the six groups are treated as arithmetic.

8. It should be pointed out that the regression-line index artificially straightens out the line across income groups. For examples of the actual percentage of AGI paid in government revenue, see Figure 8.1 of Stephens and Wikstrom 2000, p. 153.

9. A good example is transportation development districts (TDDs) in Missouri (Chapter 238, *Missouri Revised Statutes*). These TDDs were allowed in the mid-1990s to fund transportation facilities. The first was created for the Station Casino in Kansas City, Missouri, in 1996 to improve Highway 210 for access to the casino. Another was created to provide an interchange on an interstate highway for a new shopping center. Some two dozen TDDs have been created since 1996. In some places special districts have been used to construct convention centers and sports stadiums for privately owned baseball and football teams.

10. From www.brookings.nap.edu/books/0815752452/html22.html.

11. One of the authors, who lives in a suburb and works in the core city (passing through the domain of eight discrete and overlying state and local governments), has experienced at least fifteen increases in state and local, particularly local, sales and excise taxes, franchise fees, and service charges during the first six months of 2004.

12. At www.publicdebt.treas.gov.

13. The actual debt may be higher because of expenditures in the pipeline that have yet to be counted or acknowledged by those who job this is in Washington. See www.publicdebt.gov.

14. From www.census.gov/govs.

15. From CardWeb.com.

5 FEDERALISM AND INTERGOVERNMENTAL RELATIONS: THE NATIONAL POLICY PROCESS AND PUBLIC POLICY

1. See its comprehensive final report, *The Final Report of the Commission on Intergovernmental Relations* (Washington, DC: The Commission, 1955).

2. For one example of these well-crafted reports, see House Committee on Government Operations, *Government in Metropolitan Areas* (Washington, DC: The Committee, 1961).

3. For a fascinating account of the founding and evolution of the Council of State Governments and the key role played by Henry Toll in the early stages of this organization, see John C. Teaford, *The Rise of the States: Evolution of American State Government* (Baltimore: The John Hopkins University Press, 2002), pp. 149–52.

4. For an excellent overview of the implementation, overview, and demise of the GRS program, see Bruce A. Wallin, *From Revenue Sharing to Deficit Sharing: General Revenue Sharing and Cities* (Washington, DC: Georgetown University Press, 1998).

5. Indeed, some scholars argued that because a preponderance of the Supreme Court's decisions in the period from 1940 to 1980 promoted and favored national authority the principle of federalism ceased to be a viable judicial doctrine. See, for example, Jesse H. Choper, *Judicial Review and the National Political Process* (Chicago: University of Chicago Press, 1980), pp. 255–56.

6 REGULATION IN THE INTERGOVERNMENTAL SYSTEM

1. See also the following comment of John Kincaid concerning cooperative federalism, in general, and grant programs, in particular, in stimulating the use of mandates: "[T]he habit of federal activism and the national momentum built up under cooperative federalism continued forward. Substantial political, policy, and financial investments had been made in federal power, such that any idea of changing course was viewed by beneficiaries as a turn back to the Dark Ages." John Kincaid, "From Cooperative to Coercive Federalism," *The Annals of the American Academy of Political and Social Science*, 509 (May 1990), 148.

2. For examples of each of these types of preemption statutes, see Joseph F. Zimmerman, *Contemporary American Federalism: The Growth of National Power* (New York: Praeger, 1992), pp. 65–66.
3. For a detailed listing of preemption statutes that provide responsibilities and powers to the governors, see Zimmerman, *Contemporary American Federalism*, pp. 71–74.
4. For an excellent account of the Boston school crisis, see J. Anthony Lukas, *Common Ground: A Turbulent Decade in the Lives of Three American Families* (New York: Alfred A. Knopf, 1985).
5. For a brief explanation of each of these types of state mandates, see Zimmerman, *Contemporary American Federalism*, pp. 180–82.
6. In an exhaustive and perceptive study of the town meeting form of government in Vermont, Frank M. Bryan notes that the state has increasingly taken away from the towns important decision-making powers: "[I]mportant elements of local discretion have been taken (or given) away. These have been replaced with ever increasing layers of administrative complexity as the state tries to ensure (correctly) that those policies it seeks to control are properly delivered." See Frank M. Bryan, *Real Democracy: The New England Town Meeting and How It Works* (Chicago: University of Chicago Press, 2004), p. 285. See also Bryan Shelly, "Gold Towns and Shark Pools: The Effect of School Finance Reform on Vermont's School Boards" (presented at the Annual Meeting of the American Political Science Association, Chicago, September 2, 2004), in which he reported that unfunded state mandates served to erode the policy autonomy of Vermont's local schools.

7 THE RESURGENT STATES IN THE INTERGOVERNMENTAL SYSTEM: COOPERATION AND CONFLICT

1. This paragraph and the following paragraph have been heavily drawn from Ann O'M. Bowman and Richard C. Kearney, *State and Local Government*, 5th ed. (Boston: Houghton Mifflin, 2002), pp. 6–12. For a more complete statement concerning their position regarding the resurgence of the states, see Ann O'M. Bowman and Richard C. Kearney, *The Resurgence of the States* (Prentice-Hall: Englewood Cliffs, NJ, 1986); this position is also set forth in Mavis Mann Reeves, "The States as Polities: Reformed, Reinvigorated, Resourceful," *The Annals of the American Academy of Political and Social Science*, 509 (May 1990), pp. 83–93. Jon Teaford presents a counter argument in which he asserts that the modernization of state government actually commenced at the beginning of the twentieth century. See Jon C. Teaford, *The Rise of the States: Evolution of American State Government* (Baltimore: The Johns Hopkins University Press, 2002).
2. For an exhaustive inventory and discussion of the various types of interstate compacts, see Joseph F. Zimmerman, *Contemporary American Federalism: The Growth of National Power* (Westport, CT: Praeger, 1992), pp. 141–45.

8 STATE-LOCAL RELATIONS

1. For an excellent comprehensive reference work centering on the relationship of the various states to their local governments and the powers enjoyed by the latter, see Dale Krane, Platon N. Rigos, and Melvin Hill, *Home Rule in America: A Fifty-State Handbook*. Washington, DC: Congressional Quarterly Press, 2000.
2. For a comprehensive listing of the various types of state mandates, see Joseph F. Zimmerman, *Contemporary American Federalism: The Growth of National Power*. Westport, Connecticut: Praeger, 1992, pp. 180–182.
3. A detailed elaboration of the methodology employed by Stephens is found in G. Ross Stephens, "State Centralization and the Erosion of Local Autonomy," *The Journal of Politics*, 36 (February, 1974), pp. 51–66.

4. For an excellent discussion, from a historical perspective, involving the cultural, social, and historical tensions and conflicts between the states and the cities, see David R. Berman, *Local Governments and the States: Autonomy, Politics, and Policy*. Armonk, NY: M. E. Sharpe, 2003, pp. 53–69.

9 LOCAL GOVERNMENTS IN THE AMERICAN INTERGOVERNMENTAL SYSTEM

1. The centralization index was originally developed in 1974 to use available data to measure the changes in the roles played by state and local governments over time and later updated through 2002 (State Centralization and the Erosion of Local Autonomy, *Journal of Politics*, 36: 1. (February 1974), 44–76.

2. As former residents of the state, the authors believe the Census Bureau is in error in its classification of these school districts as separate units of local government. They do not seem to be independent entities when the individual towns retain control of the finances; they are more of a cooperative agreement among selected town governments.

3. As was mentioned earlier, the Census Bureau is publishing much less information about local governments than in the past. As a result we are using 1997 data for this section of the chapter.

4. All of the data in this section of the chapter are taken from a paper by the authors delivered to the annual conference of the American Political Science Association in Philadelphia in 2003.

5. This is logical. If one plots out police and road expenditures per capita for a wide range of population, one usually gets a U-shaped curve with the highest per capita expenditures for these services at the lowest and highest levels.

6. For an extended discussion of both the approach of the governmental reformers and the public choice advocates, see Chapters 3 and 6 of G. Ross Stephens and Nelson Wikstrom, *Metropolitan Government Governance: Theoretical Perspectives, Empirical Analysis and the Future* (New York: Oxford University Press, 2000).

10 INTERGOVERNMENTAL RELATIONS: PRESENT AND FUTURE

1. For instance, David M. Van Slyke in his summary of some of these studies notes: "Privatization may lead to cost savings in the areas of waste removal, some types of transportation (street repair, snow removal, etc.), towing and data processing. . . . The evidence is less clear about the cost savings achieved by privatizing social services such as foster care, child welfare, domestic violence care, substance abuse treatment, homeless and emergency shelters, job training, HIV/AIDS services, Medicaid case management, and food pantries." He concludes: "Privatization successes appear to depend on the specific types of services, the existence of highly developed and competitive markets, the specificity of the contract, and the ability to enforce accountability and evaluate program outcomes." See David M. Van Slyke, "The Mythology of Privatization in Contracting for Social Services," *Public Administration Review*, 63 (May/June, 2003), p. 297.

2. See this series of articles by Paul von Zielbauer, "As Health Care in Jails Goes Private, 10 Days Can Be a Death Sentence," *New York Times*, February 27, 2005, pp. 1, 26–28; "Inside City's Jails, Missed Signals Open Way to Season of Suicides," *New York Times*, February 28, 2005, A1, pp. A18–19; and "A Spotty Record of Health Care at Juvenile Sites in New York," *New York Times*, March 1, 2005, pp. A1, A20.

3. For a particularly intensive personal conflict and struggle within one nonprofit organization, see Stephanie Strom, "Battle in an Omaha Charitable Group Reflects Issues Raised in Corporate Scandals," *New York Times*, January 9, 2004, p. A11.

4. For two vastly different interpretations of the 1960s "urban crisis," see Mitchell Gordon, *Sick Cities: Psychology and Pathology of American Urban Life* (Baltimore, MD: Penguin Books, 1963), and Edward C. Banfield, *The Unheavenly City* (Boston: Little, Brown, 1968), and *The Unheavenly City Revisited* (Boston: Little, Brown, 1974).

5. For an excellent study comparing the federal and state governments in managing the forests, see Thomas M. Koontz, *Federalism in the Forest: National Versus State Natural Resource Policy*. (Washington, DC: Georgetown University Press, 2002).

6. Survey results released in August 2003 reported that 52 percent of the nation favored a law banning gay marriages, while 41 percent opposed such a law. See Associated Press, "Majority Against Gay Marriages, Poll Says," *Richmond Times-Dispatch*, August 19, 2003, A2.

Selected Bibliography

BOOKS

Allen, Robert S. 1949. *Our Sovereign State.* New York: Vanguard Press.

Anderson, William. 1960. *Intergovernmental Relations in Review.* Minneapolis: University of Minnesota Press.

Anton, Thomas. 1989. *American Federalism and Public Policy.* New York: Random House.

Banfield, Edward C. 1968. *The Unheavenly City.* Boston: Little, Brown.

———. 1974. *The Unheavenly City Revisited.* Boston: Little, Brown.

Barron, David J., Gerald F. Frug, and Rick T. Su. 2004. *Dispelling the Myth of Home Rule: Local Power in Greater Boston.* Cambridge, MA: Rappaport Institute for Greater Boston, John F. Kennedy School of Government, Harvard University.

Beard, Charles A. 1935. *An Economic Interpretation of the Constitution of the United States.* New York: Macmillan.

Beer, Samuel H. 1993. *To Make a Nation: The Rediscovery of American Federalism.* Cambridge, MA: Harvard University Press.

Bentley, Arthur F. 1908. *The Process of Government: A Study of Social Pressures.* Chicago: University of Chicago Press.

Benton, J. Edwin. 2002. *Counties as Service Delivery Agents: Changing Expectations and Roles.* Westport, CT: Praeger.

Berman, David R. 2003. *Local Government and the States: Autonomy, Politics, and Policy.* Armonk, NY: M. E. Sharpe.

Bowman, Ann O'M. and Richard C. Kearney. 1986. *The Resurgence of the States.* Englewood Cliffs, NJ: Prentice-Hall.

———. 2002. *State and Local Government.* 5th ed. Boston: Houghton-Mifflin.

Box, Richard C. 1998. *Citizen Governance: Leading American Communities into the 21st Century.* Thousand Oaks, CA: Sage Publications.

Bryce, James. 1891. *The American Commonwealth.* 2nd ed. London: Macmillan.

Choper, Jesse H. 1980. *Judicial Review and the National Policy Process.* Chicago: University of Chicago Press.

Citizens Conference on State Legislatures. 1971. *The Sometimes Governments: A Critical Study of the 50 American Legislatures.* Kansas City, MO: Citizens Conference on State Legislatures.

Clark, Jane Perry. 1938. *The Rise of a New Federalism: Federal-State Cooperation in the United States.* New York: Columbia University Press.

Conlan, Timothy. 1998. *From New Federalism to Devolution: Twenty-Five Years of Intergovernmental Reform.* Washington, DC: The Brookings Institution.

Council of State Governments. 2002, 2003. *The Book of the States.* Lexington, KY: Council of State Governments.

——. 2002, 2003. *Directory of Administrative Officials.* Lexington, KY: Council of State Governments.

Derthick, Martha A. 2005. *Up in Smoke: From Legislation to Litigation in Tobacco Politics.* 2nd ed. Washington, DC: CQ Press.

Derthick, Martha and Gary Bombardier. 1974. *Between State and Nation.* Washington, DC: Brookings Institution.

Dicey, A. V. 1915. *Introduction to the Study of Law and the Constitution.* 8th ed. London: Macmillan.

Dillon, John F. 1911. *Commentaries on the Law of Municipal Corporations.* Boston: Little, Brown.

Dye, Thomas R. 1990. *American Federalism: Competition Among Governments.* Lexington, MA: Lexington Books, D.C. Heath and Company.

El-Ashry, Mohammed T. and Diana Gibbons. 1986. *Troubled Waters: New Policies for Managing Water in the American West.* Washington, DC: Water Resources Institute.

Elazar, Daniel J. 1962. *The American Partnership: Intergovernmental Co-operation in the Nineteenth-Century United States.* Chicago: University of Chicago Press.

——. 1966. *American Federalism: A View from the States.* New York: Thomas Y. Crowell Company.

——. 1984. *American Federalism: A View from the States.* 3rd ed. New York: Harper & Row.

——. 1987. *Exploring Federalism.* Tuscaloosa: University of Alabama Press.

Foster, Kathryn A. 1997. *The Political Economy of Special-Purpose Government.* Washington, DC: Georgetown University Press.

Friedrich, Carl J. 1968. *Trends of Federalism in Theory and Practice.* New York: Frederick A. Praeger.

Friesema, H. Paul. 1971. *Metropolitan Political Structure: Intergovernmental Relations and Political Integration in the Quad-Cities.* Iowa City: University of Iowa Press.

Gaus, John Merriam. 1947. *Reflections on Public Administration.* Montgomery: University of Alabama Press.

Gottman, Jean. 1961. *Megalopolis: The Urbanized Northeastern Seaboard of the United States.* New York: Twentieth Century Fund.

Graves, W. Brooke. 1964. *American Intergovernmental Relations: Their Origins, Historical Development and Current Status.* New York: Charles Scribner's Sons.

Greer, Scott. 1962. *Governing the Metropolis.* New York: John Wiley and Sons.

Grodzins, Morton. 1966. *The American System: A New View of Government in the United States.* Chicago: Rand McNally.

Haider, Donald. 1974. *When Governments Come to Washington.* New York: Macmillan.

Hall, William K. 1989. *The New Institutions of Federalism.* New York: Peter Lang.

Harrigan, John H. and William C. Johnson. 1978. *The Metropolitan Council in Comparative Perspective.* Minneapolis: University of Minnesota Press.

Heclo, Hugh. 1977. *A Government of Strangers: Executive Politics in Washington.* Washington, DC: The Brookings Institution.

Jones, Charles O. 1999. *Separate but Equal Branches: Congress and the Presidency.* 2nd ed. New York: Chatham House.

Jones, Victor. 1942. *Metropolitan Government.* Chicago: University of Chicago Press.

Kettl, Donald F. 1983. *The Regulation of American Federalism.* Baton Rouge: Louisiana State University Press.

——. 1993. *Sharing Power: Public Governance and Private Markets.* Washington, DC: Brookings Institution.

——, ed. 2004a. *The Department of Homeland Security's First Year: A Report Card.* New York: The Century Foundation Press.

——. 2004b. *System Under Stress: Homeland Security and American Politics.* Washington, DC: CQ Press.

Kingdon, John F. 1995. *Agendas, Alternatives, and Public Policies.* 2nd ed. New York: Longman.

Koontz, Tomas M. 2002. *Federalism in the Forests: National Versus State Natural Resource Policy.* Washington, DC: Georgetown University Press.

Kramer, Ralph M. 1981. *Voluntary Agencies in the Welfare State.* Berkeley: University of California Press.

Krugman, Paul. 1994. *The Age of Diminished Expectations.* Cambridge, MA: MIT Press.

Light, Paul C. 2003. *The True Size of Government.* 2nd ed. Washington, DC: The Brookings Institution.

Maass, Arthur, ed. 1959. *Area and Power: A Theory of Local Government.* Glencoe, IL: The Free Press.

MacIver, Robert M. 1947. *The Web of Government.* New York: Macmillan.

Macmahon, Arthur W., ed. 1955. *Federalism: Mature and Emergent.* New York: Columbia University Press.

Martin, Roscoe C. 1957. *Grass Roots.* Tuscaloosa: University of Alabama Press.

———. 1965. *The Cities in the Federal System.* New York: Atherton Press.

McConnell, Grant. 1966. *Private Power and American Democracy.* New York: Alfred A. Knopf.

Mumford, Lewis. 1961. *The City in History: Its Origins, Its Transformations, and Its Prospects.* New York: Harcourt, Brace, and World.

National Conference of State Legislatures. 2005. *NCSL Task Force on No Child Left Behind Report.* Washington, DC: National Conference on State Legislatures.

Oates, Wallace E. 1972. *Fiscal Federalism.* New York: Harcourt Brace Jovanovich.

Phillips, Kevin. 1990. *The Politics and Rich and Poor: Wealth and the American Electorate in the Reagan Aftermath.* New York: Random House.

Polsby, Nelson W. 1986. *Congress and the Presidency.* 4th ed. Englewood Cliffs, NJ: Prentice-Hall.

Posner, Paul L. 1998. *The Politics of Unfunded Mandates: Whither Federalism?* Washington, DC: Georgetown University Press.

Pressman, Jeffrey L. and Aaron Wildavsky. 1984. *Implementation.* 3rd ed., expanded. Berkeley: University of California Press.

Putnam, Robert D. 2000. *Bowling Alone: The Collapse and Revival of the American Community.* New York: Simon & Schuster.

Rivlin, Alice. 1992. *Reviving the American Dream.* Washington, DC: The Brookings Institution.

Sanford, Terry. 1967. *Storm Over the States.* New York: McGraw-Hill.

Savas, E. S. 1982. *Privatizing the Public Sector.* Chatham, NJ: Chatham House.

———. 1987. *Privatization: The Key to Better Government.* Chatham, NJ: Chatham House.

———. 2000. *Privatization and Public-Private Partnerships.* Chatham NJ: Chatham House.

Schattschneider, E. E. 1960. *The Semi-Sovereign People.* New York: Holt, Rinehart, and Winston.

Seidman, Harold. 1975. *Politics, Position, and Power.* London: Oxford University Press.

Selznick, Philip. 1949. *TVA and the Grass Roots.* Berkeley: University of California Press.

Singer, Peter W. 2003. *Corporate Warriors: The Rise of the Privatized Military.* Ithaca, NY: Cornell University Press.

Stephens, G. Ross and Gerald W. Olson. 1975. *State Responsibility for Public Services and General Revenue Sharing.* Report to the National Science Foundation. University of Missouri–Kansas City.

———. 1979. *Pass-through Federal Aid.* Report to the National Science Foundation. Two Volumes. University of Missouri–Kansas City.

Stephens, G. Ross and Nelson Wikstrom. 2000. *Metropolitan Government and Governance. Theoretical Perspectives, Empirical Analysis, and the Future.* New York: Oxford University Press.

Syed, Anwar. 1966. *The Political Theory of Local Government.* New York: Random House.

Teaford, Jon C. 2002. *The Rise of the States: Evolution of American State Government.* Baltimore: The Johns Hopkins University Press.

Truman, David B. 1940. *Administrative Decentralization.* Chicago: University of Chicago Press.

———. 1951. *The Governmental Process: Political Interests and Public Opinion.* New York: Alfred A. Knopf.

Walker, David B. 1981. *Toward a Functioning Federalism.* Boston: Little, Brown.

———. 1995. *The Rebirth of Federalism: Slouching Toward Washington.* Chatham, NJ: Chatham House.

Wallin, Bruce A. 1998. *From Revenue Sharing to Deficit Sharing: General Revenue Sharing and Cities.* Washington, DC: Georgetown University Press.

Wheare, Kenneth C. 1964. *Federal Government.* London: Oxford University Press.

White, Leonard D. 1933. *Trends in Public Administration.* New York: McGraw-Hill.

Wikstrom, Nelson. 1977. *Councils of Governments: A Study of Political Incrementalism.* Chicago: Nelson-Hall.

Wood, Robert C. 1958. *Suburbia: Its People & Their Politics.* Boston: Houghton Mifflin.

Wright, Deil S. 1978. *Understanding Intergovernmental Relations.* North Scituate, MA: Duxbury Press.

——. 1982. *Understanding Intergovernmental Relations.* 2nd ed. Belmont, CA: Brooks/Cole.

Zimmerman, Joseph F. 1992. *Contemporary American Federalism: The Growth of National Power.* Westport, CT: Praeger.

——. 1996. *The Neglected Dimension of Federalism: Interstate Relations.* Westport, CT: Praeger.

——. 2004. *Interstate Economic Relations.* Albany: State University of New York Press.

——. 2006. *Interstate Disputes: The Supreme Court's Original Jurisdiction.* Albany: State University of New York Press.

ARTICLES

Agranoff, Robert and Michael McGuire. 1998. The Intergovernmental Context of Local Economic Development. *State and Local Government Review.* 30 (Fall), 150–64.

Anderson, Totton J. 1965. Pressure Groups and Intergovernmental Relations. *Annals of the American Academy of Political and Social Science.* 359 (May), 116–26.

Beam, David R. 1981. Washington's Regulation of States and Localities: Origins and Issues. *Intergovernmental Perspective.* 7 (Summer), 8–18.

——. 1983. From Law to Rule: Exploring the Maze of Intergovernmental Regulation. *Intergovernmental Perspective.* 9 (Spring), 2, 7, 22.

Beard, Charles A. and William Beard. 1946. The Case for Bureaucracy. *Scribner's Magazine,* 1933. Republished in the *Public Administration Review* 46 (March–April), 209.

Beer, Samuel H. 1977. Political Overload and Federalism. *Polity.* 10 (Fall), 5–17.

——. 1978. Federalism, Nationalism, and Democracy in America. *American Political Science Review.* 72 (March), 9–21.

Bickers, Kenneth N. and Robert Stein. 2003. Inter-local Cooperation and the Distribution of Federal Grant Awards. Paper presented at the Annual Meeting of the American Political Science Association. Philadelphia. September.

Bowman, Ann O'M. 2004. Trends and Issues in Interstate Cooperation. In *The Book of the States: 2004 Edition.* Lexington, KY: The Council of State Governments. 34–40.

Conlan, Timothy J. and David R. Beam. 1992. Federal Mandates: The Record of Reform and Future Prospects. *Intergovernmental Perspective.* 18 (Fall), 4, 1–11.

Crihfield, Brevard and H. Clyde Reeves. 1974. Intergovernmental Relations: A View from the States. *Annals of the American Academy of Political and Social Science.* 416 (November), 99–107.

Croy, James B. 1975. Federal Suppression: The Road to Domination. *State Government.* 48 (Winter), 32–36.

Dean, Debra L. 1989. Residential Community Associations: Partners in Local Governance or Headaches for Local Government. *Intergovernmental Perspective.* 15 (Winter), 36–39.

DeSoto, William 1995. Cities in State Politics: Views of Mayors and Managers. *State and Local Government Review.* 27 (Fall), 188–94.

Dilger, Robert Jay. 2000. The Study of American Federalism at the Turn of the Century. *State and Local Government Review.* 32 (Spring), 98–107.

Dubnick, Mel and Alan Gitelson. 1979. Intergovernmental Relations and Regulatory Policy. Paper presented at a Symposium on Regulatory Policy. Houston, Texas. November 19–20.

Elazar, Daniel J. 1961. Local Government in Intergovernmental Perspective. In Lois M. Pelekoudas, ed., *Illinois Local Government.* Urbana: Institute of Government and Public Affairs, University of Illinois. 24–25.

——. 1990. Opening the Third Century of American Federalism. *Annals of the American Academy of Political and Social Science.* 509 (May), 11–21.

Frederickson, H. George. 1999. The Repositioning of American Public Administration. *PS: Political Science and Politics.* 32 (December), 701–11.

Gladfelter, David. 1961. The Political Separation of City and Suburb: Water for Wauwatosa. In Michael N. Danielson, ed., *Metropolitan Politics: A Reader.* Boston: Little, Brown. 75–85.

Grodzins, Morton. 1960. The Federal System. In *Goals for Americans: Programs for Action in the Sixties.* Report of the President's Commission on National Goals. Englewood Cliffs, NJ: Prentice-Hall. 265–82.

Grossback, Lawrence J. 2002. The Problem of State-Imposed Mandates: Lessons from Minnesota's Local Governments. *State and Local Government Review.* 34 (Fall), 183–97.

Jenks, Stephen S. and Deil S. Wright. 1993. An Agency-Level Approach to Change in the Administrative Functions of American State Governments. *State and Local Government Review.* 25 (Spring), 78–86.

Johnston, Jocelyn M. 1998. Changing State-Local Fiscal Relations and School Finance in Kansas: Pursuing Equity. *State and Local Government Review.* 30 (Winter), 26–41.

Kincaid, John. 1990. From Cooperative to Coercive Federalism. *Annals of the American Academy of Political and Social Science.* 509 (May), 139–52.

Koch, Edward I. 1980. The Mandate Millstone. *The Public Interest.* 61 (Fall), 42–57.

Jones, Charles. 1976. Regulating the Environment. In Herbert Jacob and Kenneth Vines, eds., *Politics in the American States.* 3rd ed. Boston: Little, Brown. 388–427.

Kincaid, John. 1990. From Cooperative to Coercive Federalism. *Annals of the American Academy of Political and Social Science.* 509 (May), 139–52.

Lord, William and Douglas Kenney. 1993. Resolving Water Conflicts: The Compact Approach. *Intergovernmental Perspective.* 19:1 (Winter), 19–25.

Miranda, Rowan and Karlyn Andersen. 1994. Alternative Service Delivery in Local Government. In *The Municipal Year Book 1994.* Vol. 61. Washington, DC: International City/County Management Association. 26–35.

Murphy, Jerome. 1973. The Education Bureaucracies Implement Novel Policy: The Politics of Title I of ESEA, 1965–72. In Allan Sindler, ed., *Policy and Politics in America.* Boston: Little, Brown. 160–99.

Nathan, Richard P. 1996. The Devolution Revolution: An Overview. *Rockefeller Institute Bulletin 1996.* Albany, NY: Nelson Rockefeller Institute of Government.

Netzer, Dick. 1991. An Evaluation of Interjurisdictional Competition Through Economic Development Incentives. In Daphne A. Kenyon and John Kincaid, eds., *Competition Among State and Local Governments.* Washington, DC: The Urban Institute Press. 221–45.

Ostrom, Vincent, Charles M. Tiebout, and Robert Warren. 1961. The Organization of Government in Metropolitan Areas: A Theoretical Inquiry. *American Political Science Review.* 60 (December), 831–42.

Pagano, Michael A. 1990. State-Local Relations in the 1990s. *Annals of the American Academy of Political and Social Science.* 509 (May), 94–105.

Posner, Paul L. 1997. Unfunded Mandates Reform Act: 1996 and Beyond. *Publius.* 27 (Spring), 53–71.

Reed, B. J. 1983. The Changing Role of Local Advocacy in National Politics. *Journal of Urban Affairs.* 5 (Fall), 287–98.

Reeves, Mavis Mann. 1990. The States as Polities: Reformed, Reinvigorated, Resourceful. *Annals of the American Academy of Political and Social Science.* 509 (May), 83–93.

Schmandt, Henry J. and John C. Goldbach. 1969. The Urban Paradox. In Henry J. Schmandt and Warner Bloomberg, Jr., eds., *The Quality of Urban Life.* Beverly Hills, CA: Sage. 473–98.

Shannon, John F. 1984. Dealing with Deficits—Striking a New Fiscal Balance. *Intergovernmental Perspective.* 10:1 (Winter), 5–9.

Sloan, John W. 1997. The Reagan Presidency, Growing Inequality, and the American Dream. *Policy Studies Journal.* 25 (Fall), 371–86.

Snider, Clyde F. 1937. County and Township Government in 1935–36. *American Political Science Review.* 32 (October), 909.

Stephens, G. Ross. 1974. State Centralization and the Erosion of Local Autonomy. *Journal of Politics.* 36 (February), 44–76.

——. 1985. New Federalism by Default, Little OPEC States, and Fiscal Darwinism. In Dennis R. Judd, ed., *Public Policy Across States and Communities.* Greenwich, CT: JAI Press. 49–68.

——. 1989. The Least Glorious, Most Local, Most Trivial, Homely, Provincial, and Most Ignored Form of Local Government. *Urban Affairs Quarterly.* 24:4 (June), 501–12.

——. 1996. Urban Underrepesentation in the U.S. Senate. *Urban Affairs Review.* 31 (January), 404–18.

Stephens, G. Ross and Karen T. Parsons. 1989. Rich States, Poor States: An Addendum. *State and Local Government Review.* 21 (Spring), 52–53.

Stephens, G. Ross and Nelson Wikstrom. 1998. Trends in Special Districts. *State and Local Government Review.* 30 (Spring), 129–38.

Thomas, Clive S. and Ronald J. Hrebenar. 1999. Interest Groups in the States. In Virginia Gray, Russell L. Hanson, and Herbert Jacob, eds., *Politics in the American States: A Comparative Analysis.* 7th ed. Washington, DC: CQ Press. 113–43.

Thurmaier, Kurt and Curtis Wood. 2002. Interlocal Agreements as Overlapping Social Networks: Picket-Fence Regionalism in Metropolitan Kansas City. *Public Administration Review.* (X) (September/October), 585–98.

Vines, Kenneth. 1976. The Federal Setting of State Politics. In Herbert Jacob and Kenneth Vines, eds., *Politics in the American States.* 3rd ed. Boston, MA: Little, Brown. 3–48.

Walker, David B., Albert J. Richter, and Cynthia Cates Colella. 1982. The First Ten Months: Grant-in-Aid, Regulatory, and Other Changes. *Intergovernmental Perspective.* 8 (Winter), 8–9.

Walker, Jack. 1969. The Diffusion of Innovation Among the American States. *American Political Science Review.* 63 (September), 880–99.

Wikstrom, Nelson. 2002. The City in the Regional Mosaic. In H. George Frederickson and John Nalbandian, eds., *The Future of Local Government Administration.* Washington, DC: The International City/County Management Association. 21–38.

Williams, Oliver P. 1967. Life-Style and Political Decentralization in Metropolitan Areas. *Southwestern Social Science Quarterly.* 48 (December), 299–310.

Wise, Charles. 1998. Judicial Federalism: The Resurgence of the Supreme Court's Role in the Protection of State Sovereignty. *Public Administration Review.* 58 (March/April), 95–98.

Wright, Deil S. 2003. Federalism and Intergovernmental Relations: Traumas, Tensions, and Trends. Paper presented at the 64th National Conference of the American Society for Public Administration.

Young, Scott. 2003. The Challenge of NCLB. *State Legislatures.* 29 (December), 24–26.

Zimmerman, Joseph F. 1981. Frustrating National Policy: Partial Federal Preemption. In Jerome J. Hanus, ed., *The Nationalization of State Government.* Lexington, MA: Lexington Books, D.C. Heath and Company. 75–104.

——. 1990. Regulating Intergovernmental Relations in the 1990s. *Annals of the American Academy of Political and Social Science.* 509 (May), 48–59.

——. 1994. State Mandate Relief: A Quick Look. *Intergovernmental Perspective.* 20:2 (Spring), 28–30.

——. 2001. National-State Relations: Cooperative Federalism in the Twentieth Century. *Publius.* 31 (Spring), 15–30.

——. 2002. Trends in Interstate Relations: Political and Administrative Cooperation. In *The Book of the States: 2002 Edition.* Lexington, KY: The Council of State Governments. 40–47.

——. 2004a. Trends in State-Local Relations. In *The Book of the States 2004.* Volume 36. Lexington, KY: The Council of State Governments. 28–33.

——. 2004b. The United States Federal System: A Kaleidoscopic View. Paper prepared for presentation at a Research Seminar, Rothermere American Institute. Oxford University, Oxford, England. November 23.

GOVERNMENT DOCUMENTS

Council of State Governments. 2002–2004. *Book of the States.* Lexington, KY: CSG.

U.S. Advisory Commission on Intergovernmental Relations. 1977. *The Intergovernmental Grant System as Seen by Local, State, and Federal Officials.* Washington, DC: The Commission.

——. 1979–1993. *Measuring State Fiscal Capacity; RTS: State Revenue Capacity and Effort.* Washington, DC: The Commission.

——. 1981, November. *Studies in Comparative Federalism: Australia, Canada, the United States, and West Germany.* Washington, DC: The Commission. M-130.

——. 1984. *Regulatory Federalism: Policy, Process Impact, and Reform.* Washington, DC: The Commission.

——. 1989. *Residential Community Associations.* Washington, DC: The Commission.

——. 1992, 1993. *Characteristics of Federal Grant-in-Aid Programs in State and Local Governments.* Washington, DC: The Commission.

——. 1993. *RTS: State Revenue Capacity and Effort.* Washington, DC: The Commission.

——. 1995. *The Role of Federal Mandates in Intergovernmental Relations: A Draft Report.* Washington, DC: The Commission. [Printed Document Not Approved by the Commission]

U.S. Bureau of the Census. 1953–2005. *Statistical Abstract of the United States.* Washington, DC: Government Printing Office.

——. 1961. *Historical Statistics of the United States: Colonial Times to 1957.* Washington, DC: Government Printing Office.

——. 1982. *Census of Governments, Historical Statistics on Government Finances and Employment.* Washington, DC: Government Printing Office.

——. 1957–2002. *Census of Governments.* Compendium of Public Employment. Washington, DC: Government Printing Office.

——. 2000. *County and City Data Book.* Washington, DC: Government Printing Office.

——. 2001–3. State and Local Finances. www.census.gov/govs/estimate01s100us.html.; www.census.gov/govs/estimate02s100us.html; www.census.gov/govs/estimate03s100us.html.

——. 1952–2002a. *Census of Governments: Government Organization.* Washington, DC: Government Printing Office.

——. 1952–2002b. *Census of Governments: Compendium of Government Finances.* Washington, DC: Government Printing Office.

——. 1957–2002. Selected *Census of Governments* publications: *County Governments, Municipalities and Townships, Special Districts,* and *School Districts.* Washington, DC: Government Printing Office.

——. 1980–2004. *Consolidated Federal Funds Report: State and County Areas.* Washington, DC: Government Printing Office.

——. 1953–2004–5. *Statistical Abstract of the United States.* Washington, DC: Government Printing Office.

U.S. Council of Economic Advisors. 1991–2005. *Economic Report of the President.* Washington, DC: Government Printing Office.

U.S. Department of Homeland Security. 2004. *Securing Our Homeland: Vision, Mission, Core Values & Guiding Principles.* Washington, DC: The Department.

U.S. Department of the Treasury. 2000–2005. www.publicdebt.treas.gov/opd/opdpdodt.htm.

U.S. Office of the Federal Register, National Archives and Records Administration. 2003. *The United States Government Manual 2003/2004.* Washington, DC: Government Printing Office.

U.S. Office of Management and Budget. 2003–2005. *FY 2004–FY2006 Budget of the United States Government: Historical Tables.* Washington, DC: Government Printing Office.

Author Index

A

Aberbach, J., 130
Agranoff, Robert, 199
Allen, R. S., 49
Anderson, K., 66
Anderson, W., 46
Anton, T., 132, 139

B

Bacque, P., 52, 62, 69
Baker, A., 260
Banfield, E. C., 282n.4
Barron, D. J., 193
Beam, D. R., 90, 143, 145–46
Beard, C. A., 20, 41, 93
Beard, W., 20, 41, 93
Beer, S. H., 130, 247
Bentley, A. F., 129
Benton, J. E., 37, 192, 195
Berman, D. R., 154, 198–202, 282n.4
Bickers, K. N., 239
Bowman, A. O'M., 239
Box, R. C., 257
Bryan, F. M., 281n.6
Bryce, J., 26–27

C

Cabe, D., 162–64
Campbell, A., 49, 74
Choper, J. H., 280n.5
Clark, J. P., 109
Cohen, L., 266
Conlan, T., 49, 53, 69, 90, 108, 137
Croy, J. B., 150–52

D

Dean, D. L., 14
Derthick, M., 141, 171, 184
DeSoto, W., 202–3
Dicey, A. V., 6
Dilger, R. J., 64, 67
Dillon, J. F., 188–92
Dubnick, M., 141
Dye, T. R., 2, 67

E

Egan, T., 71–72
Eikenberry, A. M., 257
El-Ashrey, M. T., 178
Elazar, D. J., 1, 4–5, 43, 45, 48–49, 52, 70,
    127, 135, 188, 266, 278n.2
Elling, R. C., 256

F

Fenno, R., 128
Foster, K. A., 7, 228–29, 231
Frederickson, H. G., 63
Friedrich, C. J., 2, 30
Friesema, H. P., 68
Frosch, D., 268
Frug, G. P., 193

G

Garreau, J., 47
Gaus, J. M., 24
Gitelson, A., 141
Gladfelter, D., 72

Subject Index

A

Advisory Commisson Intergov't Relations (ACIR), *see* U.S. Advisory Commission on Intergovernmental Relations
aid to families with dependent children (AFDC), 39, 131–32, 161–65
Albany Plan, 7
Articles of Confederation, 8, 9, 28, 84

B

Baker v. *Carr*, 1962, 49, 69, 135–36, 160
balance, vertical and horizontal, 4–5, 73
Brown v. *Board of Education*, 1954, 69, 136, 152
Bush v. *Gore*, 2000, 133

C

Chisholm v. *Georgia*, 1793, 134
Citizen's Conference on the State Legislatures, 1, 14–15, 160
Clean Air Act, 1970, 113, 262
coercive federalism, 20, 126, 137, 156–57, 254
colonial government, 6–8, 32
Community Development Block Grant (CDBG), 197, 260
condominium associations, *see* residential community associations
Conference of Mayors (USCM), *see* U.S. Conference of Mayors
Conference of State Legislatures, 130
Congress, 16, 27, 125–28, 141–42, 144, 250, 252, 259, 265, 268, 270, 272, 274
Constitution, the U.S., *see* U.S. Constitution
Continental Congress, 8–9
contract employees
cooperative federalism, 11, 17, 46, 51–52, 109–10, 169–73, 247, 260–61
core cities, 260–61

Council of Economic Advisors (CEA), 279n.2
Council of State Governments (CSG), 86, 130, 152, 176, 234, 267, 280n.3
councils of governments (COGs), 48, 238–39
creative federalism, 111, 247
cross-cutting requirements, 149
cross-over sanctions, 149

D

debt, public and private, 41, 99–100, 105, 266–70
delegated powers, 3, 27–28
dependent cities, 260
devolution revolution, 274
Dillon's Rule, 26–27, 189–90
divided power, 4, 7, 10, 23
dual federalism, 12, 46, 134, 246

E

Eighteenth Amendment, 16
Eisenhower's iniatives, 30–31, 110–11
elected officials, 23, 25, 35–37
electoral system, 35–37
environment, 113, 261–65
Equal Employment Opportunity Act, 1972, 143
evolution of federalism, 11–18

F

family income, 98
faux middle-class, 266–70
Federal Aid Road Act, 1916, 16, 130
federal grants, *see* grants-in-aid
federalism, defined, 2–4, 25, 28–31, 33, 159
fiscal federalism, 76–77, 254–56
full–faith and credit clause, 167
functional triads, *see* iron triangles

CPSIA information can be obtained
at www.ICGtesting.com
Printed in the USA
BVHW022005230123
656913BV00006B/198

9 780195 172027